4

HITLER'S FORTUNE

HITLER'S FORTUNE

by

Cris Whetton

Pen & Sword
MILITARY

First published in Great Britain in 2004 by
Pen & Sword Military
an imprint of Pen & Sword Books
47 Church Street,
Barnsley,
South Yorkshire,
S70 2AS

ISBN 1 84415 023 2

Typeset in 11/13pt Centaur by
Phoenix Typesetting, Auldgirth, Dumfriesshire

Printed in England by
CPI UK

For a complete list of Pen & Sword titles please contact
PEN & SWORD BOOKS LIMITED
47 Church Street, Barnsley, South Yorkshire, S70 2AS, England
E-mail: enquiries@pen-and-sword.co.uk
Website: www.pen-and-sword.co.uk

CONTENTS

	Preface	vi
	Notes	vii
	Acknowledgements	x
I	Introduction	I
2	Father to the Man	9
3	Beginnings	19
4	Hitler's Press	38
5	Munich to Berlin	62
6	Hitler's Women	88
7	Hitler the Writer	109
8	The Golden Goose	124
9	Big Business	139
10	The Tangled Web	166
11	The Years of Plenty	194
12	Business-Like Dwarfs	209
13	The *Adolf Hitler Spende*	225
14	The *Berghof*	239
15	Hitler's Art Collection	262
16	The Last Days	283
17	The Inheritors	298
18	*Eine Abrechnung*	315
A1	The Hitler Family	323
A2	The *Thule Gesellschaft*	339
	References	343
	Index	351

PREFACE

This book began in 1996, following the German authorities' intervention to prevent the publication of a new Swedish edition of Hitler's book *Mein Kampf*. Knowing that I had read widely on certain aspects of the Second World War, a Swedish-Finnish friend brought this event to my attention and asked whether I knew who owned the copyright to Hitler's work. Investigations in my own library revealed very little, but excited my interest. The more I dug into the subject, the more contradictions I found and the more interested I became. Seven years later, as this work was delivered to the publisher, still much remains unresolved. The chase, however, has been rewarding on a personal level; I hope it is as rewarding to the reader.

Finally, the author wishes to make one thing clear: he is not a neo-nazi apologist. However, an historian must be honest: where Hitler behaved honestly, I have noted the fact; where he stole, or had others steal on his orders, I have noted that; where he was cheated by others, I have recorded it. I consider this to be accuracy, rather than apology, and where Hitler's possessions were looted by others at the end of the war, that too has been recorded.

Tampere, July 2003
Cris Whetton

NOTES

SOURCES

Where possible, I have tried to use original written material as sources. This includes contemporary documents, accounts written by people who participated in these events and, on a few rare occasions, interviews with survivors. The latter, almost sixty years after the end of the Second World War, are becoming increasingly rare. In some cases, I have been forced to rely on material collected by others and for which I cannot, or have not, verified the source. This could be for the following reasons: the information is of minor importance and the cost of verifying it is disproportionate to its value; or because I have been refused access to the sources or because the original source is lost, proved incorrect, or has died. In all of the above cases, appropriate comment has been added to the footnotes.

TERMINOLOGY

In general, all the terms used in this book have their conventional meanings. However, for reasons of space and clarity I have chosen to use several capitalised phrases, such as Big Business, Patrons etc. These are defined on first occurrence in the text.

One word which deserves some clarification is the German word *Völkisch* and the English equivalent 'folkic' which has been used by some writers and is here preserved in direct quotations. Perhaps the best definition of the term is 'nationalistic with racist overtones'.

CONVERSIONS

All the amounts concerning Hitler's Fortune are given in *Reichsmarks* (RM), unless otherwise noted. However, such numbers are essentially meaningless to the average reader and somehow these values must be converted to contemporary values; this is not easy. No attempt has been made to convert amounts prior to 1933 for two reasons: firstly, because the bulk of Hitler's fortune was amassed after that time and secondly because for much of 1920-33 the *Reichsmark* was unstable. After 1933, amounts have been converted using the 'shopping basket' method.

The shopping basket method

The shopping basket method uses the costs of a basket of common groceries then and the cost of an equivalent basket today to establish a conversion from *Reichsmarks* to Euros and Dollars. The basket used is:

Item	RM[1]	Euro[2]	$
Bread, 1kg loaf	0.36	0.50	3.50
White flour, 1kg	0.44	0.76	0.79
Butter, 1kg	3.20	14.86	8.12
Sugar, 1kg	0.76	1.50	1.54
Beef, 1kg	1.62	10.43	7.68
Lamb, 1kg	1.87	11.60	7.24
Pork, 1kg	1.60	5.52	8.78
Milk, 1 litre	0.24	0.75	1.67
Eggs, 12	1.44	1.32	1.05
	11.53	47.24	40.37
		4.10	3.50

These prices lead to the following approximate conversion factors: 4 €/RM; 3.5 $/RM. These have been used in the text.

Concerning the values quoted in Chapter 2 in Austrian *kronen*, the following figures provide a frame of reference[3] (overleaf):

[1] 1938 prices from SCHO89, p. 16.
[2] Based on Finnish supermarket prices, July 2001.
[3] All taken from MASE73, p. 43.

	Annual income
Assistant teacher, secondary school, Vienna	984
Provincial lawyer, 1 year experience	840
Teacher, less than five years' experience	792
Post office official	720

REFERENCES

Major reference works, which occur throughout the text, are given a code consisting of the first four letters of the author's name and the date of publication, e.g. HALE64 Details of these are collected in the section entitled 'References'. References which only occur a few times are given in full in the relevant footnote.

SPELLING

Throughout the text I have attempted to keep consistent German spelling, except in quotations where the original form is used. Thus, 'Göring', rather than 'Goering'. One exception is the use of 'Munich' rather than 'München'; this has been used simply because it is so common. I have also used the German 'ß' rather than 'ss', where appropriate.

ACKNOWLEDGEMENTS

I am eternally grateful for the assistance of the following (in alphabetical order).

Hannu and Cristina Ahonen, for reading the manuscript, helping with research into the Finnish aspects of this work, and for substantial quantities of wine, Grappa and Calvados; *Bayrisches Hauptstaatsarchiv*; William Carmody; Charles DeCicco; the US Federal Bureau of Investigation (FBI); Jarrett R. Fifield; Ben Frank, who read the early drafts and compiled the index; Russ Folsom, for his encyclopaedic knowledge of personalities in the Third Reich; Ryland Gibbs-Harris; John Gray of the Historical and Records Section of the Cabinet Office, London; Tom Hickox; Sinikka Hietala; Bob Ilett; Philippe Jacob; Cheryl Jaffee, National Library of Canada; Pertti Julin; Greg Kelley; Helena Kortelainen for some translations; Ilmari Lahti, for sharing his knowledge of the von Seidlitz family; Tim Lanzendorfer, without whom many of the original German documents would probably not have been found; Steve Lehrer, for permission to use his photograph of the Hitler family home in Leonding; Jack McKillop; Old Bushmills distillery, for sustenance in moments of despair; Pentti Parvio; the staff of the Public Records Office, Kew, UK, for whom no praise is too high; John Riegsecker; Matti Rosvall, for reading some of the chapters, making many helpful suggestions, transliterating faded Gothic script, helping with translations, and for sustained moral support; Timothy Ryback; Jochen von Seidlitz, for sharing his knowledge of the von Seidlitz family; The *Staatsarchiv München*, notably Dr. Bachmann; Tampere Public Library and all its staff, for superb service; Tuomo Virkkunen; Kari Uuttu, for reading some parts of the manuscript and suggesting clarifications; Hannu Vetola, of *Postimerkkipalvelu*, Tampere, for the loan of stamps; and finally WWIItalk@yahoogroups.com – and all who sail in her.

Lastly, but far from least, Eija who has done everything: from making coffee, through tracking down books, to standing over me with a whip while I struggled with the hard parts.

The maps in this work were prepared by the author, based on originals courtesy of The General Libraries, The University of Texas at Austin, USA.

Chapter One

INTRODUCTION

If you really want to make a million, the quickest way is to start your own religion.
Anonymous.

On 24 April 1945, one day before Lancaster bombers of the RAF made a serious dent in his real estate holdings and six days before his suicide in Berlin, Adolf Hitler was probably the richest individual in Europe[1], with a fortune worth between €1.35 and €43.5 billion at 2003 prices. This book sets out to answer three questions:

Where did Hitler's <u>personal</u> fortune come from; how much was it; and where did it go?

On Tuesday, 8 August, 1950, the following item appeared on page seven of the *Washington Evening Star*.

Hitler's Bankroll Found!
Legal action is now under way for disposing of a secret $42 million bank account maintained since 1939 in the United Kingdom by Adolf Hitler.[2]

Not surprisingly, this raised eyebrows in Washington and London and letters flowed between the relevant Treasuries. According to Vinton W. Mitchell, Office of the Treasury Representative, US Embassy, London:

The Department of State inquired of the paper concerning this item and was informed that it was obtained by that newspaper from one of its filler services. There was no further information than this and to the Department's knowledge the item appeared in no other newspaper either in Washington or in New York.

. . . If the story has any substance to it, the Department is particularly interested in being advised as to the name or names in which the account referred to in the item was maintained in England so that a check can be made of such names with respect to accounts in the United States.[3]

S. E. Wigmore, a British Treasury official, sent a memo to his colleague F. C. Wells at the Administration of Enemy Property Department:

. . . We are not disposed to treat this matter very seriously but I should welcome your comments before we reply to the Americans which we want to do in the immediate future.[4]

I

The following day, F. C. Wells replied:

> . . . *I have canvassed likely sources here but no one in A.E.P.* [Administration of Enemy Property] *Department has any knowledge of the matter. It is true, I believe, that voice has been given from time to time in this country – and even I believe in the House of Commons – to suggestions of the kind – or parallel suggestions about Goering – but only in the vaguest terms of rumour.*
>
> *It can at once be said with assurance that no such account <u>in Hitler's name</u> exists* [emphasis added by author]. *And I would not like to assume that the resources of the Treasury would be inadequate to the discovery long before this in the U.K. of any likely account of the magnitude in question in any other name, existing, as this would presumably have had to exist, since the beginning of the war in 1939.* [5]
>
> *For your personal information* [Author's comment: i.e. not to be revealed to the Americans] *the only germ of fact which might conceivably underlie this report from the pen of some imaginative American journalist is that (as indeed you may already know) a writ in the High Court has been issued against the Administrator of Hungarian Property in respect of a portion (about £1¾ million) of the Thyssen Gold; and legal proceedings against the German Administrator in relation to the balance of about £1¼ millions of Thyssen Gold will conceivably before long supervene.*
>
> *Anything else, so far as our knowledge goes, is pure fiction.*
>
> *But of course we are always open to receive information and suggestions for specific inquiry from any source.* [6]

Based on this, Wigmore replied to Mitchell:

> *You wrote to me on 20th October about a report which appeared in the Washington Evening Star concerning an alleged $42 million bank account in this country owned by Adolf Hitler.*
>
> *Your letter raised our hopes considerably, and we all set out in an effort to find this cash. Alas, we have not been successful!*
>
> *Not only would our Administration of Enemy Property Department be interested in getting this cash . . . but we, of the Treasury, might be just as interested in getting hold of this dollar sum. . . .* [7]

Wigmore presumably meant that the account, not the country, was owned by Adolf Hitler. But there the correspondence on this matter ends, leaving open the question: **did Hitler have a bank account in the UK?** To which this book answers: **very probably, but not in his name.**

This is a book about Adolf Hitler's <u>personal</u> fortune. It is about what Hitler owned and could legally have left to his heirs. That is the criterion: if it could be bequeathed, it is part of his personal fortune; if not, not. Where that fortune came from, what its extent was, and how it was finally disposed of has never been investigated in detail. But one may well ask: Why bother about his personal fortune? Why indeed. Part of the reason is curiosity, the desire to know about a subject which has hardly been addressed by other writers. This book attempts to provide some answers and also challenges some accepted 'facts', notably:

- Hitler personally received large sums of money from German 'Big Business' – he did not.

- Henry Ford subsidised Hitler – he did not.
- The Shell oil company subsidised Hitler – they did, but only by accident.
- Hitler did not own the *Eher Verlag*, the dominant publishing company in Nazi Germany – new evidence suggests that he did.

Adolf Hitler liked money. However, he did not like working for it, and his general attitude seems to have been that the world owed him a substantial fee in return for the privilege of its enjoying his existence. There is nothing unique or revolutionary about such an attitude; what *is* extraordinary is that Hitler managed to use it to amass such an enormous fortune. He did it, as he managed his political career, with a mixture of deceit, bluff, and arrogance.

Some authors have suggested that 'loot and plunder' were the primary motives behind Hitler's politics.[8] This is improbable: looting and plundering on a grand scale require skills in organisation and planning that Hitler just did not have. Hitler did very little to amass his fortune, beyond letting it be known to his followers that he expected one; once that had been made clear, the money flowed in.

Hitler always presented himself as a simple soldier, a man of the people. Only two persons close to him saw through the myth: Otto Wagener, a self-made businessman, and Franz Xaver Schwarz, the quintessential bookkeeper. The majority of those close to Hitler – Speer, Lüdecke, Hanfstaengl, Dietrich – shared this 'simple soldier' view of their *Führer*. As Dietrich wrote in his self-serving post-war memoir:

> *There can be no doubt that Hitler had no selfish desires for private riches or superficial comforts. In his whole mode of life he remained amazingly modest and undemanding.*[9]

Heiden was one of the first to suggest the reality behind the image, though even he missed some essential features:

> *All his life Hitler never had conducted a household, never had a budget; for him money is something you give away or borrow, but never earn; in his youth his receipts were tiny, in his maturity they were immense; but he never established any relation between them and his work, for he worked, not to earn money, but to secure his public position, to win the applause and admiration – shared, to be sure, with a glass of beer – of his audience.*[10]

The reference to beer is not an error; Hitler certainly drank the occasional glass of beer before his imprisonment in 1923 and later drank a special low-alcohol brew at public appearances.

> *There was always pomp around him, and it was one of his master accomplishments that he was able to conceal his own comfortable person in a grey legend of frugality and even asceticism.*[11]

And further:

> *Hitler, who indulged himself in everything, was fortunate enough not to be plagued with conspicuous desires. His inclination to conceal his private life helped him to enhance the legend of his monastic frugality, giving it a quality of the pitiful, saintly, and awe-inspiring.*[12]

One might take issue with Heiden as to whether Hitler's desire for grandiose buildings, opera, and paintings was or was not 'conspicuous'. As Toland says:

> [Hitler] *was publicised as construction worker, artist and student; as a man of the people who sat next to his chauffeur and ate simple meals. He refused to accept any honorary doctorates and would address workers in plants with the intimate plural form* Ihr, *boasting that he too was without estates or stocks — but neglecting to note that* Mein Kampf *had made him a millionaire.*[13]

In fact, it was neither *Mein Kampf* nor the royalties exacted for the use of his portrait, especially on postage stamps, that made Hitler a millionaire, though they certainly helped. Rather, it was the *Eher Verlag*, the Nazi publishing company, and the *Adolf Hitler Spende*, the fund to which German industry willingly contributed that gave him the income necessary to amass a valuable art collection and to purchase and run his extensive mountain estate, the *Berghof*.

Hitler even boasted that he was the only major European statesman who did not have a bank account, but anyone who received a personal letter from him in the nineteen-twenties knew where Hitler's bank account was. The number of his Munich checking account was printed on his notepaper, presumably as a convenience to those eager to send him money. There is also evidence, revealed here for the first time, for at least one foreign bank account in Hitler's name — in the Netherlands — and that this was known to the British government in March of 1939. Possibly because of a simple spelling mistake, but probably because they were busy at the time with more militarily important matters, the Secret Intelligence Service (SIS or MI6) does not seem to have followed this up. Another account has been found in London, under the name of one of his proxies.

Where did it come from?

Between 1919 and his assuming power in 1933, Hitler personally received money from sources as diverse as the German Army and a major shareholder in Finnish paper mills. For a variety of reasons, Hitler was very attractive to women and many women contributed to his personal financial needs. Hitler had some very powerful patrons and, as Kershaw notes:

> . . . *Hitler would have remained a political nonentity without the patronage and support he obtained from influential circles in Bavaria.*[14]

He would also have remained much poorer. During the late 1920s and early 1930s, Hitler was in trouble with the tax authorities and certainly made false statements about his income. (His 1925-32 letters to the tax authorities, headed 'From the Chancellery of Adolf Hitler', take the attitude that a person of his importance should be granted tax concessions not normally allowed to lesser mortals.) By the time Hitler became Chancellor of Germany in 1933, his arrears of taxes and penalties ran to millions of marks. On his accession to power, these were cancelled and it was decided that the *Führer* should be exempt from all taxes. A grateful Hitler announced that he would give his salary to charity – and did so, but only for only one year.

Hitler and Max Amann, the wealthy publisher of Nazi material, drew enormous sums from the profits of the *Eher Verlag*. This money financed Hitler's personal art collection and the decoration of the *Berghof*. After coming to power, the *Adolf Hitler Spende*, a fund set up by German 'Big Business' to support the political activities of the Nazi party, was hijacked by Hitler and Bormann to fund the construction of the *Berghof*. After 1934, Hitler received a royalty on the use of his image, including postage stamps. This, and royalties from the books and postcards produced by Hoffmann, also went to fund his art collection, though Hitler, the self-styled art expert, was often cheated by dealers.

How much was it?

Only one person seems to have made any serious attempt to estimate Hitler's wealth and that was a journalist covering the Nuremberg Trials who estimated that Hitler's known expenditure during his 12-year dictatorship was at least RM 305 million.[15] Drawing on neglected 'back door' sources and using simple statistical techniques, I have been able to estimate the extent of Hitler's personal fortune. In 2003 terms, his real estate holdings were between 244 and 566 million Reichsmarks at the end of 1944 – between €1 and €2.2 billion – his income from the *Eher Verlag* was between 2 and 68 million Reichsmarks in 1944 – between €4 and €272 million – his income from the *Adolf Hitler Spende* was between 23 and 99 million Reichsmarks in 1944 – between €92 and €400 million.

Where did it go?

At least four men controlled Hitler's income on his behalf: Amann; Heinrich Hoffmann, Hitler's photographer; Martin Bormann, Hitler's personal secretary; and Julius Schaub, Hitler's personal servant. The first three of these men made millions for their *Führer* (and, in the case of Amann and Hoffmann, for themselves); what became of this money has never been satisfactorily resolved. Previous attempts to investigate Hitler's Fortune have not paid sufficient attention to these characters. Hitler certainly had a secret Swiss bank account, controlled by Max Amann. The contents of this account and its subsequent disposition are not yet fully known.

Who inherited what? Hitler's descendants – collateral or self-styled – are still arguing over the remnants of his estate. Who are they? This book presents the most comprehensive investigation of Hitler's heirs that has so far been published. Despite the efforts of the Bavarian authorities to gain control of foreign copyrights, Hitler's works are still being published and still sell. Who is getting the royalties?

Hitler spent a fortune on his personal art collection; its final disposition remains uncertain because few historians have taken the trouble to distinguish between pictures collected by Hitler personally and destined for the proposed museum in Linz, Austria after his death, and pictures acquired by the *Sonderaktion Linz* for the immediate use of the museum. The former were paid for out of Hitler's own pocket, the latter out of secret state funds.

The German authorities are less than open about the question of Hitler's Fortune and, as time goes on, documentary evidence is coming under tighter and tighter control. The author of this work is not a 'conspiracy theorist' – he tends to subscribe to the 'cock-up theory' of history – but the German attitude is, to say the least, disturbing.

Hitler and Money

What does this study tell us about Hitler the man? As a youth, Hitler took more than his share of his father's inheritance and squandered it, and he fraudulently received an orphan's pension to pay for an education that he never took. His attitude to work – and its reward, money – show a fundamental laziness; money, in his view, was due to him for the simple reason that he was Adolf Hitler, Artist and *Führer*.

Much of the responsibility for the lack of knowledge about Hitler's financial affairs lies with Hitler himself – he was notoriously secretive about his private life – and with his two lieutenants, Bormann and Amann.[16] This latter pair vied for control over Hitler's personal financial affairs, with neither ever claiming final victory. Significantly, the one person who knew least about Hitler's personal finances – and who complained bitterly about the situation – was the treasurer of the Nazi party, Franz Xaver Schwarz. Turner suggests that Hitler wanted his affairs kept separate from those of the party because:

> . . . *he was obviously an unscrupulous tax evader who sought all possible means to minimize the amount of income he reported on his yearly returns. As Party Treasurer Schwarz explained to Otto Wagener at the time, Hitler feared that the republican tax officials would pry into the account books of the party and so did not want his name to appear there.*[17]

This is plausible before 1933, but not afterwards since Hitler, as Chancellor, was declared exempt from taxes. More probably, Hitler did not want the party to know just how much he was getting, though an astute accountant such as Schwarz could make an educated guess.

It is interesting to note that Hitler could be quite generous, providing handouts and jobs (at state expense, of course) to old comrades and picking up the occasional bill, such as those for Unity Mitford's medical and other expenses after her 1939 suicide attempt. He was also a generous tipper, as Hanfstaengl recalls:

> He was certainly beginning to give himself airs in financial matters at the time, and at the Hotel Hauffe, where we were staying, when I thought I was being particularly generous in giving the maid-servant a 20 per cent tip of about three marks, I saw him give her ten marks. In my travels with him he always gave three or four times the amount that was necessary, and claimed that it had a very good effect, as the staff showed the notes around in the kitchen and sometimes even got him to autograph them.[18]

He could also be very mean and petty, especially to those whom he owed for past help. Again, Hanfstaengl writes, referring to 1935 or 1936:

> Frau Bechstein, a fellow-sponsor of Hitler a dozen years before, who had received from him a miserable bunch of flowers on her birthday, went up to him at a reception and called him "a shabby sort of Chancellor" to his face. I take my hat off to her.[19]

Structure

Hitler's finances are a complex subject which exists not only in time but also in 'space'. This makes it difficult to present the material as a simple narrative, without losing the impact of detailed treatments of particular topics. Consequently, some notes on the structure of this work are appropriate. Chapter 2: *Father to the Man*, describes Hitler's early life and his early attitude to money. A chronological account of the growth of Hitler's Fortune is provided by Chapters 3: *Beginnings*, which covers 1920-23; 5: *Munich to Berlin*, which covers 1924-1932; 11: *The Years of Plenty*, which covers 1933-45; and 16: *The Last Days*, which covers Hitler's suicide and the months following. The finances of Hitler and the Nazi party form a series of interlocking networks stretching around Germany, across Europe, and even to the United States. These are described in Chapters 8: *The Golden Goose*; 9: *The Tangled Web*; and 10: *German Big Business*. Hitler's income came from three principal sources: publishing, speaking and writing, and special funds. These are examined in detail in Chapters 4: *Hitler's Press*; 7: *Hitler the Writer*, and 13: *The Adolf Hitler Spende*. Management of the fortune is described in Chapter 12: *Business-like Dwarfs*. Chapter 6, *Hitler's Women*, examines the women who gave money to Hitler and offers new information on Frau Gertrud von Seidlitz, a woman who laid the foundations for a large part of his personal fortune. Apart from tawdry gifts to a few women and trips to the opera, Hitler spent his money on two things: real estate and art. Hitler's real estate is described in Chapter 14: *The Berghof*. Hitler's personal art collection which, as his wills clearly show, were destined for the Linz Collection after his death, but were his personal possessions during his lifetime, is described in Chapter 15: *Hitler's Art Collection*. What happened to the money is examined in Chapters 17: *The Inheritors* and 18: *Eine Abrechnung*.

Notes

1 Thyssen (THYS41, p. 204) makes the same claim for a much earlier date.

2 Text taken from a letter dated October 20, 1950, from Vinton W. Mitchell, Office of the Treasury Representative, US Embassy, London, to his counterpart at the British Treasury, Mr. S.E. Wigmore. File T236/6136 in the Public Record Office (PRO), Kew, UK. The Washington Evening Star was subsequently absorbed by the Washington Post.

3 ibid.

4 Memo dated November 1, 1950. File T236/6136 in the Public Record Office (PRO), Kew, UK.

5 F.C. Wells' prose style recalls that of Sir Humphrey Appleby, one of the central characters in the British satirical comedy 'Yes, Minister', which aired on BBC TV in the 1970s.

6 Letter Reference F.I.1482, dated November 2, 1950. File T236/6136 in the Public Record Office (PRO), Kew, UK.

7 Letter dated November 16, 1950. File T236/6136 in the Public Record Office (PRO), Kew, UK.

8 Notably Pool, POOL97, p. ix.

9 DIET57, p. 13.

10 HEID44, p. 211.

11 HEID44, p. 223.

12 HEID44, p. 561.

13 TOLA76, p. 406; POOL97, p. 139. Neither gives a source for these assertions.

14 KERS98, p. 133.

15 LANG79, p. 90. von Lang identifies the journalist as Karl Anders, but I have been unable to find any trace of him.

16 KERS98, p. xxv and *passim*; TURN85B, pp. 152-153. See also GORD72, pp. 59–60 for a discussion on Hitler's financial secretiveness, though I cannot agree with Gordon's assertion that all funds to the NSDAP passed through Hitler's hands.

17 TURN85B, p. 153.

18 HANF57, p. 154.

19 HANF57, p. 275.

Chapter Two

FATHER TO THE MAN

The child is father to the man.
Nineteenth century, attributed to Wordsworth.

Most historians begin a book on Hitler with a description of his childhood and excellent general accounts are given by authors such as Hamann, Kershaw, Maser and Toland.[1] Being concerned with Hitler's financial affairs, this chapter examines only one aspect of Hitler's early life: his attitude to money. His ancestors and collateral descendants, who are important to later questions of inheritance, are covered in Appendix I.

Hitler generally described his early life as one of poverty, such as in a letter of 29 November 1921, written to the archivist of the NSDAP– the Nazi party – who had asked for a memoir of his early life:

> *I was orphaned with no father or mother at seventeen and left without any financial support. My total cash at the time of the trip to Vienna[2] was about 80 kronen. I was therefore forced immediately to earn my bread as a common labourer. I went, as a not yet eighteen year old, as a worker's helper on construction jobs and had in the course of two years experienced almost all types of work of the common daily wage earner. . . . After indescribable effort, I succeeded to educate myself so well as a painter that I, through this activity from my twentieth year on, was able to make out in this work even if at first scantily. I became an architectural draftsman and architectural painter and was practically completely independent by my twenty-first year. In 1912 I went in this capacity to Munich.[3]*

While this is not the truth, it is not quite the pack of lies that some authors have suggested. While no one has ever been able to uncover a shred of evidence that Hitler worked as 'a worker's helper on construction jobs', it seems fairly certain that he once shovelled snow from the pavement in front of the Vienna Opera House and offered himself as a porter at Vienna's Westbahnhof. At neither task was he notably successful. Hitler was never an 'architectural draftsman' in any formal sense, though he was a fair artist. Since his needs were modest, he may have been 'practically completely independent' by his twenty-first year, though not entirely through money he had earned.

For political reasons, Hitler tried to paint a picture of an impoverished young man, struggling against the odds to make his way in the world. Even Heiden seems to have accepted Hitler's account and it was not until 1956 that Jetzinger challenged such statements, claiming that Hitler was moderately well-off.[4] Jetzinger's thesis has been repeated by many subsequent authors, bolstered by the later claims of the German historian Werner Maser.[5] In 1999, Brigitte Hamann challenged these long-held views.[6] Consequently, this dispute needs to be examined for, although it has little direct effect on the amount of Hitler's subsequent fortune, it is some of the most important evidence available as to Hitler's ability to manage money.

According to Maser, Hitler's mother's illness did not absorb the 'little' money that her husband had left and Hitler hid the fact that his mother left a substantial sum. When, in June 1905, Klara, Hitler's mother, sold the rather large family house in Leonding, she received 7,480 *kronen*; the court assessed Adolf's and his sister Paula's share at 652 *kronen* each, leaving Klara with 6,176 *kronen* – perhaps slightly less, allowing for legal expenses.[7] Hamann, however, claims that Klara Hitler received 10,000 *kronen* for the house which, after deduction of various expenses, including Adolf's and Paula's share and mortgage deductions, left her with about 5,500 *kronen*.[8]

Whoever is correct, counting Klara's widow's pension of 100 *kronen* per month and the 40 *kronen* per month she received in state aid towards the education of Adolf and Paula, this would have given her an annual income (depending upon whether or not the interest on her capital was compounded and over what periods) of between 1,952 and 1,984 *kronen*. Since this is over 50% more than the annual salary of an assistant teacher in a Vienna secondary school, it should have been adequate to support herself and two children; consequently, there seems little likelihood that she needed to touch her capital.

In addition, Klara might have been receiving interest on capital which she is said to have inherited from her aunt, Walburga Rommeder (see Appendix 1.) This latter bequeathed her estate to her sister, Johanna Pölzl, with the proviso that if Johanna predeceased her – which she did – the estate was to be divided between Johanna's children, Klara, Johanna and Theresia. The exact amount of Walburga's estate is not known, but since Johanna left 3,800 *kronen* when she died in 1911, it seems likely that Adolf and Paula would each have received half of a similar amount via Klara. Klara, too, should have left a substantial sum to Paula and Adolf and this is unlikely to have been less than 2,000 *kronen*. However, the only source for this story is Maser and the documentary evidence – said to be an undated will – remains in his possession and has never been published in facsimile.

Against Maser's claims must be set those of Dr. Eduard Bloch, the Linz physician who cared for Klara in her final illness. According to Bloch, Klara and her children lived extremely modestly.[9] Hamann cites this as evidence that the family was poor, but makes no allowance for the fact that the family were peasant stock, with all the attendant habits of frugality, especially when living in 'the big city', Linz. Jetzinger's extensive analysis also supports the view that the Hitler family were quite well off.[10]

Let us assume that Maser is correct. Hitler received an orphan's pension of 50 *kronen* a month until his twenty-fourth birthday. This was shared with his sister Paula and was supposed to help with his education. It was administered by his legal guardian, Josef Mayrhofer, Mayor of Leonding. Interest rates at the time were about 4%, so a balance sheet of Hitler's income immediately after his mother's death could be drawn up as in Table 2-1.

Thus, from April 1907 to early 1908, his income – unearned – was over 80 *kronen* a month, a sum which compares very favourably with the 82 *kronen* a month salary of an assistant teacher in a Vienna secondary school.[11] A prudent man might have made such funds last longer, but Hitler was far from prudent and by 1909 the funds had evaporated, spent on opera tickets, kid gloves, and ivory-handled canes. In January 1908, shortly after his mother's burial, Hitler asked Mayrhofer for an accurate account of the money he was likely to inherit. On being told that it was 652 *kronen* (plus interest), and being asked what his plans were, he is said to have replied: *Herr Guardian, I'm going to Vienna.*[12] He also told his Aunt, Theresa Schmidt, that he would neither return nor write to her or his other family members until he had made something of himself.[13] Shortage of money caused by his extravagant spending and inability to manage his affairs forced him to modify this promise fairly quickly, though Hitler would not officially – officially as far as Hitler and the NSDAP were concerned – return to his *Heimat* until after the *Anschluß* in 1938.

Hitler made his first try for admission to the Vienna Academy of Fine Arts in October 1907, but was rejected. Shaken, but undeterred, he began to take lessons from Rudolf Panholzer, a sculptor and an experienced teacher. At the beginning of 1908, a woman from whom Klara had rented a house took a friendly interest in the young Hitler and arranged for him an introduction to

---

Table 2-1: Hitler's income: 1907-08

Source	Min.	Max.
Orphan's pension	300	300
Income from father's legacy	696	696
Income from mother's legacy	0	80
Income from Walburga's legacy	0	76
Total	996	1152
Monthly	83	96

Prof. Alfred Roller, a well-known stage designer at the Vienna Handicrafts School (now the Academy of Applied Arts). Hitler failed to meet Roller.[14] There is also evidence that some time in 1908, probably during August, Hitler received a loan (the document is explicit on this point) of 924 *kronen* from his aunt Johanna.[15] There is no evidence that this was ever repaid. In October 1908, he again applied for admission to the Academy; this time, he was not even allowed to take the tests.

He was now definitely discouraged: twice rejected by the Vienna Academy of Fine Arts, and lacking the technical qualifications to train as an architect, the world had failed to provide him with the living he felt he deserved. By the autumn of 1909, Hitler's various inheritances were exhausted, and the 25 *kronen* a month he was still receiving as his share of the orphan's pension were insufficient to maintain the standard of living that he felt he merited. Hitler went rapidly downhill.

In November 1909, Hitler was forced, through lack of money, to give up his room and spent the winter of 1909-10 living with drop-outs in the *Asyl für Obdachlose* (Shelter for Homeless Persons) in Meidling, an inner-city district of Vienna.[16] During that winter, which was exceptionally cold, he received 50 *kronen* – equivalent to two months of his orphan's pension – probably from his Aunt Johanna, and treated himself to a second-hand overcoat.[17] With this money, he also bought artists materials and began painting again, moving on 9 February 1910 to the *Männerheim* (Men's Home), on Meldmanstraße, in the north of Vienna. (The *Männerheim* was not, as it is sometimes portrayed, a home for drop-outs; rather it was a cheap, but eminently respectable, hostel for men in reduced circumstances. It still exists.) Here, Hitler entered into a loose business partnership with Reinhold Hanisch: Hitler would paint, Hanisch would take care of sales and marketing, and the profits would be shared. According to Hanisch's account – the only first-hand account that exists for this period – Hitler was too lazy to produce more than one picture a day, which they sold for about 5 *kronen*.[18] This period has also been documented by Hitler himself (most unreliably), and discussed at length by most authors.[19]

One might expect the experience of abject poverty in the winter of 1909-1910 to have induced some inclination towards thrift on Hitler's part; it did not. If Hanisch is to be believed, Hitler – and it seems true to his character – would only work as much as was necessary to maintain a minimal standard of living. Any windfalls bringing in extra cash, such as the sale of two paintings, would be immediately squandered.

On 21 June 1910, Hitler left the *Männerheim*, re-registering five days later. We do not know where Hitler spent these five days. Hamann suggests, on slim evidence, that Hitler may have gone to visit his aunt Johanna. Certainly, if Hanisch is to be believed, Hitler painted less and less after his mysterious five-day disappearance, suggesting that he may have had another source of income.[20]

Inevitably, the relationship with Hanisch deteriorated, finally collapsing over the sale of a picture Hitler had painted, apparently larger than his usual postcard size, of the parliament building in Vienna. Hitler accused Hanisch of withholding 50 *kronen*, allegedly received for the picture, plus a further 9 *kronen*, allegedly for a watercolour.[21] The police became involved and Hanisch received a few days in gaol, not for defrauding Hitler, but for using the false name of 'Fritz Walter'. Hitler's complaint against Hanisch has survived in the archives of the Vienna police, one of the few relevant documents to do so, since the files were purged on Hitler's orders following the *Anschluß* in 1938. It reads:

> *Royal and Imperial District Police Commissariat*
> *Brigittenau, August 5, 1910*
>
> *Adolf Hitler, artist-painter, born in Braunau, 20/4, 1889. Permanent address, Linz. Catholic, single. Now resident XX Meldemann Strasse 27, declares:*
>
> *It is not correct that I advised Hanisch to register as Walter, Fritz. I knew him only as Fritz Walter. Since he was destitute I gave him the pictures I painted to sell. He regularly received fifty percent of the proceeds from me. For about two weeks Hanisch has not returned to the Home for Men, and stole from me the picture of parliament, valued at fifty* kronen, *and a water-colour, valued at nine* kronen. *The only document of his that I ever saw was the working booklet in question in the name of Fritz Walter. I know Hanisch from the lodging-house in Meidling where I once met him.*
>
> *(Signed) ADOLF HITLER*[22]

The document is important not so much for the case against Hanisch but for the fact that it provides an authentic Hitler signature, useful in establishing the authenticity of later documents and paintings. At the trial, on 11 August, Hitler changed his testimony and admitted that he had received the nine *kronen* for the watercolour. Around this time, Hitler made a third attempt to gain a place at the Academy of Fine Arts; again, he was unsuccessful.[23]

Hitler returned to life at the *Männerheim*, but without Hanisch he was unable to sell any of the few paintings he produced and his financial state again became desperate. According to some accounts, he again applied to his aunt Johanna Pölzl for aid, possibly even travelling to her home in Spital to appeal in person.[24] According to Toland, they had been estranged for several years (which does not correlate with her having given him 50 *kronen* the previous winter) but Johanna was dying and may have felt that she had treated Adolf rather harshly. Accordingly, on 1 December 1910, she withdrew her life savings, about 3,800 *kronen*, and probably gave a large part of this to her nephew. According to Jetzinger, there is no evidence that the Schmidt family received anything. She died the following March, possibly without leaving a will.[25] When Hitler's half-sister Angela Raubal learned that he had received the lion's share of Johanna's estate, she was incensed and applied to the court in Linz for his half of the orphan's pension.[26] She had a good case: she was recently widowed and supporting not only her own two children, but Hitler's younger sister Paula. Furthermore, Adolf had been collecting the money under false pretences, since it was supposed to support him in his education. Hitler appeared in court and announced that, since he could now support himself, he was quite agreeable to the whole pension going to Angela. He also admitted that he had received 'significant amounts from his aunt Johanna Pölzl'.[27] He had earlier written to their guardian, Herr Mayrhofer, saying that he renounced all claim to the money. Accordingly, in May 1911, shortly after Hitler's twenty-second birthday, the court authorised Mayrhofer, who later commented to his daughter that Adolf had behaved very decently in the affair, to pay the full sum to Angela.[28]

Back in the *Männerheim*, Hitler's life continued as before: he painted a little, mostly advertising posters, and sold steadily. By 1912 he was modestly successful, selling most of his output to Samuel Morgenstern, a frame maker, Jacob Altenberg and other minor dealers, though this prosperity – if such it was – did not reflect itself in his clothing. An eyewitness describes him as wearing a knee-length 'bicycle coat' of indeterminate colour, an old, grey, soft hat with the ribbon missing, hair down to his shoulders, and an unruly beard.[29] The witness adds that Hitler owned no shirt, his coat was worn through at the elbows, and the soles of his shoes were patched with paper. Hamann estimates Hitler's income at this time at 20-40 *kronen* per month.[30] Such a sum would have been impossible to live on, considering that the monthly rent at the *Männerheim* was about 12 *kronen* a month. It is difficult to believe that, if Hamann's estimate is correct, Hitler did not have another source of income and the most likely source is his aunt Johanna.

By now the question of military service was beginning to worry Hitler. So far, he had managed to avoid conscription, but it was only a matter of time before the authorities caught up with him, though he made no attempt to conceal his where-abouts. Accordingly, Hitler made plans to leave Austria for Munich. All he lacked was the necessary money. On his twenty-fourth birthday, 20 April, 1913, Hitler became eligible to receive his outstanding share of his father's inheritance (which had been earning interest in the bank since 1 February 1904) which amounted to about 820 *kronen*. On 16 May, the District Court in Linz granted him the money, sending the cash on by mail, and Hitler immediately left Austria, arriving in Munich on 26 May. Before leaving, he carefully notified the police that he was leaving the *Männerheim*, but gave no indication of where he was bound. Once in Munich, he registered as a 'stateless person' – falsely, since he had not yet formally renounced his Austrian citizenship – and describing himself as a 'writer'. The Austrian authorities finally tracked him down and, on the afternoon of 18 January 1914, a Sunday, came the prophetic knock on the door. Opening it, he was confronted by two policemen; arrested, he was taken next day by the police to the Austro-Hungarian consulate. The consul-general, persuaded by Hitler's 'obvious sincerity', had him write a letter to the Austrian authorities to explain why he had not registered for military service. Hitler did so, painting a picture of abject penury:

. . . And as far as appertains unto my sin or omission in the autumn of 1909, this was an infinitely bitter period for me. I was a young inexperienced man without any financial support and too proud to accept it from no matter whom, let alone ask for it. Without monetary help, cast out on my own resources, the few kronen *often only* heller *obtained through my work barely sufficed to give me somewhere to sleep. For two years I had no other friend[31] but care and want, no other companion but everlasting insatiable hunger. . . .*

The letter continued:

I earn my living as a self-employed artist, but I do so only in order to continue my education, being otherwise quite without means (my father was a civil servant). I can only devote a very small part of my time to earning as I am still learning to be an architectural painter. So my income is very modest and only just enough to meet my expenses. In proof of this, I enclose my tax certificate which I should be grateful if you would return to me without delay. My income is estimated on the high side at 1,200 marks which should not be taken to mean that my monthly income is exactly 100 marks.[32]

This, as has been noted above, is far from the truth. The letter, which covered three and a half pages, was accompanied by a note from the consul-general:

Hietler [sic] *. . . was suffering from a complaint which renders him unfit for military service and at the same time removes all motive for evading it . . . He seems very deserving of considerate treatment.*

The consul-general seems to have been a gullible man. Hitler made a brief trip to Linz, was medically examined and declared unfit for military service.

Hitler returned to Munich, where he continued to live in some comfort; certainly, he later described this period as 'the happiest and most contented' of his life.[33] He rented a room on Schleißheimerstraße, in Munich's artists quarter of Schwabing, from a tailor, Josef Popp. The room, which cost only 20 *marks* a month, was pleasantly furnished and had a private entrance from the street. Popp was a kindly, well-travelled man and made sure his tenant was well dressed, so as not to reflect badly on his own establishment, which dealt in dresses *á la mode de Paris*. Hitler was also befriended by a local baker, Herr Heilmann, who had a shop nearby at Gabelsbergerstraße 66, and sold him slightly stale cakes and buns for a few *pfennig*. In a 1952 interview, Heilmann recalled that he had bought two paintings from Hitler, whose works sold regularly for about 10 to 20 *marks* each.[34] NSDAP archives record other sales: a Dr. Schirmer, who bought a small oil painting and commissioned Hitler to make watercolour copies of two postcards of alpine scenes; and a Herr Würsler, who bought a small oil painting for 25 *marks*.[35] Doubtless there were many others.

All this came to an end on 28 June 1914 when a Serb terrorist, Gavrilo Princip, assassinated Archduke Franz Ferdinand and Sophie, his morganatic wife, thereby precipitating World War I. On 3 August, the day Germany declared war on France, Hitler – still an Austrian citizen – petitioned King Ludwig III of Bavaria for permission to enlist in his army. He was accepted, and on 16 August he was inducted into the 1st Bavarian Infantry Regiment.

Hitler's wartime service is of little relevance to a history of his financial affairs, but one thing is most significant: the friendships which he made in the trenches. Of these, Max Amann is the most important and the Hitler-Amann collaboration was of enormous profit to both parties (see Chapters 4 and 12). His other friendships from this period show a side of Adolf Hitler that many would like to ignore: his generosity. Most of those with whom he served in the trenches later benefited from Hitler's rise to power: Amann, as noted above; *Leutnant* Fritz Wiedemann, who later became Hitler's adjutant from 1935 to 1939; Ernst Schmidt, and others. The major exception was *Leutnant* Hugo Gutmann who recommended Hitler for the Iron Cross First Class; Gutmann was Jewish.

On the morning of 14 October 1918, near Comines, in the Ypres sector, Hitler's active service ended when he was temporarily blinded by gas.

Notes

1   HAMA99, *passim*; MASE73, pp. 1-69; KERS98, pp. 3-105; TOLA76, pp. 3-76.
2   This statement is confusing. Hitler's mother died on 21 December 1907, when Hitler, who was born on 20 April 1889, was eighteen. Hitler was 'not yet eighteen' at the time of his <u>first</u> trip to Vienna in 1906, but he was clearly eighteen when he became an orphan and almost nineteen when he <u>moved</u> to Vienna, some time between 14 and 17 February, 1908. It is thus impossible to decide which trip to Vienna – 1906 or 1908 – Hitler is referring to. Since Hitler was supported by his mother during the 1906 visit, references to work suggest the 1908 move.
3   WAIT77, p. 193. Waite quotes HAP, folder 17a, reel 1. The translation is Waite's.
4   JETZ58, *passim*.
5   MASE73, p. 41 and following pages.
6   HAMA99, pp. 3-59.
7   MASE73, p. 42; JETZ58, pp. 81-83.
8   HAMA99, p. 21. JETZ58, pp. 50, 82-3. Jetzinger notes that the house had an existing mortgage of 2,520 *kronen* which Alois assumed when he bought the property and did not discharge because the mortgage made the house more readily saleable.
9   Bloch, Eduard (as told to J.D. Radcliff). *My Patient , Hitler*. Colliers Magazine, 15 and 22 March, 1941.
10 JETZ58, pp. 79-81.
11 Jetzinger (JETZ58, p. 113) arrives at the same minimum figure as the author.
12 JETZ58, pp. 101-22. Hitler had already visited Vienna for two weeks in May 1906.
13 HEID44, p. 50.
14 MASE73, pp. 43-5. SPOT03, p. 223, citing Fraunfeld, A.E., *Der Weg zur Bühne*, 1943, p. 290.

15 JETZ58, p. 129, merely shows that Hitler visited his aunt Johanna, who was then living with Theresia Schmidt in Spital, in August 1908.

16 Hamann (HAMA99, p. 141) casts grave doubts on the NSDAP official position that Hitler occupied furnished rooms at 11 Simon Denk Gasse.

17 KERS98, p. 53; TOLA76, p. 42 have Hitler, prompted by his some-time friend Reinhold Hanisch, writing to his aunt to ask for the money. See also Hamann (HAMA99, p. 156) who seems to accept this part of Hanisch's story. However, this seems at odds with Toland's later assertion (p. 47) that Hitler and his aunt were estranged. Heiden (HEID44, p. 52), who may not have had access to the Hanisch material, seems to confirm the story, but makes no mention of any estrangement. JETZ58, pp. 134-5 tells a similar story.

18 Hanisch, Reinhold. *I was Hitler's Buddy*. A three part series, published in The New Republic, 5, 12, 19 April, 1939, pp. 239-42, 270-72, 297-300. Also in HAP, reel 3, file 64. The article in The New Republic was published two years after Hanisch's death.

19 E.g. Kubizek, August. *Adolf Hitler. Mein Jugendfreund*, Graz (1953), 5th edition 1989; *Mein Kampf, passim*; BULL62, Ch.1; TOLA76, Ch. 2, *The School of My Life*; MASE73, Ch. 3, *Artist and Architect*; KERS98, Ch. 2, *Drop-out*; HAMA99, Ch.6, *As a Painter in the Men's Hostel*.

20 Several authors have cast doubts on Hanisch's memoirs and those of Josef Greiner; e.g. SPOT03, p. xviii.

21 These are somewhat higher than the 3-4 *kronen* (about €10-12 in 2003) that he normally received.

22 Taken from HEID44, p. 62.

23 SPOT03, p. 129.

24 WAIT77, pp. 195-6; TOLA76, p. 47. However, Kershaw (KERS98, p. 57) disputes the story and Hamann (HAMA99, p. 174) offers no evidence to support it.

25 Waite (WAIT77, p. 196) citing Jetzinger, says that the will was probated in the District Court of Linz. However, JETZ58 merely notes that no will was found in documents available in 1952. Toland (TOLA76, p. 47) says she died intestate.

26 Jetzinger (JETZ58, p. 138) claims that it was the Linz authorities who initiated the case.

27 JETZ58, pp. 139-42.

28 TOLA76, p. 48.

29 Paraphrased from HAMA99, p. 379, itself based on the well known account of one of Hitler's colleagues in the *Männerheim*, 'Anonymous from Brünn'.

30 HAMA99, p. 380. Hoffmann, however, relates a story (HOFF55, pp. 168-9) of Hitler receiving 500 *kronen* for a watercolour of the interior of Vienna's Capucin church, but there is nothing to substantiate the story, which may well be a typical bit of Hitler boasting.

31 The translation here is from Waite (WAIT77, p. 70) but similar text is quoted by many authors. The original German uses the word '*Freundin*', or female friend, and some authors have been tempted to render this by the more poetic 'mistress'.

32 MASE73, p. 71. KERS98, p. 84 implies that Hitler was questioned by the

authorities in Linz for non-payment of taxes. However, Maser (MASE73, p. 53) makes it quite clear that this figure of 1,200 marks (equivalent to about €800 in 2003) a year comes from his tax returns. Since Hitler was living in Munich, it is odd that the Linz authorities should have been interested in his taxes.

33 Hitler, *Mein Kampf*.
34 *Münchener Revue*, 46, November 15, 1952.
35 HAP, folder 30, reel 2; folder 31, reel 2.

Chapter Three

BEGINNINGS

Get money; still get money, boy,
No matter by what means.
Ben Jonson (1572-1637)
Every Man in his Humour. Act ii. Sc. 3.

On 19 November 1918, eight days after the armistice, Hitler left the military hospital at Pasewalk, near Berlin, where he had been recovering from being gassed. Two days later, he arrived in Munich, home of his regiment. At that time, his Munich savings account totalled 15 *marks* 30 *pfennigs*.[1] Five years later he was in prison, awaiting trial for leading an attempted coup, his political career apparently over. In the meantime, he had established a network of friends and admirers who, in addition to funding the Nazi party, supported him financially. He had also laid the foundations for a business empire that would later bring him – and his buddy, Max Amann – hundreds of millions of *Reichsmarks*. How did he do it?

When the First World War ended, Hitler's eyes had been damaged by gassing, at least to the extent of becoming more sensitive to light, and he would have been eligible for discharge from the army and a disability pension. He did not apply for release. At least one author sees this as evidence that Hitler exaggerated the effects of his gassing and knew that medical records would not support his claim.[2] More probable is that he passionately wanted to stay in the army, the only stable home he had enjoyed in the past ten years. Possession of the Iron Cross, First Class, probably helped him remain in the army despite his injury.

1919 was a strange time in Germany. The Munich to which Hitler returned was in turmoil: the Bavarian monarch had abdicated and an uneasy left-wing coalition government formed under the leadership of Kurt Eisner, a Jewish socialist and pacifist. It did not last long. On 21 February, Eisner was assassinated by *Graf* (Count) Anton von Arco-Valley, a former army officer whose Jewish ancestry had led to his being refused admission to right-wing circles. Anarchists and 'Red Guards' took over the former royal palace, a 'dictatorship of the proletariat' was declared, and a 'Red Army' raised. Where Eisner fell, the Communists placed his picture on the wall, guarded by one of their members, and passers-by were forced to salute the icon.[3] Members of the right-wing *Thule Gesellschaft* (see Appendix 2) splattered the area with a bag of flour, soaked with the secretions of two bitches in heat. Within hours the scene became a bedlam of excited dogs and the picture was quietly removed.

On 13 April, the *Kampfbund*, a paramilitary organisation with close ties to the *Thule Gesellschaft*, staged a coup which was rapidly overwhelmed by a left-wing counter-coup. That rebellion was put down by regular soldiers from Prussia and Württemberg, under the command of Colonel Ritter von Epp and assisted by paramilitary Bavarian *Freikorps* units. The period is well documented, and a good account is given by Kershaw; suffice it to say that that period passed into popular memory as the *Schreckensherrschaft* (rule of horror), a state imposed by 'Jewish-Bolshevik elements, acting on orders from Moscow'.[4] What, then, of Adolf Hitler in this time?

On 20 February, Hitler and his wartime comrade Ernst Schmidt were assigned to guard duty at the main railway station in Munich, where they stayed for about two weeks. Hitler and Schmidt had found a 'cushy billet': they received about 40 *marks* a month, plus food and accommodation, and earned an additional 3 *marks* per day testing gas masks – a curious choice for Hitler, whose horror of gas as a weapon would remain throughout the Second World War.[5]

On 3 April, a routine order for the 2nd Demobilisation Company refers to Hitler as the company's *Vertrauensmann* – literally Man of Confidence – and he may have held this position since 15 February.[6] Since his duties included propaganda and political education of the troops, and the providers of the propaganda and politics were the revolutionary SPD (*Sozialdemokratische Partei Deutschlands*), Hitler was acting for the extreme left. In this, Hitler was not alone: Josef 'Sepp' Dietrich, Julius Schreck, Hermann Esser, and Gottfried Feder – all later ardent Nazis – also served the Communist regime in one way or another. Subsequently, Dietrich supervised the executions in the 1934 Blood Purge and commanded a *Waffen SS* division in the field. Schreck, Hitler's near double, became his chauffeur and founded the *Stoßtrupp Adolf Hitler* (forerunner of the SS). Esser rose in the ranks of the NSDAP and, as Bavarian Economics Minister, became an expert on rape and pillage – especially the former. Feder became the Nazis' 'economic expert', though his theories were crackpot in the extreme. Following the proclamation of the Communist *Räterepublik* on 14 April, Hitler was re-elected as Deputy Battalion Representative by his colleagues, suggesting that they had confidence in his revolutionary sympathies. This, and other evidence of left-wing sympathies, was suppressed by Hitler in later accounts, where he claimed that he acted against the leftists and was marked down for arrest. He was arrested, though not by the leftists, but by the right-wing *Freikorps* and was only released on the intervention of his officers.[7]

On 2 May, the regular army began an investigation into the uprising; one of those who testified was Adolf Hitler. As one of his friends later stated:

The consequences, though hardly due to Hitler's testimony alone, were predictable: hundreds were summarily executed.

On 11 May, following the crushing of the *Räterepublik*, the *Bayerische Reichswehr Gruppenkommand Nr. 4* (Gruko) was created, under the command of *Generalmajor* von Möhl, with orders to re-educate the troops in a nationalist, anti-Bolshevik fashion. In early June, as part of this effort, Captain Karl Mayr was ordered to organise training courses for persuasive speakers who would remain in the army and indoctrinate the troops. Mayr had far more power and influence than his low rank of Captain might suggest and he was given considerable funds to finance agents and informants, patriotic parties, and publications. These funds came from the *Reichswehr* headquarters in Munich and Berlin, and from private sources.[9] Hitler came to Mayr's attention on several occasions and records suggest that he was recruited into Mayr's organisation in late May or early June.[10] By August, Hitler was one of 26 instructors specially selected to conduct a five-day course at the *Reichswehr* camp at Lechfeld, near Augsburg, most of whose inmates had been prisoners of war in Russia and who had pro-Bolshevik sympathies. The course ended on 25 August and a row blew up about 500 *marks* which the commandant of Lechfeld, Rudolf Beyschlag, had failed to pay to the instructors.[11] The spokesman for the instructors was Adolf Hitler. By the beginning of September, Hitler appears to have been held in high esteem by Mayr and in a letter dated 10 September, Mayr addressed Hitler with the salutation *Sehr verehter Herr Hitler*, a formal 'Dear Sir' address used by equals and hardly to be expected from a Captain to a Lance Corporal.[12]

On Friday, 12 September, Hitler, acting under orders to monitor political groups, attended his first meeting of the *Deutsche Arbeiterpartei* (DAP – German Workers' Party) in the *Leiber* room of the *Sterneckerbrau* beerhall, Munich. The origins of the DAP are obscure, but most historians agree that it was founded by the *Thule Gesellschaft*, as a subordinate club more appropriate to the masses than its 'intellectual' parent. Whatever its origins, it was more of a club than a political party. As Hitler later said:

In the year 1919 when I met the handful of men who held their little meetings under the name of German Workers' Party, there was neither a business office nor any employee. There was no paper with letterhead; in fact, even rubber stamps were lacking. The entire property of this seven men's club consisted of a briefcase, in which the incoming and outgoing mail were kept, and a cigar box which served as cash-box. This portable party office in the form of a brief-case travelled under the arms of party comrade Harrer, our "president", into every conceivable beer hall and café in which the party committee — which at that time was the party itself — met. [13]

Harrer was also a member of the *Thule Gesellschaft*. Acting under orders from Mayr – and not, as he later claimed, after many days of agonised soul-searching – Hitler joined the DAP with instructions to ensure its growth.[14] For this he was provided with 20 gold *marks* (*marks* backed by gold and thus protected against inflation) a week and was permitted to stay in the army, against standing orders which forbade serving soldiers from belonging to political parties. In addition to drawing his army pay – about 40 *marks* a month, probably more by this time – Hitler received speaker's fees from the party, which he was apparently allowed to keep, thus establishing what would become one of his important early sources of income. How much of the 20 gold *marks* a week found its way into Hitler's pockets is not known, but some of it certainly came back as speaker's fees.

Hitler's connection with the newspaper the *Völkischer Beobachter* (then the *Münchener Beobachter*) may have begun with the placing of an advertisement (paid for after some protest by his fellow DAP members) for a meeting to be held on 16 October in Munich's *Hofbräukeller*.[15] This meeting, one of the first to be publicly advertised, drew 111 attendees and raised 300 *Reichsmarks* (RM) when the hat was passed around for a collection.[16] By the end of 1919, Hitler was speaking to several DAP meetings a week, attracting audiences of up to 400 and being paid accordingly. Since an audience of about 100 brought in a collection of about RM 300, an audience of 400 might bring in a proportionate figure of RM 1,200. Just what proportion Hitler received as 'speaker's fees' is not known, but 20-30 *marks* a week seems a reasonable guess and would be a significant addition to his army pay of about 10 *marks* a week, which he continued to draw until 31 March, 1920.

Towards the end of the autumn of 1919, Hitler met Alfred Rosenberg. Rosenberg, with his Russian-speaking Baltic German background, immediately became the party's expert on 'Jewish Bolshevism' and was later editor of the *Völkischer Beobachter*.

For Hitler's personal finances, the most significant event of 1920 was his acquisition of the *Eher Verlag*, a publishing company, and with it a newspaper, the *Völkischer Beobachter*. Almost equally important was the beginning of his friendship with Dietrich Eckart.

Some 20 years older than Hitler, Eckart had an established relationship in right-wing circles, especially with the *Thule Gesellschaft*. It was Eckart who provided the struggling Hitler with some of the introductions to Munich society which were later to be such important sources of finance. It was Eckart who first took Hitler in hand, smartened up his appearance, and gave him the elementary social skills that he would soon need in polite society. Eckart, though hardly wealthy, was comfortably off, thanks to royalties from some of his translations, particularly of *Peer Gynt*, and often paid for Hitler's meals and minor expenses. Of the party's finances in general and Eckart in particular, Hitler later said:

> *The party was financed almost exclusively by my meetings. The membership dues stood in no relation to the money brought in by my speeches. To be sure, the party did have one big backer at that time; our unforgettable Dietrich Eckart.* [17]

Kurt Lüdecke (see Chapter 8) suggests that Eckart contributed to Hitler's personal expenses.[18] Otto Dietrich, however, portrays Eckart more as a conduit for funds for the party than a source:

> It was he who obtained financial support for Hitler in the early days when he was building up his party. Eckart was acquainted with a group of wealthy men to whom he had appealed for subsidies for his newspaper; he introduced Hitler to these men. They were the first backers who, out of general patriotic considerations, lent aid to Hitler.[19]

Hoffmann, too, implies that Eckart's support was for the Nazi party, rather than for Hitler personally, though at that time he was probably not in a position to know.[20] To speak, as Hitler did, of Eckart being a 'big backer' is to exaggerate his importance and to obscure the other sources of funding at this time: the Army, minor German industrialists, wealthy families such as the Bechsteins and the Bruckmanns, anti-Bolsheviks, White Russians, idealistic playboy wheeler-dealers such as Lüdecke and romantic ones such as Scheubner-Richter (see Appendix 2). The latter not only provided Hitler with access to wealthy patrons in Munich society, but also offered somewhat murky links to White Russian émigrés with money to spend on anti-Bolshevik causes. According to Pool, an official report claimed that he raised 'enormous sums of money' for the NSDAP; this is possible, but has not been substantiated.[21]

On 24 February 1920, the DAP rented the hall at Munich's famous *Hofbräuhaus* for the first time. Thanks to astute advertising, a capacity crowd of over 2,000 packed the hall. It was here that Hitler publicly announced the new party manifesto; a bold move, for he was not yet leader of the party. (Anton Drexler had recently taken over from Harrer as president.) There was some heckling, probably from Communists, but order was soon restored by a squad of armed soldiers that Hitler, still an employee of the political bureau of the Munich District Army Command, had brought along. A week later, the DAP changed its name to the *National Sozialistische Deutsche Arbeiter Partei* (National Socialist German Workers Party or NSDAP), the name under which it was to become notorious and bring a new word to the lexicon of obscenity: Nazi.

Towards the end of the abortive right-wing *Kapp Putsch* in Berlin, which lasted from 12 to 18 March, Hitler and Eckart made the hazardous journey to Berlin as representatives of Bavarian monarchists who were planning their own coup. They stayed for several days in Berlin, meeting General Ludendorff, members of the ultra-right *Stalhelm*, and the Bechstein family who were later to play a prominent part in financing both Hitler and the NSDAP. Hitler also met Ernst von Borsig, head of the famous locomotive manufacturing company.[22] However, despite assertions at Hitler's 1924 trial, Borsig's contributions should not be overestimated. Borsig considered himself an enlightened employer who sought ways to bring management and workers closer together. The NSDAP intrigued him, with its idea of 'patriotic workers' and its anti-Communism, and he certainly contributed to it; however, he also contributed to just about every other political party that was not on the extreme left. There is no evidence that Borsig knowingly contributed to Hitler's personal finances.

Hitler and Eckart returned to Munich on 31 March 1920, the day Hitler formally left the army with a ready-made career as a political agitator and with Mayr's continued patronage and influence in Munich circles. Hitler received his demobilisation pay of 50 *marks* and moved into a small room in a house at Thierschstraße 41[23], in a middle-class district near the Isar River. The room – hardly bigger than a closet and sublet from one of the other tenants, a Frau Reichert – was just a few doors from the offices of the *Eher Verlag*, publisher of the *Völkischer Beobachter* and destined to play a major role in Hitler's subsequent political and financial career.[24]

On 24 September, Mayr wrote to Wolfgang Kapp, now exiled to Sweden after his failed *putsch* in March:

> *The national workers' party must provide the basis for the strong assault-force we are hoping for . . . I've set up very capable young people. A Herr Hitler, for example, has become a motive force, a popular speaker of the first rank. In the Munich branch we have over 2,000 members, compared with under 100 in summer 1919.[25]*

If correctly dated, the letter suggests that Hitler was still working for Mayr at that date, and presumably being paid. Mayr, apparently, continued to provide funds towards the staging of these mass meetings.[26] As 1920 went on, Mayr began to lose his influence with Hitler, being supplanted by Captain Ernst Röhm, adjutant and political adviser to Colonel von Epp.

Röhm, a homosexual bully and a brave fighting soldier, had excellent connections within the army and with the many paramilitary and patriotic organisations which made up the Bavarian extreme right. Röhm soon began to act as a link between Hitler and the NSDAP and these larger organisations, particularly in the area of funding. He also continued the financial assistance begun by Mayr, paying for various items directly and indirectly from Army funds. Pool gives a convincing – if unoriginal – account of one of Röhm's stratagems, which are also hinted at by Lüdecke:

> *Two privately-owned corporations were created, one dependent on the other. The basic corporation, the very existence of which was top secret, was the* Feldzeugmeisterei, *directed by Ernst Röhm. The other, the dependent corporation, was the Faber Motor Vehicle Rental Service, operated openly as a business by Major Wilhelm Faber, who was under Röhm's command. Röhm had the initial approval of his military superiors in setting up these corporations because they were an ideal cover for concealing extra armaments and vehicles forbidden by the Versailles Treaty. The corporations also served the purpose of making this illegal equipment available to the clandestine reserve Army – the Free Corps units. The Nazi S.A. as one of the many Free Corps regiments was entitled to occasionally use some of this equipment and receive a few small subsidies from Röhm's corporations.[27]*

In mid-1920, the NSDAP was still struggling financially, with subscriptions not yet covering the costs of meetings. Additional funding came from a variety of sources: from Lehmann, publisher of many of the German Navy's books; from the *Reichswehr*, via Mayr and later Röhm; and from Eckart.[28] Funds were also obtained from Dr. Gottfried Grandel, an industrial chemist from Augsburg, of whom more later.

In December 1920, Hitler acquired the debt-ridden *Eher Verlag*, and its newspaper, the *Völkischer Beobachter* (approximately: Folk-race Observer), which had earlier been a vehicle for the *Thule Gesellschaft*. The *Eher Verlag* was to play a most important part in Hitler's financial affairs, as described in Chapter 4.

One minor encounter occurred in 1920, which was later to have a significant impact on Hitler's political career, as well as his finances: Heinrich Hoffmann, later to become Hitler's personal photographer, art adviser, and significant source of income, had his first glimpse of his future master. He was not impressed:

> On one occasion I attended a district meeting of the local Citizens' Army. Among other speakers was one Adolf Hitler. I saw no reason for wasting a [photographic] plate on this nonentity . . . [29]

Throughout 1921, Hitler expanded his sources of personal finance to include minor industrialists and, something which was to be of great importance to him, rich older women. However, in the long term his most important act was to place Max Amann (see Chapter 12) at the head of the *Eher Verlag*. It was the beginning of a mutually profitable collaboration.

On 2 February, Hitler spoke at Munich's *Zirkus Krone*, a circus arena that could hold 6,000 people. The arena cost little to rent – the manager was a party member – and was packed to capacity. If Hitler was getting a percentage of the admission price and any collection that was taken, he must have been very pleased.[30]

Gustav Ritter von Kahr, Minister President of Bavaria, invited a delegation from the NSDAP to talks on 14 May, hoping to enlist their aid in gaining the support of 'national forces' in the region. The meeting was not a great success, nor was their long-term relationship: Kahr was murdered in the purge of June 1934. Three days later, in an attempt to smooth the way for collaboration between Hitler and Kahr, Rudolf Heß wrote to Kahr, praising Hitler's spirit of self-sacrifice and maintaining that he received no salary from the NSDAP but lived only on the fees that he received for his speeches and journalism.[31]

By mid-1921, Hitler was bringing in most of the party's funds from a variety of sources: collections at meetings, contributions from wealthy individuals, and secret accounts within the German Army. At no time did he draw a salary from the party; to have done so would have prejudiced his intention to take over the NSDAP. This did not mean that he received no money from the NSDAP; he did, but in the form of generous 'expenses' for speaking at meetings. However, Hitler made very few speeches to organisations other than the NSDAP at this time and 'expenses', plus gifts and journalism, must have been his main source of income. As an example of Hitler's journalism, between January and June he wrote 39 articles for the *Völkischer Beobachter*, for which he was paid, and from September onwards, he regularly contributed to the NSDAP's internal news-sheet, for which he was also probably paid.

In June-July, Hitler went on another fund-raising expedition to Berlin, accompanied as always by Eckart. Through Eckart's contacts, and others opened up by Max Maurenbrecher, editor of the newspaper *Deutsche Zeitung*, Hitler attempted to tap Pan-German supporters for funds to support the *Völkischer Beobachter*.[32] In this he was not very successful. While in Berlin, Hitler stayed with the Bechsteins (see Chapter 6) where, among others, he met the anti-Communist Count Yorck von Wartenburg who offered him financial support if he would move his headquarters to Berlin. Hitler, well aware that most of his support was in the south and equally aware of competition in the north from the Strasser brothers, declined the offer. It was probably at the Bechsteins that Hitler first met Dr. Emil Gansser, a former employee of *Siemens und Halske*. Gansser, who moved in wealthy, right-wing Protestant circles and would later play an important part in Hitler's finances, took Hitler to speak at Berlin's National Club, where he made a favourable impression. It was through Gansser that Hitler met Admiral Schröder, former commander of the German marines, who was one of the first high-ranking officers to join the NSDAP. Schröder is said to have channelled funds from the Navy, via J.F. Lehmann – a publisher with close links to the Navy and to the *Thule Gesellschaft* – to Hitler and the NSDAP.[33]

The trip to Berlin had to be cut short when certain members of the NSDAP rebelled against Hitler's leadership. On 11 July, in an attempt to force the party to appoint him leader, with dictatorial powers, Hitler announced his resignation from the party. Three days later, speaking before the party's general membership committee, he said:

> *I make these demands not because I am power hungry, but because recent events have more than convinced me that without an iron leadership the party . . . will within a short time cease to be what it was supposed to be: a national socialist German Workers' Party and not a western association.*[34]

Hitler gave the committee eight days to respond to his demands. The situation was further complicated by a leaflet, published by left-wing[35] members of the party's ruling committee and entitled *Adolf Hitler – Verräter?* (Adolf Hitler – Traitor?). It was made public in a special edition of the left-wing *Münchener Post* of 3 August 1921, and levelled several accusations against Hitler, including:

> *If any member* [of the party] *asks him how he lives and what was his former profession, he always becomes angry and excited. Up to now no answer has been supplied to these questions.*[36]

The pamphlet also questioned Hitler's relationships with women. Finally, on 29 July, after much drama, Hitler was confirmed as chairman of the party, replacing Drexler, who was given the post of 'honorary chairman' and now began the slide into obscurity. The pamphlet led to a libel action against the *Münchener Post* and Hitler, to his evident embarrassment, was forced to answer questions in court about his sources of income. Asked if he had received money for sixty-five speeches given in Munich he is said to have replied:

If I speak for the National Socialist Party, I take no money for myself. But I also speak for other organisations such as the German National Defence and Offensive League, and then, of course, I accept a fee. I also have my midday meal with various Party comrades in turn. I am further assisted to a modest extent by a few Party comrades.[37]

This suggests that at this time Hitler was living a hand-to-mouth existence. This is far from true; nor is it true, as he later claimed, that he was existing off stolen apples. He was shortly to start receiving substantial funds – personal and party – from prominent German names such as Bruckmann and Bechstein. Nor was the party in bad shape; shortly after he assumed control, in November, Hitler moved the party to new headquarters in an old abandoned inn in Corneliusstraße, near the Gärtnerplatz.[38] These offices had new desks, a safe, a telephone and a full-time, paid secretary. Within six months the NSDAP would have thirteen full-time salaried employees; not one of them was Adolf Hitler.

1922 was marked by the appearance of a number of key figures who were to play a significant part in Hitler's financial affairs: the well known Hermann Göring, the less well known Ernst Hanfstaengl and Kurt Lüdecke, and the almost unknown Frau Gertrud von Seidlitz. Of this quartet, the latter may have been the most significant in the long term.

Dr. Emil Gansser continued to raise money for Hitler, particularly in Switzerland where he had connections with wealthy, anti-Catholic Protestants. On 2 April he wrote to a Swiss evangelical:

[I] observed with keen delight on my last journey through Switzerland that among the influential German families Hitler's great ideological struggle is followed with far more attention and sympathy than in my own country . . .[39]

There are rumours that Hitler went to Switzerland with Gansser at about this time, in 1921 and 1923, to collect money to lead a crusade against the Catholic Church in Germany. The 1923 trips, at least, have been corroborated by Lüdecke and Hanfstaengl and further evidence was presented at Hitler's 1924 trial.[40]

On 24 June, the day that Walther Rathenau, Foreign Minister in the Weimar Government, was murdered, Hitler began a three month sentence in Stadelheim prison. Hitler had been convicted of 'inciting a riot' in breaking up a political meeting being addressed by a Bavarian separatist named Bellerstedt. He was given a cell with a private toilet, a cell which the warder took pains to point out was generally reserved for 'celebrities'. He was released on 27 July, with two months suspended against future 'good behaviour' – behaviour which never materialised.

On 11 August, Hitler came to the attention of Kurt Lüdecke, who became

Hitler's principal, though not very successful, fundraiser outside Germany. This idealist, though ultimately a rather pathetic figure, is described in Chapter 8.

Julius Streicher, leader of the Nuremberg branch of the right-wing *Deutsche Werkgemeinschaft* (DWG – German Work Community) wrote to Hitler on 8 October 1922, offering to bring the organisation, together with his newspaper the *Deutscher Volkswille*, into the NSDAP. The offer was not quite so straightforward as it seemed: the Nuremberg branch of the DWG was almost bankrupt and owed considerable sums to Dr Otto Dickel, who had founded the DWG in Augsburg, in March of 1921. The NSDAP granted Streicher RM 70,000 with which to pay off these debts, together with a loan for the outright purchase of the *Deutscher Volkswille*. Clearly the NSDAP was not short of funds and it may be assumed that Hitler's bank balance was equally healthy.

Foreign governments began to pay attention to Hitler. The US embassy in Berlin dispatched Captain Truman-Smith, an Assistant Military Attaché, to Munich to make discreet inquiries. Warren Robbins, a Counsellor at the embassy, had been at Harvard with Ernst Hanfstaengl in 1908 and suggested to Truman-Smith that he contact him for information. Robbins telephoned Hanfstaengl and asked him to give Truman-Smith what gossip he could about the political situation in Bavaria. Hanfstaengl agreed and introduced Smith to Cossmann, editor of the newspaper *Münchener Neueste Nachrichten*, and he in turn introduced Truman-Smith to such well-known political figures as Crown Prince Rupprecht, Ludendorff and Kahr. On Truman-Smith's last day in Munich, he lunched with Hanfstaengl and mentioned the name of a young politician called Hitler. At this time, Hanfstaengl was so ignorant of Bavarian politics that he thought Truman-Smith had confused the name with that of Hilpert, a well-known German nationalist. Truman-Smith, with a train to catch, gave Hanfstaengl his press ticket for a meeting that evening at which Hitler was scheduled to speak and asked him to report on what Hitler had to say. It was 22 November.

Hanfstaengl describes in some detail his first impressions of Hitler at the meeting, which took place in the *Kindlkeller* beerhall, and how, at the end of the meeting he introduced himself to his future master.[41] Lüdecke, however, claims that Hanfstaengl left the meeting with him, and without meeting Hitler, though it is doubtful whether this discrepancy has any significance.[42] Captain Truman-Smith made a detailed report to his superiors and on 5 December, Robbins sent a report to the US Secretary of State in which he noted:

> Hitler . . . is working very slowly and I should say efficiently along the same lines as Mussolini. . . .
> He is obtaining a great deal of money from the manufacturers just as Mussolini did . . . He told
> Truman Smith . . . that he is collecting funds and equipment and that all was going well.[43]

The report was filed away and forgotten. Just who the 'manufacturers' were is not explained; it could be a reference to Borsig, Grandel and Gansser. Hanfstaengl, attracted by Hitler's ideas and convinced that he could influence him for good against the influence of crackpots such as Rosenberg, whom he grew to detest, began to invite Hitler to his home.

Ernst 'Putzi' – the nickname can best be rendered in English as 'Titch' – Hanfstaengl was a lumbering giant of a man, with a remarkable resemblance (except for the teeth) to the actor Richard Kiel, who played 'Jaws' in the James Bond film 'Moonraker'. The gossip columnist Bella Fromm has left her own – not very flattering – impressions of the man:

> Another guest was the absurd looking giant, Dr. Ernst Hanfstaengl. His hands, of almost frightening dimensions, accompany every phrase in violent gesticulation. A jerk of his strangely distorted head drives every point home. The party members love him as a court jester is loved. "Putzi" is Nazi-struck. He has neglected his family business for years to follow the trail of his master like a faithful hound. It is said his American mother has helped the Nazi cause with donations of no mean dimensions.[44]

Son of a wealthy Munich family of art publishers with US connections, Hanfstaengl not only had money – and access to dollars, a major bonus in times of rampant inflation – but also important social connections. In the long term, these were to prove every bit as useful as cash. However, if Lüdecke is to be believed, Hanfstaengl's dollars were initially his major source of interest to the NSDAP, and especially to Max Amann, who was the party's business manager at the time:

> At last Amann and I succeeded in getting him to sign, most reluctantly, on the dotted line. We put him down for one American dollar a month – not so absurd as it sounds, for at that time the dollar was worth about six thousand marks.[45]

Once again, Lüdecke's version conflicts with that of Hanfstaengl, who claims that he did not actually join the NSDAP until August 1931. Since all the NSDAP records were hastily destroyed in the aftermath of the November 1923 *Putsch*, it is possible that Hanfstaengl did join the party in 1922, only re-joining it later. However, it seems more likely that Hanfstaengl merely signed on as a supporter, rather than as an actual member.[46]

It was Hanfstaengl who introduced Hitler to the Bruckmanns, another family of Munich publishers and, possibly, to Gertrud von Seidlitz, who was to play an important role in the success of the *Völkischer Beobachter*. It was Hanfstaengl who introduced Hitler to William Bayard Hale, leading European correspondent for the Hearst press which would later pay generously for the articles he wrote and interviews that he gave, and to Wilhelm Funk, who would become one of Hitler's link-men to German Big Business. In the early days of their acquaintance, Hanfstaengl, like Göring, bought Hitler meals and gave him small amounts of cash, as Eckart had done earlier.

Shortly after, Hitler bought his first motor car, a vehicle of decrepit appearance which nevertheless gave him a moral edge over the Communists who either walked or used public transport. This vehicle was quickly replaced by a slightly less ramshackle, green *Selve*, which Hanfstaengl describes as: . . . *a rattling monster and each end looked as if it was going in different ways* . . . [47] Hoffmann is hardly less flattering, but more colourful:

> *As a car it wasn't much to look at; it was already pretty ancient, and the sea-weed stuffing with which it was upholstered was sprouting out of the back seat. A cart pulled up immediately behind it, and the horse, mistaking it for hay, pulled out a goodly mouthful of the upholstery. He quickly found, however, that it was by no means to his taste* . . . [48]

Both cars were Hitler's personal property (as were all his vehicles until 1933, as confirmed by his tax returns) though where he found the money remains a mystery. It is possible that at least one vehicle was a gift.

In November, Hitler met Hermann Göring who would become Commander in Chief of the Luftwaffe, creator of the Gestapo and the concentration camps, and Hitler's designated successor.[49] A war hero, who brought an additional air of respectability to the NSDAP, Göring had money and, through his wide circle of friends in Germany and abroad, access to more money. Although he had been rendered virtually penniless by the hyperinflation of that time, Göring was still able to live comfortably on the foreign income of his wife. Göring, like Hitler, loved money; unlike Hitler he did not mind having to do a little work to get it. In the middle of the First World War, with the help of his friend Prince Philipp of Heße, he set up a shoe factory to supply the German Army. This association was later to bring funds to Göring, Hitler, and the NSDAP, as was his friendship with Crown Prince Friedrich Wilhelm. At their elegant villa in the Munich suburb of Obermenzing, near the Nymphenburg palace, it was the Görings who persuaded General Erich Ludendorff that Hitler's views deserved serious consideration.

In late 1922, a group of Bavarians, including some *Freikorps* units, plotted a coup against the Bavarian government. According to Lüdecke, Hitler supported the plotters, but when they developed cold feet and the plot was abandoned he railed against what he called 'mediocrities and cowards'.[50] This failed coup was the beginning of the end of the *Freikorps* movement. From here on, those who had previously given financial support to the *Freikorps* would increasingly transfer that support to Hitler, the NSDAP, and the SA. So too would many Freikorps leaders.[51] Former Naval Lieutenant Hans Ulrich Klintzsch, a prominent member of the *Freikorps Eberhardt Brigade*, was the first official leader of the SA in 1921.[52] The *Freikorps* movement enjoyed a brief resurgence in September 1923 when Hitler succeeded in organising a loose Bavarian *Kampfbund* (Fighting League) of some 70,000 men. It came to nothing and most of its members joined the SA, which was probably what Hitler intended.

Apart from the failed putsch in November 1923, which ended with Hitler in prison, the most important event of that year was the conversion of the *Völkischer Beobachter* to daily publication and from 'tabloid' to 'broadsheet' format. This gave the newspaper an air of respectability which not only brought increased sales but also increased advertising revenues. Increased profits began to find their way into the pockets of Hitler and Amann.

Nineteen twenty-three was a year of rampant inflation in Germany, conditions which brought many people to Hitler and the NSDAP. Though the NSDAP could not have been receiving much of value from its rank and file members, it certainly acted as if it did. The only explanation that can account for this is that both the NSDAP and Hitler had access to hard currency: American Dollars; British Pounds; Czech Koruna; French Francs; even Finnish Markka. The NSDAP was doing well with the collections which it made at meetings (and from which Hitler received a percentage) and one police informant reported money being collected 'by the bushel', though given the rate of inflation at the time this was not quite so spectacular as it might seem.[53] Hitler later claimed, possibly with some exaggeration:

> *We, with our two and a half million members, banked two and a half million marks every month. Many members paid more than the subscription demanded (at first it was fifty pfennig a month, then it was raised to a mark). Fräulein Schleifer, from the post-office, used to pay ten marks a month, for example. Thus the Party disposed of considerable sums. Schwarz was very open-handed when it was a question of large matters, but extremely thrifty in small ones. He was the perfect mixture of parsimony and generosity.* [54]

Lüdecke was arrested on January 27, 1923, on the eve of the Nazis' *Parteitag*, and attempts were made to link him to various rumours of French espionage. It was around this time that rumours began to circulate that Hitler was also in the pay of the French – a topic examined in Chapter 10. These rumours were no doubt ignited by the allegations surrounding Lüdecke and fuelled by Hitler's apparent ambiguity over the French occupation of the Rhineland.[55]

In February, the *Völkischer Beobachter* was re-launched as a daily paper. Most of the money needed to expand the paper, especially the purchase of a rotary press, came from Frau Gertrud von Seidlitz (see Chapter 6.) Commenting on this period, Hanfstaengl says:

> *I simply have no idea where the Party revenues came from. There is little doubt that, in its early stages, the German army command in Bavaria had provided subsidies for an organization which gave every promise of fighting the Communists, but by 1923 I suspect this source was drying up, as the Nazis were becoming too independent.* [56]

It is *chutzpah* for Hanfstaengl to claim that he did not know where funds were coming from, since he claims to have been one of the principal fund-raisers. Around the beginning of April, Hitler and Hanfstaengl, driven by Emil Maurice in the famous *Selve* and accompanied, for no obvious reason, by the eighteen-year-old Fritz Lauböck, drove off to see Dr. Emil Gansser in Berlin.[57] In Berlin, accommodation had been arranged for Hitler by Wilhelm Ohnesorge, then an official with the post office and Postmaster-General after 1933, where he was instrumental in arranging for a royalty to be paid to Hitler for the use of his image on postage stamps. They visited the Bechsteins, but they were not forthcoming, pleading hard times. Whether Hitler actually met Gansser and extracted support from him, Hanfstaengl does not say. Gansser *did* go to Switzerland on a fund-raising tour and may have been accompanied by Hitler who is said to have returned from a trip to Zurich 'with a steamer trunk stuffed with Swiss francs and American dollars'.[58] Unless it was a very small 'steamer trunk' or the notes were low denomination, or both, this seems highly unlikely.[59] On another trip to Switzerland, Hitler was accompanied for at least part of the journey by Prince Ahrenberg.[60]

One of the first recorded instances of gifts being showered on Hitler comes with his birthday in 1923. It also offers an interesting insight into the mind of Adolf Hitler:

> I went along during the morning to congratulate him and found him alone, though the grubby little flat was stacked from floor to ceiling with flowers and cakes. Yet Hitler was in one of his curious wary moods and had not touched a single one of them. There they were, with swastikas and eagles in whipped cream all over them, looking like the bakers' pavilion at a village fair. It was not much to my taste, I am a beer and sausage man myself, but even my mouth watered. "Well, Herr Hitler," I said, "now you can really have a feast". – "I am not at all sure they are not all poisoned", he replied. "But they are all from your friends and admirers", I told him. "Yes, I know", he replied. "But this house belongs to a Jew and these days you can drip slow poison down the walls and kill your enemies. I never eat here normally". "Herr Hitler, you've been reading too many of those Edgar Wallace thrillers", I answered, but nothing would persuade him, and I literally had to take a taste myself before he would touch them.[61]

Hitler was also unwilling to accept gifts if he thought it was good propaganda to refuse them. Referring to Christmas of 1922, Lüdecke writes:

> To Hitler I gave an etching of Frederick the Great, which seemed to please him. I had intended giving him a warm blanket, because I remembered that when the nights grew cold on the trip to Coburg, he had wrapped himself in a tattered old covering which obviously had reached the retirement age. But when I offered him a new one for Christmas, he refused it, saying he could not part from the one that was his shelter all through the war. If there was an object-lesson in that for me, I saw none.[62]

Some time in early 1923, Röhm's corporate fiddling to divert funds and equipment to the SA was noticed by his superiors. Nothing happened except that the dummy companies were quietly wound up and the loophole closed. To have dismissed or prosecuted Röhm would have revealed what the Army fervently wished to conceal: that it was breaking the Versailles Treaty. There may have been a little more to it: Röhm was accused of profiting from illegal arms sales, possibly to the NSDAP or remnants of the *Freikorps*. Nothing was ever proven but the events did lead to a split between Röhm and Epp, each accusing the other of disloyalty. Epp was replaced by General Otto von Lossow, an incorruptible member of the military 'priesthood' advocated by de Vigny, and there was no place for the likes of Röhm in the type of organisation envisaged by von Lossow. Hitler's army funding was over; it did not matter, he no longer needed it.

In September, using jewellery lent by Frau Bechstein as surety, Hitler was able to borrow 60,000 Swiss Francs from Richard Frank, a wealthy Berlin coffee merchant.[63] To what use the money was put – and if it was not for his own use, at least it was borrowed in Hitler's own name – or whether the loan was ever repaid, is uncertain, but the timing suggests that it was connected with the following affair. Needing larger premises for the NSDAP, Hitler and Frank went to see Dr. Kuhlo, director of the Association of Bavarian Industrialists and a Nazi sympathiser, to discuss a scheme whereby Kuhlo would form a syndicate to buy the *Hotel Eden*, a large property near the Munich main railway station, and Frank would provide the deposit in Swiss Francs – a condition of the hotel's current owners.[64] Once the deal was concluded, the NSDAP would have exclusive use of the premises in return for a modest rental. According to Hitler:

> *When all was ready, the syndicate met, with Kuhlo in the chair. The latter rose to his feet and announced that the hotel would be put at the Party's disposal for a modest rental. He suggested, in passing, that perhaps the Party might suppress the article in its programme concerning Freemasonry. I got up and said good-bye to these kindly philanthropists. I'd fallen unawares into a nest of Freemasons![65]*

Hitler and the NSDAP were almost as violently opposed to Freemasonry as they were towards Jews. Since this deal did not go through, the 60,000 Swiss francs must have been used for other purposes, possibly to support the *Völkischer Beobachter*, as described in Chapter 4.

At the German Day rally in Nuremberg, on 1-2 September, Ludendorff pledged his support to Hitler and the NSDAP. From a propaganda point of view, this was great news: what could be better than a General, a war hero, who was regarded by many as the true leader of German nationalism? Hitler began to exploit his Ludendorff connection: a propaganda film was made in which Hitler and Ludendorff appeared side-by-side, as equals. The implications were obvious to potential Hitler supporters. Ludendorff's support naturally had financial consequences, though the old general himself was far from wealthy. According to Lüdecke:

> *Many people of wealth and social position suddenly discovered their patriotic hearts and made common cause with us, in the belief that Hitler might, after all, come out on top and share the spoils with them. Many others gave money to the movement without actually joining it.[66]*

Hitler, possibly on his own initiative, possibly at the suggestion of Hoffmann, began to have his photograph everywhere and Hoffmann, the only person permitted to photograph Hitler, began publishing and selling photographs of his master. It was the beginning of a lucrative association for both men, as described in Chapter 12. Scheubner-Richter took over from Amann as business manager of the NSDAP in September. He was not to hold the post for long, being killed a few weeks later during the *Putsch*.

Some time in October, Fritz Thyssen, of the Ruhr steel family, gave 100,000 gold *marks* to Ludendorff to finance his political activities.[67] Thyssen later admitted that he gave the money with the instruction to divide it amongst nationalist groups as he saw fit. Hitler and the NSDAP are known to have benefited, but probably only in a minor way.

On November 9, Hitler and his followers, including Ludendorff, staged an abortive *Putsch* in Munich and on November 11, Hitler was arrested at Hanfstaengl's house — and taken away in his pyjamas, his Iron Cross, First Class, pinned to his chest.[68] There, Hitler composed the first of his 'political testaments' (it is not known whether he also made a personal will) transferring leadership of the party to Rosenberg, with Amann as his deputy. During the *Putsch*, Amann was involved in a robbery for which he was later briefly jailed. On Hitler's orders, Amann and a group of SA men seized 14,605 trillion *marks* in notes from the *Parcus* and *Mühlthaler* printing companies. Though the amount sounds astronomical, it was actually worth very little: the Nazis had stolen about $3,500 at the then exchange rate. Hanfstaengl recalls seeing the money in the *Putsch* headquarters at the *Bürgerbräu*:

> In the anteroom there was a little orchestra platform and on it, in a pile about five feet high, thousands of million- and billion-mark notes in neat banker's bundles, which the brownshirts had "requisitioned" somewhere during the night. I could have done with a few of them myself, for my hospitality the night before had left me without a penny in my pocket, but evidently they were to be expended in a legal and formal fashion whatever their origin.[69]

On the day of the Putsch a copy of the *Völkischer Beobachter* cost 8 billion *marks*. Six days later, the German Mark finally stabilised and the country entered a period of stability and prosperity that was far from Hitler's liking. In future, he would have to find other causes of discontent to attract support.

Notes

1   KERS98, p. 105.
2   WAIT77, p. 204.
3   HEID44, p. 24.
4   KERS98, pp. 110-116.
5   KERS98, p. 117, quoting Heinz, Heinz A., *Germany's Hitler*, London (1934), second edition, 1938, p. 90.
6   DAVI77, p. 124; KERS98, p. 118.
7   MASE73, p. 103.
8   HEID44, p. 26, but with no citation for the source of the statement. MASE73, p. 104, citing Viktor von Körber, *Hitler, sein Leben und seine Reden*, Munich, 1923.

9   MASE73, p. 104. These 'private sources' are not known, but many suspect that they were connected with the *Thule Gesellschaft*.

10   KERS98, p. 122. Fromm (FROM43, p. 83) claims that Himmler was also "co-spy with Hitler for the Reichswehr".

11   KERS98, p. 126.

12   DAVI77, p. 124.

13   HEID44, pp. 77-78. No citation, but said to be 'ten years later', so possibly a quotation from *Mein Kampf* or from a speech.

14   KERS98, p. 127, quoting Mayr and Jäckel. Another who joined the DAP around the same time as Hitler was the expressionist artist Emil Nolde, later to be banned by Hitler as a 'degenerate'. (MASE73, p. 63.)

15   KERS98, p. 140. Some authors describe this meeting as being in the cellar of Munich's famous *Hofbräuhaus*; it was not. As Kershaw rightly points out, the *Hofbräuhaus* is in the city centre, but the *Hofbräukeller* was part of a brewery, on Wienerstraße, east of the city centre.

16   KERS98, p. 140.

17   HEID44, p. 96; no source is given for the statement.

18   LÜDE38, p. 87.

19   DIET57, p. 163. The 'newspaper' referred to was an anti-Semitic weekly entitled *Auf gut Deutsch* (In Plain German).

20   HOFF55, p. 42.

21   POOL78, p. 53. The reference cited cannot be traced; perhaps it is incomplete.

22   POOL78, p. 29; TURN85B, p. 51.

23   Some authors have '51', but '41/1' is the number that appears on all Hitler's tax returns.

24   Toland (TOLA76, p.102) believes that Hitler's choice of room was determined by its proximity to these offices, but Hitler did not acquire the *Eher Verlag* until nine months later and it seems more likely that cost played a significant part in the decision.

25   KERS98, p. 129.

26   KERS98, p. 153, quoting Mayr, Karl (Anon.), *'I Was Hitler's Boss'*, *Current History*, Vol. I, No. 3, (November 1941), pp. 198-6. Mayr was killed in Buchenwald in 1945.

27   POOL78, pp. 46-47; the first two sentences are copied almost exactly from Gordon (GORD72, p. 161). LÜDE38, p. 145, merely notes Röhm's access to secret Government funds and his mastery of 'arms bootlegging'.

28   KERS98, p. 155.

29   HOFF55, p. 39. Hoffmann, as he notes, was present as a press photographer.

30   TOLA76, p. 109.

31   KERS98, p. 159, quoting from Deuerlein, Ernst, *Der Aufsteig der NSDAP in Augenzeugenberichten*, Munich, 1974, pp. 132-4.

32   Pan-Germanism was an extreme right movement which aimed to unite all who were 'racially German' in the struggle against 'evil', as personified by those who were not 'racially German', such as Jews, Slavs, Freemasons, Socialists, and abstract artists.

On a practical level, the movement advocated press censorship, restriction of voting rights to those who were 'racially pure', and laws against Jews and Socialism.

33 POOL78, pp. 36-37; however, this is based only on Sebottendorf's evidence, which cannot be corroborated.

34 TOLA76, p. 111, quoting Franz-Willing.

35 i.e. committee members who took the expression 'Socialist' in the party's title literally, even to the extent of wanting to abolish interest on bank accounts, nationalise all major industries, etc.

36 Elements of this story are quoted by BULL62, p. 83; SHIR60, p. 73; TOLA76, p. 111.

37 BULL62, p. 83; SHIR60, p. 73; KERS98, p. 160.

38 HEID44, pp. 96-97, without any source for the quote.

39 HEID36, p. 236.

40 DEUE62, pp. 386-90.

41 HANF53, pp. 32-37. It is clear from Hanfstaengl's account that he went to the meeting on Truman-Smith's behalf and he was not, as some authors claim, taken there by Truman-Smith.

42 LÜDE38, p. 95.

43 Text taken from TOLA76, p. 130. Robbins' note implies that Hitler met Truman-Smith, but this conflicts with Hanfstaengl's account. The discrepancy has not been resolved.

44 FROM43, p. 85.

45 LÜDE38, p. 96.

46 See Lüdecke (LÜDE38, p. 147) where he writes of people giving money without actually joining the party.

47 HANF57, p. 44.

48 HOFF55, p. 44.

49 For some reason, Heiden (HEID44, p. 91) has them meeting a year earlier, in 1921.

50 LÜDE38, p. 62.

51 The following information is based mostly on information supplied to the author by Russel Folsom in a personal communication of 14 July 2001.

52 Heiden (HEID44, p.94) has his first name as Johann, so it is possible that the Hans was a diminutive, and the last name as Klintsch. Hanfstaengl (HANF57, p. 46), Gordon (GORD72, p. 62) and Lüdecke (LÜDE38, p. 102) all have the spelling as Klintzsch, which seems the more probable.

53 Report of the *Polizeidirektion, München*, dated 6 February, 1923. NSDAP HA 69/1507.

54 HITL53, p. 280. Evening of 3 February, 1942.

55 HANF57, p. 49. As usual, it is difficult to be sure just what date Hanfstaengl is referring to.

56 HANF57, p. 55.

57 It is possible, though not proven, that he was the son or grandson of Theodor Laubock, the *Reichsbahn* official who often helped Hitler in small, discreet ways. See Chapter 6, *Hitler's Women*.

58 POOL78, p. 71.

59   The author owns a trunk dating from the nineteen-twenties. It is about 100x60x30 centimetres, giving a volume of 180,000 cc. $100 in one dollar bills occupies about 120 cc – depending upon how hard one squeezes. Therefore the author's trunk could hold over $150,000 in one dollar bills – rather a large sum for the time.

60   HITL53, pp. 571-2. Midday, 5 August 1942.

61   HANF57, p. 66.

62   LÜDE38, p. 105.

63   Turner (TURN85B, p. 378) claims that the man's family name was Franck, not Frank, but the name on the loan documents is Frank.

64   POOL78, p. 70. Hitler also refers to the deal (HITL53, p. 278) though in slightly less detail.

65   HITL53, pp. 278-9. 3 February, 1942, evening.

66   LÜDE38, p. 147.

67   THYS41, pp. 133-4. Thyssen, rarely precise about many things, is vague as to the date but it must have been shortly before the November *Putsch*.

68   The affair is of little direct importance to the question of Hitler's fortune and is not detailed here. The reader may find a good account in Toland (TOLA76, Chapter 6) and a rather more fanciful one in Heiden (HEID44, Chapter 9). Deuerlein (DEUE62, pp. 357-9) is the only source for the Iron Cross story.

69   HANF57, p. 103. According to Baur (BAUR58, pp. 99-100), Hitler expressed approval of bank robbery when it was to finance a political party, even expressing approval of Stalin's actions in that respect.

Chapter Four

HITLER'S PRESS

*A cynical, mercenary, demagogic, corrupt press will produce in time a people as
base as itself.*
Joseph Pulitzer (1847-1911)
Inscription over the gateway of the Columbia School of Journalism,
New York.

Hitler was well aware of the 'power of the press' – both as a propaganda tool and
as a source of income – and one of the most significant events of his career was
the purchase of the *Eher Verlag*, a publishing company, and with it, the newspaper
Völkischer Beobachter. By the end of 1944, the *Eher Verlag* owned or controlled almost
every newspaper and magazine in Germany and was bringing its general manager,
Max Amann (described in Chapter 11) an income of RM 3,800,000 a year. There
is strong evidence that it brought Adolf Hitler an equal or greater amount.

As with most things, what Hitler declared in public differed from what he did
in private and his relations with the press are no exception. In the notorious
'Twenty-five Points', which he declared on 24 February, 1920, point twenty-
three reads:

> *We demand legal warfare against conscious political lying and its dissemination in the Press. In order
> to facilitate creation of a German national press we demand:*
>
>   *(a) that all editors of newspapers and their assistants, employing the German language, must be
>   members of the nation;*
>
>   *(b) that special permission from the state shall be necessary before non-German newspapers may
>   appear. These are not necessarily printed in the German language;*
>
>   *(c) that non-Germans shall be prohibited by law from participation financially in or influencing
>   German newspapers . . .* [1]

While Hitler almost certainly used the word 'German' in a racial sense, rather
than in the sense of legal nationality, it is amusing to note that he, an Austrian
citizen at the time, violated clause (c) by his purchase of the *Völkischer Beobachter*
and clause (a) by writing for it himself and installing Rosenberg, still a Russian
citizen at the time, as editor.[2]

When Hitler came to power, the German press was far more fragmented and decentralised than in other European countries.[3] In 1932, there were 4,703 daily and weekly newspapers, the majority of which (81% in 1928) were family-owned local publications. To a large extent, it was this fragmentation which allowed the Nazis to take over almost the whole of the German press by the early nineteen forties. Another feature of the German press was the *Interessantenpresse* – 'special interest press' – which promoted the views of a particular group; usually a sector of business, political party or religious sect. Such publications were despised for their blatant bias and were often rather shady enterprises. As Oron Hale, author of the first comprehensive study of this topic, puts it:

> *Shares were sold, traded, and acquired, and properties transferred without the true ownership being revealed. In these instances the shares would appear as vested stock in the hands of a legal trustee or bank representing an unknown, but not always unsuspected, owner.*[4]

This aptly describes the situation of the *Eher Verlag* and the *Völkischer Beobachter*. To quote Hale again:

> *The press mirrored the mood of the country – confusion, uncertainty, and fear, and the clash of irreconcilable parties and ideologies.*[5]

It was such a climate as this which permitted newspapers such as the *Völkischer Beobachter* to flourish.

Purchase of the *Eher Verlag*

By 1943, according to one estimate, the *Eher Verlag* had an annual turnover exceeding that of the chemical combine *IG Farben*.[6] The company had its offices at Thierschstraße 11, Munich, in a modest three-storey building in a pleasant, if rather run-down, middle-class street close to the river. From here it controlled about 150 publishing companies, employed about 35,000 persons, and raked in annual profits of over RM 50 million in its best years (see Table 12-2). Most of this money found its way into the pockets of Hitler and Amann, though some went to the NSDAP to finance the election campaigns of 1932-3. After 1933, the party had no further need of such funds and the entire profits became available for Hitler's and Amann's personal use.

The *Eher Verlag* was founded by Franz Eher, who in 1900 acquired the *Münchener Beobachter*, a four-page, suburban weekly newspaper in a format that we would now call tabloid, the paper itself having been founded in January 1887. By the time of Eher's death in 1918, the paper was publishing two editions, one within Munich, the other outside. Shortly after Eher's death, the external edition was re-named the *Völkischer Beobachter* and in 1919, the title of *Völkischer Beobachter* was adopted for all editions. In 1920, his heirs sold the *Eher Verlag* and the *Völkischer Beobachter* to Sebottendorf, President of the *Thule Gesellschaft* (see Appendix 2). One of

Sebottendorf's first steps was to incorporate the *Eher Verlag* as a legal entity. Incorporation required a declaration of the shareholders and it is from this point that we begin to get glimpses of the company's ownership.

It is alleged that most of Sebottendorf's financial backing was provided by his mistress, Fräulein Käthe Bierbaumer, and the list of stockholders filed with the corporation court in Munich on 20 March, 1920 shows her as the principal share-holder.[7] The full list is given in Table 4-1. Of this octet, Dora Kunze was Sebottendorf's sister. Gottfried Feder was one of the ideological founders of the Nazi party, and Eder was, for a time, business manager of the *Eher Verlag*. Heuß was a Munich paper manufacturer and should not be confused with the first President of the post-war Federal Republic of Germany. As many have found, before and since, publishing often absorbs far more money than it produces; by December 1920, the *Eher Verlag* was on the brink of bankruptcy. Whether this was the result of general mismanagement and the poor profitability of the publishing industry at that time or, as Toland suggests, because of the large number of libel actions filed against the *Völkischer Beobachter*, is unclear.[8] Whatever the reasons, the owners were ready to sell.

There are several versions of how Hitler acquired the *Eher Verlag* and the earliest is probably that of Lüdecke, who wrote in 1938:

> In December [1920] the Voelkischer Beobachter, *an insignificant folkic weekly, was acquired with funds obtained from the* Reichswehr *by Dietrich Eckart and Captain Ernst Roehm, Hitler's staunchest supporters.*[9]

Lüdecke here fails to distinguish between the *Völkischer Beobachter* and its publisher, the *Eher Verlag*, but the only minor error in Ludecke's bald account is that the paper

---

Table 4-1: Ownership of the EV on 20 March 1920

Shareholder	Amount (RM)
Bierbaumer, Käthe	46,500
von Feilitzsch, Franz Freiherr	20,000
Kunze, Dora	10,000
Feder, Gottfried	10,000
Eder, Franz Xaver	10,000
Gutberlet, Dr Wilhelm	10,000
Heuß, Theodor	10,000
Braun, Karl Alfred	3,500
Total:	**120,000**

actually appeared twice a week, on Wednesdays and Saturdays. Heiden's 1944 account gives essentially the same information.[10] Bullock adds the information that the purchase price was RM 60,000, of which he claims Dietrich Eckart provided half and part of the rest came from 'Army secret funds'.[11] The next account comes from Shirer, who tells essentially the same story, adding that it was Major General Ritter von Epp who was thought to have provided most of the money from 'Army secret funds'.[12] Shirer, too, fails to distinguish between the paper and its publisher. He also gives no sources for his information, but the unusual phrase 'Army secret funds' – rather than 'secret Army funds' – is exactly as in Bullock. The next, and up to that time the best researched, account of the purchase of the *Eher Verlag* comes from Hale, much of whose information is acknowledged to be due to the unpublished 1956 doctoral thesis of Sonja Noller and Franz-Willing's study of Hitler's rise to power:

> With dwindling income and mounting debts, the Verlag was on the brink of bankruptcy by December 1920, when a controlling interest was acquired by the National Socialist party. The purchase price was 120,000 RM and assumption of debts amounting to 250,000 RM.[13]

Note that Hale refers to a 'controlling interest', rather than outright purchase, of what he correctly identifies as the *Eher Verlag*. It is apparent from Noller's investigations (see below) that at least two of the original shareholders kept some of their investment. Hale's account continues:

> Dietrich Eckart, Hitler's friend and sponsor in the party, played the decisive role in that he found the money to make the down payments on the majority shares. Eckart got the cash – 60,000 RM – from Reichswehr General Ritter von Epp, acknowledging receipt and pledging repayment in a personal note dated December 17, 1920.

In a footnote to this latter comment, Hale states:

> It is generally assumed that Von Epp used special Reichswehr funds. In 1923, when the matter was exposed in the Social Democratic press – Von Epp called it a "stink bomb" – he claimed that this was a personal loan which had been repaid, a statement of doubtful validity.[14]

Hale concludes:

> While the loan from Epp was decisive, others also contributed. Dr. Gottfried Grandel, an early supporter of the party, and Simon Eckart, an official of the Hansa Bank, advanced part of the purchase money or pledged their credit to consummate the deal.[15]

Grandel and his activities were described in the previous chapter. Simon Eckart (see Chapter 10) was actually a wealthy farmer. There is no hard evidence that he was an executive of the Munich Hansa Bank, despite Hitler's claims, but there is documentary evidence that he backed a loan made by that bank to the *Eher Verlag* or the *Völkischer Beobachter*.[16] In an ironic footnote to the affair, Grandel sued the *Eher Verlag* in 1940 for the return of the guarantee that he had pledged in 1921.

In 1976, with the advantage of many interviews with survivors, Toland gave his version of the acquisition of the *Völkischer Beobachter*, failing, like many authors, to distinguish the paper from its publishing company:

The Völkischer Beobachter *was on the brink of bankruptcy because of numerous libel actions. This was the paper Hitler wanted. A financial crisis was the opportunity he had been waiting for. At 2 A.M. on the morning of December 17 Hitler burst into Eckart's* [sic. It was actually Drexler that he went to visit] *apartment excitedly announcing that the Beobachter had to be sold because of debts and was "in danger" of falling into the wrong hands. . . . The asking price was reasonable only 180,000 marks; and Hitler was positive Eckart could raise this from wealthy friends.*[17]

For Toland, the asking price is RM 180,000, RM 60,000 more than for Hale, but, at this point, he makes no mention of any debts to be assumed. Toland continues:

At eight the next morning Drexler was at Eckart's door. It was an unspeakable hour for a man of the latter's habits and "at first" recalled Drexler, "he was bad tempered. Then we started off." By noon they had collected 60,000 marks from General von Epp . . . and 30,000 more from an anti-Semitic doctor. Drexler himself signed a note for the paper's debts of more than 100,000 marks and at four that afternoon the purchase of the Beobachter *was properly registered.*

The 'anti-Semitic doctor' was almost certainly Grandel, who was a real doctor, rather than a physician, as Toland seems to think. Pool tackled the subject in 1978, adding the following to previous accounts:

On December 17, Hitler made a personal appeal to Dr. Gottfried Grandel, an industrialist from Augsburg, Bavaria, who had recently made a few moderate contributions to the Party. Surprisingly, Grandel agreed to help. He and Simon Eckart, an official of the Hansa Bank, advanced part of the purchase money and pledged their credit to consummate the deal. Not long after the transaction had taken place, Fräulein Bierbaumer and Frau Kunze came to Grandel for payment in full and received a total of RM 56,500. Although the bulk of the necessary money was supplied by Grandel and von Epp, others also contributed. For example, Dr. Gutberlet made Hitler a present of shares valued at RM 5,000 and Dietrich Eckart probably put in a small amount of his own money.[18]

Pool is one of the first to mention Gutberlet's contribution, yet the evidence for that had been available since the publication of the book *Hitler's Secret Conversations* in 1953, where Hitler claimed that Dr Gutberlet had given him RM 5,000 worth of shares as a gift and that he – Hitler – had bought other shares.[19] Whether these shares were bought in Hitler's name or on behalf of the NSDAv[20] – or even if they were bought at all – is not known. Finally, one of the most recent historians to address the question is Kershaw, who writes:

Grandel later served as guarantor for the funds used to purchase the Völkischer Beobachter *and turn it into the party's own newspaper in December 1920.*

The party leadership had been looking to buy the near bankrupt Beobachter *since the summer to provide the wider publicity that was needed. But it was only in mid-December, when rival bidders for the newspaper emerged, that Hitler moved. Together with Hermann Esser and the deputy party-chairman Oskar Körner*[21]*, he turned up in an agitated state at Drexler's flat at two o'clock in the*

*morning claiming the Beobachter was "in danger", that it was about to fall into Bavarian separatists'
hands. Drexler's mother was wakened up to make coffee, and around the kitchen table it was decided
that Drexler would first thing the next morning call on Eckart to persuade him to encourage his wealthy
contacts to provide the financial backing to acquire the newspaper. Hitler, meanwhile, would seek out
Dr Grandel in Augsburg. Six hours later, Drexler was drumming an irritable Eckart out of bed,
disgruntled at being awakened so early. They were soon on their way to see General von Epp. Eckart
convinced the latter how vital it was to gain possession of the Beobachter and stood guarantee with his
house and property for the 60,000 Marks which Epp provided from the funds of the Reichswehr.
Other sources yielded a further 30,000 Marks, and Drexler himself, earning 35 Marks a week, took
over the remaining debts of 113,000 Marks before, that afternoon, becoming the legal owner of the
Völkischer Beobachter.*[22]

Given these different accounts, several of which stem from essentially the same sources, some estimate of the truth can be had by appealing to the numbers: whatever numbers make sense are probably the right ones. There is no question that the share capital of the *Eher Verlag* was RM 120,000 and that this was the asking price, plus assumption of the company's debts of between RM 100,000 and RM 250,000.[23]

Eckart definitely received RM 60,000 from von Epp, which was almost enough to pay for the combined holdings of Braun, Eder, Feder, von Feilitzsch, Gutberlet, and Heuß, which amounted to RM 63,500. If Hitler is correct in saying that Gutberlet gave him RM 5,000 worth of shares and he purchased others, then von Epp's funds were more than sufficient to buy a controlling interest. The 17 December, 1920 records of the Munich corporation court show that ownership was then in the hands of Käthe Bierbaumer, Dora Kunze – and Anton Drexler, listed in the document as chairman of the NSDAv, holding a clear majority, as shown in Table 4-2. What probably happened is this:

- Braun, Eder, Feder, von Feilitzsch, Gutberlet, and Heuß were bought out in 1920 using the RM 60,000 from von Epp and the RM 5,000 worth of shares given to Hitler by Gutberlet.
- The remainder of von Epp's RM 60,000 – at least RM 1,500, possibly more if Hitler really had bought some shares – was applied towards the *Eher Verlag's* outstanding debts.

Table 4-2: Ownership of the EV on 17 December 1920

Shareholder	Amount (RM)
Bierbaumer, Käthe	46,500
Kunze, Dora	10,000
Drexler, Anton	63,500
Total:	**120,000**

- Bierbaumer and Kunze agreed to defer payment for their shares.
- Grandel provided RM 30,000, which went towards payment of debts. He and Simon Eckart guaranteed the outstanding amount to Bierbaumer and Kunze. This was paid off some time between December 1920 and November 1921, possibly by Grandel.

Thus, at least RM 31,500 went towards debt repayment, so that if Drexler assumed responsibility for RM 113,000 (as Kershaw says) the original debt would have been at least RM 144,500 or, alternatively, that the debt was reduced to RM 81,000 or less. Nonetheless, evidence as to the ownership of the *Eher Verlag* at the point when Hitler gained control remains confusing, or, as Noller puts it, 'unclear and opaque' (*unklar und undurchsichtig*).[24] Hitler took care to ensure that it was to remain so. The question is further complicated by a statement made by Max Amann, in 1951, that when he became a director of the *Eher Verlag*, on 4 April 1922, the shares were held by Gottfried Feder, a *Freiherr* von Reitzenstein from Garmisch, and by the NSDAv.[25] We will probably never know, since most of the relevant records were destroyed during the war. However, as shown later in this chapter, there is strong evidence that Hitler alone owned the *Eher Verlag*. On 18 December 1920, the day after the share transfer was recorded, the *Völkischer Beobachter* announced that it had been bought by the NSDAP.

In July of 1921, Hitler gained control of the NSDAP. It must be presumed, though it is not certain, that Hitler also assumed control of the NSDAv. Certainly, it would have been logical for him to do so. On 16 November 1921, an entry appears in the register of the Munich corporation court listing Adolf Hitler as chairman of the board of the *Eher Verlag* and noting that he 'declares that he possesses all the shares of the Eher company'. This statement implies that Hitler may have been – at that instant – the legal owner of the *Eher Verlag* and, through it, owner of the *Völkischer Beobachter*. On the other hand, it may simply mean that he was registered owner in his capacity as chairman of the NSDAv – just as it had earlier listed Drexler. What is without a doubt is that Hitler was, at that time, chairman of the board of the *Eher Verlag* and his name appears as publisher on the masthead of the *Völkischer Beobachter* from 1925 to 1933. As such, it must be presumed that he at least received director's fees.

In 1929, a lawsuit was brought against the *Eher Verlag* in which Amann was named as a defendant. This prompted Hitler to publish a statement of ownership in the *Völkischer Beobachter* of 11 April 1929, in which he declared that Amann was not a private stockholder in the company and that:

> The firm of Eher is an incorporated company whose total shares are held by the NSDAv, a registered society in München. There are no private stockholders in the firm.

Subsequently, in December of 1933, the Nazis promulgated the 'Law for the Safeguarding of the Unity of Party and State'. Paragraph 1 of this law made the NSDAP a legally incorporated body whose constitution was determined by the Führer. In March, 1935 a law was issued dissolving the NSDAv and transferring its assets to the NSDAP. These laws made no changes to the status of the *Völkischer Beobachter* and the *Eher Verlag*: **they were not and were never to be under the control of the party treasurer**. To all intents and purposes, the *Eher Verlag* and the *Völkischer Beobachter* were answerable only to Hitler, with chairmanship of the board delegated by him to Amann. In such a situation it was not necessary for Hitler to own shares in the company: he could do whatever he liked and only he and Amann would know about it. It is significant that Amann's income did not begin its meteoric rise (see Chapter 12) until 1935 – concurrent with the dissolution of the NSDAv.

One further incident strengthens this conjecture. When the Nazi press was reorganised in 1933-34, an order by Hitler expressly forbade any party official from holding a financial interest in the press. Even Goebbels, who had substantial investments in a variety of publishing ventures, was barred from such holdings. Yet Amann alone retained his shares in the Müller printing company and continued to receive a five percent share of the profits from the *Eher Verlag*. That he could have done so without Hitler's knowledge or approval is possible, but highly unlikely. The whole of the *Eher* enterprise seems to have been hedged around with exceptions and there had to have been a reason.

A History of the *Eher Verlag* and the *Völkischer Beobachter*

On its take-over, the *Eher Verlag* and the *Völkischer Beobachter* could hardly have been in worse shape, if Hitler is to be believed:

> . . . when I took it over the Völkischer Beobachter *had no more than seven thousand subscribers, not a single advertising contract in its pocket, and not a penny in the till for the purchase of the paper it was printed on.*[26]

This latter statement, while probably true, is not necessarily relevant. From its earliest days under Hitler's ownership, the *Völkischer Beobachter* benefited from the generosity of its printer, Adolf Müller, a Nazi supporter who carried on printing no matter how large the arrears of payment had become (Müller is described in Chapter 12). What remains an open question is whether or not Hitler received a percentage of the profits, and if so, how much. If he did receive a share, it is unlikely that it was less than Amann's 5% and could have been the full balance of 95%. Hitler certainly paid a lot of attention to the *Völkischer Beobachter*, even after it had served its purpose in bringing the Nazis to power. As Hale notes:

> . . . one sometimes has the impression that Hitler was more interested in new subscriptions to the V-B [Völkischer Beobachter] *than in new party members.*[27]

As will be seen in the following brief history, the party – directed by Hitler – went to great lengths to boost the circulation of the *Völkischer Beobachter*, even going so far as to employ door-to-door salesmen and forcing other officially approved Nazi papers to advertise in its own pages.

It seems to have been late in 1921 that Hitler and Hanfstaengl discussed plans for the *Völkischer Beobachter*, as Hanfstaengl recalls:

> *I told [Hitler] of the effective use in American political life of telling catch-phrases and explained how this was buttressed by snappy headlines in the newspapers, putting ideas over with a phonetic, alliterative impact.*
>
> *"You're absolutely right," Hitler replied. "But how can I hammer my ideas into the German people without a Press. The newspapers ignore me utterly. How can I follow up my successes as a speaker with our miserable four-page Völkischer Beobachter once a week? We'll get nowhere until it appears as a daily." He told me of the great plans they had for this if only they could find the funds.*
>
> *It must have been that evening that I decided to render more substantial help.*[28]

Hanfstaengl certainly did render 'substantial help', but his contribution may be a little exaggerated. There is also a story, so far unsubstantiated, that Hitler floated a loan within the party to finance the *Völkischer Beobachter*, issuing some sort of promissory note which would be redeemable once the NSDAP came to power. Heiden gives a graphic description of these notes:

> *The note was a rectangle the size of a dollar bill, and was intended to look like a bank note. The text, framed in a maze of swastikas, obligated the N.S.D.A.P. to pay back ten marks. The left quarter of the note was taken up by a little picture – and what a picture! A young man with an open shirt and a head covering not clearly recognizable (though the moustache was lacking, the grave, threatening face had the features of a self-portrait) held by the right hand a sword dripping with blood; the left hand grasped the curls of a severed female head. Head and sword seemed to lie on the page of a newspaper, perhaps the Völkischer Beobachter. In the background a banner with a swastika; beneath the picture in Gothic letters: 'Warriors of truth, behead the lie!'*[29]

Unfortunately, for it would make an excellent illustration, no example of such a note has been found. The idea that the note was to finance the *Völkischer Beobachter* is greatly weakened (though not rendered impossible) by the fact that it was issued by the NSDAP and, as this chapter shows, Hitler always ensured that the finances of the party were kept separate from those of the *Eher Verlag* and the *Völkischer Beobachter*. If such a note existed, it was most probably a means of financing the NSDAP itself.

On 8 February 1923, the *Völkischer Beobachter* converted to a daily publication. This was a bold move on Hitler's part since the paper did not have the finances necessary for such expansion. The conversion to a daily – and later to the larger 'broadsheet' format – were to have far-reaching consequences, both for Hitler and the Nazi party. Indeed, it can be fairly argued that the change was an important catalyst to the events which brought Hitler and his cronies to power.

The circulation of the *Völkischer Beobachter* – between 20,000 and 30,000 in 1923 and quite respectable for a journal of that type – was far from sufficient to support the move to daily publication, let alone from tabloid to broadsheet format. These important moves could only have been made with the aid of outside capital. In fact, the paper was in financial difficulties and Hitler later remarked:

Doctor Gansser deserves eternal gratitude from the Party. I owe him a whole series of very important relationships. If I hadn't, thanks to him, made the acquaintance of Richard Frank, the wheat man, I wouldn't have been able to keep the Beobachter *going in 1923. The same's true of Bechstein.* [30]

Hitler – or rather, Bormann's stenographer – refers to Frank as 'the wheat man', suggesting that he was a corn merchant, when in fact he was a coffee dealer and manufacturer of a coffee substitute made from barley. The exact timing is impossible to determine from Hitler's account, but it does suggest one possible use for the 60,000 Swiss francs which Hitler obtained from Frank in September of 1923.

In August, again at Hitler's insistence, the format of the *Völkischer Beobachter* was changed from the small, 'tabloid' size to the larger 'broadsheet' format. Lüdecke suggests that Hitler first became interested in the idea of a broadsheet newspaper after seeing both the British *Times* and Mussolini's *Popolo d'Italia* in early January.[31] The story of this move from tabloid to broadsheet format has an important bearing on the question of Hitler's finances. In one of his 1941 monologues, Hitler is recorded as saying:

The best trick I ever played on [Müller] *was the adoption of the large format for the* Völkischer Beobachter. *Müller had thought himself the cunning one, for he supposed that, by being the only man who possessed a machine corresponding to our new format, he was binding us to him. In reality, it was he who was binding himself to our newspaper, and he was very glad to continue to print us, for no other newspaper used our format. Müller had become a slave to his machine.* [32]

As with most of Hitler's statements, this is not exactly 'the whole truth and nothing but the truth'. The key phrase is 'no other newspaper used our format'. In Germany at that time, broadsheet was known as the 'Berlin' format and had a size of 46.5 by 31 cm (18.3 by 12.2 inches). Müller already owned a machine that could print a sixteen-page paper in this format, a rotary press that he had purchased in 1920 (he also owned a sixteen-page rotary press for the smaller tabloid format).[33] Hitler, however, was determined to go one better: the Berlin format was not sufficient for him, he wanted the 'American' format – 21 inches by 18 inches (approximately 53 by 46 cm). The *Völkischer Beobachter* was to be the biggest newspaper in Germany. According to Hoffmann:

There was considerable criticism within the Party, which regarded this format as unusual for a German newspaper and unwieldy to handle. These views, however, did not influence Hitler, who was determined that the originality of his newspaper should burst the bounds of normal complacency. [34]

Müller, Amann and Hitler bought a large 16-page rotary machine in the American format from a company in Würzburg, though just what it was doing there remains a mystery. None of the other small newspapers could afford this much more expensive format (neither could the *Völkischer Beobachter*, so this move was something of a gamble) and the consequent impression – wrongly – was of a large, well financed, serious newspaper. As a result, the *Völkischer Beobachter* began to attract a wider readership and more paid advertising. The gamble paid off. But who got the press?

Even a modest-sized rotary press requires a large industrial building with substantial foundations. Such a large machine cannot just be stood on the floor of an office. Prior to 1933, neither the *Eher Verlag* nor the *Völkischer Beobachter* ever owned any plant and all printing was subcontracted to the printing plant of *M. Müller und Söhn*, which later became the main printer for the *Eher Verlag* and exclusive printer of the southern German editions of the *Völkischer Beobachter*. Hitler offers a hint, saying: . . . *Müller, who ran the printing presses for the* Völkischer Beobachter *in his own name, and for his own profit* . . . [35] It seems certain that Müller got the press, but who paid?

Hanfstaengl implies that his loan of $1,000 provided most of the money to buy the press, but admits that Frau von Seidlitz (see Chapter 6) helped with her shareholdings in the Finnish paper industry.[36] The 'American' format was not a standard German size and paper for its printing would have to be ordered specially. It is most unlikely that paper was imported from America, but quite probable that it was imported from Finland which had – and still has – a substantial export trade in pulp and paper. Since Finland provided most of Germany's paper supplies until late 1944, it is possible that the *Eher Verlag* and the *Völkischer Beobachter* obtained its paper at a preferential rate. Another who may have been involved in the supply of paper to the *Eher Verlag* was Theodor Heuß (not to be confused with the first President of the German Federal Republic, 1949-59), a wealthy Munich paper manufacturer who was one of the original shareholders in the *Eher Verlag* and also one of the earliest members of the DAP. Heuß was also involved with the *Thule Gesellschaft*. In his memoirs, Hanfstaengl makes it clear that he made a loan of one thousand dollars to the *Eher Verlag*.[37] Note that this was a loan, not a gift, to be repaid in 1924, and it is said that Hanfstaengl claimed to have made Hitler pledge the assets of the *Völkischer Beobachter* as security.[38] This makes little sense and there seems to be no evidence to support it; certainly Hanfstaengl makes no mention of any security in his memoir. Firstly, any assets would be those of the *Eher Verlag*, rather than the *Völkischer Beobachter*. Secondly, the evidence suggests that Hanfstaengl's money provided only part of the cost of the rotary printing press, the bulk being provided by Gertrud von Seidlitz, so it is unlikely that Amann, the *Eher Verlag*'s hard-headed general manager, would have permitted the pledging of assets greater than the value of the original loan. What Hanfstaengl does say is:

. . . *I was really very short of money. The same could not be said of Hitler and his immediate clique.*
. . . *I thought well, I helped them out of a hole once over the* Beobachter, *which after all was only ever a loan. I will see if I can get at least some of it back.*

I went down to Amann and explained the position, but he was first stupid and then rude. . . . and when I said that was neither here nor there and that I needed the money he just turned obstinate again, the Party had no funds and so on and so forth. I was not even asking for the dollars back . . . I was perfectly prepared to accept the equivalent in new marks.

. . . My wife even brought up the subject once to Hitler himself in Berchtesgaden, where we happened to be early in 1926. . . .

In the end I lost patience and went along to see Christian Weber, the tough, brawling horse-dealer who had still managed to keep his position in the Hitler circle . . . We had always got on very well together and he thought I was being scurvily treated so, good horse-dealer that he was, he agreed to take over my claims at a twenty percent discount and paid me the balance in cash. He had made a good bargain and of course got the whole amount back in no time. He knew exactly how to deal with Amann, who was, needless to state, absolutely furious.[39]

According to Heiden, on 8 February, 1923 (the day the *Völkischer Beobachter* first appeared as a daily) Hitler and Amann went to buy office furniture for the new premises and paid for it in Czech *koruna*, supposedly received by Hitler for speeches made in Czechoslovakia. On noting the salesman's surprise at seeing so much hard currency, Hitler is said to have remarked:

The Ratsch-Kathel [Rats Nest; an offensive Nazi term for the left-wing Munich Post newspaper] *are always wanting to know where we get our money from. You see where it comes from: the Germans in other countries all over the world send us foreign currency because they begin to cherish hopes for Germany again, since we appeared on the scene.*[40]

Rosenberg tells a similar story, also dating it at 8 February 1923, though here it is he – not Amann – who is accompanying Hitler:

Hitler went shopping with me. I was to select a desk. I picked one with a roll top, since my untidiness made this desirable. Hitler was almost childishly pleased.[41]

Lang and von Schenk, Rosenberg's editors, add the comment:

Even today [presumably 1948-9] *people in Munich remember that incident. Hitler came into the store, instructed Rosenberg to choose what he wanted and pulled out a pocketbook crammed with Czech Korun* [sic]*. In answer to Rosenberg's sidelong glance, he volunteered: "The* Münchener Post . . *. would give a great deal to know where this money comes from. Do you know? The Germans abroad once again have faith in us and want to help.*[42]

These anecdotes, if true, are interesting. All descriptions of Hitler and his daily habits make the idea of him going on a shopping trip, even with his close associate Amann, let alone Rosenberg, most unlikely. However, there could have been a good reason for Hitler to do so: the money was not NSDAP money, but Hitler's own. The likelihood of this is strengthened if the money really did come from giving speeches in Czechoslovakia, since Hitler certainly demanded a fee for speaking outside the NSDAP. But why would Hitler spend his own hard-earned cash on office furniture for the *Eher Verlag* and the *Völkischer Beobachter*? A plausible explanation is that he was buying for himself, as owner of the *Eher Verlag*.

By November 1923, at the time of the abortive *putsch*, circulation of the *Völkischer Beobachter* had reached about 30,000. In 1924, following Hitler's imprisonment, publication of the *Völkischer Beobachter* was banned and the authorities attempted to shut down the *Eher Verlag*.[43] In this, they were unsuccessful as German corporate law required that all the directors of a company be present to vote for its closure and, according to Hitler, one director, Sebottendorf, was frequently absent, on business in Turkey.[44] Lüdecke, who had returned to Germany from the USA in May 1924, states:

> Max Amann had kept his private publishing concern when the Nazi offices were dismantled by the police.[45]

Although too much should not be made of Lüdecke's statements, it is interesting that he refers to Amann's 'private publishing concern', though without making it explicit to what he is referring. Hitler offers a clue:

> Very intelligently, for reasons of camouflage, Amann created on the side the Hoheneichen Publishing Co., whose name covered certain publications.[46]

Amann struggled to keep the *Eher Verlag* from bankruptcy by maintaining and expanding its small book-publishing department. He was also aided by Wilhelm Weiß, later editor of the *Völkischer Beobachter*, who published a small daily newssheet – the *Völkischer Kurier* – as a substitute for the banned *Völkischer Beobachter*, though there are some suggestions that the paper was published by Ludendorff.[47] Again, it was a fortunate move and the *Eher Verlag* was consequently well placed to publish *Mein Kampf* when it finally appeared on 18 July, 1925. This side of the business grew rapidly with the publication of *Mein Kampf* and other Nazi works and its profits were to subsidise the *Völkischer Beobachter* until it too achieved financial self-sufficiency around 1930. Hanfstaengl claims to have given further financial assistance to the *Eher Verlag* during this time:

> . . . although the publishing company and offices were still intact under Amann, there was no money coming in. Bills were unpaid and the creditors were about to move in and seize all the office furniture and property and put them up for auction. Amann rang me up one day and begged me to come to see him. . . . "You are the only man who can help us, Herr Hanfstaengl. You must do it if you believe in Hitler at all. Otherwise it is the end." I had a great many obligations at the time myself. I had received another instalment from the States, but part of it had gone in helping the families of those killed and injured [in the November Putsch] . . . Amann was so insistent that in the end I gave way. There were about half a dozen notes of hand of three or four hundred marks each but I paid some of them and backed others and this sufficed to keep the offices going. I was not alone in this. I think Gansser helped again, but the fact that Hitler found a functioning staff when he was released from gaol was entirely due to our efforts.[48]

Another who may have helped was Müller, the printer, who certainly printed the paper on credit and is even said to have advanced the editor's wages. When Hitler was released from jail on 20 December 1924, of the two persons who came to meet Hitler at the prison gates, one was Heinrich Hoffmann, Hitler's photographer, and the other was Adolf Müller. Immediately, Hitler enlisted the aid of his old friend Pöhner, the former Police President of Munich, to persuade Gürtner, the Bavarian Minister of Justice, to lift the ban on the *Völkischer Beobachter*. The ban was lifted on 16 February, 1925 and publication began again on 26 February, with an editorial by Hitler entitled *A New Beginning*. Initially re-launched as a weekly, on 24 March it was again converted to a daily publication. The circulation had now fallen to a meagre 4,000 from a high of 30,000 in 1923 – a level it was not to reach again until mid-1930.

By 1926, the *Völkischer Beobachter* was rapidly becoming the sole propaganda organ of the Nazi party and there are signs that even at this early stage it was striving towards a monopoly position. Three of the editorial staff of the *Völkischer Beobachter* – Buchner, Stolzing-Czerny (who helped with the editing of *Mein Kampf*), and Gengler – refused to sign an undertaking not to write for other journals, nor even to pass on information to other journals supporting the NSDAP. For their refusal, they were dismissed; only Rosenberg signed the agreement. The staff were not well paid and salaries were often in arrears:

> In 1926, with tears in his eyes, [Hitler] assured a journalist to whom he owed money that he had no funds at all, not even for his most urgent needs; the next day he started on a pleasure trip to Bayreuth in an automobile. When the journalist complained, Hitler screamed at him: how could such an incompetent good-for-nothing even dare to open his mouth? [49]

Heiden does not identify the journalist, but circumstantial evidence suggests that it was Weiß. 1926 also saw the launch of the *Illustrierte Beobachter*, an illustrated journal, founded on the initiative of Amann and Hoffmann. Initially, the magazine appeared monthly, then fortnightly, finally weekly. As usual, Hitler profited both from the general sales of the magazine and from the editorial which he wrote, though it is doubtful whether Hitler 'made his living' from these editorials, as Heiden suggests.[50] There is, however, no reason to disagree with Heiden's claim that these editorials were the dullest spot in a lacklustre magazine.

On 26 January, the *Völkischer Beobachter* carried a special supplement in which Hitler personally called for a campaign to recruit more subscribers to the journal and on 1 February, as part of this drive to boost circulation of the *Völkischer Beobachter*, the party propaganda office issued a directive to all officially approved Nazi journals to carry a reprint of this supplement in their next editions. In effect, journals were being forced to advertise one of their principal rivals – and at their own expense.

Hitler issued a lengthy message, via the party's propaganda office on 17 September 1928, to all Nazi-approved newspapers, stating the official position with regard to competition between such journals. At the end of the document is a list of the thirty-one approved publications, including [51]:

- Two daily papers: The *Völkischer Beobachter* and Goebbels' *Der Angriff*, which appeared in the afternoon.

- Twenty-seven weeklies, of which seven were published by Gregor and Otto Strasser through their Berlin based *Kampfverlag*. Three – possibly four – were published by the *Eher Verlag*, and the rest were local publications. Nineteen carried the swastika, which was rigorously protected by copyright, giving them the status of official Nazi party publications.
- One fortnightly publication, the *Nationalsozialistische Briefe*.
- One monthly publication, the *Hitler Jugend Zeitung*.

Hitler's message closed with a reminder that it was the duty of all party offices and party members to promote circulation of the *Völkischer Beobachter* and its weekly companion the *Illustrierte Beobachter*.

In 1929, circulation of the *Völkischer Beobachter* reached 18,400. Under Amann's astute management, the paper had cleared all its debts and was financially independent, no longer needing support from the *Eher Verlag*. By this time, the *Verlag* itself was benefiting greatly from the increased sales of Hitler's *Mein Kampf*. The *Eher Verlag* began printing a new monthly, *Deutscher Wehrgeist* (German Military Spirit) aimed specifically at the Army and intended to show that the Nazis were the party that the Army ought to support, and that failure to do so would be a betrayal of the Army's own traditions and detrimental to its future expansion. [52]

By the 1930 election campaign, the *Eher Verlag* had become hugely profitable and enjoyed a virtual monopoly on the printing of party material. In addition to *Mein Kampf* and the now profitable *Völkischer Beobachter*, the *Eher Verlag* published the National Socialist Library, a series of booklets written by Gottfried Feder and many single volumes by Nazi or Nazi-inspired authors. Much of this material was required to be purchased for *Gau* and *Kreis* offices and any NSDAP member who could afford to do so was expected to subscribe to the *Völkischer Beobachter*. South German and Berlin editions of the *Völkischer Beobachter* were added and circulation reached 39,000.

Following the break between the Strasser brothers and Hitler, which resulted in the closure of their publishing house, the *Kampfverlag*, Goebbels hoped to dominate the north German scene with his afternoon journal *Der Angriff*. According to Strasser, Hitler offered to buy the *Kampfverlag* outright, though whether this was with the funds of the *Eher Verlag*, his own money, or NSDAP funds is not clear.[53] The offer was declined, and not politely. Goebbels held Amann and Rosenberg in great contempt, referring to them as 'Sergeant director Amann' and 'Almost Rosenberg' and expected to prevail against the 'bumpkins' of Munich.[54] It was not to be. The Berlin edition of the *Völkischer Beobachter* was instituted to thwart Goebbels' plans and *Der Angriff* never achieved much of a circulation. Corruption within its offices led to financial difficulties and, in a final irony, it was rescued by Amann and absorbed into the *Eher Verlag*.

Following the September 1930 elections, in which the NSDAP won 107 seats, sales of the *Völkischer Beobachter* rose rapidly. More importantly, so did the number of businesses placing advertisements in the paper. Hitler, however, with his lack of commercial common-sense, caused problems:

> *I once did myself incalculable harm by writing an open letter to an inn-keeper. I reproached him with the commercial demagogy of the brewers, who made themselves out to be benefactors of the small man, struggling to ensure him his daily glass of beer. Very soon I saw Amann appear, completely overwhelmed, to tell me that the big beer-halls were cancelling their advertising contracts with the newspaper. That meant an immediate loss of seven thousand marks, and of twenty-seven thousand over a longer period. I promised myself solemnly that I would never again write an article under the domination of rage.*[55]

It is interesting to note that Hitler refers to himself – rather than the party – as the one who suffered for this error. In late 1930, while making discreet enquiries as to the sources of Hitler's personal finances, Otto Wagener asked Schwarz, the NSDAP treasurer:

> *"Do you know how the profits of the* Völkischer Beobachter *are apportioned?"*
> *"Since the* Völkischer Beobachter *does not own its own press but has a contract with another printing plant to produce it, the net profit is very small. The* Eher *publishing house is owned by the party. Party enterprises are generally known to be registered as a corporation, and Bouhler is the manager. Profits are taxed according to the corporation tax laws. What is left is spent on expanding the enterprises, to support other newspapers, and, at the present time, for the acquisition and improvement of the building. The building is itself a kind of party enterprise.*[56]

Schwarz's idea that the major profits in publishing accrue to the printer seems a little naïve. The reference to 'the building' is ambiguous, since all the evidence suggests that the offices of both the *Eher Verlag* and the *Völkischer Beobachter* were rented. It is possible, given that Wagener dates his conversation with Schwarz as late in 1930, that this is a reference to the *Braunes Haus*. Writing on his return to Germany in 1932, Lüdecke states:

> *During my absence from Germany, the* Eher Verlag *had mushroomed out to a huge concern, and now was one of the largest publishing houses in the Reich. Amann was its manager, Hitler the principal owner.*[57]

He then goes on:

> *Most of the effective placards, hand-bills, and pamphlets which were poured over Germany in gigantic quantities came from the* Eher Verlag, *as did most of the Nazi literature. This was already impressive in bulk, and consisted chiefly of Hitler's* Mein Kampf, *Feder's dogmatic economical essays, Goebbels' clever and scurrilous lampoons, Strasser's political-economic studies, and Rosenberg's political-philosophical treatises and polemical pamphlets.*[58]

In fact, all these things were published by the *Eher Verlag*, but the printing was mostly done by Müller. In 1932, overall circulation of the *Völkischer Beobachter* fell slightly to 116,200, from 128,000 in the previous year. Interestingly, the circulation for the Munich and South Germany editions – the traditional seat of Nazi party support – fell by 23,000, while that for the Berlin edition almost doubled. It is a measure of the paper's success that, during the numerous elections held during this year the *Völkischer Beobachter* contributed RM 3,900,000 to Nazi party funds.[59] This should be compared with the estimated profit for the *Eher Verlag* of between 440,500 and 800,500 in 1933 (see Chapter 12, Table 2.) If Hale's estimate of the contribution to NSDAP funds is correct, this suggests that all of the profits went to finance the elections, leaving nothing for distribution to Amann and Hitler.

One reason the *Völkischer Beobachter* was so profitable was advertising revenues. As circulation grew, companies flocked to advertise in its pages, and in the pages of other Nazi periodicals. They had little option; these were the publications their customers were reading. Some very well known names advertised in the Nazi press – Dunlop and Continental (car tyres); Daimler-Benz, Auto Union and Ford (motor vehicles); Shell (oil products) – and this has led to claims that such advertisements were a form of backdoor subsidy to the NSDAP. Such arguments collapse when it is realised that the same companies were advertising on a similar scale in the Social Democratic press and in other, decidedly non-Nazi, journals.

An interesting example of attitudes to advertising in the Nazi press is offered by the case of Philipp Reemtsma, at the time Germany's largest manufacturer of cigarettes. By 1932, it has been estimated that his companies were making two thirds of the cigarettes sold in Germany.[60] Reemtsma was a favourite target of the NSDAP, which saw his huge company as the sort of monopoly to which they were opposed, and of the SA, which had its own cigarette making concern and saw Reemtsma as their major competitor. SA cigarette packets carried the slogan *Gegen Trust und Konzern!* (Against Trust and Combine). By 1932, it was obvious to Reemtsma that the Nazis were a potential future government and that he needed to protect his position. Some time in July, Reemtsma arranged to meet Hitler. As far as is known, this is the only time the two met and Hitler's later comments suggest some mild disdain for Reemtsma, though similar disdain can be perceived in his comments about Hoffmann:

> *Hoffmann often speaks of his desire to have me visit his model farm. I can see from here what would happen. He'd photograph me entering a barn. What publicity for the sales of his milk! I'd be posted up in all the dairies.*
>
> *If I agree to be photographed with a cigar between my teeth, I believe Reemtsma would immediately offer me half a million marks!*
>
> *And why not just as well some publicity for a master furrier? A pelisse on my back, a muff in my hand, on the look-out to shoot rabbits!*[61]

Whatever their feelings for each other, Reemtsma's proposed advertising in the *Völkischer Beobachter* was accepted; between 20 July, 1932 and the Reichstag elections on 31 July, a half-page advertisement for Reemtsma's cigarettes appeared every day. Such conspicuous advertising by a company to which the NSDAP was officially opposed naturally excited some comment and at least one small independent snuff and cigarette manufacturer and NSDAP supporter wrote to the party court, the Uschla (*Untersuchungs- und Schlichtungs-ausschüsse* – Committee for Examination and Adjustment) to complain. The reply included the phrase:

> . . . *acceptance of the Reemtsma advertisement in the* Völkischer Beobachter *took place on the order of the Führer after personal consultation with Herr Reemtsma, following thoroughgoing scrutiny by the central National Socialist advertising office.*[62]

It is curious that Hitler, who forbade smoking in his presence, ordered the *Völkischer Beobachter*, a paper he controlled, to carry adverts for cigarettes by a company to which the NSDAP was officially opposed. One is led to presume that whatever agreement was made between Hitler and Reemtsma it was mutually profitable. Yet another instance of Hitler's keeping the *Völkischer Beobachter* and its affairs separate from the party and manipulating them to his own advantage. Similar behaviour can be seen in the case of advertising by Royal Dutch-Shell. To a complaint from the NSDAP Dresden branch, Amann replied:

> *We accept Shell advertisements because not even we National Socialists can drive with water.*[63]

In 1933, a North German edition of the *Völkischer Beobachter* was added, complete with its own editorial offices and printing plant in Berlin. Whether this plant formed part of Müller's empire or was a separate entity is not clear. Again, the Munich edition suffered a drop in sales, falling to 11,645. The circulation figures for the *Völkischer Beobachter* need to be seen in the light of Nazi party policy. All party officials – and there were thousands of them – were required to subscribe and ordinary party members – along with non-members – were 'encouraged' to subscribe through aggressive sales drives.

Prior to 1933, the *Völkischer Beobachter* had served simply as a party propaganda organ. Once the journal had fulfilled its purpose – the Nazis came to power in that year – Amann and Weiß, who was promoted to deputy editor, set about turning it into a profitable newspaper. Weiß broadened the paper's coverage, improved journalistic standards, and developed its news service, the *N-S Korrespondenz*. Between 1933 and 1939, Weiß accomplished a great deal and was amply rewarded: Golden Party Badge; the Blood Order; the Service Cross; and the rank of *Obergruppenführer* in the SA.

In 1934, total circulation of all editions of the *Völkischer Beobachter* reached about 200,000 and that of the Munich edition suddenly surged to about 50,000. Between 1935 and 1937, total circulation of all editions of the *Völkischer Beobachter* rose from 300,000 to about 500,000. Amann boasted at the party congress that none of the various Nazi-affiliated *Verlagen* was operating at a loss. This may have been true but the Nazi press – and especially the *Völkischer Beobachter* – was notoriously mean in paying its staff, particularly foreign correspondents. In 1934-35, the total budget of the *Völkischer Beobachter* for foreign representation was no more than RM 12,650 and the German community in Stockholm held a collection to buy a telephone for the local *Völkischer Beobachter* representative.[64]

Following the 1938 *Anschluss*, an Austrian edition of the *Völkischer Beobachter* was founded. Preparations for this were made well in advance, with the purchase in 1934 of the Waldheim-Eberle printing plant. Within hours of German troops arriving in Austria, Amann and Müller flew to the capital to supervise the purging of the Austrian press and the establishment of the *Völkischer Beobachter*. The first edition rolled off the Waldheim-Eberle presses less than a week later. Subsequently, Waldheim-Eberle was transferred to the Müller company which, by this time, was one third owned by Amann. Total circulation of all editions of the *Völkischer Beobachter* reached about 600,000.

An incident then occurred which, had it been developed further, might have shed some much needed light on the ownership of the *Eher Verlag*. On 22 March 1939, Nevil Bland, of the British Legation in the Hague, wrote to Sir William Strang at the Foreign Office in London:

> My dear William,
>
> You may be interested to know that the father of the Commercial Secretary's Dutch clerk, who is employed in the local Tax Collector's Office, has informed Laming that there is an account with the Netherlands Postal Cheque and Clearance Service in the name of
>
> Eher [sic] Nachfolger G.m.b.H.,
>
> Thierstrasse 11,22,
>
> Munich
>
> Giro number 211846
>
> and that, according to an Inspector of Taxes who in the course of his investigations discovered the fact, this account belongs to Herr Hitler.
>
> I am sorry that I have been unable to find out any further details about the account, but the regulations naturally make this almost impossible.[65]

Apart from the name being misspelled, all the details are correct.

Total circulation of all editions of the *Völkischer Beobachter* reached 741,714 in 1939, but the outbreak of war brought restrictions to the newspaper industry: tabloids were limited to eight pages, broadsheets to 16 pages and illustrated weeklies to 28 pages. Despite this, in 1941 total circulation of all editions of the *Völkischer Beobachter* peaked at 1,192,542. By 1944, restrictions on the use of newsprint became increasingly tight; all newspapers were restricted to a maximum of four pages and six editions per week. Single issue sales were restricted to within 25 km of the place of publication and subscription sales restricted to 100 km. The distribution of papers through the military postal system was prohibited. All weeklies classed as 'entertainment' were suspended and only two illustrated news weeklies were permitted: the *Illustrierte Beobachter* and the *Berliner Illustrierte* – both of which were published by the *Eher Verlag*.

In March of 1945, as a result of newsprint shortages and other restrictions, all newspapers were reduced to a single page, issued whenever conditions permitted and distributed locally. The reign of the *Eher Verlag* was over.

On 10 October 1945, Law No. 2 of the Allied Control Council formally dissolved the NSDAP and the *Eher Verlag*, which was held to be a subsidiary of the NSDAP.[66] Liquid assets in bank accounts, stocks and bonds totalled RM 600 million; it is estimated that total assets could have been as high as RM 10 billion.[67] The assets were subsequently transferred to the State of Bavaria. According to the *Bayerische Staatsministerium der Finanzen*, no records remain of when these assets were transferred or how much they amounted to.

Who owned the *Eher Verlag*?

This vexed question has been long discussed. For example, Bullock implies that the *Völkischer Beobachter* had been purchased 'for Hitler' in 1921 though it may be that he means the Nazi party, rather than Hitler the individual.[68] The conclusion of this author is that there is a strong case that Hitler personally owned the company after 1935, though he may have held ownership on behalf of the NSDAv from 1920 or 21 to 1935. In practice, actual ownership may not have mattered much; throughout his career, Hitler always acted as if he owned it. The evidence for Hitler's ownership is as follows:

- Hitler's 1942 claim that Dr Gutberlet had given him RM 5,000-worth of shares in 1920 as a gift and that he had bought other shares.
- The 16 November, 1921 entry in the register of the Munich corporation court listing Adolf Hitler as chairman of the board of the *Eher Verlag* and noting that he 'declares that he possesses all the shares of the Eher company'.
- The appearance of Hitler's name as publisher on the masthead of the *Völkischer Beobachter* from 1925 to 1933. Its removal after 1933 was probably linked to Hitler's becoming Chancellor.
- The March 1935 law which dissolved the NSDAv and transferred its assets to the NSDAP while specifically making no changes to the status of the *Völkischer Beobachter* and the *Eher Verlag*. The *Eher Verlag* and its holdings were to be under Hitler's direct control, with their finances completely hidden from party treasurer Xaver Schwarz.
- Amann's retention of his shares in the Müller printing company and his share in the profits of the *Eher Verlag* even after Hitler expressly forbade any party official from holding a financial interest in the press. This is not evidence for any holdings on Hitler's part, but is further evidence that Amann and the *Eher Verlag* were treated as a special case.
- The existence in 1939 of the Netherlands bank account of the *Eher Verlag*, which was in Hitler's name.
- The statements of Konrad Heiden, a writer in Munich at the time:

Hitler's strongest hold on his party in these times [i.e. the late nineteen twenties] *was the owner-ship of the party's newspaper, the* Völkischer Beobachter.[69]

The owner and publisher of the paper was Adolf Hitler; for two years he was to devote the main strength of his Party to advertising his paper.[70]

- Lüdecke's statement:

During my absence from Germany [i.e. from 1925 to 1932], *the* Eher Verlag *had mush-roomed out to a huge concern, and now was one of the largest publishing houses in the Reich. Amann was its manager, Hitler the principal owner.*[71]

- Otto Dietrich's statement:

The administrator of his property and his money was Max Amann in his capacity as director of the Eher Verlag, *which published* Mein Kampf. *Once or twice a year Amann would drop in on Hitler to present his accounts. At such times he would always bring up his wishes with regard to newspapers and book publishing and would ask Hitler for authority in various matters. He was seldom if ever refused.*[72]

Dietrich does not make any direct claim for Hitler's ownership, but why other-wise would Amann be asking Hitler for authority on matters concerning the *Eher Verlag*? The phrase 'his accounts' is, alas, ambiguous: were they the accounts of royalties for *Mein Kampf* or those of the *Eher Verlag*?

- Thyssen is more direct:

Hitler holds most of the stock in the party publishing house – Franz Eher, of Munich, Berlin, and Vienna. . . . All this is very profitable. Herr Hitler, man of letters, publisher, owner of several papers, earns several million marks yearly . . .[73]

The evidence against Hitler's ownership is:
- Hitler's statement of ownership in the *Völkischer Beobachter* of 11 April 1929, in which he declared that Amann was not a private stockholder in the company and that all shares were held by the NSDAv.
- Schwarz's 1930 statement that the *Eher Verlag* was owned by the party, with Bouhler as manager. This must be a reference to Bouhler's time as head of the NSDAv, since no one other than Amann ever managed the company's affairs on a day-to-day basis.

The balance in favour of Hitler's control of the *Eher Verlag* is overwhelming; that for his actual ownership seems strong enough for a jury to convict.

Notes

1   Translation from LÜDE38, p. 701. This quotes 'the official English translation by E.T.S. Dugdale, published by Frz. Eher Nachf., Munich, 1932.'

2   Rosenberg became a German citizen in February of 1923 [ROSE49, pp. 49, 70]; Hitler did not become a German citizen until 25 February, 1932.

3   HALE64, Introduction and *passim*.

4   HALE64, pp. 5-6.

5   HALE64, p. 13.

6   HALE64, p. 15.

7   NOLL56, p. 232.

8   TOLA76, p. 108.

9   LÜDE38, p. 58.

10   HEID44, p. 83.

11   BULL62, p. 79.

12   SHIR60, p. 67.

13   NOLL56; Franz-Willing, Georg. *Die Hitler Bewegung: Der Ursprung, 1919-1922*, pp. 180-85.

14   von Epp papers, US National Archives, Micro-copy T84, R-24, frame 9692 and R-25, frames 9695 ff.

15   HALE64, p. 19.

16   Eckart's obituary in the *Völkischer Beobachter*, Bavarian Edition, 23 April 1936 and a letter from Bernhard Schick, a former director of the Hansa Bank, dated 6 June 1935, now in the *Bundesarchiv*, Koblenz, Ref. NS 26/1218. HITL53, p. 291. evening, 5 February, 1942.

17   TOLA76, p. 108. Toland gives no source for his information, except for the quoted statement by Drexler.

18   POOL78, p. 33.

19   HITL53, p. 333. Night of 27-28 February 1942.

20   The *Nationalsozialistische Deutsche Arbeitverein, e.V.* (National Socialist German Workers' Society – NSDAv) was an incorporated body which held property in trust for the unincorporated NSDAP. Prior to 1933, when the NSDAP was incorporated and the NSDAv dissolved, all members of the NSDAP were also members of the NSDAv.

21   Oskar Körner owned a small toy shop and was one of the founders of the DAP. He was killed during the *Putsch* of 9 November 1923.

22   KERS98, pp. 155-6. Kershaw [KERS98, p. 651, note 121], citing Tyrell, *Trommler*, 110, 177, notes that Grandel had been an NSDAP member since August and had brought the members of his own organisation into the party.

23   This is corroborated in Noller (NOLL56) by a quote from Adolf Dresler (p. 236) giving the purchase price as '120,000 paper Marks' and a second quote (pp. 237-8) from Amann's memoir *Ein Leben für Führer und Volk* where he gives the same figure.

24   NOLL56, p. 233.

25   Amann's appeal against his denazification sentence, Munich, 2 November 1951.

26   HITL53, p. 438. 6 May, 1942.

27   HALE64, p. 42.

28   HANF57, p. 53. When Hanfstaengl gives a date for an event, he is usually accurate; unfortunately, Hanfstaengl does so only rarely, so it is often necessary to infer dates from other, dated, events, with consequent loss of accuracy.

29 HEID44, pp. 303-4.

30 HITL53, p. 223. Night of 16-17 January, 1942.

31 LÜDE38, p. 107.

32 HITL53, p. 154. Evening of 30 November, 1941.

33 NOLL56, p. 243. Noller cites as her source a history of Adolf Müller and his company, published in 1934 on the occasion of his fiftieth birthday. Other authors refer to the purchase of the rotary press, notably HANF57, p. 53; KERS98, p. 189; KERS98, p. 660, footnote 122, citing Hanfstaengl's *15 Jahre*; Franz-Willing, *Ursprung*, pp. 277-8. All of these references can be traced back to Hanfstaengl. Curiously, Hale makes no mention of any rotary press.

34 HOFF55, p. 63.

35 HITL53, p. 437. 6 May, 1942.

36 HANF57, p. 55.

37 HANF57, p. 53. It is not quite clear where this American money of Hanfstaengl's came from. On p. 28 he tells of the forced sale of his family's US assets by the Custodian of Enemy Property for $8,000 in 1918. He then, p. 28, talks of setting up his own business, the Academy Art Shop, which he ran until his return to Germany in 1921, selling the business to his partner.

38 POOL78, quoting his own interview with Hanfstaengl's son. Lüdecke adds some support to the idea that Hanfstaengl received security for the loan when he writes (LÜDE38, p. 173) of Hanfstaengl, immediately after the failure of the November *Putsch*, wailing: "What good is it now to have a receipt and a mortgage on the office furniture?" Heiden (HEID44, p. 110) says that Hanfstaengl borrowed the money, but this is incorrect.

39 HANF57, p. 138.

40 HEID36, p. 131.

41 ROSE49, p. 62.

42 Ibid., p. 63. Since it is their comment – not Rosenberg's statement – it is possible that the story has been lifted from Heiden. But who was Heiden's source? Certainly not Hitler; probably not Amann or Rosenberg; which only leaves the store clerk.

43 In December of 1923, the Müller company seems to have made an unsuccessful attempt to get the ban on the VB lifted. DEUE62, pp. 468-9, letter from M. Müller u. Sohn to *Generalstaatskommissar* Kahr, dated 5 December 1923.

44 HITL53, p. 333. Night of 27-28 February, 1942. Sebottendorf would not necessarily have been a shareholder to be a director.

45 LÜDE38, p. 219.

46 HITL53, p. 334. Night of 27-28 February, 1942. From the context, Hitler seems to be referring to the period of his imprisonment in 1924.

47 LÜDE38, p. 249.

48 HANF57, p. 116.

49 HEID44, p. 292.

50 HEID44, p. 234.

51 HALE64, pp. 40-41.

52 BULL62, p. 164.

53 Strasser, Otto. *Hitler und Ich*. Buenos Aires, no date but possibly 1941. p. 101.

54 According to one source, Goebbels was fond of saying that: "Rosenberg almost managed to become a scholar, a journalist, a politician – but only almost." CECI72, p. 5.

55 HITL53, p. 185. Midday, 4 January, 1942.

56 TURN85a, p. 130.

57 LÜDE38, p. 366.

58 LÜDE38, p. 367.

59 HALE64, p. 32.

60 TURN85B, p. 268.

61 HITL53, p. 185. Midday, 4 January, 1942.

62 Letter from Emil Weiß to Uschla, 30 September, 1932 and a reply from Grimm, 30 September, 1932. US National Archives RG 242 Microcopy T-81, 91/105163-66.

63 Letter from Amann to NSDAP Bezirk Dresden, dated 11 February, 1932. Berlin Document Centre; *Oberstes Parteigericht.*

64 HALE64, p. 250.

65 Letter dated March 22 1939, received at the Foreign Office on March 25, with index number C3982. In file FO371/23083 in the PRO, Kew, UK.

66 STMF03. See Chapter 17: *The Inheritors* for a detailed discussion of when the NSDAP ceased to exist.

67 POOL97, p. 152. No source is given for these figures.

68 BULL62, page 80.

69 HEID44, p. 226.

70 HEID36, p. 200.

71 LÜDE38, p. 366.

72 DIET57, p. 196.

73 THYS41, pp. 204-5.

Chapter Five

MUNICH TO BERLIN

There is a tide in the affairs of men
Which taken at the flood, leads on to fortune;
William Shakespeare (1564-1616)
Julius Cæsar. Act iv. Sc. 3.

Adolf Hitler began 1924 in prison and ended 1932 on the verge of becoming Chancellor of Germany. In the eight years between, he spent an enormous amount of money on himself, buying several top-of-the-range supercharged Mercedes and a nine-room luxury apartment in the centre of Munich. To go with these, he personally employed a secretary, a chauffeur, a housekeeper, and several domestic servants. The income he declared on his tax returns, which have survived, was nowhere near sufficient to support his lifestyle. Not surprisingly, questions were asked, and not only by the tax authorities but in the press. These many allegations in the press led to several libel suits, each of which Hitler won, though since the cases were heard in Munich, where most of the judiciary were Nazi party members, this is not as surprising as it may seem. Even the tax authorities were remarkably lenient.

The trial of Hitler and his co-defendants began in Munich on 25 February, 1924. At the trial, several witnesses spoke of Hitler's and his party's finances and these statements have been well documented by Deuerlein (DEUE62) and Franz-Willing (FRAN62). The contributions – such as they were – of such figures as Hermann Aust, Dr. Kuhno, and others are discussed in Chapter 10.

Frau Gertrud von Seidlitz also testified at the trial, where she proudly admitted to having helped Hitler financially for some time and to have persuaded others, in Germany and abroad, to contribute to Hitler and the NSDAP. When pressed, she steadfastly refused to disclose any details. Police inquiries suggested – though did not prove – that the Borsig and Daimler companies had contributed either to Hitler directly or to party funds. There were also allegations of foreign funding, described in Chapter 10.

The trial verdict was rendered, perhaps appropriately, on April 1; Hitler received five years' 'fortress detention' – with the proviso that he could be released on parole after six months if his behaviour were satisfactory – and a fine of 200 gold *marks*. With Hitler in prison, the NSDAP was in disarray and Hitler was content that it should be so: the last thing he wanted was the emergence of a serious rival to his leadership. What else can explain the appointment of the ineffectual Rosenberg to manage the party during Hitler's enforced absence? Amann was probably appointed deputy leader so that he could keep an eye on both Rosenberg and what remained of the party's shattered finances. Hanfstaengl was surprised to be nominated by Hitler as the chief fund-raiser for the virtually non-existent party; Hanfstaengl was already owed $1,000 by the *Eher Verlag*, and had no spare cash to give.[1] According to Heiden, the party leadership was in serious disarray:

> *The movement had fallen apart; the leaders . . . fought for a share in sudden fame, for the approval of the masses, for frequent mention in the newspapers; and most of all they fought over money. This was one of the main reasons why they suddenly participated in parliamentary elections . . . For a member of parliament received a monthly remuneration of four hundred to eight hundred marks . . .*[2]

It is worth asking just what money they were fighting over. Following the failure of the *Putsch*, someone – probably Amann – destroyed all the NSDAP records to prevent their falling into the hands of the police. Whatever money there was in the party coffers was presumably spirited away to a safe place. Just how much money remains a mystery, but it is possible that there was a significant sum. Fighting an election costs money and it seems most likely that this was the money that was fought over, if fighting there was. The surviving Nazi leadership met in Vienna to try to plan some sort of recovery; in desperation, Lüdecke was dispatched to the USA on a fund-raising expedition, described in Chapter 8. Göring, his own German bank accounts frozen, was recovering from wounds received during the Putsch and was tasked with encouraging wealthy Austrians to contribute to the Nazi coffers. He met with little success.

Hitler served nine months of his five year sentence in a prison in the small town of Landsberg, about 100 km west of Munich. It was at Landsberg that he dictated the first volume of *Mein Kampf*, initially to Emil Maurice, his chauffeur, but later to the mad, but more literate, Rudolph Heß who had voluntarily left exile in Austria to join his *Führer*. Hitler's time in prison sounds quite idyllic and he was showered with gifts on a grander scale even than on his birthday. Hanfstaengl tells of his young son gorging on Hitler's chocolates and later describes how such gifts were used as bribes in Landsberg:

> *He received favoured treatment, which included freedom to accept gifts of food from outside, and this again gave him a further hold over his warders. It was very easy to say "take this box of chocolates home to your wife" when he had almost unlimited quantities available. . . . People were sending presents from all over Germany and Hitler had grown visibly fatter on the proceeds. Frau Bruckmann had been one of the most generous donors, but food supplies and money had also come in from Siegfried and Winifred Wagner . . .*[3]

Hitler occupied a ground-floor apartment where he could entertain as many visitors as he wished. There were no restrictions on his correspondence.

In the long term, perhaps the most important visitor Hitler received was Xaver Schwarz, treasurer, or deputy-treasurer, of the Munich city council. Announcing that he was dissatisfied with being treasurer of the right-wing Popular Block, whose leadership he felt to be lacking in drive, Schwarz offered himself to Hitler as treasurer of the NSDAP. The offer was accepted and it was thanks to Schwarz's astute – and strict – financial management that the NSDAP was as financially successful as it was. As Toland notes:

> He brought to his job the talents of an adding machine and the spirit of a miser.[4]

This is perhaps a little unfair. Schwarz was everything an accountant should be: short, fat, bespectacled, pedantic, fussy, and tight-fisted. The ideal bureaucrat to manage the financial affairs of a sprawling organisation such as the NSDAP. He also seems to have been wise to every financial fiddle ever conceived and was one of the few in the Nazi hierarchy who was totally opposed to corruption and rigorously fought it. Turner claims Schwarz put the NSDAP finances on such a sound basis that Hitler no longer needed to solicit subsidies from wealthy patrons or from industry.[5] This may have been true after 1930, but there is little evidence for it before.

Hitler was released on 20 December 1924. He said goodbye to those of his comrades who remained in prison (several had already been released) and gave them all the money that he had on him: 282 marks.[6] At his own request, only two persons came to meet Hitler at the prison gates: Adolf Müller, the Munich printer, and Heinrich Hoffmann, Hitler's photographer.[7] It was a cold, raw day and Hoffmann snapped a quick picture before the trio drove off to Munich. At Pasing, on the edge of Munich, they were met by a group of Nazi motorcyclists and escorted into the city. According to Hoffmann, it was at this point that Hitler decided to make the new Nazi party headquarters at Schellingstraße 50 – the building in which Hoffmann had his studios and opposite Müller's printing plant. Thirteen rooms were available in the building, of which Hitler, who was very superstitious, rented twelve:

> One of his most ardent supporters, a wealthy member of a famous aristocratic family and the wife of a highly respected businessman, arranged a personal office for him and furnished it with furniture of her own which for years had been in a depository. But the moth-holes in the ancient upholstery worried him so much that he could never work there, and preferred to work in his furnished room in the Thierschstraße.[8]

Hitler had now tasted power, from his involvement in the *putsch*; fame, from the subsequent trial; and, to some extent, luxury – waited on by his followers, provided with three square meals a day (at the taxpayer's expense), and showered with gifts. After Landsberg, there was no question of going back to a simple existence, let alone the poverty of the pre-war years:

> *The first thing I did on leaving the prison at Landsberg, on 20th December 1924, was to buy my supercharged Mercedes. Although I've never driven myself . . . I discovered* [my new car] *by reading a prospectus. At once I realised that it would have to be this one or none. Twenty-six thousand marks, it was a lot of money!*[9]

Hitler's statement about his not driving is ambiguous, for in the same conversation he goes on:

> *Adolf Müller* [the printer] *had taught me to drive all right, but I knew that at the slightest accident my conditional liberty would be withdrawn, and I also knew that nothing would have been more agreeable to the Government. In November 1923 I was already the owner of a marvellous Benz. On the 9th* [i.e. the day of the *Putsch*], *it was in Müller's garage under lock and key. When the police came to seize it, they must have filed through the chain. But they dared not use it in Munich, for the whole population would have risen in revolt, shouting: "Car-thieves!" So they sent it to Nuremberg, where it immediately had an accident. I've bought it back since, and it can be seen amongst our relics.*[10]

It is in 1924 that the first existing records of Hitler's tax affairs begin, though judging by the tone of some of Hitler's letters there may have been earlier correspondence.[11] In 1924, a tax assessment form for Hitler was compiled by the authorities, but the amounts were left blank and the form annotated 'Presently in Landsberg prison', followed by a (presumably) later annotation 'Still in Landsberg prison'.

Beginning 4 January 1925, several meetings took place between Hitler and Held, the Bavarian Minister President. Although no record exists of what was said, it seems clear that Hitler distanced himself from Ludendorff and promised that he would never again attempt to seek power by force. These promises were accepted; the ban on the *Völkischer Beobachter* was lifted and the remaining prisoners were released. Hitler not only had a party again, but also the means to publicise and finance it – and himself.

An early new supporter was Albert Pietsch, a director and major shareholder in the *Electrochemische Werke München*, who contributed RM 1,000 and repeated the contribution on other occasions. Party dues were re-established at one *mark* a month, of which ten percent went to the Munich headquarters. Nonetheless, the party was short of money, or at least sufficient money to satisfy Hitler's ambitions. As Hanfstaengl recalls:

> *One day he came to me and said: "We must have 100,000 marks, with that money everything could be built up again." His chief hope lay in the success of his book, the manuscript of which was now complete.*[12]

Hitler's hopes certainly rested on the success of *Mein Kampf*, but these were not hopes for the party; the only one to profit directly from the sales was Hitler himself. In February, Hitler bought a new car, a supercharged Mercedes from

Jakob Werlin, the Munich sales representative for the Daimler Works in Stuttgart, a far cry from the rickety old Selve. Although he told the tax authorities that he had raised a bank loan, Otto Dietrich says that the car was purchased on credit direct from Mercedes.

> *He considered the Mercedes the foremost German quality automobile; moreover, at the beginning of his political career the firm had obligingly permitted him to acquire his first automobile by instalment payments.*[13]

Dietrich also relates that later – he seems to be referring to post-1933, but is not specific – Hitler owned six or seven Mercedes, kept in Munich, Berlin and other cities.[14] One source of funds for Hitler as he struggled to re-establish himself and his party was the notorious anti-Semite Julius Streicher. Streicher was not culpably implicated in the *Putsch* and retained his liberty, his newspaper, and his loyalty to Hitler. According to Heiden, and the author has found no evidence to confirm this, profits from Streicher's newspaper *Der Stürmer* and from his speaking engagements at anti-Semitic meetings provided funds to sustain both Hitler and the party.[15] There is also a suggestion (see Chapter 6) that Hitler raised a loan of RM 45,000 for his personal expenses.

The *Völkischer Beobachter* began publication again on 26 February 1925, with an editorial by Hitler entitled 'A New Beginning' in which he promised to act within the law, a promise that he would break within 24 hours. The next day, Hitler, still on parole, made a violently anti-government speech at a party meeting. The authorities response to the speech was to ban Hitler from public speaking for two years and threaten him with deportation to Austria. Hitler solved the deportation problem on 27 April when he applied to renounce his Austrian citizenship. He paid the requisite 7.5 *Schillings* and three days later was issued an emigration permit freeing him from allegiance to Austria. Although he told the authorities in Linz that he intended to become a German citizen, he did not do so, but became a stateless person. In the matter of deportation, he was now fireproof.

The NSDAP was allowed to hold public meetings, but only on condition that Hitler did not speak at them. This ban had two unforeseen consequences. Firstly, permitted only to speak in private, Hitler began using the salons of his wealthier patrons as places to make political speeches. While this did not go down well with his hosts, it did allow more and more of the moneyed classes to hear his views. The second consequence was that Hitler now had plenty of time and energy to organise the party and to travel around raising funds. He did both, with conspicuous success.

Hitler was not, however, banned from writing. Since some of Hitler's personal fees came (by his own admission) from speaking at other organisations, this loss of income must have been a problem and it is clear that he made up some of the deficit by writing. Indeed, there were complaints from those associated with the party finances and with those of the *Völkischer Beobachter* that his journalism fees were excessive. Whatever the state of his finances at this point, Hitler clearly had sufficient funds to stay regularly at the Platterhof Inn and the Pension Moritz, Berchtesgaden where, over the next two years, he put the finishing touches to *Mein Kampf*. Rudolf Heß assisted him as his personal secretary, at a salary of RM 300 a month, paid for out of his master's pocket. Göring, however, was still in exile and short of money. In desperation, his wife Carin went to Munich and met with Hitler on 15 April, pleading for help. According to one account, Hitler opened a cupboard in his office and handed Carin several bundles of marks, lira and Austrian Schillings.[16]

Hitler's birthday on 20 April became the traditional day on which to shower the *Führer* with gifts, from hand-painted greetings cards to new Mercedes. Some of these gifts came from supporters abroad: in 1925 *Teutonia*, a society of German-Americans, sent what seems to have been a gift of cash to Hitler for his birthday. Hitler wrote to their leader, Fritz Gissibl:

> *If the affluent ones among the Germans and Germans in foreign countries would sacrifice in equal proportion for the movement, Germany's situation would soon be different.* [17]

It was also in 1925 that Martin Bormann joined the NSDAP and by 1928 had got himself attached to the Supreme Command of the SA. By 1933, Bormann had entered Hitler's entourage as Secretary to Rudolf Heß. From this springboard, Bormann was to become Hitler's Secretary and controller of a large part – but not the only part – of his personal finances.

Tax affairs – 1925

On 1 May 1925, the Munich Finance Office notified Hitler that not only had he failed to file a tax return for 1924, but that his first quarterly declaration for 1925 was overdue. The authorities enclosed the appropriate forms, along with an order that the forms be returned within eight days; failure to do so would result in a fine of RM 10 or one day in gaol. Characteristically, displaying the cavalier attitude that he showed towards all financial authorities throughout his life, Hitler did not reply until 19 May – eighteen days after the serving of the notice. He returned the form with the marginal note:

> *Munich, May 19, 1925. I had no income in 1924 or in the first quarter of 1925. I have covered my living expenses by raising a bank loan.*[18]

Hitler seems to have ignored the order to complete a quarterly return; however, the tax authorities were not ready to ignore Hitler. In February, he bought a super-charged Mercedes for RM 20,000; not unnaturally, this piqued the interest of the authorities. On 23 July, the Munich Finance Office wrote to the man with no income demanding that he write, '*at the earliest possible, to inform this office of the source of the funds used to purchase this automobile*'. Almost a month later, on 14 August, Hitler curtly replied that he had raised a bank loan. Noting that he had not yet filed a quarterly return, the authorities issued an order against Hitler, imposing the usual fine of ten marks, with the alternative of one day in gaol. Hitler returned the form, with a statement of income, on 16 September, explaining that he had been away from Munich for several months and that, on his return, the notice had lain undiscovered under a pile of mail. Hitler requested that the order be revoked. The authorities were not impressed, as such notices were sent by registered mail; furthermore, since he had written to the authorities from Munich on 14 August, he could hardly claim to have been away 'for several months'. Finally, on 31 October – fourteen days after the deadline – Hitler, writing from Dresden, filed a tax return for the third quarter of 1925. In summary, the return claimed:

Gross income	11,231		
Professional expenses	6,540	Comprising	
		Repayment of loan	3,000
		Travel expenses	1,500
		Salary, private secretary	900
		Salary, assistant	600
		Salary, chauffeur	540
Interest payments	2,245		
Net taxable income	2,446		

Judging from the suspiciously round figures for travel expenses, Hitler did not keep his receipts. The declaration was accompanied by a three-page, typewritten statement detailing and attempting to justify the claim for RM 6,540 as deductible professional expenses. Hitler's argument was that he needed the money from the loan to live while writing *Mein Kampf*, which he describes as 'a political work'. To write a political work, he needed to engage in politics, both to gather material for the book and to promote its sales. Politics was, for Hitler, a legitimate business activity. To engage in politics, he needed to travel; hence the need for a car and chauffeur. He also, he claimed, needed an assistant and a private secretary. Hitler noted that research costs were an allowable deduction for a scientific work and that travel costs were similarly allowed for a writer on travel, therefore a political writer should be allowed similar deductions. In the final paragraph of the letter, Hitler appealed to the authorities, presenting an image of himself as a man of honour with no thoughts of financial gain from his activities:

I am quite willing at any time to make a sworn statement with regard to my personal expenses and expenditures. The Finance Office can then see that out of the income from my book, for this period, only a very small fraction was expended for myself; nowhere do I possess property or other capital assets that I can call my own. I restrict of necessity my personal wants so far that I am a complete

abstainer from alcohol and tobacco, take my meals in the most modest restaurants, and aside from my
minimal apartment rent make no expenditures that are not chargeable to my expenses as a political
writer. I instance all this so that the Finance Office will see in my representations not an attempt to
avoid a tax obligation, but rather a sober proven statement of the actual circumstances. Also the auto-
mobile is for me but a means to an end. It alone makes it possible for me to accomplish my daily work.[19]
[Emphasis added.]

His tax returns for 1925 describe him as a 'writer' and his gross income is recorded as RM 19,843. Again, Hitler got into dispute with the authorities and half of his claimed deductions were disallowed. Hitler protested this decision and the matter eventually went before the tax review committee of the Finance Office which decided, on 27 January, 1927 that:

This taxpayer travels mainly in order to spread his political ideas among the people and to attend to
Party affairs. Also, his employees are for the most part engaged in work of this kind. The stated expen-
ditures are not in and of themselves professional expenses within the meaning of the income tax law.
Since, however, this activity at the same time provides material for his work as a political writer and
increases the sales of his book, one half of the claimed expenses for travel and salaries is allowed as a
deduction from income.[20]

As well as income tax, Hitler was liable for 'turnover' tax (*Umsatzsteuer*) on sales of *Mein Kampf* and for property tax (*Vermögenssteuer*). In regard of the latter, he filed his only property tax return on 15 December, dating the return from Kissingen. In the section for reporting property used in connection with professional work, Hitler recorded:

Owned on 1 January, 1925, besides a writing table and two bookcases with books, no property.
Highest value 1000.

A close examination of the text reveals that it is not quite so simple. Hitler's '1000' actually reads '10.000,0', where the last two digits and the decimal comma have been deleted by a jagged line resembling an 'M'. The period as thousands separator and the comma as decimal point – common practice in some European countries – are quite clear, suggesting that Hitler had second thoughts.

On 26 February 1926, Hitler took a significant step towards gaining serious financial support for the NSDAP: he addressed a meeting of Hamburg's socially exclusive *Nationalklub von 1919*, held in the city's elegant *Hotel Atlantic*.[21] (This was a private meeting; Hitler was still banned from public speaking.) His audience on this occasion differed sharply from the beer hall rabble that he was used to addressing, these were the *haute bourgeoisie*: businessmen, lawyers, high civil servants, and military officers. He spoke quietly, but forcefully, about the need to eliminate Marxism and socialism, and to curb the power of the trade unions. Hitler made a good impression and the meeting ended with a standing ovation and cries of *Heil!* It was the beginning of the chain of events that would eventually lead to the establishment of the *Adolf Hitler Spende* (see Chapter 13).

May saw Hitler on another fund-raising mission, this time in the north of Germany, where he spoke at many private meetings. It was probably on this trip that Hitler met the astrologer Erik Jan Hanussen who is said to have taught the *Führer* his notorious 'body language'. Hanussen would later cast Hitler's horo-scope (see Chapter 14) and himself die in mysterious – and presumably unpredicted – circumstances.[22]

Another step towards an association with Big Business occurred on 18 June 1926, when Hitler addressed a group of businessmen in Essen. The Nazis put it about that Hitler was invited to speak by local business leaders, but this was a lie. It was Hitler who sent out the invitations. Other, similar meetings took place in the following months, marking the beginning of Hitler's attempt to solicit the support of industrialists in the Ruhr.

The annual Party Rally was held 3-4 July in Weimar and saw the emergence of a new-style Hitler: a remote, authoritarian figure, high on a distant podium, surrounded by guards. It was the beginning of the *Führer* cult. From this time on, Hitler withdrew behind a protective screen of close friends – Schaub, Maurice, Heß, Hoffmann – who not only separated him from the general public but also began to run his daily life, including his financial affairs. Even though these were going fairly well, they were not going well enough for Hitler:

> In 1926 he told Gauleiter Munder in Württemberg that Mussolini had invited him to call on him in Italy. 'Go at once!' was Munder's advice. 'No,' was the Führer's answer; 'to impress Mussolini I would have to arrive with at least three automobiles – I just haven't got them yet.'[23]

Munder was later to raise embarrassing questions about Hitler's lifestyle and expenditure, being dismissed from his post in 1928 in consequence. According to Heiden, who is not always reliable on financial matters, much of the funding for the NSDAP still came from Streicher, who is said to have boasted that one of his sources was the wife of a wealthy party member who happened to be his mistress.[24] This led to a row with Hermann Esser, who claimed the woman as <u>his</u> mistress (there seems little reason why she should not have serviced both men) and who had to be reprimanded by Hitler and banished to the editorship of the *Illustrierte Beobachter.*

Tax affairs – 1926

In January of 1926, Hitler wrote to the tax authorities nominating his secretary, Rudolf Heß, as his agent and giving him full access to all of his records. However, Hitler must have continued to see the returns since most of them bear his signa-ture. Hitler's tax return gives his income as RM 15,903 and the royalties received from *Mein Kampf* as RM 14,707 – leaving RM 1,196 from other sources, presum-ably journalism. (Publishers accounts were audited by the tax authorities so it was impossible for him to declare an income less than his royalties.[25]) Hitler's publishing royalties were paid every six months and when he received the necessary forms for declaring liability for turnover tax he merely signed the form and returned it – blank.

On 24 July Heß wrote to the tax authorities under the rather pompous letterhead 'Chancellery of Adolf Hitler, Munich 2, Schellingstraße 50. Private Secretary (R. Heß)'.[26] Heß acknowledged the notice of payment due for the second quarter of 1926, but pointed out that RM 100 had already been paid and asking for a deferment. When protesting his assessments, Hitler was not so tardy. On 19 August 1926, he wrote to the Finance Office objecting to the level of quarterly advance payments that had been demanded, noting that although he had received an advance against sales of *Mein Kampf* in 1925, this was a one-time payment and would not be repeated. Ever reasonable, the authorities reduced his annual advance payment from RM 1,500 to RM 750.

On 23 September, Hitler personally wrote to the authorities, acknowledging arrears of RM 275 and asking for a further deferment until December, by which time he expected to have received income from the second volume of *Mein Kampf*. The Finance Office graciously granted him a postponement to 10 December, provided that interest was paid at six percent. It was not to be. On 28 December, Hitler again wrote to the Finance Office, asking for a further deferment because all his royalties had not yet been collected and he had had to pay unexpectedly high 'church taxes'.[27]

Hitler's tax records claim that he paid Heß RM 300 a month as private secretary and RM 200 a month to a chauffeur/assistant (presumably Emil Maurice). Hitler claimed expenditures of RM 31,209 for 1926 – against declared income of RM 15,903. In correspondence with the authorities, he claimed that he had made up the difference through a loan, but offered no documentary evidence of this. Amongst his other claimed expenses were: social security and insurance payments of around RM 800/year; car insurance and tax at about RM 2,000/year; and RM 240/year for 'continuation of professional training' (*Ausgaben für die Fortbildung in dem Beruf*). This might have been for speech and 'body language' lessons that he received from Hanussen.

At the end of January 1927, Saxony became the first major German state to lift the ban on Hitler speaking in public. The other German states followed; only Prussia and Anhalt maintained a ban until late 1928. From a financial, as well as a political, point of view this was good news; the way was again open for Hitler to receive substantial fees for speaking appearances. However, audiences at meetings were dwindling, often to less than a quarter of what they had been in 1926, so collections – for party funds and fees to Hitler – cannot have been large. In fact, between 1925 and 1929 he gave few speeches: 31 in 1925; 32 in 1926; 56 in 1927; 66 in 1928; but only 28 in 1929. Most of the 1928 speeches were in the five-month run-up to the Reichstag elections, and most of them were in Bavaria.

It was at about this time that questions again began to be asked in the press: Who was this Hitler and where did he get his money? His tax returns only serve to underline the mystery because they only report income from audited sources such as publishers. Hitler was still living in a single room, presenting an image of the pure, ascetic *Führer*, dedicated to the German people, while privately guzzling cream cakes and travelling the country in his chauffeur-driven Mercedes, staying at the best hotels. Towards the middle of the year, a story went around – possibly fostered by Hitler himself – that he shared his modest supply of shirts and socks with the poor.[28]

On 27 April, Hitler gave another of his series of speeches in Essen, this time with the title *Leader and Mass*. One of those present was Emil Kirdorf, a major industrialist (see Chapter 9). Shortly after, at the provincial *Parteitag* in Stuttgart, Hitler issued one of his regular public denials that he received any support from Big Business.

In October 1927, Hitler brought his step-niece and lover Geli Raubal to Munich and installed her in furnished rooms in Königinstraße, on the west side of the *Englischer Garten*. Quite where he found the money to do so is a mystery, at least if his tax returns are accurate, which they certainly are not.

Tax affairs – 1927

In July, irritated by his failure to file a turnover tax statement for 1926, the authorities assessed Hitler for 1926 and added an additional assessment for 1925. Naturally, Hitler contested the decision, but now the NSDAP had its own lawyer, Hans Frank, later to become notorious as the brutal governor of part of occupied Poland. Frank wrote to the Finance Office on 5 October, claiming that all of Hitler's writings were handled by the *Eher Verlag* and that that organisation having paid its turnover tax, Hitler was no longer responsible. What the authorities' response was, we do not know; what is certain is that several telephone calls were made between Frank's office and the Finance Office and that as a result Hitler admitted liability and paid the tax. Barring occasional penalties for late filing, Hitler paid the turnover tax without complaint until 1934.

On I October, Hitler still owed RM 1,245 in current taxes and unpaid taxes from 1926. Enclosing a contribution of RM 300, Hitler again requested an extension and offered to pay the arrears in monthly instalments; the proposal was accepted. The offer to pay monthly suggests that his income was becoming more regular; certainly he seems to have had less difficulty paying after 1928.

Hitler's tax return gives income as RM 11,494, corresponding exactly to the royalties received from *Mein Kampf* which sold 5,607 copies. His tax return claims deductions of RM 13,452 of which RM 7,979 was allowed, leaving a theoretical net income of RM 3,515. He was assessed for RM 351 of taxes and penalties.

Hitler claimed to have paid RM 1,706 in interest charges and his claims for professional expenses were roughly the same as in 1926.

On 20 May 1928, twelve NSDAP members were elected to the Reichstag. While politically significant only as a beginning, this also had an effect on NSDAP finances, though probably not those of Hitler personally. Reichstag deputies received generous daily allowances and were entitled to free first-class travel on the state railways; some trips on party business were now being financed by the state.

In July, Hitler's lover Geli Raubal returned briefly to her native Austria to renew her passport. On her return to Munich, Hitler rented for her a furnished room in the house of Adolf Vogl, a Nazi party member, at 43 Thierschstraße – next door to his own apartment at 41. Hitler's chauffeur Emil Maurice developed a passion for Geli, who wanted to marry him. Hitler's relationship with Maurice, who had served him faithfully since 1919, collapsed. Maurice had to sue Hitler in the Munich *Arbeitsgericht* for arrears of salary; he was awarded RM 500 out of a claim for 3,000.

During the summer of 1928, Hitler rented a villa, *Haus Wachenfeld* in the Obersalzberg, for RM 100 a month from the widow of an industrialist in Buxtehude called Winter. (Wachenfeld was the lady's maiden name.) Hitler's tax returns for 1929 and the corresponding land registry records show the house as being rented jointly by Hitler and his half-sister Angela Raubal; presumably there were financial advantages in doing so.[29] It was also around this time that the controversy developed between Hitler and *Gauleiter* Munder of Württemberg over the large sums which Hitler and his friends took as expenses from party funds. Munder also complained that Hitler was 'being excessively diverted by the company of his niece from his political duties'.[30] The argument ended in Munder's dismissal.

Tax affairs – 1928

Hitler's tax return for 1928 gives his income as RM 11,818, of which RM 8,318 was royalties received from *Mein Kampf*. RM 3,500 therefore came from other sources – presumably journalism. His claims for professional expenses were roughly the same as in 1926, though without the claim for 'training'. Hitler claimed total deductions of RM 9,991 of which RM 5,493 was allowed, leaving a theoretical net income of RM 6,325. He was assessed for RM 605 of taxes and penalties. Financially, if his tax records are to be believed, this was Hitler's lowest point since 1921; however, there appears to have been no change in his lifestyle.

In 1929 the NSDAP, like Hitler, was also in financial straits. Membership numbers were stagnant and attendance at public meetings was well down on previous years. If the NSDAP were to become a serious force in national politics, money would have to be found from somewhere. Hitler had to go on a fund-raising drive. This he did, but it left him little time for making speeches. It did not, however, discourage him from making personal appeals for money to fund one of his pet projects, the construction of a new and magnificent opera house in Munich.[31] The fund raising trips were not very successful: who was going to put money into a party that was losing support? Some were: faithful patrons such as the Bechsteins and Bruckmanns, and the occasional industrialist, such as Emil Kirdorf, who is said to have given RM 100,000 to the NSDAP at about this time, but most were not. The situation was made worse in April by Otto Strasser's public support for a metalworkers' strike in Saxony, which led to an ultimatum from Fritz Thyssen: curb the Strasser brothers or lose funding.[32]

In April 1929, a curious incident occurred which has been much discussed and which shows Hitler acting in a thoroughly corrupt manner, using NSDAP money to cover up a scandal of his own making. The affair is well recorded, if not exactly documented.[33] Early in 1929, Hitler wrote a sexually explicit letter to Geli Raubal.[34] Somehow, the letter fell into the hands of a Dr. Rudolph – said to have been the son of Hitler's landlady, though her name was Reichert – and never reached Geli; perhaps it was never meant to, being more in the nature of an exercise in fantasy. Whatever its purpose, the letter was damaging and Hitler took steps to recover it. Rather than sending a couple of SA thugs to retrieve the letter, Hitler arranged to buy it back through a rather devious route. There was in Munich at that time an eccentric collector of political documents called J.F.M. Rehse. Rehse was an NSDAP member and a friend of Fr. Bernhard Stempfle who had helped to edit *Mein Kampf*. Schwarz, the party treasurer, approached Rehse and Stempfle and asked them to buy the letter for their collection. Sensing a good opportunity, the pair agreed, but on condition that the NSDAP purchase the whole collection, re-house it, and install them as curators. Hitler and Schwarz agreed. Schwarz apparently handed over money to Stempfle, who bought the letter and handed it over to Schwarz, who presumably turned it over to Hitler for destruction. Rehse does not seem to have seen the document, which may have been as well for him as Stempfle was murdered during the Blood Purge of 30 June 1934. By 1930, the archive was housed in a building next to the Munich *Führerbau* and Hitler consulted the archive at least once, suggesting that it was considered a useful resource.[35]

Most other writers[36] examine the story for evidence of Hitler's sexuality; none examine it for evidence of Hitler's willingness to spend party funds to clean up his own mess. To do so, one must assume that the essentials of the story are true. One thing is certain: the NSDAP definitely acquired the Rehse-Stempfle archive. Heiden gives the reaction of party members to news of the acquisition:

> . . . the National Socialist Party was still insignificant, it was sorely in need of money, and when highly deserving party comrades of the old guard came to the offices of the Völkischer Beobachter,

Leaving aside the idea of Rosenberg kicking anything larger than a harvest mouse downstairs and the lack of connection between the finances of the NSDAP and the *Eher Verlag*, it is perhaps a little fanciful to assert that 'even the best informed did not suspect its true motives'. Schwarz knew; Hanfstaengl knew; Wagener knew; Strasser knew something; Rehse and Stempfle knew, though they were not high in the party hierarchy; probably many others knew, but the reaction of the high party members, rather than the rank and file, was, "Well, what of it?"

The first week of August also saw the Nuremberg rally, attended by 30–40,000, including Winifred Wagner, William Patrick Hitler, with his father, Alois, Otto Wagener, and Emil Kirdorf, who was Hitler's guest of honour despite the fact that he had resigned from the party the previous year.[38] Around the same time, still concerned about the socialist elements of the NSDAP, Kirdorf met with Hitler to discuss the problem. Kirdorf is said to have sent his gofer Josef Terboven to Hitler, bearing RM 5,000 and a request that Hitler come to see him as soon as possible.[39] Hitler, accompanied by Heß, arrived with Terboven the following night and the next day the four sat down for a working breakfast. Hitler is said to have told Kirdorf that he needed three things to control the NSDAP and limit any socialist tendencies: a little time; a lot of money; and an end to the ban on his speaking openly in Prussia. Given these three things, Hitler would allow the industrialists to determine NSDAP economic policy. In the end, neither really got what they wanted: Hitler got some money, but not much from Kirdorf (the NSDAP got very little), and the industrialists progressively lost what control they had after 1933 as Germany headed towards war. Pool asserts that Kirdorf may have given Hitler RM 1,000 every two or three months; it is difficult to prove otherwise.[40]

While the NSDAP was short of money, Hitler was not. Having previously occupied a two-room apartment in a lower-middle class area, in September of 1929, Hitler suddenly rented a large apartment, occupying the whole of the second floor at Prinzregentenplatz 16, in a fashionable part of Munich. He also installed a housekeeper and, eight weeks after moving in, provided a room for his niece, Geli Raubal. Initially, he employed his former landlady Maria Reichert as housekeeper, and she lived in with her mother Frau Dachs. Georg Winter, formerly valet to General von Epp, was taken on as manservant and when he married, his new wife, the 24-year old Anni, entered the household, becoming cook/housekeeper, one of Hitler's confidantes, and a beneficiary under his will.

Tax affairs – 1929

Hitler's tax return gives his income as RM 15,448, again corresponding exactly to the royalties received from *Mein Kampf*. He claimed deductions of RM 9,411 of which RM 4,613 was allowed, leaving a theoretical net income of RM 10,835. He was assessed for RM 1,264 of taxes and penalties.

In 1930 there were again rumblings within the party that Hitler was spending too much of party funds for his own benefit – especially the purchase of yet another new supercharged Mercedes. On 5 February, Hitler went to court in yet another libel trial over his sources of income:

> With trembling passion in his voice, he swore in court that he had never made an attempt to obtain money from Henry Ford; the man who could have had him sent to prison for perjury by producing a document, and might thus have spared the world its encounter with Hitler, unfortunately kept silent.[41]

Hitler's statement is probably true, since it was Lüdecke and the Wagners who approached Ford. Furthermore, if Hitler had indeed been jailed for perjury, it would not have been for long, since the courts – especially in Munich – were generally sympathetic. More drastic measures would have been needed at that point if the world were to be spared the Third Reich.

In February or March, Wagener, who had a successful businessman's nose for finance, though his ideas on economics and science are best described as 'cranky', completed his reorganisation of the financing of the SA.[42] The success of this exercise brought praise from Hitler and for the next three years Wagener acted as his confidant on economic matters. Later events, recounted in Chapter 9, were to bring him to enquire into the sources of Hitler's personal finances.

Hitler now wanted a 'proper' party headquarters and had his eye on the *Barlow Palace*, a building on Munich's aristocratic Briennerstraße. Lacking the money, Hitler turned the task of raising funds over to Heß, who approached Kirdorf, who passed Heß on to Fritz Thyssen.[43] Thyssen arranged and guaranteed a loan from the Bank voor Handel en Scheepvaart N.V. in Rotterdam. Although Thyssen claimed in his Nuremberg testimony that the loan was for RM 250,000, some claim that it was for as much as RM 1,250,000.[44] According to Thyssen's account, the NSDAP repaid only RM 100,000, leaving himself, as guarantor, to repay the balance.[45] The building was purchased in May – the purchase price is unknown – and over the next two years was transformed into the *Braunes Haus* or Brown House. The building was formally opened on January 1, 1931. One witness has put the cost of remodelling at RM 800,000, but there is nothing to say how he arrived at this figure.[46]

By mid-1930, the NSDAP had come to the attention of the man (and woman) in the street; party membership began to rise, and more members meant more party funds. More NSDAP members also meant more subscribers to the *Völkisher*

Beobachter and more purchasers of *Mein Kampf*, in both cases, to Hitler's direct benefit.

In September, the trial in Leipzig of three young Reichswehr officers accused of conspiring with the NSDAP to mount a military coup, brought the bonus of world-wide publicity for Hitler. Hanfstaengl milked the affair for all it was worth and even succeeded in placing three articles by Hitler in the US-based Hearst press, for the high fee of $1,000 each, with Hanfstaengl getting a 30% cut. Hitler was delighted; henceforth he announced that he would be able to stay at the *Kaiserhof*, one of Berlin's most elegant and most expensive hotels – though not as expensive as Hitler liked to pretend.[47] He also wrote an article for Britain's *Sunday Express* and was interviewed by the *Times*.[48]

Elections were held on 14 September 1930 and resulted in the NSDAP winning 107 seats in the Reichstag – a gain of 95 seats. Hitler must have breathed a sigh of relief, as must Schwarz, the NSDAP treasurer, who had mortgaged most of the party's property and borrowed heavily to finance the election campaign. This unexpected electoral triumph naturally aroused much comment, particularly assertions that the Nazis were clearly incapable of making such gains on their own, so they must have had help. And the only source of help most of their opponents could imagine was Big Business. To a columnist in a leftist weekly:

> *National Socialism is in the pay of industrialists who seek to split the proletariat into warring factions according to the principle of "divide and rule".*[49]

The Communists were even more vehement:

> *. . . the hired agents of finance capitalism . . . the last card of the German bourgeoisie.*[50]

Neither was right. As Chapter 9, *Big Business* shows, the two sources most often alleged to have financed the Nazis' 1930 election campaign – Kirdorf and Hugenberg – do not stand up to scrutiny. In fact, the answer was simple: the NSDAP raised most of the money itself. How they did so is not relevant to this work and has been well described by others.[51] Briefly, they benefited greatly from the unpaid activities of its vast army of members and from the willingness of many of its members – especially printers – to contribute the services of their companies.

It is not often fully appreciated just how much rallies and public meetings contributed to NSDAP funds and, through generous 'expenses', to Hitler's pocket. While all political parties staged rallies and mass meetings – their only effective means of communication in an age before television – Nazi events were bigger and better. A typical Nazi event would be preceded by a march of SA men, accompanied by a band. The event, held in a large hall, marquee or sports arena, often included side-shows, such as films, plays, and entertainment for children – something most of the other parties never thought to do. For these and other reasons, NSDAP events were generally well attended. Another feature of Nazi events not copied by the other parties was an admission charge; the NSDAP made people pay to listen to its propaganda. Admission charges were typically one mark (approximately the cost of a pair of socks), but could be as high as two. Once inside, collecting boxes would circulate for additional contributions.

There were many people in 1930 who were interested in how much the Nazis were making from their events, especially the other parties, journalists, and the Prussian political police. A 1930 report by the latter estimated that at a rally in Essen, at which Hitler spoke, 10,000 attended and the NSDAP made a profit of RM 12,000.[52] In 1931, two journalists estimated that at three rallies which the Nazis held in the Berlin *Sportpalast* during the 1930 election campaign, the total gate was 38,000 persons, each of whom paid between one and two marks admission.[53] On the basis of this, the two estimated that the NSDAP made a profit of RM 30,000 on the three meetings, to which must be added whatever was obtained by 'passing the hat' inside the meeting.

Not only did the Nazis hold better meetings than their opponents, they also held more of them, even holding events where no election was scheduled. True to their ideas of 'perpetual struggle', they waged a perpetual campaign. For an election campaign, such as in 1930, the intensity increased to an estimated 100 rallies a day throughout Germany – rather short of the Nazis' boast of 34,000 meetings (800 a day) in six weeks, but nonetheless substantial. Only a few of these meetings were actually addressed by Hitler, typically those in major cities such as Berlin and Essen, the rest being addressed by second-level Nazis such as Rosenberg or Heß, or, at the lowest level, by itinerant orators trained by the party. These latter might receive a fee as low as seven *marks*, plus free board and lodging and travel expenses.

What did Adolf Hitler personally get out of all this? Although he was never an employee of the NSDAP and publicly claimed that he received no fees for speaking at party meetings, he received generous expenses for his party speeches. It has also been suggested – and is probably true – that these 'expenses' were a percentage of the profits, rather than a fixed amount. Just what that percentage might have been, we can only speculate. Taking the figure of RM 10,000 to RM 12,000 as the typical profit for a meeting at which Hitler spoke, it would hardly have been worthwhile speaking for less than 2%; similarly, 10% seems quite large. These give an income to Hitler of between RM 200 and RM 1,200 for a typical public meeting addressed by him during the 1930 election campaign. Note that this does not take account of any contributions made at the gathering, rather it is simply based on attendance.

Tax affairs – 1930

Hitler's tax return gives his income as RM 48,472, of which RM 45,472 were royalties from *Mein Kampf*. Other income came to the suspiciously round figure of RM 3,000. He claimed deductions of RM 26,892 of which RM 14,292 were allowed, leaving a theoretical net income of RM 34,179. He was assessed for RM 6,575 of taxes and penalties. Against his income, Hitler claimed the usual professional expenses, but added RM 1,692 for books purchased and greatly increased his travel expenses to RM 4,980 for transport and RM 12,000 for 'general travel expenses'. About this time, Hitler began noting – for the tax inspector's benefit – that his claimed travel expenses were only a fraction of the actual expenses incurred.

1931 saw the start of Hitler's real rise to power and the end of what the Nazis called the *Kampfzeit* – the Time of Struggle. Recalling this period, Hitler is recorded as saying:

> *When I visited Berlin before we came to power, I used to stay at the Kaiserhof* [a large and fashionable hotel]; *and as I was always accompanied by a complete general staff, I generally had to book a whole floor and our bill for food and lodging usually came to about 10,000 marks a week. I earned enough to defray these costs mostly by means of interviews and articles for the foreign press. Towards the end of the Kampfzeit, I was being paid as much as two or three thousand dollars a time for such work.* [Emphasis added.] [54]

Otto Dietrich confirms Hitler's statement:

> *In Berlin Hitler often put up for weeks, with his entire staff, at the Hotel Kaiserhof – which cost sizeable sums. Several times he raised the money for the hotel bill only by granting exclusive copyrighted interviews to American news agencies or newspapers, for which he received several thousand dollars.* [55]

The implication of these statements is that Hitler was meeting these expenses out of his own pocket, not out of party funds. Most probably they were paid from the travelling funds kept by Julius Schaub. In any case, Hitler grossly exaggerates the costs of his stays in the *Kaiserhof*; surviving bills tell a different story. In 1931, Hitler and his entourage took seven rooms and stayed three days, at a cost of RM 650.86, including meals.[56] In 1932, a room could still be had there for six marks a night.

On 5 January, Hitler was introduced to Hjalmar Schacht at Göring's Berlin home, at a dinner also attended by Fritz Thyssen. Schacht, a former director of the Reichsbank and a banker of international repute, seems to have been a supporter of Nazism as early as 1930, if Fromm's diary is correct:

> *February 12, 1930 Silver wedding at house of important banker. . . . Reichsbank president, Hjalmar Schacht, and his wife present. I understand she adorns, or rather amplifies, her bosom with an expensive swastika in rubies and diamonds whenever the occasion appears suitable politically or socially. Although Schacht was helped to his present position by* [various prominent Jews] *he is not above using the swastika as his insignia whenever he thinks it will suit his purpose.* [57]

Hitler met with Hugenberg on 9 July, and the pair agreed to cooperate, though whether this led to any financial arrangement is not known. Some time in the early autumn of 1931, Otto Dietrich was appointed Chief of the Press Bureau of the National Socialist Party. Like Hanfstaengl, Dietrich was also an important fund raiser for Hitler and the NSDAP, though while Hanfstaengl provided funds from his own resources, Dietrich sought them from business and industry. Dietrich was moderately well known as a business and financial journalist; he had been commercial editor of the *Essener Allgemeine Zeitung* and later business editor of the *München-Augsburger Abendzeitung*. He was also the son-in-law of the owner of the *RhenischWestfälische Zeitung*, a newspaper that was generally considered to speak for heavy industry in the Ruhr. Hugenberg and Dietrich are discussed in detail in Chapter 9.

On 14 October 1931, Kurt von Schleicher arranged a first meeting between Hitler and President Hindenburg. The meeting, to the disappointment of both von Schleicher and Hitler, did not go well, though, according to Toland, von Schleicher was not discouraged, but continued to have high hopes of Hitler.[58] But hopes for what? It is alleged that von Schleicher ' . . . was in charge of a secret informal political department of the army [and] gave over ten million marks to Hitler'.[59] There is no reliable evidence for this and the truth is more prosaic; von Schleicher was simply an ambitious politician who hoped to replace the Brüning government with something further to the right. Such a government was to include Hitler and the Nazis, but von Schleicher thought the Nazis were 'merely little children who had to be led by the hand'.[60]

Tax affairs – 1931

Hitler's tax return gives his income as RM 55,132, of which RM 40,780 were royalties received from *Mein Kampf*; the sources of the rest of his income – RM 14,352 – are not itemised. He claimed deductions of RM 26,488 of which RM 14,644 were allowed, leaving a theoretical net income of RM 40,488. He was assessed for RM 9,130 of taxes and penalties. Hitler's claims for expenditure against taxes were substantially the same as for the previous year.

On 26 (or 27) January 1932, Hitler spoke at the Industry Club in Düsseldorf.[61] The meeting was a modest success, though as is shown in Chapter 9, its effects were greatly exaggerated for propaganda purposes. In his memoirs, Thyssen writes:

> *I have personally given altogether one million marks to the Nazi Party. Not more. My contributions have been very much overestimated, because I have always been rated the richest man in Germany . . . It was during the last years preceding the Nazi seizure of power that the big industrial corporations began to make their contributions. But they did not give directly to Hitler; they gave them to Dr Alfred Hugenberg, who placed about one fifth of the donated amounts at the disposal of the National Socialist Party. All in all, the amounts given by heavy industry to the Nazis may be estimated at two million marks a year.* [62]

It seems from the context that when Thyssen refers to 'Hitler' he really means 'the Nazi party' though this is not entirely clear. Indeed, from this period on it becomes increasingly difficult to separate Hitler's finances from those of his party. Dietrich offers a similar story in his 1957 memoir. Fromm, recording what her friend Conrad von Frankenberg said, claims:

> *Dr. Gustav Krupp von Bohlen-Halbach, Director Kloeckner, and the big men of I.G. Farben, made considerable donations on the spot. General Ludendorff, who could not afford to part with any important sum, had pledged to take payment for interviews with foreign, especially American, reporters — and he will give the money to the National Socialist party. There was a rumour that the ore and coal potentates even suggested legislation for a ten percent tribute of their incomes to the good cause.*[63]

The entries in Goebbels' diary suggest that this meeting brought about a radical change in the fortunes of the party and, presumably, of Adolf Hitler.[64] What proportion went to the Nazi party and what to Hitler personally is uncertain, but during the election campaign the Nazis were spending up to RM 200,000 per week on propaganda alone.

On 25 February, a minor matter was finally regulated: Adolf Hitler became a German citizen, opening the path for him to become Chancellor. Hitler had been stateless since renouncing his Austrian citizenship in 1925. Now, in a typical piece of chicanery, Hitler was appointed by Klagges, the pro-Nazi Minister of the Interior in Braunschweig (Brunswick), to the post of *Regierungsrat* (government counsellor) in the *Landeskultur- und Vermessungsamt* (Office of Agriculture and Land Measurement).[65] As Bella Fromm noted in her diary for 27 February:

> *His aged Excellency, poor Dr. Boden, Minister of Brunswick, never knew what hit him. . . . The English don't think it funny, as Hanover and Brunswick are the soft spots of all history-loving Britishers, and to have the Austrian house-painter naturalized by the Brunswick government seemed a personal affront to every wearer of the old school tie.*[66]

Presumably those British — the majority — who did not wear an 'old school tie' felt less strongly about the matter. According to Hanfstaengl:

> *The original plan had been to give him a nominal post as professor of arts in the Brunswick education service. However, when I threatened to greet him with "Heil, Herr Professor" after all the years he had spent making fun of academicians, the idea was modified. He displayed his warrant when he returned in the evening, and from that time on I sometimes addressed him by his new title as a joke. I must have been the only person to get away with it.*[67]

In fact, the authorities at the Brunswick *Technische Hochschule* balked at the idea, citing Hitler's lack of formal education and their fears of possible student unrest; another appointment was quickly found. This appointment immediately entitled him to citizenship, which he took; as Kershaw remarks: *he swore an oath as a civil servant to the German state he was determined to destroy.*[68] The position carried a salary, which Hitler drew until 10 November, when he took indefinite leave to fight further elections.[69]

On 26 February, Hitler announced his candidacy in the forthcoming elections. Hitler flew from meeting to meeting, descending dramatically (for the times) from the sky in a campaign that was dubbed, with deliberate ambiguity, 'Hitler over Germany'. Hitler engaged a personal pilot, Hans Baur, who would stay with him faithfully to the end, and a second chauffeur, Erich Kempka, to supplement the existing chauffeur Julius Schreck. Kempka was responsible for chauffeuring Hitler in the west of Germany, Schreck in the east. All this cost money – lots of money.

On 31 July, election day, the Nazis won 13,732,779 votes – half a million more than the combined totals of the Social Democrats and the Communists. Delighted, Hitler announced his intention to run for Chancellor. Göring and Goebbels were less than enthusiastic about the idea; they could imagine what it would cost.

The next month, on August 30, Göring was elected President of the *Reichstag*, a post which brought with it a palatial palace opposite the *Reichstag*. Hitler moved in too; no longer would he need to spend money on suites at the *Kaiserhof*. The move also had its propaganda value.

Hitler declared on October 15 that he had no intention of claiming any salary when he became Chancellor, one of the few promises he actually kept, if only for a year.[70] In this context he criticised Papen, the then Chancellor, for drawing his salary while owning property worth over RM 5 million. Within a few years, Hitler would have assets worth many times those of Papen and his Chancellor's salary would be a drop in the ocean of money flowing from the *Eher Verlag*, the *Adolf Hitler Spende* and other sources, but he took it, all the same.

By the end of the year, after four elections and faced with a fifth, the Nazis were again in financial difficulties. On 3 November, Goebbels made a big mistake: he and NSDAP members in Berlin joined the Communists in a wildcat transport strike. Side by side, they threw rocks at strike-breakers and tore up tram-lines. Middle-class Berliners were disgusted and election contributions from bourgeois sources dried rapidly to a trickle. Hitler was furious.

It is generally acknowledged that the latter months of 1932, before Hitler achieved power in January of 1933, were one of the Nazis' lowest points financially. Hitler spoke of the early financing of the party and the *Völkischer Beobachter* with reference to the 1932 election campaign:

> It has been from the beginning one of my most potent sources of strength that I made all the newspapers of the NSDAP, unlike all the other newspapers of similar importance, completely independent of the Jewish advertising agencies and thus impervious to economic pressure of this nature.
>
> This happy success with the press of the Party encouraged me to set about making the whole party, in every branch of its activities, economically impregnable. I was all the more readily able to accomplish this as I found in the person of Schwarz, the then Treasurer of the Reich, a colleague so skilled in the management of the revenues of the Party derived from subscriptions, collections, and the like, that our movement was able to launch the decisive campaign of 1932 from its own financial resources.[71]

This seems to contradict Goebbels' various statements that money was difficult to come by. Hitler's monologue continues:

> *Apart from Mutschmann it was Dr. Ley who collected the most money for the Party. By describing me as a genuine monster, he made the industrialists and their ladies so curious to see me that they were willing to pay anything up to two hundred marks for a seat at one of my meetings. Unfortunately, a great deal of the money thus collected was later lost in Ley's subsequent activities in the newspaper industry, for he failed to realise that the printing-presses owned by the Party were bringing ruin to the newspapers of the Party.*[72]

It was at this time that SA men were sent onto the streets to beg for money and Heiden claims the NSDAP had debts of 12 million marks; others of up to 20 million.[73] There is no suggestion that this refers in any way to Hitler's personal finances.

Part of the problem was 'election fatigue'. The Nazis – and Hitler, who got a percentage whenever he spoke – depended heavily on the money they collected at mass rallies, but by the end of 1932 attendance was down. People were tired of attending such meetings. The major problem was that while the Nazis were gaining votes, they were not gaining power and people began to become disenchanted. The numbers joining the NSDAP began to fall off and may even have been exceeded by the numbers resigning; they were certainly exceed by the aggregate of those resigning and those who failed to pay their dues. Newspaper circulation also declined. The Nazis lost more than two million votes and thirty-four seats in the Reichstag. Hitler was despondent. 1932 ended in financial crisis, as Hitler stated:

> *My most tragic moment was in 1932, when I had to sign all sorts of contracts in order to finance our electoral campaign. I signed these contracts in the name of the Party, but all the time with the feeling that, if we did not win, all would be forever lost. In the same way, I to-day sign contracts in the name of the Reich, quite confident in our ultimate success, but equally conscious of the fact that, if the war is lost, then the German people is inevitably and irretrievably lost with it. No expense, therefore, is too great provided that it contributes to the assurance of our final victory.*[74]

These factors ought to have affected Hitler's personal income, but they did not; even as the NSDAP faced ruin, Hitler continued to take his lavish expenses without regard for the financial health of the party. It was an ominous portent for the future.

Tax affairs – 1932

Hitler's tax return gives his income as RM 64,639, of which RM 62,340 were royalties from *Mein Kampf*. Other income fell to a mere RM 2,299. He claimed deductions of RM 35,188 of which RM 19,894 were allowed, leaving a theoretical net income of RM 44,745. He was assessed for RM 12,130 of taxes and penalties. Hitler's claims for expenditure against taxes were substantially the same as for the previous year except that his claims for travel expenses rose from around RM 17,000 to RM 26,000. However, as Chapter 11 shows, Hitler's relations with the fiscal authorities, following his appointment as Chancellor, were about to take a turn for the better.

Notes

1   Heiden (HEID44, p. 203) seems to think that Hitler owed Hanfstaengl 'thousands of dollars' who was seeking repayment in 1924. However, Hanfstaengl (HANF57, p. 138) refers only to the 1923 loan of $1,000 and is clear that he did not seek repayment and sell the debt to Weber until 1926 or later. On p. 204, Heiden refers to Hitler owing $1,000 to Weber, implying that this was in 1924; while this confirms Hanfstaengl's figure it conflicts again with his date.

2   HEID44, pp. 201-2.

3   HANF57, p. 114.

4   TOLA76, p. 210.

5   TURN85B, p. 119.

6   HOFF55, p. 61; TOLA76, p. 202, no source given, but probably Hoffmann.

7   Hoffmann (HOFF55, pp. 59-61) has left a detailed description of the event, in which he makes it clear that the well-known photograph of Hitler standing beside Müller's car was taken outside the gates of Landsberg city and not, as it is often miscaptioned, outside the fortress itself, where photography was forbidden.

8   Ibid, pp. 61-62. Hoffmann does not identify the woman, but it seems probable that it was either Frau Bechstein or Frau Bruckmann.

9   HITL53, pp. 280-1. Night of 3-4 February, 1942.

10   Ibid.

11   The records, now in the Bavarian State Archives, were maintained in the Munich Finance Office from 1925 to 1935 and comprise some 200 items. A microfilm copy of these papers is in the Alderman Library of the University of Virginia, USA, and a full copy is in the author's possession. A detailed analysis has been made by Hale (HALE55).

12   HANF57, p. 127.

13   DIET57, p. 166.

14   DIET57, p. 167.

15   HEID44, p. 204.

16   MOSL74, p. 98.

17   DIAM74, pp. 96-7, citing Hitler to Gissibl, May 20, 1925, in USNA T-81/144/183160.

18   Hitler's marginal note to the Tax Declaration Notice, dated 1 May, 1925. Copies of the entire tax archive are in the author's possession, but, owing to the extreme difficulty of deciphering Hitler's handwriting, Hale (HALE55) has been used for some translations.

19   HALE55, pp. 832-833.

20 HALE55, p. 833.

21 Toland (TOLA76, p. 216) has this as 'the last day of February' and Maser (MASE73, p. 327) as 28 February, but most other authors give the date as the twenty-sixth.

22 Heiden (HEID44, p. 577) claims that Hanussen's real name was Steinschneider and that he was murdered on the orders of SA *Obergruppenführer* Count Wolf Helldorf, who owed Hanussen/Steinschneider a considerable sum of money. Fromm (FROM43, p. 73) seems to add credence to this when she writes: *Hitler's* [astrologer] *is Jan Hanussen, known in certain circles to be of Jewish origin, but he manages to conceal his origin successfully in circles where concealment is considered necessary. He is a close friend of Count Helldorf.* See also FROM43, p. 96, which seems to put the murder at 2 or 3 April, 1933.

23 HEID44, p. 223.

24 HEID44, p. 233.

25 This seems to have changed after 1933 and it is clear (GOEB48, pp. viii-ix) that Goebbels was blatantly under-reporting *his* income from publishing. It is also noteworthy that Goebbels advances exceeded the income from his books by over 226,000 marks!

26 This was also the address of the editorial offices of the *Völkischer Beobachter*, with which the NSDAP was sharing premises at the time, and not to be confused with the address of the *Eher Verlag*, which remained at Tierschstraße 11.

27 In many European countries, churches collect money through the tax system. Payment is required unless a person specifically declares him/herself a non-church-goer. It seems strange that Hitler should have happily paid church taxes in preference to those due to the state.

28 TOLA76, p. 226.

29 HEID44, p. 223.

30 ROSE98, p. 127; no source given.

31 HEID44, p. 283.

32 TOLA76, p. 239.

33 Heiden (HEID44, p. 304) gives the earliest account of the affair, but other sources, with varying details, are given by Hanfstaengl and Strasser.

34 Heiden has '1919', but this is almost certainly a typo as Geli would have been eleven years old at the time.

35 TURN85a, p. 19.

36 HANF57, pp. 162-3; WAIT77, p. 238; ROSE98, pp. 128-134. Waite more-or-less paraphrases Heiden's original account, though he seems to credit Stempfle for it.

37 HEID44, p. 305. Heiden never mentions the journalist by name, but later (HEID44, p. 449) he writes: 'That the man whom his own party comrade Rosenberg had kicked through the doorway when he came begging for ten marks had suddenly become Minister of the Interior . . . ', suggesting that the journalist was Frick.

38 Hanfstaengl (HANF57, p. 148) implies that this was the first time Hitler and Kirdorf met, but he is clearly mistaken since Kirdorf later admitted to meeting Hitler in 1927. Although he refers to payments by Kirdorf and Thyssen as being 'more regular' than anything previously received, this can be treated with some scepticism as he admits in the same sentence that he had "no intimate knowledge of these transactions".

39 POOL78, p. 151, but no source is given.

40 POOL78, p. 153.

41 HEID44, p. 293. 'Steel' claims (STEE37, p. 268) that Hitler brought over 1,600 libel actions.

42 TURN85a, p. 15.

43 Heiden (HEID44, p. 283) claims that Kirdorf paid for the purchase of the *Barlow Palace* but later evidence shows that this is not true. Kirdorf merely introduced Heß to Thyssen. (THYS41, p. 129).

44 POOL78, p. 169. Turner (TURN85B, p. 148) seems to think that this all took place in 1931, but by then the *Braunes Haus* had been officially opened and most of the work was complete. Late 1928 seems to be the earliest date that fits the chronology of events, though it is equally likely that this occurred in 1929.

45 THYS41, p. 129. von Lang [LANG79, p. 53] implies that the NSDAP insurance fund (*Hilfskasse*) provided some of the money.

46 LÜDE38, p. 434.

47 KERS98, p. 338, citing Hanfstaengl, *15 Jahre*. However, the Kaiserhof story does not appear in HANF57.

48 TOLA76, p. 244, quoting 'Baynes' who does not seem to appear in Toland's list of sources.

49 Kurt Hiller, *Warnung vor Koalitionen, Die Weltbühne*, 23 September 1930. Translation from TURN85B, p. 112.

50 From *Die Rote Fahne*, the official journal of the German Communist Party, as quoted in *Internationale Presse-Korrespondenz*, 16 September 1930. Translation from TURN85B, p. 112.

51 TURN85B, p. 115 ff.

52 Report of the *Polizeipräzident*, Essen, to the *Regierungspräzident* (Government President), Düsseldorf, 28 November, 1930. *Hauptstaatsarchiv* Düsseldorf, *Regierung* Düsseldorf, 30653.

53 Öhme, Walter and Kurt Caro. *Kommt "Das Dritte Reich"?* Berlin, 1931. p. 92.

54 HITL53, p. 527. Dinner, 6 July 1942.

55 DIET57, p. 172.

56 US Library of Congress, Manuscript Division. Bill for a stay from 1 to 4 September 1931.

57 FROM43, p. 29. Schacht had resigned his post in March 1930, but would re-occupy it under Hitler.

58 TOLA76, p. 259.

59 POOL97, p. 27.

60 TOLA76, p. 265; no clear reference is given to the source of this apparent quotation.

61 Most writers give the date as 27 January, as do Lüdecke (LÜDE38, p. 326), who was not even in Germany at the time, and Fromm (FROM43, p. 43), noting that it was the ex-Kaiser's birthday. According to the invitation (TURN85B, p. 205), the meeting was held on 26 January. Two local newspapers, *Kölnische Volkszeitung* and the Düsseldorf *Volkszeitung*, printed accounts of the meeting in their 27 January editions, strengthening the view that the meeting was on 26 January.

62 THYS41, pp. 133-4. 'Steel' (STEE37, p. 157) claims that Thyssen gave Hitler (i.e.

the NSDAP) 3.5 million marks just prior to the 1932 election. No other writer makes such a claim and 'Steel' offers no supporting evidence.

63 FROM43, pp. 43-4.
64 BULL62, p. 196.
65 Hanfstaengl (HANF57, p. 176) has the post as *Oberregierungsrat*, but most other writers have the lower designation; in practical terms, it hardly matters.
66 FROM43, pp. 45-6.
67 HANF57, p. 176.
68 KERS98, p. 362.
69 In a speech at Frankfurt am Main on 7 April, Hitler said that he had arranged for his salary to be distributed to the 'disqualified unemployed'. However, the Braunschweig authorities refused to accept this arrangement.
70 KERS98, p. 388, citing NSDAP records.
71 HITL53, p. 437. 6 May 1942.
72 Ibid. Martin Mutschmann, an industrialist who owned several lace factories, was *Gauleiter* of Saxony from 1925 to 1945. Goebbels (GOEB48, pp. 127, 178 and 179) seems to have had a very low opinion of him.
73 BULL62, p. 242, but no other reference.
74 HITL53, p. 438. 6 May 1942.

Chapter Six

HITLER'S WOMEN

When lovely woman stoops to folly,
And finds too late that men betray,
What charm can soothe her melancholy?
What art can wash her guilt away?
Oliver Goldsmith (1730?-1774)
On Woman. Chap. xxiv

Women were financially important to Hitler. In the early days of his political career many women supported him directly and many more, by attending Nazi party meetings in great numbers, indirectly contributed to his personal funds. However, as this chapter shows, with only three exceptions womens' contributions to Hitler's personal funds were modest, though many gave significant sums to the NSDAP and helped Hitler in other ways. Of these three women (Bechstein, Bruckmann, and von Seidlitz), one may even have helped him to such an extent, at such a critical point in his career, that without her Hitler might never have come to power and would certainly not have become so rich. Therefore, the principal questions of this chapter are: Who gave him money?; and how much did they give?

There is no doubt that Hitler was attractive to women and he was aware of this from an early age. Even his enemies emphasised the women who were said to pursue him. However, the ideas of Hitler and the NSDAP must also have had some attractions for women. In 1920, it was being reported that a quarter of those attending NSDAP meetings were women – and this at a time when women's involvement in politics was barely tolerated, especially in right-wing circles. Hitler deliberately pitched the opening lines of many of his early speeches at women, referring to food shortages and the effects of inflation, and this emphasis on financial hardship seems, paradoxically, to have made women even more eager to contribute. Lüdecke tells that, some time in 1922, a fifty-ish woman of modest means donated the whole of a recently received inheritance to the NSDAP.[1] In a speech, Hitler revealed a somewhat practical attitude to women in general and Nazi followers in particular:

The key to the heart of the people is not "if you please" but power. In this the masses are like women: It is not for nothing that you see so many women here in this hall.[2]

It was also NSDAP policy to attract women and Dietrich Eckart, Hitler's political mentor, once remarked that a bachelor was the ideal leader for the party since a bachelor would naturally attract women.[3] The famous 'Traitor' pamphlet, published in the *Münchener Post* of 3 August 1921, stated:

So his conscience cannot be clear, especially as his excessive intercourse with ladies, to whom he often describes himself as the King of Munich, costs a great deal of money.[4]

It must be assumed – though it is not absolutely certain – that the word 'intercourse' refers to the 'social' rather than the 'sexual' variety. On 3 April 1923, another article in the *Münchener Post* claimed that women were regularly making gifts of money to Hitler and the party, together with jewellery and antiques which were subsequently auctioned.[5] In Hitler's 1927 series of speeches in the Essen region, although the audience consisted nominally of invited businessmen, the number of women present was so much greater than expected that it attracted the notice of the press.[6]

Many have assumed that the attraction which Hitler held for women was something 'of its time', something peculiar to the society of Munich and Berlin, with their *salons* where polite, but trivial, conversation mingled with political intrigue. This is not so. One need only look at more recent times to see a similar situation, one captured so finely in Tom Woolfe's book *Radical Chic and Mau-Mau-ing the Flak Catchers*.[7] It was Woolfe who coined the phrase 'Radical Chic' and like the 'revolutionaries' of Woolfe's book, Hitler, the 'Radical Chic' of his time, was dangerous; no society hostess could resist a man who advocated revolution and arrived at the *salon* wearing a pistol and carrying a whip. Hanfstaengl noted the effects, but not the causes, at the first of Hitler's meetings he ever attended:

I looked around the audience. . . . Only a few yards away was a young woman, her eyes fastened on the speaker. Transfixed as though in some devotional ecstasy, she had ceased to be herself and was completely under the spell of Hitler's despotic faith in Germany's future greatness.[8]

Lüdecke offers a similar impression:

His meetings were attended by many women, who responded even more enthusiastically – and generously – than the men. Frankly, I did not fail to note that some of these devoted females were of the hysterical type, who found an emotional ecstasy in surrender to the man on the platform. He could twitch their very nerves with his forcefulness. But many of the women were as intelligently interested as the men, and without their financial aid the Party's early years would have been much more difficult.[9]

Such adulation could go to extremes, as Waite notes:

When Hitler made an important speech in Düsseldorf in January 1932, the wives of industrialists paid a cloakroom attendant a mark each for the privilege of holding the bouquet that had been presented to him on entering the hall – they were thrilled by the thought that they could actually smell the same flowers the Führer had sniffed.[10]

While power helps to explain Hitler's attraction to younger women, it seems insufficient to explain his attraction to older women, especially in his younger days when the positions of power were reversed. It was these older women who provided him with funds at a crucial stage in his career. Many of them seem to have looked upon Hitler as a 'favourite son', a rough diamond that they could take and polish into an ideal child; not for nothing were such women known as the *Hitler-Mutti* – Hitler Mothers. Characteristically, once Hitler had achieved power and financial stability, he forgot about them completely.

Hitler could be notably rude to his women, even to his intimates, especially after he came to power. Hitler liked his women to be attractive – by his own standards – and preferred them unadorned by makeup. His ideal seems to have been the simple, blonde, full-busted country maiden, in peasant costume. His dislike of makeup was expressed on several occasions – especially to Eva Braun, whose main interests were cosmetics, clothes, and jewellery – claiming that lipstick was variously made from sewage, human fat, and kitchen waste.[11] He could, of course, be charming, though in his own, schmaltzy Austrian manner: kissing women's hands, presenting them with huge bunches of flowers, and addressing them by pet-names and endearing terms such as 'little princess'.[12] And at the same time, flourishing a rhinoceros hide whip and inviting them to share the thrill of his supercharged Mercedes. Somehow it worked, with young and old alike.

Some idea of his attitude towards women is given by an incident which occurred during the 1932 election campaign. While resting in Weimar, Hitler, who was talking with his pilot, Baur, ordered one of his assistants to go into town and bring back fifteen young ladies for afternoon coffee. The ladies duly arrived and Hitler commented to Baur on their attractiveness. Baur in turn remarked that it was a pity that Hitler could not enjoy their favours. Hitler agreed, saying:

> Now if you make a little side trip, no rooster will crow about it, but with me the ladies advertise and I can't afford that. [13]

The party later moved on to a more discrete rendezvous in the Artists' Café, every member of the group provided – except Hitler – with a willing companion. It is to be hoped that someone told Hitler that roosters are not ladies.

Naturally, rumours abounded about Hitler's relationship with women. It is not the purpose of this book to investigate Hitler's sexuality; that has been done with varying degrees of credibility by many authors.[14] The simplest summary of Hitler's position with regard to women is that he deliberately suppressed the majority of his romantic feelings and played the part of the dedicated bachelor, wedded only to Germany. For example, he told his adjutant Wiedemann that he missed family life, but that marriage would lose him too many votes. Consequently, he said, he had a girl at his disposal in Munich.[15]

For someone who could discipline his behaviour as well as Hitler could – moving from *gemütlich* charmer to raving demagogue and back again in a matter of seconds – such subjugation of the flesh may have been easy. It was almost certainly unpleasant and, in unguarded moments Hitler admitted to those closest to him that he missed the pleasures of the opposite sex. Perhaps what Hitler came to enjoy, as a result of this self-imposed public celibacy, was the pleasure of flattery: in the short term, to see the gratified reaction of the object of his flattery; in the long term, to receive flattery's rewards, both emotional and concrete. Unfortunately, flattery can become boring with time and, as can be seen in the case of some of Hitler's women, lead to diminishing returns.

Who gave what?

One of the first women to support Hitler was Frau Carola Hoffmann (no relation to Hitler's photographer) the elderly, though trim and attractive, widow of a Munich headmaster and generally considered to have been the first *Hitler-Mutti*.[16] Indeed, Hitler himself referred to her as 'my beloved and devoted *Mütterchen*'.[17] After first hearing him speak in 1920, she became an ardent supporter and even started a branch of the NSDAP in her neighbourhood. In the early nineteen-twenties, at her country house in Solln, near Munich, she fed him on cream cakes, did his laundry, organised his wardrobe, and lectured him on how to behave in polite society.[18] At age sixty-six, she never failed to pay Hitler a monthly visit during his imprisonment in Landsberg.[19] If she gave money to Hitler, it was probably only small amounts, as she was far from wealthy.

Another early *Hitler-Mutti* was Frau Theodor Lauböck, the wife of a *Reichsbahn* (State Railways) official who founded the Rosenheim branch of the NSDAP and later moved to Munich. According to Hanfstaengl, who went to tea and played the piano there several times, their support was faithful, though not very effective, and probably rarely involved money, though Herr Lauböck did hide arms and ammunition for the NSDAP and SA.[20]

Hitler's next patroness, Frau Hélène Bechstein, was far more wealthy and effective. Hitler was introduced to the Bechstein family in Berlin by Dietrich Eckart in March 1920. Both of the Bechsteins became frequent contributors to Hitler and the NSDAP, though perhaps not on such a large scale as has sometimes been assumed. Frau Bechstein is said to have been a domineering, possessive woman, though her behaviour towards Hitler only hints at this. She apparently took an immediate liking to Hitler and he was a frequent visitor to their various homes in Berlin, Munich, and Berchtesgaden. Indeed, according to one author, Frau Bechstein was so taken with the young Hitler that she seriously considered adopting him as her son, a project which foundered on her husband's opposition to the idea. Others claim that, when Hitler was in prison at Landsberg, she told the authorities that she was his adoptive mother so as to have more frequent access to her 'son'. More plausibly, she is said to have been convinced that she would succeed in marrying off her daughter Lotte to Hitler.[21]

She also gave Hitler his first dog whip, a gift that was to be repeated by several of his female admirers and to lead to some jealousy between them. Another who gave him a whip was Frau Elizabeth Büchner, wife of the owner of the *Pension Moritz*, the hotel at which Hitler regularly stayed in the Obersalzberg. As Hanfstaengl describes it:

> [She] *was a towering Brünhilde type with a flashing gold tooth, and Hitler had developed for her one of his unproductive, declamatory passions. He used to play the romantic revolutionary for her benefit, stamping around and cracking a rhinoceros-hide whip she had given him.* [22]

Hitler found the Bechsteins dazzling and after one visit to their suite in a Munich hotel he told Hanfstaengl how embarrassed he had felt, wearing his worn, blue suit while Herr Bechstein was wearing a dinner jacket and the servants were all in livery. Even little things astonished him:

> *And you should have seen the bathroom, you can even regulate the heat of the water.* [23]

It may have been after this visit that Frau Bechstein persuaded Hitler to wear, maybe even bought for him, an evening outfit of dinner jacket, starched shirt, bow tie, and patent leather shoes, though Hanfstaengl says he advised against this, claiming it would not be good for his 'common man' image. As with so many women, Hitler encouraged her to call him 'Wolf', a name which he claimed was the old German form from which 'Adolf' was derived and which he reserved for intimate friends.

In April of 1923, the Bechsteins received a visit from Hitler and Hanfstaengl. As they were leaving, Hitler found that his battered black, floppy hat had been replaced by an elegant greyish-yellow fedora. According to Hanfstaengl it had belonged to Herr Bechstein; it is surprising that it fit, for Hitler's head was rather large. It was the only profit they got from the meeting and, when the Bechsteins pleaded hard times, Hanfstaengl suggested she pawn some of her jewellery to aid the party's finances.[24] Four months later she effectively did so, giving Hitler some jewellery which he used as security for the loan of 60,000 Swiss Francs from Richard Frank, dated 20 August 1923. The list of goods given in security is impressive:

> *As security for the loan, Herr Adolf Hitler transfers to Herr Richard Frank property deposited in the banking house of Heinrich Eckert in Munich in the name of Max Amann the following articles:*
> *No. 1 An emerald pendant with platinum and diamonds and a small platinum chain.*
> *No. 2 A platinum ruby ring with diamonds.*
> *No. 3 A sapphire ring in platinum with diamonds.*
> *No. 4 A solitaire diamond ring, with diamonds set in silver, the ring 14-carat gold.*
> *No. 5 One Venetian relief-point, hand made, 6½ metres long, 11½ centimetres wide (seventeenth century).*
> *No. 6 One red silk Spanish piano shawl with gold stitching (size 4x4 metres).*
> *A certificate of deposit from the banking house of Heinrich Eckart in Munich is handed to Mr.*

Richard Frank herewith. It is expressly stated that the depositor Max Amman acts with this deposit as the business manager of Herr Hitler, on his order and authority.[25]

This list is quoted by many authors, almost all of whom omit any mention of Amann in their translation. In her testimony to the police prior to Hitler's 1924 trial, Frau Bechstein said:

In addition to the regular financial support which my husband channelled to the NSDAP, I also gave Mr. Hitler a number of contributions — not in the form of money. Instead, I gave him art objects with the remark that he could do with them what he wanted. These were art objects of great value.

Their value can be gauged from the above list, but her statement that she never gave cash to Hitler appears to be false, for Hanfstaengl claims to have seen money pass between them and Lüdecke implies something similar. Equally important, Frau Bechstein was instrumental in ensuring Hitler's financial security on his release from prison in 1924 by persuading her husband to guarantee a personal loan of RM 45,000 from the Hansa Bank, Munich. Typically, though Hitler offset the interest payments against taxes, he defaulted on the loan which had to be made good by Carl Bechstein. He did, however, present the Bechsteins with the manuscript copy of the first book of *Mein Kampf*, though whether it was worth RM 45,000 is a matter of opinion. Another area where Frau Bechstein helped was in furnishing the *Haus Wachenfeld*, after Hitler first took up residence there, though it seems unlikely that she did more than donate a few sticks of used furniture from the Bechsteins' own nearby villa.

As Hitler rose to power and more and more women began to compete for his attention — rather than Hitler competing for theirs — relationships with Frau Bechstein began to deteriorate and by the mid-thirties she had begun to scold him openly. Relationships between Hitler and the Bechsteins further deteriorated after his coming to power and by 1936 or 1937 she was sufficiently disenchanted to call Hitler 'a shabby sort of Chancellor' to his face.[26]

Shortly after entering the Bechsteins' circle, Hitler also entered that of the Bruckmanns. Born Princess Cantacuzène of Romania, Elsa Bruckmann was the wife of Hugo, a wealthy right-wing publisher and anti-Semite. In addition to her husband's money, Elsa had ample funds of her own. Although some writers say it was Hanfstaengl who introduced Hitler to the Bruckmanns, Hanfstaengl, who knew the Bruckmanns well, says that Hitler already knew them before he came along at the end of 1921.[27] The Bruckmanns introduced Hitler to Emil Kirdorf, a major contributor to the NSDAP, to Professor Alexander von Müller, a Munich historian whose ideas clearly influenced *Mein Kampf*, Domhöfer, director of the Pinakothek art gallery, and to Ludwig Troost, the architect.

Frau Bruckmann was enchanted by Hitler, whose ingratiating manners and social naïveté seem to have brought out a motherly instinct in her — though few mothers fondly present their child with a dog whip. Hitler in turn is said to have been impressed by her family title and by her passion for Wagner. As with the Bechsteins, Hitler seems to have been troubled by a certain lack of social *savoir faire* in their presence; according to Lüdecke:

> I can still see Frau Bruckmann's eyes shining as she described Hitler's truly touching dismay before an artichoke. "But madam," he said in his softest voice, "you must tell me how to eat this thing. I never saw one before." In those days that naivety was sincere and genuine. [28]

There seems to have been an element of jealousy in Frau Bruckmann, for Hitler is reported as saying:

> One day I detected an unexpected reaction even in Frau Bruckmann. She had invited to her house, at the same time as myself, a very pretty woman of Munich society. As we were taking our leave, Frau Bruckmann perceived in her female guest's manner a sign of an interest that she doubtless deemed untimely. The consequence was that she never again invited us both at once. As I've said, the woman was beautiful, and perhaps she felt some interest in me — nothing more. [29]

Just what gifts she and her husband gave to Hitler and the NSDAP is not known, and whatever they were they were modest, but frequent. Like the Bechsteins, the Bruckmanns played a significant role in expanding Hitler's circle of contacts.

Another who expanded Hitler's social circle was Hélène Hanfstaengl, wife of Ernst. She is of interest not for any material gifts to Hitler — she probably gave him nothing beyond a little moral support — but because she offers a contrast to the other women. She was <u>not</u> older than Hitler, <u>not</u> domineering, <u>not</u> an ardent German nationalist, <u>not</u> rich, and <u>not</u> a fanatical devotee of Wagner. With most of the other givers, it was they who introduced Hitler to their husbands; with the Hanfstaengls, it was the other way around. In her unpublished memoirs, Hélène describes her first meeting with Hitler, whose constant companion her husband had recently become:

> He was at the time a slim, shy young man, with a far-away look in his very blue eyes. He was dressed almost shabbily — a cheap white shirt, black tie, a worn dark blue suit, with which he wore an incongruous dark brown leather vest, a beige-coloured trench coat, much the worse for wear, cheap black shoes and a soft, old greyish hat. His appearance was quite pathetic. [30]

Even Hélène, who quickly became disenchanted with Adolf and his politics, seems to have had her maternal instincts stirred by this little ragamuffin. She admitted to seeing a certain warmth in Hitler, especially in his relationships with children in general and with her young son, Egon.

Gottfried Feder once accused Hitler of preferring beautiful women over his obligations to the party and Hanfstaengl claims this referred to his sister Erna and more especially to his wife Hélène.[31] Hitler was somewhat besotted with her and, as Hanfstaengl describes it:

> On one occasion at the Pienzenauerstrasse house, when I had gone out to call a taxi, he went down on his knees in front of my wife, proclaimed his love for her, said what a shame it was he had not met her while she was still free and declared himself her slave. [32]

When Hélène told her husband of this, he laughed off the incident and put it down to Hitler's general loneliness and romanticism. Hitler, however, seems not to have lost his liking for Hélène. When she and Putzi divorced in 1936, Hitler is alleged to have been on the point of sending her a congratulatory telegram.[33] However, on reflection he decided not to do so, remarking that Frau Hanfstaengl was one of the few real ladies in Germany. Until her escape from Germany in 1938, Hitler continued to send her flowers on her birthday.

Hitler was also attracted to Hanfstaengl's sister Erna, and rumours began to circulate in Munich to the effect that not only were they romantically involved, but that Erna was part Jewish. Hitler solved this problem in his usual romantic fashion by publishing a notice in the *Völkischer Beobachter* declaring that they were not engaged and that Erna had no 'Jewish blood'. Erna immediately severed all ties with Hitler and married a surgeon. Hanfstaengl tells another anecdote of Hitler being banned from the home of Wilhelm Ohnesorge after professing love for his daughter. Though Kershaw expresses doubts as to the story's truth, it seems in keeping with Hitler's general behaviour towards women.[34]

Frau Winifred Wagner, the English-born wife of Siegfried Wagner, the son of the composer, was an early friend and supporter of Hitler and possibly an early member of the NSDAP. While she certainly contributed something to Hitler's upkeep, the Wagners were not in good financial shape in the nineteen-twenties, since Richard's music was far from popular in the aftermath of the First World War. Her efforts to raise large sums of money for Hitler and the NSDAP came to nothing and there is more evidence of her support for Göring than for any other individual. Like Hélène Bechstein, Winifred Wagner also contributed to the furnishing of *Haus Wachenfeld*, providing linen and china. As with the Bechsteins, these were probably cast-offs from the Wagners' own house in the area. Hitler was certainly close to Winifred, but there is little evidence to support one author's assertion that, after the death of Geli Raubal, Hitler seriously considered marrying Winifred, who had been widowed in 1930. Certainly, the Wagner family was well rewarded: Hitler became the principal patron of the Bayreuth festival, supporting it with money from the *AH Spende*, and Winifred's son, Wieland, was excused military service.

Even when famous, Hitler was happy to receive little trifles, especially if they came from women. During the final elections before his coming to power in 1933, Hitler and Hanfstaengl paid a visit to the Villa Silberblick, where Nietzsche had died and where his elderly sister still lived:

> Hitler had gone in carrying his whip, but, to my astonishment, came tripping out with a slim little turn-of-the-century cane dangling from his fingers: "What a marvellous old lady", he said to me. "What vivacity and intelligence. A real personality. Look, she has given me her brother's last walking stick as a souvenir, a great compliment. . . ."[35]

95

The image smacks a little too much of Charlie Chaplain to be entirely credible and may be malicious invention on Hanfstaengl's part – especially as he implies the unthinkable: that Hitler left his whip behind.

Some of Hitler's patronesses are less well documented. One such was Frau Viktoria 'Tory' von Dirksen, a socially ambitious matron who ran a Berlin *salon* whose frequent visitors included Crown Prince August Wilhelm ('Auwi'), heir to the exiled Kaiser and a close friend of Hanfstaengl who, curiously, fails to mention her in any of his works. It is alleged that she was a supporter of Hitler from the early twenties and that her habit of wearing a large diamond brooch in the shape of a swastika earned her the title of 'Mother of the Movement'.[36] According to one rather obscure source, she was 'Hitler's greatest woman friend' and 'gave most of her late husband's fortune to promoting Hitler's career'.[37] There is little evidence to support either allegation.

Not surprisingly, a man like Hitler was unwilling to leave such a promising source of funds as the German aristocracy untapped, though his efforts do not seem to have met with much success. Princess – sometimes incorrectly styled 'Empress' and referred to by many as the 'Quotation mark Empress' – Hermine was the second wife of the exiled Kaiser. A wealthy Silesian landowner in her own right, she is said to have been a passionate supporter of Hitler after 1930, making her support somewhat late compared to the other women. Heiden claims she gave 'large sums' to her Berchtesgaden neighbour Adolf Hitler, but offers no proof.[38] The widow of Prince Schönaich-Carolath, she married the widowed Kaiser in November 1932. It is not clear whether she contributed to Hitler before her marriage. After her marriage, she seems to have acted as the Kaiser's agent in aristocratic circles, especially in Berlin. Bella Fromm recounts one embarrassing incident at the *salon* of the elderly Countess von der Gröben, in the autumn of 1932, when the latter asked:

> *Your Majesty, I have been told that your sympathies are with the National Socialists. Is it true that His Majesty has made a donation to the National Socialists?*[39]

Rather than rebutting the allegation, the Princess is said to have remained in embarrassed silence. Another aristocrat for whose contributions there is more solid evidence was the Duchess Eduard von Sachsen-Anhalt. Divorced from her wealthy husband, she received from him the rather modest sum of RM 2,000 a month. Apparently she was not over intelligent and in 1926 Hitler was able to persuade her to give him RM 1,500 a month, having allegedly convinced her that he would restore her to her former glory once he came to power.[40] This story, which seems to originate with Heiden, has been partly mangled by later authors, at least one of whom asserts that this sum represented three quarters of Hitler's income.[41] It was certainly three quarters of the Duchess's income; what proportion of Hitler's income it represented is not known. Whatever the proportion, if this anecdote is true, it would give him an income in 1926 of at least RM 18,000 – somewhat above the RM 15,903 declared for taxes.

There were many other women who are said to have given money or jewellery to Hitler, though probably not on the scale of Bechstein, Bruckmann, and von Seidlitz. Grand Duchess Victoria, wife of Grand Duke Kyrill, the playboy heir to the Russian throne, is said to have raised money for the NSDAP and contributed jewellery to the Nazi cause, though whether any of this came through Hitler personally is uncertain. The Duchess of Coburg, a relative of Grand Duchess Victoria, is said to have helped Hitler and the NSDAP with occasional gifts.[42] None of this appears to have matched the contributions of Frau von Seidlitz.

According to Hanfstaengl:

> There was a Frau von Seidlitz who had helped over the printing presses and two Finnish ladies living in Munich who subsidised what they assumed was an anti-Bolshevist crusade, probably under the influence of Rosenberg.[43]

Hanfstaengl is not the only person to mention these 'two Finnish ladies'; Amann, in his 1924 interrogation by the Munich police, mentions a Finnish woman. It would not have been in the least surprising to find one or more Finnish ladies living in Munich, a city which even today has strong ties to Finland, nor would it be unlikely, in the wake of Finland's civil war, to find them funding an anti-Communist cause. Their existence and level of support remains unproven. Turner somehow manages to conflate Hanfstaengl's statements with Gertrud von Seidlitz's testimony at Hitler's trial into:

> Some of Hitler's well-to-do early followers also provided funding for the young party. Among them one finds a motley assortment of persons that included obscure noblemen, White Russian émigrés, Swiss sympathisers, and a wealthy widow from Finland.[44]

Adding in a footnote that she was apparently 'Gertrud von Sedlitz', Gun refers to the 'Finnish Frau von Seydlitz', whilst Maser refers to a Finnish divorcée 'Frau von Seydl'; in all probability, these are erroneous references to Gertrud von Seidlitz.[45] Which brings this story to Frau Gertrud von Seidlitz and the questions: Who was she?; why was she so important?; and where did her money come from?

Gertrud von Seidlitz

Until now, little is known about Frau von Seidlitz, but, as described in Chapter 4, she played a pivotal role in the fortunes of Hitler, the NSDAP, and the *Eher Verlag* by providing most of the money (Hanfstaengl claims to have provided the rest) to purchase a rotary printing press capable of broadsheet format. Without this press, Hitler would not have attracted such a wide audience for his views so rapidly. In statements to the police following the 1923 *Putsch*, she admitted that she had been a contributor to Hitler and the NSDAP since 1921 and claimed to have raised funds from foreign sources, especially from Finland.[46]

Born Gertrud Krause (or Kruse) in Königsberg (now Kaliningrad), in 1872, Frau Gertrud von Seidlitz was a 'Baltic German', and almost certainly not Finnish.[47] She married the rather exotically named Gerhard Karl Lamarck Darwin von Seidlitz; unfortunately, when and where are not known, but presumably in Königsberg, where her husband was a partner in a psychiatric hospital. Her husband was the only son of Georg Karl Maria von Seidlitz, a renowned scholar and disciple of Charles Darwin, then living near Munich. She is known to have been active in right-wing circles in Munich and it is even said that she was one of the intermediaries between the White Russians and Hitler.[48]

Frau von Seidlitz is said to have held investments in Finnish paper mills; whether it was the sale of these shares which provided the funds to buy the rotary press for Hitler or income from these shares is in some doubt, because her statements to the Munich police in the aftermath of the November *Putsch* are somewhat ambiguous.[49] She said that she had recruited backers from Finland and guaranteed them with her own shares in Finnish paper mills. This suggests that Finnish sources loaned money to Hitler or the NSDAP with her shares as security. However, she goes on to say that:

> I repeatedly gave smaller sums, just to Hitler and Amann. I refuse to say what the origin of these sums was, nor their amount. In so far as I donated funds from my own purse, the money originated from interest from foreign securities that I possessed . . . [50]

In her police statement, Frau von Seidlitz also claimed to have arranged funding from Czechoslovakia, Switzerland and Sweden.

It is because of her importance that considerable efforts have been made to trace Frau von Seidlitz and her family. Chronologically, Hanfstaengl, as noted in the passage quoted above, is the first to mention her and her involvement with the purchase of the rotary press. However, Rosenberg, writing while imprisoned at Nuremberg, says:

> . . . a wealthy woman helped out. She owned, if I am not mistaken, shares in some Finnish paper mills, and she gave the party a sufficient number to make it possible for us to run the risk of getting out a daily.[51]

Rosenberg goes on to imply that Frau von Seidlitz's contribution may have been made shortly before 8 February, 1923. Note that Rosenberg gives no name for the 'wealthy woman'; in fact, it is the authors of the commentary to Rosenberg's memoirs who wrote:

> The woman mentioned above, Gertrud von Seidlitz, placed considerable sums — partly Finnish capital — at the disposal of the party.[52]

The chronology is interesting. Rosenberg implies that the von Seidlitz money was used to finance the transition to a daily paper in February 1923; Hanfstaengl suggests that the money was used to purchase the rotary press which went into operation in August 1923. The author has examined the records of the Helsinki stock exchange and identified two transactions in the weeks before these two events, transactions which can only be described as 'anomalous'. Further proof – or disproof – was lacking at the time this work was delivered to the publisher.

The following points strongly suggest that Gertrud von Seidlitz, née Krause, was the widow of Gerhard Karl Lamarck Darwin von Seidlitz:

- She was born in Königsberg.
- She is the only Gertrud so far identified amongst the von Seidlitz family.
- Her style of 'Frau Gertrud' suggests that she was a widow in the early 1920s and this would be consistent with Gerhard's death in 1912 at Wehlau, near Königsberg. He predeceased his father.
- The branch of the von Seidlitz family into which Gertrud married was based at Irschenhausen, near Munich, having moved there from Estonia in 1895. Gertrud's own address, in the Munich police files, was Villa Maria, Ebenhausen.[53] Both are within 50km of Munich, though on opposite sides of the city.
- Her father-in-law is known to have visited Finland at least once, in 1910, and to have owned property in Königsberg which may have been given to her husband, and hence to Gertrud.

It is also apparent that Gertrud was not herself a member of the aristocracy: in a von Seidlitz family history, she is listed without title and without family details, suggesting that, from the point of view of that book, she was an irrelevancy.

But was she really as wealthy as supposed? Gerhard worked as an assistant physician in a lunatic asylum, not commonly a route to riches. It is possible that Gerhard received money from his father – who was certainly wealthy – or was one of the owners of the asylum where he worked, and equally possible that Gertrud had her own fortune. Attempts to identify Gertrud and her family through her maiden name of Krause (or Kruse) have not been successful and access to records in Königsberg is difficult. There is, however, a further factor that needs to be taken into consideration: Theodor Heuß.

Heuß was one of the earliest members of the DAP (forerunner of the NSDAP), a member of the *Thule Gesellschaft*, and one of the original shareholders in the *Eher Verlag*, as described in Chapter 4. The reason Heuß is interesting is that he was a paper manufacturer in Munich, with commercial connections to Finland, source of much of Europe's wood-pulp, the essential ingredient of paper. It is also known that the *Eher Verlag* continued to receive supplies of paper from Finland until late 1944. There is thus circumstantial evidence for a much stronger connection between the Finnish paper industry and Hitler than has previously been suspected. Other significant facts have emerged about the von Seidlitz family which suggest their involvement in right-wing circles. Georg Karl – Gerhard's father – was a Baltic patriot and anti-Bolshevik who maintained a 'Baltic Home' in Dresden which was much patronised by exiled Balts after the revolution of 1905-7. He was also an art collector, who established an important collection in Dresden and moved freely in artistic circles. The von Seidlitz family had been major landowners along the Baltic coast from Riga (Latvia) to St Petersburg (Russia).

These facts lead to certain speculative conclusions, though proof of these has not been established. Family involvement in Baltic Nationalism <u>could</u> provide a link to Rosenberg and other exiled Balts. Involvement with the Baltic Nationalist movement, and general anti-Bolshevism <u>could</u> provide a link to White Russian exiles in Germany and even to the *Thule Gesellschaft*. Georg's connections to the art world <u>could</u> provide a link to Hanfstaengl who some think may have introduced Frau Gertrud to Hitler.

The receivers

No discussion of Hitler and his women is complete without some mention of his attitude as a giver of gifts. There is ample evidence that Hitler was moderately generous towards women, especially towards those younger than himself, but his generosity was often ham-fisted and unthinking. He showed a remarkable talent for turning his generous impulses into an unpleasant experience for the recipient.

Mimi Reiter was probably Hitler's first serious love, if one discounts his earlier unconsummated affairs. At the time of their relationship, she was sixteen, he thirty-seven and this difference in ages seems to have set the pattern for his two other major relationships: Geli Raubal, nineteen years his junior, and Eva Braun, twenty-three years younger. Like Geli, Mimi *avait du monde au balcon*, unlike Eva Braun, who is reported to have padded her bra with handkerchiefs. The story of Hitler's relationship with Mimi is well documented.[54] What is interesting to this study is the money he spent on her – very little. He gave her a signed, leather-bound copy of *Mein Kampf*; she gave him a pair of embroidered cushions. He gave her a wrist watch for her birthday, 23 December, the same day Hitler's mother was buried in 1908. He took her for drives in the countryside and invited her to his home a few times and she claimed to have slept with him. On more than one occasion, he took her to dinner, though always to some political function, rather than a candle-lit *tête-à-tête*, which would have been more to Mimi's romantic tastes. Besotted with him, she gave him everything she could – and got little in return. Around 1935, she married SS *Hauptsturmführer* Kubish, a member of Goebbels' personal bodyguard. In 1940, following her husband's death in the French campaign, Hitler sent her 100 red roses. It was the last contact between them. However, in a twist to the tale, after the war she shared a cottage with Hitler's sister, Paula, on the Waldsee, Bavaria.

The next major love of Hitler's life – perhaps the love – was his step-niece, Angelika 'Geli' Raubal. It is difficult to say when their affair began since it appears to have developed gradually and it was not until early 1927 that their relationship began to be noticed. At first, Hitler lodged her in a boarding house near Munich's *Englischer Garten*, but in 1928 he rented for her a furnished room not far from his own. This arrangement seems to have been less than satisfactory since it left her unsupervised and allowed her to engage in several casual affairs, including one with Emil Maurice, Hitler's chauffeur – an affair which eventually led to his dismissal and Geli's banishment for several months to live under the watchful eye of the Bruckmanns. Not for nothing did Hanfstaengl call her 'an empty-headed little slut' and he certainly held her in deep contempt:

> She went around very well dressed at his expense, or, more probably, at the Party's expense, as a lot of resentment was expressed . . . She was perfectly content to preen herself in her fine clothes, and certainly never gave any impression of reciprocating Hitler's twisted tenderness. . . . In addition, there was, of course, an unpleasant suggestion of incest about the affair, which I can only assume harked back to their in-bred peasant family. [55]

Hitler certainly 'showered her with presents', but it was all cheap stuff; Geli's tastes ran to glitter, rather than style, and Hitler was the last person to take any interest in elegant clothes or beautiful jewellery. In 1929, she moved into her own room at Hitler's new luxury apartment on Prizregentenplatz. Throughout that year, and possibly until her death, Hitler paid 100 marks a month for singing lessons for Geli, who had ambitions as an opera star – ambitions which Hanfstaengl believes were prompted by Hitler himself. Her singing lessons were not a success:

> It was arranged that [Streck] would give Geli twelve lessons a month and be paid 100 marks. "Geli is the laziest pupil I have ever had," he used to complain. "Half the time she rings up to say that she can't come and she learns very little when she does." She never practised at home and the main impression Streck derived was of Hitler's boundless tolerance of the waste of his money. [56]

Geli Raubal was found shot in her room at Hitler's flat on 18 September 1931. Whether she committed suicide or was murdered remains an open question, but the evidence is strong that it could not have been Adolf Hitler who squeezed the trigger. Other than death, what did she get out of the relationship? A few bits of cheap jewellery, clothes, food, and free lodging.

After Geli, Hitler was associated with a string of women, in parallel with his affair with Eva Braun, which was just beginning at the time of his niece's suicide. There was Sigrid – Sigi – von Laffert, the daughter of impoverished aristocrats whom Hitler is said to have supported financially.[57] She was a distant cousin of Viktoria von Dirksen, one of Hitler's alleged financial supporters, whose social ambitions may have played a part in publicising Sigrid's alleged relationship.

Eva Braun was one of the few women on whom Hitler spent substantial amounts of money, though by the time she became his mistress he certainly had more to give than earlier. Hitler met Eva in October 1929 when she was working as an assistant in the shop of the photographer Hoffman; she was just seventeen. In the early years of their relationship, he seems to have been fairly casual about providing her with money, occasionally passing it to her in an envelope, in full view of their companions in a café or restaurant. Few acts could have made anyone feel more like a 'kept woman'. In 1935, on 1 April, Eva wrote in her diary:

> I had to sit beside him for 3 hours without being able to say a single word to him. As a farewell gesture, he gave me an envelope with some money inside, as he has already done once before. How lovely it would have been if he had also written a line of greeting or a kind word. But he never thinks of such things. [58]

Eva, who seems by all accounts to have been a woman of modest tastes, may not have needed more. Before Bormann took over most of his personal finances, Hitler would take Eva on the occasional shopping trip, typically buying medium-priced jewellery; after Bormann took over, the value of these gifts increased, though they continued to reflect her relatively modest tastes. By 1932, Hitler was paying for her apartment on Munich's Wiedenmayer Straße. For her twenty-first birthday, a few days after he came to power in January 1933, Hitler gave her a matching set of ring, earrings, and bracelet of tourmalines:

> The semiprecious stones were mediocre and rather small, for Hitler was far from generous, but the setting was finely worked and gave the impression of being old. When Eva went home, she had to hide this finery in her purse. It always remained her favourite jewelry. [59]

On 9 August 1935, Eva and her younger sister Gretl moved into a three-room apartment on Wiedermeyerstraße, in Munich's Bogenhausen district, a short walk from Hitler's own Munich residence. The apartment had three comfortable rooms and central heating, but, as Gun notes:

> With his inveterate avarice, [Hitler] had bought the furniture at a reduced price. There was not a single picture on the walls and Eva had to borrow linen and cutlery from her mother. A Hungarian maid had been engaged, whose chief occupation, when she was not playing Ping-Pong in the hall, was drying the washing of her lover, an army sergeant, on the balcony of the apartment. [60]

The rental was in Hoffmann's name, but the rent was paid by Hitler. Subsequently, Hitler bought (again using Hoffmann as proxy) a house for Eva and Gretl. Situated at Wasserburgstraße 12 (now Delpstraße) in a fashionable area, the house was not large, but stood on a large plot, surrounded by high walls. When the girls took up residence on 30 March 1936, Hitler gave Eva a Mercedes and driver as a housewarming gift.

Always fashionable, Eva Braun spent lavishly on clothes, sending the bills to various people for settlement. [61] Her shoes were hand made in Italy; her dresses were made by Fräulein Heise, one of Berlin's most reputed dressmakers; her silk underwear came from Paris; and her sports outfits were made in Vienna. Even the Braun family seems to have benefited to some extent from Eva's relationship with Hitler. Gretl received presents a plenty and had her own rooms at the Berghof, while even Fritz, Eva's father, received a gold watch and a dog for his sixty-fifth birthday and was appointed to a military sinecure as director of a hospital. On 24 October 1944, Eva Braun drafted a will and compiled a list of her valuables:

> "Rings, one big and one small, bracelet of emeralds surrounded by diamonds, necklace and brooch, also of emeralds and diamonds, another brooch in the shape of a butterfly, emerald earrings, a marguerite-shaped brooch of diamonds and rubies, a solitaire diamond ring; a diamond ring, a diamond brooch, a ring, a diamond watch, a brooch in the form of flowers, another diamond ring, jewellery of beryl, an emerald set consisting of a pin, a bracelet, a pendant, another ring and earrings, a gold bracelet set with sapphires and diamonds, a brooch and a necklace . . . "
>
> The list continues with about thirty more valuable pieces of jewelry, to which must be added a dozen or so fur coats, including one of sable and one of mink.[62]

Of particular interest as an example of Hitler's generosity – because it is so well documented – is the case of Unity Valkyrie Mitford. (She would make great play on her middle name in her relationship with Hitler.) Unity was one of the daughters of Lord Redesdale, a member of a minor branch of the British aristocracy noted for producing two talented writers, Unity's sisters, Nancy and Jessica. She is of interest to this story not for the money which she gave to Hitler – she had little to give – but for the money she received.[63] Unity Mitford went to Munich in 1934, ostensibly to study art history, but also determined to meet Hitler. She did so by the simple expedient of going every day to the *Osteria Bavaria*, Hitler's favourite restaurant, and sitting quietly at a table by the door, wearing British 'Blackshirt' uniform, and waiting until she was noticed. This she was, on Saturday, 9 February 1935, after which she rapidly became part of the *Osteria Bavaria* circle and later an intermittent member of Hitler's court.[64] There is no doubt that Hitler was aware of the propaganda value of having a faithful follower drawn from the ranks of the British aristocracy; it also seems that he was amused by her liveliness and by the bluntness of some of her statements. There was no truth in the rumour that she was his mistress and Hitler seems to have treated her as he treated most women younger than himself: as a romantic but trivial plaything. To forestall any prospect of marriage to a Nazi party member, her sister Nancy, who thoroughly disapproved of Nazism, managed to spread a rumour that the family had Jewish blood, even going so far as to send a fake family tree to Himmler.[65]

In 1938, shortly after the Bayreuth Festival, Unity fell ill – with pneumonia, possibly complicated by some sort of nervous breakdown – and entered the *Clinic am Hofgarten* in Munich, close to the Wagner family's *Haus Wahnfreid*.[66] Hitler paid her medical bills but, after she had recovered, her father, Lord Redesdale, took her to the *Berghof* and insisted on repaying the bill in full.

In 1939, Unity was back at Berchtesgaden, spending the night of 6-7 May at the *Berghof* itself.[67] She had earlier made it known that she was looking for an apartment in Munich and Hitler ordered Heß to make the necessary arrangements; she was offered a choice of four apartments, all confiscated from Jews in the aftermath of the *Kristallnacht* pogrom. She inspected them all – at least two still housed their dispossessed owners – and selected Agnesstraße 26, Apartment 4. However, for some reason, she still continued to live with Hanfstaengl's wife Hélène, at a farmhouse in the Obersalzberg. But Putzi had fled the country in disgrace and on 9 June 1939, Hitler forbade her to stay any longer in the Hanfstaengl household, insisting that she move into her Munich apartment immediately, and offering to pay for new furnishings. Alas, we do not know whether this offer was accepted.

When Germany invaded Poland, on 1 September 1939, Unity wrote several farewell letters – some of which she delivered by hand – then went to Munich's *Englischer Garten* – a poetic touch – and shot herself in the head. As a suicide, it failed, but she was severely injured.[68] Found by agents of the *Sicherheitsdienst*, who had been alerted by the recipient of one of her letters, Gauleiter Wagner, she was taken to the *Chirurgische Universitätsklinik* for treatment. There she had a private room, with a nurse in constant attendance; Hitler personally guaranteed to pay for her treatment. Her apartment was sealed, again on Hitler's orders.

A record of payments and correspondence exists.[69] On 1 November 1939, the State Secretary of the Bavarian Ministry of the Interior wrote to the office of the *Führer's* Adjutant, acknowledging receipt of RM 1,039.29 and asking for a further RM 255.89 to be paid into account number 4415 at the Bayerische Gemeindebank in the name of Unity Mitford. The outstanding sum was itemised as:

- RM 161.14 for hospital treatment between 11 and 20 October.
- RM 90 for Dr. Albert Kohler, for two X-rays.
- RM 3.95 to the *Theatiner* shoe shop.

On 8 January 1940, after Unity had been repatriated to Britain, Professor Magnus, of the *Chirurgische Universitätsklinik* sent in his bill for over 3,000 marks, but this was not paid until April. In February, Unity's account was credited with RM 250 from the sale of some specially-made cupboards from her apartment. The Ministry of the Interior then notified Hitler's office that the apartment was available for re-letting. Case closed. As Unity's biographer, David Pryce-Jones remarks:

> The expenses had been high. Hitler paid. It was the least he could do.[70]

Two other women benefited to some extent from Hitler's generosity: his half-sister Angela and his sister Paula. Angela – Geli's mother and sister to Alois Jr. – acted as Hitler's housekeeper at the *Berghof* from 1928 until 1935. After Angela left the Berghof, Paula took over. Schwarzwäller maintains that she was soon dismissed for being too critical of her brother, returning to Vienna, where she had an interest in an arts and crafts shop, and adopting the name 'Wolf'.[71] Other authors, such as Waite, have claimed that Adolf and his sister were on poor terms, but there is little evidence for this. According to Toland:

> The story that Hitler treated his younger sister badly was denied after the war by Paula herself. When Hitler's notoriety spread to Vienna she changed her name to Wolf. Even so, she was dismissed from her job. "I went to Munich and described my difficult position in life to my brother. With full understanding he assured me that he would provide for me in future." He gave her 250 marks a month, raising that figure to 500 in 1938. In addition he gave her a present of 3,000 marks every Christmas and helped her buy a villa. She would occasionally visit him in the Obersalzberg but rarely for more than two weeks. [72]

Whether the monthly payment of 500 marks continued after April of 1945, and where it was paid from, are not known; answering these two questions would be a significant step towards untangling Hitler's finances.

Why did they do it?

Why did so many women give money and gifts to Hitler? What was it about these women that caused them to be attracted to this coarse, rather ugly little man with the big ideas? What did they have in common?

One answer is money. It is easy to believe that Hitler was attracted to these women because they had money, but did their access to money affect their attraction to him? It is sometimes said that wealth brings guilt. Did these women feel guilty that they had money and Hitler did not? That hardly seems likely since they were not noted for showering gifts on passing beggars in the street. Furthermore, not all of the women were wealthy; Hoffmann and Laubóck certainly were not.

Another motive that has been advanced is the joint one of anti-Communism and German Nationalism. Certainly, these would be good reasons for supporting the NSDAP, but were they sufficient to support Hitler the individual? One must conclude that they were. All the patronesses had been through the First World War and experienced Germany's humiliation in its aftermath. Each had seen their husbands' or their own finances ravaged by inflation. Each sought a restoration of Germany's 'glory'. Clearly ardent nationalism and surrogate motherhood are a potent combination.

Another common factor is age; all the patronesses were significantly older than Hitler, all were somewhat matronly in both appearance and attitude. Certainly the dishevelled, under-nourished Hitler would bring out the mother (especially the stereotypical 'Jewish mother': You'll never get to be a dictator in a suit like that! You can't make a speech to storm troopers without a decent meal inside you!) in any woman, but that seems hardly sufficient reason for the amounts given. However, one aspect of age must not be ignored: where these women had children, those children had already matured and left the family fold. Hitler, however, presented them with a fresh chance at 'motherhood'. Not only was he in need of mothering, but here was a son who might one day be leader of his country. The possibility of being known as the 'Mother of the Führer' could be a powerful incentive.

Notes

1   LÜDE38, p. 99.
2   HEID44, pp. 205-6. Heiden gives no date or other reference to the speech but the implication is that it was that of 27 February 1925 at the *Bürgerbraükeller*, Munich.
3   TOLA76, p. 99.
4   Elements of this story are quoted by BULL62, p. 83; SHIR60, p. 73; TOLA76, p. 111; HEID36, p. 97. Heiden claims that the pamphlet was written by Anton Drexler.
5   This could not refer to the Bechstein jewellery (see below) because this was not given until September 1923.
6   TURN85B, p. 89, citing the *Essener Allgemeine Zeitung*, as quoted by the *Völkischer Beobachter*, 10 December 1927.
7   New York, 1987 (re-issue edition), Farrar Straus & Giroux; ISBN: 0374246009.
8   HANF57, p. 35.
9   LÜDE38, p. 99.
10 WAIT77, p. 48.
11 WAIT77, p. 39, citing Schneider, *7 Tage* (no page given). Waite also claims that Hoffmann said that Hitler had no objection to women wearing lipstick, but gives no source.
12 It has been pointed out to the author by the Finnish writer-critic-translator Matti Rosvall that Hitler's behaviour towards women greatly resembles that of Max Bialystok in Mel Brooks's satirical film *The Producers*.
13 From Toland's interviews with Baur, quoted in TOLA76, p. 267. The story as told in Baur's own book (BAUR58, pp. 35-7) is similar, but less colourful.
14 Those interested in such speculations should read WAIT77 or HANF57.
15 TOLA76, p. 365, quoting from Wiedemann, Fritz. 1964. *Der Mann, der Feldherr weden wollte*, Velbert, p. 35.
16 GUN68, p. 71 has her 'ugly but aristocratic, the widow of a professor at Munich University', but this is at odds with all other accounts.
17 TOLA76, p. 198; HEID44, p. 210; MASE73, pp. 198-9.
18 KERS98, p. 160, quoting Auerbach; HEID44, p. 210.
19 There seems to be some doubt about her age; Toland has her as 83 in 1925, Pool (POOL78, p. 27) as 61 in 1920, Hanfstaengl simply says she was in her sixties. The lower figure has been adopted out of respect.
20 HANF57, p. 50. Kershaw (KERS98, p. 160) merely records that she 'saw to Hitler's well-being'.

21   HANF57, p. 43.
22   HANF57, pp. 82-3. Hanfstaengl is mistaken about Frau Büchner's height. A photograph of her in 1936 (CHAU01, p. 34) shows her as being of average height and rather flat-chested. The gold tooth is not visible.
23   HANF57, p. 43.
24   HANF57, p. 62.
25   Adapted from FRAN62, pp. 192-3. Translation by the author.
26   HANF57, p. 275.
27   HANF57, p. 42. Hanfstaengl claims (p. 43) that he later broke off social relations with Frau Bruckmann after learning that she had supported Rosenberg, though this seems rather a petty reason, especially in the light of Hanfstaengl's oft professed desire to exert a moderating influence on Hitler.
28   LÜDE38, p. 97.
29   HITL53, p. 344, night of 10-11 March, 1942.
30   Quoted by Toland, TOLA76, p. 135.
31   HANF57, p. 50.
32   HANF57, p. 137. Waite (WAIT77, p. 48) has the rather more explicit declaration: "If only I had someone to take care of me!" though no source is actually quoted. See also KERS98, p. 281, citing Hanfstaengl, *15 Jahre*, pp. 183-4.
33   TOLA76, p. 395.
34   HANF57, p. 137; KERS98, p. 684, note 150.
35   HANF57, p. 206.
36   MASE73, p. 198; GUN68, p. 71. Not much credence can be given to this title which was also given variously to the *Frauen* Bechstein, Bruckmann, Hoffman, Lauböck, and Wagner.
37   Flanner, Janet. *Fuehrer*. Date and publisher unknown. Extract quoted from the US Office of Strategic Services' 'Hitler Source Book'.
38   HEID36, p. 279. Heiden also has the princess implicated in the Osthilfe Scandal.
39   FROM43, p. 57.
40   HEID44, p. 231.
41   BULL62, p. 137.
42   POOL78, pp. 62 and 73. The supporting evidence for this is not clear. Schwarzwäller (SCHW89, p. 90) repeats the story, though without any reference.
43   HANF57, p. 55.
44   TURN85, p. 54.
45   GUN68, p. 71; MASE73, p. 198. Extensive research has so far failed to reveal any evidence of a Seydl, Seydlitz or Sedlitz with a Finnish connection. Tantalisingly, Williams (WILL72, p. 59) mentions a " . . . Baltic Baroness Seydlitz, the widow of a Russian officer living in Norway." However, there seems to be no connection.
46   FRA62, pp. 191-2.
47   Williams (WILL72, pp. 7-20) gives a good account of the Baltic Germans.
48   WILL72, p. 166.
49   Statement dated 13 December 1923. Extracts are quoted in FRA62, pp. 191-92.
50   Extracted from *Vermahung von Frau von Seidlitz, Protokoll von 13.12.1932, Akt den*

Polizeidirektion, München. Translation by the author. Portions of the original German text appear in Franz-Willing and in Deuerlein.

51   ROSE49, p. 62.

52   Ibid.

53   DEUE62, p. 377.

54   KERS98, pp. 284-6; WAIT77, pp. 223-5; ROSE98, pp. 109-17; GUN68, pp. 74-76. Of these, Kershaw's is the most objective account, and less clouded by psychological mumbo-jumbo than other authors.

55   HANF57, p. 162.

56   HANF57, p. 164.

57   GUN68, p. 186.

58   GUN68, p. 87; Toland (TOLA76, p. 376), quoting from the 'diary' translation in the US National Archives has a slightly different translation, but no major differences.

59   GUN68, p. 96; TOLA76, p. 364 repeats the story.

60   GUN68, p. 102.

61   Gun (GUN68, p. 176) has her sending bills to Axmann for payment. This is improbable, since Axmann spent most of his career in the Hitler Youth organisation. A tantalising possibility is that Gun is referring to Max Amann, but there is no proof.

62   GUN68, p. 206. Gun is exaggerating when he refers to the pieces as 'valuable'.

63   According to Pryce-Jones (PRYC77, p. 112) she had an allowance of about £100 a year – equivalent to about 2,000 "register marks".

64   The *Osteria Bavaria* circle consisted of Hitler, Heinrich Hoffmann, Adolf Wagner (Gauleiter of Munich), Martin Bormann, Julius Schaub, Otto Dietrich, Theodor Morell (Hitler's physician), Albert Speer, and Karl Brandt (another physician). There were also sundry aides, bodyguards, and guests. Since, according to Speer, Hitler's place in the *Osteria Bavaria* was a booth seating eight, one wonders how they could all fit in!

65   GUN68, p. 192.

66   PRYC77, p. 210-11.

67   PRYC77, p. 227.

68   A fuller account can be found in Pryce-Jones (PRYC77, pp. 245-247).

69   The following paragraph is derived from Pryce-Jones (PRYC77, p. 258); unfortunately, he gives no references as to his sources.

70   PRYC77, p. 258.

71   SCHW89, p. 159.

72   TOLA76, footnote to p. 395. Toland's source reference cites his interview with Hans Hitler, but the words reported appear to be attributed directly to Paula.

Chapter Seven

HITLER THE WRITER
(AND SPEAKER)

No man but a blockhead ever wrote except for money.
Samuel Johnson (1709-1784)
Life of Johnson (Boswell). Vol. vi. Chap. iii.

Throughout most of his life, Hitler described himself as a writer and claimed that the majority of his income came from writing. This was far from the truth, but any study of his finances must examine his work as journalist and author. His activities as a speaker are equally important, since he derived income not only from public speaking, but also by charging hefty fees for interviews.[1]

Journalism

Hitler's name appeared as the by-line for many articles, some of which – especially those in the *Völkischer Beobachter* and similar publications of the *Eher Verlag* – he actually wrote or dictated. As for what he was paid, Baldur von Schirach, leader of the *Hitlerjugend*, claimed that Hitler was receiving RM 800 per article in the early nineteen-thirties.[2] This was probably true; during the long-running argument with *Gauleiter* Munder over his expenses and lifestyle between 1925 and 1928, Hitler is reported to have said:

> *'Yes, indeed,' he said when called to account, 'I accept payment for these articles, and good payment; after all, I am not the employee of our enterprise, I am its founder and leader.'*[3]

Hitler also assiduously cultivated the press, especially those sectors of the foreign press that would present a favourable image of him. These included the British press baron Lord Rothermere, owner of the *Daily Mail*, and that paper's editor, Ward Price. In 1930, the *Daily Mail* was Britain's largest-circulation newspaper and Lord Rothermere – and the press he controlled – Hitler's most vocal admirers. However, on closer examination, Lord Rothermere's admiration seems prompted more by anti-Communism than pro-Nazism. Nonetheless, he contributed morally to Hitler's rise and, in a small way, financially, by paying well for articles and interviews. A discussion of Lord Rothermere's alleged financial support is given in Chapter 8.

Much of the success of Hitler's relations with the press, especially the foreign press, was due to the efforts of Hanfstaengl. In the United States, Hitler's mouthpiece was William Randolf Hearst, owner of a huge press empire and in the early twenties Hanfstaengl introduced Hitler to William Bayard Hale, former chief European correspondent for Hearst and then living in retirement in Munich.

Speeches

Hitler gave many speeches and it must be assumed that he wrote most of them, or at least wrote an outline; indeed, the evidence suggests that he did – or at least wrote an outline.[4] What concerns us here is whether he was paid for them and how much. There are two cases to be considered: speeches given publicly at NSDAP rallies or meetings (Public Speeches) and speeches given to outside bodies, such as business clubs (Private Speeches).

Public Speeches

Hitler always maintained that he never charged the NSDAP a fee for speaking at rallies and meetings. This is true. He did, however, receive 'expenses', from which he paid travelling costs for himself and his sizeable entourage of chauffeurs, secretaries, security men, valets, and general hangers-on. Nor were the 'expenses' simple reimbursements, rather they were a percentage of the profits. Just what that percentage was, we do not know, but it is known that Hitler left the actual bargaining to Schaub.

Private Speeches

Before becoming Chancellor, many of Hitler's speeches were made privately, as the invited guest of a club or political organisation. Sometimes Hitler spoke for a flat fee; more often it seems to have been a fee supplemented by voluntary contributions. As noted in Chapters 5 and 10, Aust described such contributions at Hitler's 1924 trial. The 1927 speeches in Essen are another example.

Interviews

From fairly early in his career, journalists sought interviews with Hitler and as they came flocking to his door Hitler, perhaps encouraged by Hanfstaengl and Dietrich, began to ration his interviews. Rationing encouraged high prices. For example, second-hand evidence suggests that Hitler wanted two dollars per printed word for an interview by the American journalist and avant-garde writer Djuna Barnes.[5] The dating of this is far from clear and could be 1924, 1931, or both. The interview never took place.

Authorship

The history of Hitler's main work, *Mein Kampf*, follows at the end of this chapter. In addition, the following works were wholly or partially written by Hitler or transcribed from his conversations:

Life and Speeches

In 1923 the *Eher Verlag* brought out a little book of 150 or so pages entitled *Adolf Hitler, sein Leben und seine Reden* (Adolf Hitler, his Life and Speeches), the only book, other than *Mein Kampf*, published in Hitler's lifetime. Technically, although Hitler wrote the speeches, which were collected from the *Völkischer Beobachter*, the book was not Hitler's but was edited by one of the newspaper's staff, Adolf Viktor von Körber. Hitler dictated a few spurious biographical comments to von Körber, who added them by way of an introduction. A second edition was issued in 1933.

What makes this work so interesting is not the content, but the editing. The speeches as they appeared in the *Völkischer Beobachter* were transcribed by a stenographer and contain all the lapses of grammar, lacunae, and minor asides by the speaker. The speeches as they appear in the book have been edited, not just in the 1923 edition, but further edited for the 1933 version. Heiden has made a useful analysis of these changes.[6] Whether Hitler received any specific royalties for this book is not known; however, he certainly benefited through its contribution to the profits of the *Eher Verlag*.

The 'Second Book'

Hitler's *Second Book* (it seems to have lacked even a working title) opens with the portentous – or pretentious – words: 'Politics is history in the making . . . ' Like most of Hitler's 'writing' it was dictated, rather than written, and there is some controversy, irrelevant to this book, over who took that dictation. However, it is clear that the work was composed during the last weeks of June and the beginning of July, 1928.

Hitler eventually forbade publication of the book probably because parts of it were out of date before the book was finished and much of it no longer fitted with the *realpolitik* of the moment. It is also possible that Amann advised against publication, afraid that it might damage sales of the second volume of *Mein Kampf* which, at that time, was not selling well. Because the book was unpublished, copyright could not be seized by the Bavarian government after the war. Some time in the 1950s François Genoud, a Swiss lawyer, acquired the copyright from Hitler's sister, Paula. Genoud took pains to secure his copyright position by bringing out a French translation, which could then be copyrighted independently of the original text. All subsequent translations are thought to have been based on the French translation, though Trevor-Roper has cast doubts on this, claiming that Genoud allowed the translator of the English version access to the original text. A German version of the book was finally published in 1961, by *Deutsche Verlagsgesellschaften* of Stuttgart, as *Hitlers Zweites Buch*. It may be assumed that Genoud received the royalties, as he did from his collection of Bormann's letters.[7] A new edition was announced in June of 2003; at the time this work was delivered to the publisher, no Hitler relative had appeared to claim copyright or royalties.

The 'Secret Conversations'

The so-called *Secret Conversations* were taken down by stenographers at Bormann's command. They are useful source material, but often inaccurate. Hanfstaengl makes an interesting comment:

> People who have read the collection of his remarks at table assume that he kept up this running fire of comment and commentary the whole time. It is simply not so. During my years at the Chancellery he would rail against the enemies of the régime in his old propaganda style, or talk about past campaigns, but there was no discussion of the progress of his revolution. It was only after the war had started, when there were no more meetings to rant at, and he had a new audience of generals, that he produced for posterity, probably at the suggestion of Bormann, the pearls of wisdom by which he wished to be remembered. It was done for deliberate effect and came long after my time.[8]

The *Secret Conversations* were not published until after the war and form no part of Hitler's estate.

Mein Kampf

Hitler's turgid political manifesto *Mein Kampf* (My Struggle) is so important to his finances after 1925 that its history deserves a section of its own – as opposed to its contents, which deserve little or nothing.

Writing

Hitler began dictating the book while imprisoned in Landsberg fortress in 1924. At first, dictation was taken by Emil Maurice, Hitler's chauffeur, later passing into the hands of the more literate – though less sane – Rudolf Heß. The most colourful account of the origins of *Mein Kampf* comes from Otto Strasser[9] According to Strasser, while Hitler was in Landsberg prison the other prisoners became irritated by his long political harangues which could last for several hours.

To protect his fellow prisoners, Strasser's brother, Gregor, hit on the idea of having Hitler write his memoirs. This Hitler eagerly seized on, retiring to his room on the first floor and leaving the other inmates, on the ground floor, in peace – until Hitler took to reading passages from his work in progress every Saturday night.[10]

More likely is Heiden's version that it was Max Amann who, sensing the profits that could made from a sensational exposé of the events surrounding the *Putsch*, persuaded Hitler to write his account of the affair. In the matter of sensation, Amann – and subsequent readers – were greatly disappointed. Heiden also maintains that the work was based on an unpublished document, begun in 1922 and entitled *Eine Abrechnung* (A Reckoning, a title adopted for the last chapter of this book), which was an attack on Hitler's many enemies within the various far-right movements. This grew into *Mein Kampf*. There is something to be said for Heiden's argument for, as described in Chapter 3, Hitler was under attack at that time in right-wing circles, partly for his profligate spending and the secrecy surrounding his sources of income. In which case, it is ironic that the attack should have resulted in its subject becoming even wealthier. The working title was *Four and a Half Years of Struggle against Lies, Stupidity, and Cowardice*; hardly the pithy title one might expect from a master of propaganda, but Hitler was still learning his trade. Heiden credits Amann with the invention of the final title under which the work became notorious: *Mein Kampf*.

The first volume of *Mein Kampf* was published on 18 July 1925 at the high price of 12 *marks*. In its first year, *Mein Kampf* sold 9,473 copies, at *8 marks* apiece, of which Hitler received 10%. The first volume was actually published under the title *Eine Abrechnung*, followed on 10 December 1926 by the second volume, *Die Nationalsozialistiche Bewegung* (The National Socialist Movement). Not until 1930 were the two parts combined into a single volume, followed by a cheap edition in 1933. Heiden gives the price as *7 marks 20 pfennigs*.[11] The first part is largely biographical, while the second, which was not begun until after Hitler's release from Landsberg prison, deals more with political and racial issues. In both cases, the prose was slipshod, ungrammatical, turgid, and rambling.[12] Otto Strasser, one of Hitler's close associates at the time, described it as:

A veritable chaos of banalities, schoolboy reminiscences, subjective judgements, and personal hatred.[13]

Several people took turns at editing it into its published form. Indeed, so many people had a hand in the work that one wonders just how close the final text is to Hitler's intentions. Amann, Müller (the printer), Hanfstaengl, and Heß all worked on the text – to little effect. In an attempt to make a best-seller out of what was clearly a non-starter, Amann arranged for parts of the book to be further 'edited' by two unusual figures: Josef Stolzing-Czerny, music critic of the *Völkischer Beobachter*, and Bernard Stempfle, a former Hieronymite monk and former editor of the *Miesbacher Anzeiger*, a provincial Bavarian newspaper with far-right sympathies.[14] Stempfle was the subject of a rather sensationalised 1995 BBC documentary entitled *Hitler Stole My Ideas*. In the mid- and late nineteen-twenties, Stempfle was a regular at Hitler's *Stammtisch* in the *Café Heck*, on Munich's Galleriestraße. Hanfstaengl has left his memory of the editing:

> . . . one morning Hitler appeared with a bunch of [galley proofs] in his hand. "Would you help me correct them?" he asked, to which I agreed only too readily until I started to read them. It really was frightful stuff. I suppose I did not see more than the first seventy pages or so . . . the style filled me with horror. . . . the book still reads like one of Fafner's monologues out of Wagner's Siegfried. [15]

Heiden, an experienced writer and critic, has given his own impressions of the work in which he echoes Hanfstaengl's comparison with Wagner. Biased and amusing, it is nonetheless worth quoting at length:

> In the first edition the first volume is written almost in dialect, and the spelling is by no means above reproach. Endless heaps of substantives are intended to cover over the jargon of the Vienna lodging-house. Hitler uses few verbs, for he seldom says what happens; he always tries to create an image with his own luminous figure striding through columns of majestic substantives. He has enriched the German language with a dozen of the most hideous foreign words (hideous especially because they are not really at home in any language of the world). But even this terrifying style is not his own creation; it is borrowed from Richard Wagner's prose writings . . . [16]

Once published, *Mein Kampf* was regarded, especially by Hitler, as 'holy writ' which could not be altered, though, as noted above, many grammatical errors were corrected over the years. The substance, however embarrassing, out of date, or inaccurate was never altered. Where Hitler subsequently adopted policies different from those he had advocated in *Mein Kampf*, the written evidence was merely ignored.

The second volume of *Mein Kampf* was published late in 1926, at a price of 12 *marks*, and combined sales for the year were only 6,913 copies. In September 1932, Kurt Lüdecke discussed with Hitler the possibility of selling the US copyright of *Mein Kampf* for $50,000, the Hearst organisation having already offered $25,000.

> "I don't see any danger in the book as it stands," said Hitler. "If you can get fifty thousand for it, go ahead — the money would be most welcome right now. Of course it would be up to the American publisher to condense and abridge, provided that doesn't falsify or distort the original meaning. I don't need to retract what I wrote years ago, like a professional writer — I make politics, not books.[17]

When, in February 1936, the French journalist Bertrand de Jouvenel asked Hitler why he did not alter anti-French statements in *Mein Kampf* to bring them into line with his current policies, Hitler is said to have replied:

> Are you suggesting that I should correct my book like an author who is bringing out a revised edition of his work? I'm a politician, not a writer. My corrections are made in my foreign policy which is directed towards an understanding with France. . . . My corrections are made in the great book of history.[18]

Since the sentiments echoed in these two quotes are remarkably similar, even though they are dated four years apart, one is forced to wonder whether these were stock answers, used regularly by Hitler, or whether Lüdecke's memory has been helped by the *Völkischer Beobachter* article.

Publication

By 1940, *Mein Kampf* had been translated into sixteen languages – plus a Braille edition in German.[19] As Figure 7-1 shows, by 1945 the work had sold 9,800,000 copies.[20] In 2003, *Mein Kampf* was more widely available than ever before – despite the efforts of the State of Bavaria to suppress its publication – with versions abounding on the Internet.

Germany & Austria

As noted earlier, the high price of the first volume – twelve marks, double the price of comparable works – did not help sales. Indeed, as Figure 7-1 shows, sales were only a few tens of thousands – respectable, but hardly 'best selling' – in the nineteen-twenties, only taking off spectacularly after Hitler became Chancellor in 1933. (Note that number of copies is in millions, on a logarithmic scale.)

It is often said, especially by those who are sympathetic to the philosophies that it propounds, that *Mein Kampf* is banned in Germany. This is untrue. Publication of *Mein Kampf* <u>without commentary</u> is formally banned in Germany

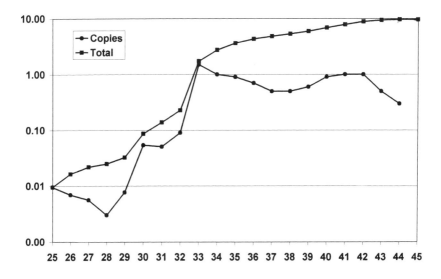

Figure 7-1. Sales of *Mein Kampf*

and appears to be tacitly banned in Austria. The book can be bought in Germany (though with difficulty) provided it is in a critical edition, with approved commentaries pointing out the errors and iniquities in the text. It is not illegal to own it, nor to read it. It is the sale of the book in its original form, without any accompanying commentary, that is prohibited and there have been several cases where the authorities have intervened in an attempt to prevent the sale of, for example, signed first edition copies.

The origin of much of the fuss surrounding publication of *Mein Kampf* stems from the Allies' decisions of 1945-46 regarding Hitler's property and the property of the Nazi party, subsequent German law – especially the 1948 *Befreiungsgesetzes* (lit. release law) and the Bavarian state government's *Einziehungsverordnung* (lit. collection regulation) – and German sensitivities in general. As noted in Chapters 17 and 18, this has left much of Hitler's personal assets in the hands of the Bavarian Finance Ministry, which transferred the copyright to the Bavarian state in 1965.[21] This includes all works published prior to his death but, by a quirk of German law, not to material which was not published at the time Hitler's assets were seized. Rightly sensitive to the feelings and opinions of groups representing those who suffered under the Nazi regime, but also conscious of the political need to present a public image of a benign Germany, the Bavarian Finance Ministry is unrelenting in its efforts to ensure that un-commented versions of *Mein Kampf* are not published, anywhere, in any language – except in Britain and the USA. One unintended side-effect of all this effort is that every time anyone attempts to publish a new version, he or she receives vast amounts of free publicity. The current German copyright expires in 2015; what will happen then remains to be seen.

Britain

In the nineteen-thirties[22], the *Eher Verlag* sold the copyright of the British and Commonwealth editions of *Mein Kampf*, through the Curtis Brown literary agency, to William Hutchinson, a major British publisher. In 1939, Hutchinson commissioned the Jewish emigré Ralph Mannheim to produce a translation – a choice that was not well received in Munich – and the first full British edition appeared in March of 1939, receiving scathing reviews. Prior to the outbreak of war, royalties were paid to Curtis Brown. Since the copyright had been sold outright, there was no question of royalties being seized by the Custodian of Enemy Property, though whether Curtis Brown held royalties in trust, forwarded them to a third party, or kept them as part of their legitimate income, the company refuses to say.

Shortly after the outbreak of war in 1939, rumours began to circulate in British publishing circles that Hurst and Blackett, a subsidiary or affiliate of Hutchinson, was to publish a cheap copy of the 'unexpurgated' English translation of *Mein Kampf*. In January of 1940, publication began and ran to eighteen weekly instalments at a price of sixpence each. Each copy (except the final instalment) bore the note: "Royalties on all sales will go to the British Red Cross Society"; on the final volume, this was amended to: "Royalties will go to the Red Cross & St John Fund".[23] According to the official British Red Cross Society (B.R.C.S.) history, there seems to have been some confusion between themselves, Hurst and Blackett, Hutchinson, and the Secretary of the Lord Mayor's Fund. Eventually, everything was sorted out and, after some hesitation on the part of the B.R.C.S. "as to the propriety of accepting the royalties, which might be regarded as 'tainted money'" the official history records:

> . . . Mr. Hutchinson explained that he had advertised that royalties on the unexpurgated edition of Hitler's "Mein Kampf" would be devoted to the funds of the B.R.C.S. The edition sold at nine shillings. He hoped that about £750 would accrue to the Fund from this source. Later, "Mein Kampf" had been issued in parts. It was stated on the cover of each part and in the advertisements that the B.R.C.S. would also receive the royalties on this edition.[24]

Just how much the Lord Mayor's Fund (and through it, the combined forces of the British Red Cross Society and the Order of St John of Jerusalem) received is unclear but a statement in *The Times* of 29 November 1940, claims that Mr. Hutchinson had donated £500 from the royalties by that date.[25] It is reasonable to assume that further royalties were paid for 1941-45.

After the war, *Mein Kampf* went on to the Hutchinson backlist, but was reprinted in 1969, reportedly selling about 3,000 copies a year. One article recounts some of the problems faced by the publisher:

> Richard Cohen, now managing director of Richard Cohen Books, was Hutchinson's trade publishing director in 1985, and he recalls the tricky issue of how to deal with the book. "The questions we faced at Hutchinson were: what were a publisher's responsibilities when confronted with such a book, and should we do anything to increase sales?"
>
> The moral dilemma was solved by describing the book as "vile" on the dust jacket. Today's version, now published by Pimlico, still calls it an "evil" book.[26]

Hutchinson was bought by Random House, which in turn was bought by the German Bertelsmann group, leading to the ironic situation that a book banned in Germany is being published in Britain by a German company.

Hutchinson offered the profits from these sales to the Bavarian Government, but the offer was refused.[27] Profits from British sales were then offered to various Jewish groups and again to the Red Cross, which offers were also refused. Finally, from 1976 a British charity agreed to accept the money through Curtis Brown on condition that it remained anonymous. Then, in 2001, a story slowly emerged. An article in the *Daily Telegraph* revealed that the mysterious charity was the London-based German Welfare Council.[28]

The German Welfare Council, a charity set up to help Jewish victims of the Holocaust, received more than £500,000 in royalties from the sales of *Mein Kampf*, but in June 2001 it decided to block any further payments because it regards the money as 'tainted'. The decision came with a rise in the book's sales: in the three years 1998-2001, *Mein Kampf* sold more than 11,000 copies in Britain. According to the chairman of the German Welfare Council:

> When we agreed to the arrangement [i.e. in 1976], *the generally accepted view was that there was a moral obligation to pass the money to Holocaust victims, but no Jewish charity would take it. The current board of trustees, however, has decided the funding is no longer appropriate — not least because we no longer deal exclusively with Holocaust victims.*
>
> *This charity was chosen because of its work with Jewish refugees from Germany, but their number has diminished greatly over the years; most have died of old age. The problem now is that no one wants anything to do with the money.*[29]

In 2001, the Council still had £250,000 of the money and its trustees were trying to decide what to do with it. The publisher, which plans a new edition in 2002 in response to increased demand, earlier justified continued publication on the grounds that the royalties went to charity; now a new reason will have to be found. According to Lord Janner, who chairs the British Holocaust Education Trust:

> *I don't think this charity should have taken the money. But giving it back is a step in the right direction. No one should profit from this book. If it must be published then it should be on a limited print run for academic purposes.*[30]

Just where Curtis Brown stands remains a mystery, as they refuse to discuss the matter, saying that they are prevented from doing so by a confidentiality agreement.[31]

USA & Canada

The first full US edition was published by Houghton Mifflin, Boston, 1943, though there was an earlier abridged edition. During the Second World War, the US Government seized the copyright of *Mein Kampf* under the Trading with the Enemy Act and made more than $20,000 from royalties. Since the seizure apparently took place in 1942, production of the full edition must have taken place with the approval of the US Government.[32] By 1979, the Justice Department had collected more than $139,000 in royalties. Eventually, the money was paid on a pro rata basis to claimants, many of them American former prisoners of war. In 1979, Houghton Mifflin, the US publisher of the book, paid the government more than $35,000 to re-secure its rights. With *Mein Kampf* selling more than 15,000 copies a year in the USA, Houghton Mifflin has made substantial profits. When questioned about the ethics of this, the publisher reassigned the profits to charity.

1. Hitler, in 1932, is in tears because 'no one will let me be dictator'.

(*Hanfstaengl's book* 'Tat gegen Tinte'; *originally from the left-wing journal* 'De Wahre Jacob', *December 31, 1932. Artist unknown.*)

2. Max Amann, 'Hitler's business dwarf'.

(*Author's collection.*)

3. Martin Bormann *(left)* with Hess *(centre)* and Ley. Although Hess was responsible for Hitler's financial affairs from the twenties onward, it was Bormann, the petty bureaucrat, who took over Hitler's financial affairs.

(Original NSDAP photograph)

4. Otto Wagener, the successful businessman who tried to get Hitler to adopt his cranky economic theories and was one of the few to question the sources of Hitler's income.

(NSDAP photograph)

? **Hanfstaengl** **Göring** **Hitler** **Röhm** **?**

5. Ernst 'Putzi' Hanfstaengl second from the left, (circa 1933).
(A cutting from an unidentified Polish newspaper.)

6. Julius Schaub *(right)*, Hitler's bag man. Bormann, as always, is hovering in the background.

7. Fritz Thyssen, heir to a steel fortune, but who never gave Hitler as much money as he pretended or as others imagined.

8. Dietrich Eckart, Hitler's early mentor who helped finance the purchase of the *Eher Verlag*.

9. Heinrich Hoffmann, Hitler's photographer (date unknown).
(US Army files.

10. Heinrich Hoffmann giving evidence at Nuremberg (circa 1946). *(US Army files.)*

11. Walter Funk, who may have channelled money from industrialists to Hitler.
(Reichsbank photograph

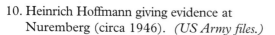

12. Kurt Lüdecke, the Golden Goose (circa 1946).
    (From his FBI file.)

13. A 1920 Selve, similar to that owned by Hitler, but in better condition. *(Author's collection.)*

14. Hitler's birthplace in Braunau-am-Inn, Austria. *(From a 1930's postcard.)*

15. Hitler's family home in Leonding, Austria, as it is today. *(Picture courtesy of Steven Lehrer.)*

16. Hitler's Munich apartment building (circa 1945). *(US Army photograph.)*

17. Eva Braun's Munich villa (circa 1945).

(US Army photograph.)

18. *Haus Wachenfeld* in its original state (circa 1928).

(Hoffmann archive.)

19. *Haus Wachenfeld*
after Hitler's
first expansion
(circa 1934).

*(From an NSDAP
postcard.)*

20. *Haus Wachenfeld*
after Hitler's
first expansion
(circa 1934).
Hitler, the self-
styled architect,
seems to have
done no more
than hang boxes
on the side.

*(From an NSDAP
postcard.)*

21. The *Berghof* in 1937.   *(From an NSDAP postcard.)*

22. The dining room at the *Berghof* (circa 1937).

(From an NSDAP postcard.)

23. The bombing of the *Berghof*, 25 April, 1945.

(RAF photograph, PRO, UK.)

24. The *Berghof* in 1945. (*US 101*[st] *Airborne archive.*)

25. The *Berghof* in 1945.   (Yank *magazine.*)

26. The *Berghof* in the winter of 1945-46. (Yank *magazine.*)

27. Soldiers of the US 3rd Inf. Div. on the terrace of the *Berghof*, 1945. The ski sticks are unlikely to have been Hitler's.
(Yank *magazine.*)

28. The *Berghof* in the 1950s. (*Contemporary postcard.*)

29. Caricature of Franz von Stuck (1863-1928) by Adolf Hengler.

(Private collection.)

30. von Stuck, *Sensuality.*

Franz von Stuck was one of Hitler's favourite painters. Although much of his work can be characterised as 'variations on a theme of a big-busted woman and a fat snake', he could occasionally produce work of charming whimsicality.

31. von Stuck, *Salome.*

32. von Stuck, *Music.*

33. *Alter Freunden*, by Eduard Grützner (1846-1925).

34. *Nepal*, by Carl Spitzweg (1808-85).

Grützner, of whose works Hitler claimed to have the largest collection, specialised in depictions of 'tipsy monks and inebriated butlers'. Hitler frequently paid inflated prices for his work,; today his paintings sell for little. Spitzweg, had a touch of pre-Surrealism and it is rather surprising that his work appealed to Hitler, the arch-traditionalist.

35. *The Poet*, by Carl Spitzweg (1808-85).

36. Caricature of Ca Spitzweg (1808-8 by J.B. Kirchner. *(Private collection.)*

37. *Die ver Elemente (The Four Elements)*, by Adolf Ziegler (1892-1959). The French Ambassador, François Poncet, dubbed painting The Four Senses 'since taste is missing'. *(Bayerischen Staatsgemäldesammlungen, Munich.)*

38. The bank account which Hitler 'did not have', Postcheckkonto Munchen 11253, clearly appears on his 1929 letterhead. It is interesting that Hitler, who was bitterly opposed to the Bauhaus and all that it stood for, should have chosen what appears to be one their type styles for his letterhead.

ADOLF HITLER
KANZLEI:
MÜNCHEN 13, SCHELLINGSTR. 50
FERNSPR. 29031 UND 297217 (NSAT)
POSTSCHECKKONTO MÜNCHEN11253

39. Hitler, the self-styled 'art expert', at an exhibition of 'degenerate art'.

40. A stamp issued for Hitler's 52nd birthday. This is a 12-pfennig stamp, with a 38-pfennig surcharge for the Cultural Fund.

41. Wilhelm Ohnesorge (date unknown, but probably after 1933), the Reich Postmaster General who created the Adolf Hitler Cultural Fund.

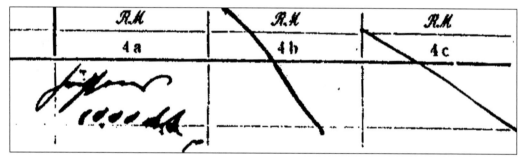

R.M.	R.M.	R.M.
4 a	4 b	4 c

42. Hitler changes his mind on his 1925 tax return. Note that '10.000,0' (ten thousand) has been reduced to '10.00' (one thousand).

43. The bill of lading for Hitler's coffee beans (1939).

```
                    C O P Y   O F   M A N I F E S T .


MPAGNI
ny Limited)


d per DANISH Motor Ship    "DANMARK"    Captain E. H. CHRISTENSEN from ADEN to HAMBURG.


        Consignees        Marks & Numbers      No of Pcs      Description      Weight


:d   H/O B/L OF HALAL         S. E.             20          Bags of Coffee   Kos. 2080
     SHIPPING Co LTD.      HERR HITLER
        Hodeidah       PRESIDENT REPUBLIQUE
                        GRAND ALLEMAGNE
                            HAMBURG
```

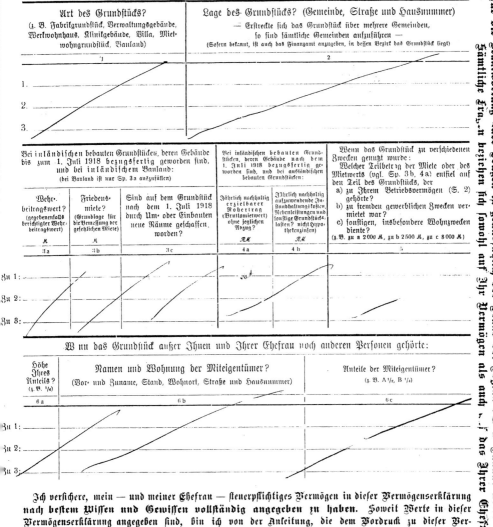

4. A page from Hitler's 1925 tax return – blank, as usual.

GLADBACHER
FEUERVERSICHERUNGS-AKTIEN-GESELLSCHAFT

Agentur: München XV, Günther

Versicherungsschein Nr. ▓▓▓

für

verbundene Feuer- und Einbruchdiebstahl-Versicherung des häuslichen Mobiliars.

Die Gladbacher Feuerversicherungs-Aktien-Gesellschaft in M. Gladbach

versichert nach Maßgabe ihrer Allgemeinen Feuerversicherungs-Bedingungen und der Allgemeinen Versicherungs-Bedingungen für Einbruchdiebstahl- und Beraubungs-Versicherung, sowie der umstehenden besonderen Bedingungen

dem Herrn Reichskanzler Adolf H i t l e r ,

in München, Obb., Prinzregentenplatz 16/II   auf Grund des gestellten

Antrags vom 8. Oktober 1934   die sämtlichen Gegenstände seines Hausrats (siehe Seite) 2
                                   einschliesslich Bücher

in der obigen Wohnung

RM ▓▓▓.▓▓▓ (in Worten) ▓▓▓▓▓▓▓▓▓▓▓▓▓▓▓

Davon entfallen auf: Sammlungen und zwar Bilder, Gemälde   RM 150.000.

Die Versicherung gilt für die Zeit vom   8 Oktober 1934   mittags 12 Uhr bis

zum   8. Oktober 1939   mittags 12 Uhr und verlängert sich bei Ablauf um ein Jahr

und weiter von Jahr zu Jahr stillschweigend, wenn sie nicht drei Monate vor jedesmaligem Ablauf von

einem der beiden Vertragsteile schriftlich gekündigt worden ist

München   den   9. Oktober   1934.

In Vollmacht der
Gladbacher Feuerversicherungs-A.-G.

45. Insurance certificate for the contents of Hitler's Munich apartment.

In October 1997, the publication of a new edition of *Mein Kampf* in Sweden by the publishing house of Hägglunds was prevented after the intervention of the Bavarian government – an act which sparked off this whole six-year investigation when a Swedish-Finnish friend asked the author if he knew who received the royalties from such publications. The first volume of *Mein Kampf* came out in Finnish in 1941, under the Finnish title *Taisteluni* (a direct translation of the original) and published by the well-known company WSOY. A 1941 advertisement promises that the second volume will be available 'soon'. Readers were offered three versions: paperback, for 60 *markka*; hardback, for 75 *markka*; and leather-bound, for 120 *markka*. In France, apparently *Mein Kampf* can legally be sold, and is; it is also freely available in Romania and Russia. In 1967, a Spanish publisher proposed to publish a new Spanish edition of *Mein Kampf*. The Bonn government apparently bought the Spanish rights to prevent publication. An Arabic translation is said to be on sale in the Palestinian territories of Israel where, in 1999, it was number six on a bestseller list.[33] *Mein Kampf* cannot legally be sold in Israel.

The last years of the twentieth century saw a sudden spate of new publications of *Mein Kampf*, notably in Bulgaria, Croatia, the Czech Republic, and Slovakia. In each case, the publisher was issuing a new translation of a work which – from their point of view at least – is out of copyright. The Bavarian State Government disagreed. A Bulgarian edition of *Mein Kampf* went on sale in December 2000. Advertised as 'the first unabridged Bulgarian version', the 584-page volume specified neither the publisher nor the number of copies printed. In mid-June of 1999, a Croatian edition of *Mein Kampf* was edited and published, with about 2,000 copies being printed. Croatia's state attorney said that there was no mechanism for banning publication and stressed that under Croatian criminal law it would only be possible to press charges against the editor of a book like *Mein Kampf* if it could be proved that the editor supported its contents.

In December of 2000, a new version of *Mein Kampf* was released in Slovakia. Unlike the Czech version, the Slovak version included a thirty-page preface condemning Nazism. According to the publisher:

> *We are bringing out this book so that people know the potential effects of dictatorship, populism, and racism* [which are] *quite widespread in Slovakia.*[34]

Five thousand copies were printed, but at least two major book stores refused to carry the work.

Mein Kampf was first sold in Czechoslovakia in 1936, in an abridged, annotated version. In March 2000, Michal Zitko, of the publishing house Otkar II, issued an unabridged Czech translation, saying he wanted to expose Hitler's 'monstrous ideology', and claiming that Nazi ideas were no worse than those of communism.[35] Zitko said Hitler was one of the best-known people of the twentieth century and everybody should have the right to read his political manifesto. The edition of 10,000 copies sold out almost immediately and announcements were made for a second printing, despite objections from human rights groups, the Czech Freedom Fighters (SBS), the Czech Federation of Jewish Communities and representatives of the Roma community. As usual, the Finance Ministry of the Bavarian government said it would use its powers to prevent publication and its statements and actions in this case throw a little light onto this controversial subject.

According to Berndt Schreiber from the press department of the Finance Ministry of Bavaria, Bavaria's goal is to prevent the distribution and publication of the book. Schreiber added that there had already been attempts to publish the book – for example, in Croatia and in Turkey at the beginning of the 1990s, in Sweden in 1993, and even in Germany in 1999, where one company had planned to release it on CD-ROM. Bavaria, however, intervened in each case to block the distribution of the book. Schreiber said that Bavarian authorities had learnt about the publication of the book in Czech and immediately demanded that the German Foreign Ministry take steps to stop the distribution of the book. Bavaria seeks to have already published copies of the book destroyed and to prevent further publication of it. Germany does not perceive the book as a literary work, but rather as much a symbol of Nazism as the swastika. According to Zitko, commenting on Schreiber's reported statements:

> Understandably, I don't have the rights to it, because in the Czech Republic these rights have already expired. In the Czech Republic, the work is freely allowed by law.

A Prague lawyer acting for Zitko added:

> Author's rights cease to exist after fifty years, and the publisher, to my knowledge, has no descendants.

Czech-language editions of the book have twice appeared, but always with commentaries and disclaimers included. The first was published in 1936, but its publication in Czech was banned by Hitler himself during the Nazi occupation. Another appeared in 1993 with remarks by former Czechoslovak foreign minister Jiri Hajek. On 11 April 2000, two Czech senators personally filed criminal charges against Zitko. At the request of the State Attorney for Prague First District, police began an investigation into whether or not the publication of the book violated Czech law. On 1 June 2000, Zitko was charged with promotion of Nazism, a crime which carries up to eight years' imprisonment. On 2 June, Czech Prime Minister Milos Zeman rejected Zitko's allegation that the government ordered the investigation to be launched, adding that the police are obliged to act if people file complaints and that as far as he was aware, that had been the case in this instance.

On 5 June, police seized 300 copies of the Czech translation in a raid on the offices of the book's distributor, Pavel Dvorak, who had been summoned by Zitko to testify as a witness in his defence. By 10 June it was being reported that Czech police had seized 12,500 copies out of a total print run of 15,000. The affair dragged on. In September 2000, Josef Stuchlik, the police investigator in charge of the affair, announced that Vit Varak, the owner of a website selling the Czech version of *Mein Kampf* on the internet, was to be charged with the 'support and dissemination of a movement advocating the suppression of human rights and freedoms'. Varak faced a sentence of between three and eight years in prison if convicted. In October, the Czech state attorney, announced that Zitko would be tried for 'support and promotion of movements suppressing peoples' rights'. Zitko was undeterred, claiming, in an interview, that a similar case had already been dismissed by the International Court in Strasbourg.

In December of 2000, Zitko was found guilty, given a three-year suspended sentence, and fined about $51,000.[36] However, on February 20, 2001, the Prague City Court overturned the sentence imposed by the Prague District Court. The City Court ruled that several 'serious judicial mistakes' were made at the earlier trial. Zitko's retrial began as this manuscript was being completed.

Where banned

Apart from Germany, *Mein Kampf* is apparently banned in Denmark, Hungary, Latvia, The Netherlands, Norway, Portugal and Switzerland. In Spain, Sweden (1993) and Turkey, publication has been banned following the intervention of the Bavarian Government.

The Internet

No discussion of *Mein Kampf* would be complete without reference to its availability on the Internet. A search made on the Internet in the course of writing this chapter brought 1,613 'hits' for the phrase '*Mein Kampf*'. The first sixty of these (which was all that this author read before making the search more specific) contained five different web sites where the text could be read: three in English, one in German, and one in what might have been Dutch or Afrikaans. In addition, copies are regularly sold at auction, through the various electronic auction services. Clearly the efforts of the Finance Ministry of the State of Bavaria are not being very successful. Nor are they being as successful as they would like in preventing an on-line bookseller in a country – such as the USA or Britain – where uncommented editions of *Mein Kampf* can be legally published – from accepting orders from a different country – such as Germany – where it cannot. Indeed, the sales lists of on-line booksellers provide an interesting insight into sales of *Mein Kampf*. According to one report, in 1999 it was the second most common title requested from a US-based company by Germans.[37] However, that same company, in response to German government pressure, did not – and does not – allow its work to be sold on the German website.

Notes

1   So too, according to Thyssen (THYS41, p. 113) did Ludendorff, but with less success.
2   Schirach, Baldur. *Ich glaubte an Hitler*. Hamburg, 1967, p. 112.
3   HEID44, p. 224.
4   For the outline notes of a typical speech, see Maser (MASE73, Appendix B).
5   Herring, Phillip F. *Djuna: The life and work of Djuna Barnes*. New York 1995, Viking Penguin. ISBN 0-670-84969-3. pp. 71 and 177. Incredibly, the bisexual Barnes had been Hanfstaengl's lover in New York during the First World War. Friendship with Hanfstaengl did not reduce the fee.
6   HEID44, pp. 116-117.
7   TREV54. Although Trevor-Roper edited Bormann's letters, copyright belonged to Genoud, who had legally acquired title from the Bormann family. Interestingly, the letters were translated by Lt. Col. R.H. Stevens, one of the MI6 officers abducted in the November 1939 'Venlo Incident'. Stevens also translated Hoffmann's memoirs (HOFF55).
8   HANF57, p. 219.
9   Strasser, Otto. *Hitler und Ich*, Buenos Aires, 1941 (?)
10 KERS98, p. 241, quoting *Monologe*.
11 HEID36, p. 340.
12 According to Waite (WAIT73, p. 72) it contains over 164,000 errors of German grammar and syntax; one wonders who took the trouble to count them, and why. At 768 pages, assuming 1,000 words per page, this comes to one error about every 5 words – probably a record. Maser (MASE73, p. 190) says that about 2,500 corrections were made between the first edition and that of 1939.
13 KERS98, p. 242, citing Strasser's *Hitler und Ich*.
14 Hoffmann (HOFF55, p. 52) describes Stempfle as "Professor". I can find no evidence of Stempfle ever having held an academic chair and the title is probably no more than an honorific bestowed by Hoffmann and his friends.
15 HANF57, p. 128.
16 HEID44, p. 227.
17 LÜDE38, p. 424.
18 MASE73, pp. 249-50. According to Maser, the quotation is taken from an interview published in the *Völkischer Beobachter* on 29 February 1936.
19 WAIT73, p. 72.
20 WAIT73, quoting *Der Zeit*, No. 26, 25 June, 1976. It is not clear whether this is German language copies or world-wide.
21 STMF03. Just when the Finance Ministry received the copyright is not clear.
22 The date is uncertain. Lüdecke implies that it was 1932/3 and this would certainly tally with Hitler's need for cash to finance the election campaigns – or to expand the Berghof. Others, including Hanfstaengl, imply that the sale was in 1938 or 39.

23 This, and the following comes from Cambray, P.G. and G.G.B. Briggs. *Red Cross &* *St John: The official record of the humanitarian services of the War Organisation of the British Red Cross Society and Order of St John of Jerusalem 1939-47.* London, 1948. pp. 785-787 of the two-volume Confidential Supplement. Additional information was kindly supplied to the author by Mr. Michael A. Meyer, Head of International Law at the British Red Cross.

24 Ibid., pp. 786-7.

25 Ibid., p. 787.

26 Pascal, Julia. *Unbanning Hitler.* New Statesman; 25 June 2001; Vol. 14, Issue 662; p. 38, 4 pp.

27 *"Mein Kampf": Germany's Modern Best Seller.* The *Salt Lake Tribune,* 21 November 1999. Story credited to the Scripps Howard News Service. STMF03, though the publisher is not mentioned by name.

28 Edwardes, Charlotte and Chris Hastings. *Jewish charity's £500,000 from Mein Kampf.* The Daily Telegraph, UK News, 17 June 2001.

29 Ibid.

30 Ibid.

31 Letter to the author from Mr. Jonathan Lloyd, Group Managing Director, Curtis Brown.

32 The Bavarian Ministry of Finance states [STMF03] that the seizure occurred in 1942, which is consistent with US entry into the Second World War. Enquiries to the US Department of Justice have not been answered.

33 *"Mein Kampf": Germany's Modern Best Seller.* The *Salt Lake Tribune,* 99.11.21 Story credited to the Scripps Howard News Service.

34 *Bookshops Snub "Mein Kampf" in Slovakia.* AFP, 14 December 2000.

35 This narrative has been constructed from about 20 news agency reports; space does not permit recording all of them.

36 Some reports have a five year sentence and $57,000 fine.

37 *"Mein Kampf": Germany's Modern Best Seller.* The *Salt Lake Tribune,* 99.11.21 Story credited to the Scripps Howard News Service.

Chapter Eight

THE GOLDEN GOOSE

goose . . . *a stupid, silly person* . . .
golden goose *the fabled layer of golden eggs, killed by its over-greedy owner.*
The Chambers Dictionary, 1998.

Kurt Lüdecke was a playboy-gambler-businessman with wide social connections and a sizeable fortune, well-travelled, and possessing foreign bank accounts through his business interests. Like Hanfstaengl, Lüdecke was close to Hitler during the nineteen-twenties and early thirties. Like Hanfstaengl, Lüdecke eventually fell out of favour and only just escaped with his life. Like Hanfstaengl, he wrote a memoir, saying in the preface:

> *Having nothing to lose, I can afford to tell the unadorned truth as I see it, limited only by my conscience and considerations of good taste, . . .*[1]

The truth, as revealed in his memoirs, is somewhat different. Lüdecke was a vicious, intellectual anti-Semite, a quasi-professional gambler, far from scrupulous in his business dealings, and, by his own admission, a convinced Nazi when he wrote his memoirs. However, in fairness, one should at least record the words with which he ends the preface:

> *I have sinned, strived, suffered, and survived. I am a free man at last. The end of this book is the beginning of a new life, which is less a process of reformation and regeneration than it is the natural realization of a new self, which I hope will be better than my former self.*[2]

Because Lüdecke was Hitler's agent for soliciting funds outside Germany, many historians have drawn extensively on his book, but, as with all such memoirs, the question must be asked: Is it accurate? Much of what Lüdecke writes has not been verified or cannot be verified; where other accounts exist, they often differ from that given by Lüdecke. Consequently, his assertions must be treated with great care.

Hitler came to Lüdecke's attention on 11 August 1922. By his own account, someone 'looking for a leader and a cause', Lüdecke was an immediate convert to Nazism and quickly became Hitler's principal, though not very successful, fundraiser outside Germany. He also seems to have become rapidly involved in NSDAP finances:

> *The Nazi organisation itself lived from day to day financially, with no treasury to draw on for lecture-hall rentals, printing costs, or the other thousand-and-one expenses which threatened to swamp us. The only funds we could count on were membership dues, which were small, merely a drop in the bucket. Collections at mass meetings were sometimes large, but not to be relied on. Once in a while a Nazi sympathizer would make a special contribution, and in a few cases these gifts were substantial. But we never had money enough.*[3]

Lüdecke made the first contacts with Mussolini, who had never heard of Hitler, about a month before the 'March on Rome' of 28 October 1922. The meeting was apparently cordial and the two men established some sort of friendship.[4] By 1923, Lüdecke claims he was supporting Hitler and others:

> *Were not my time, my energy, my heart, all dedicated to Party work without any reservation? And my bank account as well? In a quiet way I was giving money to Hitler and others, in addition to the large sums the troop was costing.*[5]

Lüdecke also took over the support, finance and training of the SA from the twenty-five year old Klintzsch who was not considered sufficiently experienced, though Lüdecke's military experience was negligible, having spent most of 1914-18 in military prisons or psychiatric hospitals as a result of 'insubordination'. Continuing the theme of the previous quotation:

> *Several times I gave them foreign notes, including some of the French money left over from the Paris trip.*
>
> *I still remember how the last of those French notes went. One afternoon I was in the Nazi office with Max Amann, Dietrich Eckart, and Adolf Müller, the printer, when in stormed Hitler aflame with an idea. . . . But Amann, shrugging his shoulders, said there was no money. . . . Acting on impulse I took out of my pocket three hundred-franc notes and tossed them to Amann, who counted them, his eyes gleaming. Then the four of us tried our higher mathematics, and found that the French money, figured in German marks, would be ample to pay the printer.*[6]

During this period of rampant inflation, Lüdecke's financial contributions in 'hard' currency were invaluable. However, such ready generosity with French currency eventually led to accusations that Lüdecke was a French spy, accusations that would eventually lead to the ruin of this anti-Semitic playboy.[7] Lüdecke was arrested on 27 January 1923, on the eve of the Nazis' *Parteitag*, which was to be held in Munich's *Löwenbraukeller*. His apartment, which contained weapons belonging to his SA troop, was searched, though not very thoroughly, if his own account is to be believed. The arrest caused a sensation in the anti-Hitler press and attempts were made to link him to various rumours of French espionage which were rife at that time. Not surprisingly, Lüdecke was questioned about his sources of money, his foreign bank accounts, and the fact that he possessed a Mexican passport – legacy of a 1920 visit – in addition to his German one.

According to Lüdecke, no charges were ever brought against him and he was released at the end of March. Why he – and no other prominent member of the NSDAP – was arrested remains a mystery. Lüdecke hints, though never actually says, that it was all a cunning plot by Göring and Amann, though what the plot was supposed to achieve is unclear.

In the early summer of 1923, Lüdecke spent several weeks in Spain recovering from his prison experiences, and returned to Germany via Italy and Austria, where he met with Dr. Walter Riehl, leader of various Pan-German groups, though he makes no mention of soliciting any funds.[8] Later that summer, he established connections with Gyula Gömbös, a member of the Hungarian parliament and leader of *Magyar Országos Véderö Egyesület* (MOVE – Association for Hungarian National Defence). At the end of August, following his trip to Hungary, Lüdecke went on to visit Mussolini again, charged by Hitler with a five-point mission:[9]

1 To encourage Mussolini to either remain neutral or ally with France in the event that Bavaria declared independence from the rest of Germany.

2 To reassure Mussolini that a Nazi government would not make any territorial claims on the South Tyrol, that part of Italy bordering on Austria and known by the Italians as Alto Adige.

3 To obtain the support of the Italian press and their agreement to use the Nazis as their source of German news, rather than the Berlin news agencies.

4 To promote the Nazi party to Mussolini and denigrate the existing German government.

5 To procure money.

Prior to the trip, Hitler and Lüdecke discussed Italian questions at a two-day meeting in Linz. According to Lüdecke, Hitler's parting words were:

Fetzen Sie aus Mussolini heraus, was Sie können! [10]

. . . which he renders as 'Rip out of Mussolini whatever you can!' On the third item on his agenda, relations with the Italian press, Lüdecke was successful, especially with those papers supporting Mussolini. On points one, two and four, he had a measure of success, but on point five, getting funding, he apparently failed. That he should fail to attract overt financial support from Mussolini is hardly surprising; Mussolini was Prime Minister of Italy and for him to be seen supporting a party that was in violent opposition to the German government would have provoked a major diplomatic row, if not a war. There is, however, anecdotal evidence that Mussolini did provide covert support to Hitler and the NSDAP during the early nineteen-twenties. This is discussed in Chapter 10.

Following his trip to Italy, after a brief stopover in Munich, Lüdecke set off once more to try his luck in Hungary, possibly at the invitation of András Mecsér, an anti-Semite and anti-Communist who is said (though not by Lüdecke) to have given a substantial donation to Hitler after hearing him speak in Germany in 1921 or 1922.[11] Lüdecke makes no mention of soliciting funds during this Hungarian interlude. Towards the end of September 1923, Lüdecke returned to Budapest, partly to warn his Hungarian contacts to be prepared for major events in Germany in the coming months. Lüdecke makes no mention of any fundraising on this trip, but it is said (again, not by Lüdecke) that Gömbös sent gifts of horses and cattle to Hitler during the few months between Lüdecke's visit and the *Putsch*.[12] Such gifts would not have been quite as silly as they sound since beasts could be readily sold and Hitler had a suitable salesman in Christian Weber, a horse dealer and one of Hitler's inner circle at that time.

After the failure of the *Putsch*, Lüdecke went again to Hungary, this time with the intention of getting some much-needed money. Although he was well received, spending Christmas with Gömbös on his country estate, Gömbös regarded Hitler as a spent force and no money seems to have been forthcoming. Unnamed Hungarians are said to have tried to interest Lüdecke in a rather wild scheme: the wholesale counterfeiting of French francs with the assistance of the Hungarian government.[13] If the scheme ever existed, it came to nothing.

In the middle of December, following the failed *Putsch*, the surviving leadership – Lüdecke, Hanfstaengl, Esser, and others – met in Vienna to try to plan some sort of recovery. Two NSDAP members from Prague also attended:

> Jung and Knirsch, Nazi deputies from Prague, were splendid, contributing all their party could spare. But they had problems of their own, and though their generosity warmed our hearts and lifted our spirits, it scarcely altered our financial status.[14]

Such money as there was went into the party coffers; Hitler did not need it – he was in prison. Various proposals were made, including counterfeiting (an idea abandoned because they lacked the funds to do it) and armed robbery, but, as Lüdecke puts it:

> Finally some one hit on an idea which the others enthusiastically seconded. I was asked to use my connections and persuasive power to raise money in the United States, that Eldorado where every citizen owned a roc which laid mountainous golden eggs.[15]

Of all those who were close to Hitler in the mid nineteen-twenties, only Hanfstaengl and Lüdecke had any first-hand knowledge of the USA. Lüdecke, however, had only visited the USA as a tourist and wheeler-dealer and scarcely had the business connections of Hanfstaengl. Hanfstaengl would have been the logical choice – he was personally acquainted with such figures as Pierpont Morgan, Ford and Roosevelt – but it was Lüdecke who went, instructed by Hitler in a letter sent from prison on the notepaper of his lawyer, Lorenz Roder:

4 January 1924

Much Esteemed Herr Lüdecke:

First expressing my heartiest thanks for your representation of the movement in Italy. I ask you to solicit in the interests of the German Liberty movement in North America and especially to assemble financial means for it. I ask you to receive these means personally and, if possible, to bring them over in person. Thanking you in advance for your efforts, I greet you most heartily.

(Signed) Adolf Hitler[16]

This letter is ambiguous, even in the German (see endnote) and, after exhaustive linguistic analysis, the author is unable to offer a better translation. The second sentence reads as if Hitler is asking Lüdecke to arrange financing <u>for</u> the Nazi movement in America, rather than <u>from</u> it. The third sentence could either mean that Lüdecke was to collect funds in Germany and carry them to the USA, or from the USA and bring them home to Germany; the latter seems more probable. In addition, Lüdecke was provided with credentials for his visit to the USA, an imposing document, the German text of which reads (with illegible characters replaced by '*'):

Nationalsozialistische Partei Grossdeutschlands

Zwischenstaatliche Kanzlei

Wien, 6. Bezirk, Matrosengasse 9

Fernsprecher Nr. 75.81   *Postsparkassenkonto 147.7**

VOLLMACHT und LEGITIMATION

Herr Kurt Georg Luedecke [sic, no umlaut], *geboren am 5. Februar 1890 zu Berlin, wird hiedurch mit d*r Vertretung der National-Sozialistischen Partei Gross Deutschlands in den Vereinigten Staaten von Nord-Amerika betr**t.*

Herr Luedecke ist ermächtigt, für die Nation-Sozialistischen Partei Gross Deutschlands Geldsammlungen einzuleiten und Spenden in jeder Höhe entgegenzunehmen. Ebenab Geldb*tr*ge an das ***k*nto "Germaniaspende" Wiener Bankverein Zweige*ll* [illegible word] *überwie*en werden.*

Wir bitten, Herrn Luedecke in diesen Eigenschaft anzuerk**nen und ihm auf seiner Propagandareise jederzeit Unterstützung mit Rat und Tat zu gewähren.[17]

A translation of which gives:

Herr Kurt George Luedecke, born February 5th, 1890, in Berlin, is hereby entrusted with the representation of the National Socialist Party of Greater Germany in the United States of North America.

Herr Luedecke is authorised to initiate money collections and to receive donations of any amount. Also sums of money [can?] *be transferred to the cash account "Germaniaspende" Wiener Bankverein,* [?] *branch.*

We ask to recognise Herrn Luedecke in this capacity and to aid him on his propaganda tour at any time with advice and support.

Thus armed, Lüdecke set sail for New York, where he hoped to harvest the Roc's giant golden eggs. Unfortunately, Lüdecke seems not to have been well versed in mythology: the Roc's eggs, while gigantic, were not golden; it was the goose that laid the golden eggs and it was Lüdecke who was about to become a goose.

With the help of Siegfried and Winifred Wagner, son and daughter-in-law of the composer, Lüdecke hoped to get funding from Henry Ford, the automobile manufacturer and anti-Semite, but his attempts, described in Chapter 10, came to nothing.

Lüdecke gave up and reset his sights on his second target, the German-American immigrant community. Shortly after his meeting with Ford in Detroit, Lüdecke was invited to address a meeting of a society of German-Americans in Washington on the subject of the allocation of welfare funds in Germany. The distribution of such funds provided by German-American societies had become the province of leftward-leaning organisations in Germany and little of these funds reached those on the right, however pitiful their financial situation. Lüdecke's attempt to play on this fact was a big mistake:

> I tried to give a fair picture of the true situation. These people, who knew nothing about the Nazis, listened with wide eyes when I pleaded the tragedy of Hitler's setback, which temporarily had thrown so many of his followers into distress. At first it seemed as though I had won my case; I began to hope that this prosperous group of German-Americans would divert at least a few hundred dollars to the Nazi poor.[18]

Unfortunately for Lüdecke, a well-informed German-American then attacked him point-by-point and the crowd soon turned hostile; Lüdecke was almost thrown from the room. In his own words:

> Had the Sirens themselves sung my cause, results would have been just as negative. The eloquence I wasted might easily have raised a fund to rescue moths from the sun; but Hitler and the Nazis rated nothing better than a perpetually empty collection plate. I was howled down in derision each time I spoke of him as a coming world power. It is grim satisfaction now to remark that simply as fortune-telling, my talks were worth the money I asked – and didn't get.[19]

Lüdecke toured the US with equally disappointing results:

> In Pittsburgh, Cleveland, Chicago, Milwaukee, St. Louis, and other cities, experiences were just as disheartening. It was a hopeless business to interest people in a movement which had become the butt of the Press. Also, while a considerable minority of my expatriate countrymen shared the Nazi outlook, a majority misunderstood and condemned it. In other words, I discovered that the situation abroad was simply the home situation in little, and no more rewarding from a financial standpoint.[20]

Still not completely discouraged, Lüdecke headed for New York, where he knew of 'a wealthy German-American who showed active sympathy' but who failed to arrange anything of significance. Some German-American organisations were more forthcoming. The first seems to have been the short-lived *Barbarossa Bund*, where Lüdecke was suspected of being a mysterious French spy with the same name. Once the *Barbarossa Bund* had received assurances from a Herr von Kursell, Ludendorff's spokesman, they were more forthcoming and 'sent a few dollars each month to the address in Munich'.[21] Alas, Lüdecke fails to say just what that 'address in Munich' was; possibly it was NSDAP headquarters at the offices of the *Eher Verlag*. There Lüdecke's 1924 fundraising trip to America ended, though he went on to make one further effort at propaganda: he approached the Ku Klux Klan. Here, as elsewhere, he came away sadly disillusioned.[22]

In 1924, Lüdecke returned to Germany via Britain. Here he made a number of contacts among the aristocracy, of which the most potentially influential may have been the Duke of Northumberland, though he clearly had little interest in Lüdecke's presentation:

> Northumberland was a leading shareholder in the Morning Post, *the most important Tory paper, anti-German by tradition. Though he listened courteously to my exposé of the German situation, it was at once apparent that he was too aloof and faraway from the real demands of our time to take a practical interest in the German world struggle.*[23]

What Lüdecke does not seem to have noticed is that while the Duke was everything that an aristocrat should be in manners, he was also intelligent. However, most of those he met seem to have been anti-Semitic cranks such as Lord Sydenham of Combe, author of a scurrilous tract somewhat ambiguously entitled *The Jewish World Problem*, and W.A. Peters, secretary of a tiny anti-Semitic society called *The Britons*, whose imaginative slogan was *Britain for the Britons*. Like Americans, Britons were prepared to listen, but not to act:

> *In London, as in New York and Washington, all my interviews were sterile. The motto of the men who received me was 'My time is your time' — but time wasn't money.*[24]

Continuing on to Germany via France, Lüdecke, who had been given a letter of introduction by Boris Brasol, called on the White Russian community in Paris. He met with no success and hastened south to Nice for a meeting with Grand Duke Kyrill and his wife, Victoria. Sensing that Victoria controlled the purse-strings, Lüdecke directed his efforts towards her, also suggesting that she try to interest her relatives at the Spanish court in supporting Hitler. Their response was typical:

> *. . . their somewhat Imperial Highnesses' reaction to each discreet suggestion was so stiff-necked that I abandoned hope long before they had a chance definitely to refuse, and dropped the matter. . . . Politics had become for these landless lords and ladies merely a pastime, not a matter of life and death.*[25]

Lüdecke's response was also typical: with his last two thousand Francs he went to Monte Carlo to recoup his losses at the gaming tables. He lost the lot, and had to borrow money for the train fare to Munich.

Lüdecke made another trip to France during the summer of 1924, to attend an anti-Semitic conference organised by the Roman Catholic church. The only result was that Lüdecke – the alleged French *espion* – was arrested and interrogated by the Sûreté, the French counter-espionage agency.[26] His unbelievable account of the affair reads like a Feydeau farce. Annoyed, he left for Switzerland.

Over Christmas of 1924, Lüdecke again went to Hungary and had another lengthy meeting with Gömbös, at which he tried to repair the damage caused by the failed *Putsch*. The meeting was stormy, but ended on a friendly note, with Gömbös again inviting Lüdecke to spend Christmas at his country home, where he dined with one of the German murderers of Mathias Erzberger, the minister who had signed the Armistice in 1918. No money was forthcoming and Gömbös pointedly reminded Lüdecke that it was Hungary who was caring for the wanted killer, not Hitler.[27]

On 8 April 1925, Lüdecke agreed to act as Hitler's representative in Berlin and as representative for the *Eher Verlag* in northern Germany. Lüdecke, a Berliner by birth and upbringing, set about re-establishing old contacts and, through Count Ernst zu Reventlow, he was introduced to Dr. Class and Dr. Bang, two close colleagues of President Hindenburg:

> *Dr. Class and Finanzrat* [financial consultant] *Dr. Bang, the financial expert of the Pan-German Association and an important figure as founder and head of a new folkic association of industrialists, listened to me with understanding and declared that they were ready at any time to discuss with Hitler a basis for co-operation if his men would cease their defamations and malicious attacks.*[28]

Unfortunately, Lüdecke does not identify this 'folkic association of industrialists', though it seems likely that they were associated in some way with Hugenberg. The job as representative for the *Eher Verlag* did not last long and Lüdecke took a position as US and Canadian representative of 'a German art-publishing house'.[29] Once more, Lüdecke set off for North America.

In 1925-32, Lüdecke worked in North America, first as the representative of a German art-publishing company, though he seems to have given up that work in April 1926. After many romantic adventures, the 'penniless' Lüdecke – who always seemed to find some way of raising money for himself, if not for Hitler – went off to Detroit in September of 1926 to observe a 'Jewish libel suit against Henry Ford'. The suit was settled out of court, with an apology by Ford and an end to his overt anti-Semitism; it also, presumably, marked the end of any possible support for Hitler.

In the course of 1927, he met with Dr. Günther Quandt, brother of one of his old school-friends, and now a wealthy businessman. As usual, Lüdecke failed to extract any financial commitment but did succeed in converting Quandt's wife to Nazism, to which she responded with such fervour that she eventually left her husband and married Dr. Josef Goebbels. Now married himself, and with some savings from his various business enterprises, which included a pro-Nazi newspaper *The American Guard*, Lüdecke returned to Germany in June of 1932.

The Germany that Lüdecke returned to had changed dramatically; the Nazi flag was on display everywhere, the *Heil Hitler!* greeting, with its characteristic salute, had become common, and neither the NSDAP nor its leader were short of funds, or at least, of credit. With grandiose plans for a Nazi organisation and propaganda machine in America, Lüdecke hastened to party headquarters at Munich's *Braunes Haus*. He was greatly disappointed; at the NSDAP HQ, intrigue had replaced organisation as the primary business. Lüdecke's ideas called for the establishment of both a branch of the NSDAP and a publishing company; consequently, he sought the financial support of Schwarz, the NSDAP treasurer, and Amann, the managing director of the *Eher Verlag*. However, Lüdecke and Amann were on bad terms, partly because of Lüdecke's unfortunate attempts to represent the *Eher Verlag* in Berlin, but also because of his growing suspicion that Amann might have been responsible for his 1923 imprisonment.

A further complication was the perjury trial of Werner Abel in early 1932, which had been badly handled in the *Völkischer Beobachter* by Rosenberg. Apparently referring to Hitler's 1930 lawsuit, Lüdecke reports Rosenberg as saying that Hitler had declared in court that he had never received foreign money from any source and never even asked for it. Lüdecke, of course, was well placed to recognise this for the lie that it was. Rosenberg went on to explain that Christian Weber was called as a witness against Abel and accidentally referred to another witness as 'Kurt Ludecke' when the man was neither 'Kurt' nor was he a 'Lüdecke', but bore a name of similar spelling but having the 'u' without an umlaut. The *Völkischer Beobachter* had perpetuated the mistake. The real Kurt Lüdecke was far from pleased, and was only slightly appeased when Weber agreed to make a public apology. Lüdecke then went to put his American proposals to Amann, and here makes some very definite and revealing statements:

> Max Amann . . . was Hitler's banker and close friend; to my knowledge, he and Roehm were the only Nazis to whom the Fuehrer ever said 'du'. Amann was in on Hitler's personal financial affairs as well as his secrets. . . . During my absence from Germany, the Eher Verlag had mushroomed out to a huge concern, and now was one of the largest publishing houses in the Reich. Amann was its manager, Hitler the principal owner.[30]

Amann's response was encouraging, though hardly generous:

> "I'll use any influence I have to put your idea over with Hitler," he promised. "As for money, you can draw two thousand marks (nearly one hundred pounds) a month from the Verlag treasury. But I'm afraid you'll have trouble getting the rest from Schwarz, even if Hitler asks for it."[31]

Goebbels, too, doubted whether Lüdecke would get funds from Schwarz, noting that the recent series of elections – with more probably to come – had seriously depleted the party's funds. Lüdecke's interviews with Hitler, which generally took place at the *Braunes Haus*, appeared encouraging. The *Braunes Haus* itself, however, gave Lüdecke cause for concern, especially as he began to find that, despite Hitler's support, money was not forthcoming. Yet money was available to equip the building with a meeting room for party leaders, which was never used, and a private lift serving Hitler's own office, another room which was rarely used. Still, Lüdecke persevered in his attempts to create his 'Foreign Bureau' but was forced to place the idea under Rosenberg, who expected to be Foreign Minister when Hitler came to power.

Lüdecke also proposed setting up an office in Washington, to lobby on behalf of NSDAP interests. Hitler liked the idea and Amann agreed to provide $500 a month. Again, Lüdecke was promised a matching sum from the party treasury; again, he was disappointed. He did, however, get funds from Amann, including a three month advance.

In September of 1932, Lüdecke discussed with Amann and Hitler the possibility of selling the copyright of *Mein Kampf* to an American company. Shortly afterwards, he met with Hitler at his Munich apartment, and again raised the question of finance for his proposed Washington office:

> . . . I took the plunge, fortified by the thought that he could not have forgotten the financial sacrifices I had made for the Party or the donations I had given him personally in the lean years. I told Hitler I was in a dilemma: I had been forced to borrow money to make this trip; the advance received from Amann was my allowance for October, November, and December, and did not cover my travelling expenses or my expenses in Germany. . . . Then he took a thousand-mark note from his pocket and handed it to me with a significant look. Mon Dieu, I thought ruefully, scarcely boat fare – what magnificence. But he autographed a copy of Mein Kampf for me, and gave me some photographs of himself.[32]

No doubt Lüdecke could have sold the copy of *Mein Kampf* and the photographs for a modest sum, but the 'significant look' that Hitler 'handed' to him – assuming it was his own – should have commanded a very high price.

In October 1932, Lüdecke returned to America via Canada, then on to New York, where he received an unpleasant surprise. Intent on building a US organisation of his own pattern, he had been told by Strasser that the existing NSDAP affiliate organisations in America would be ordered to disband. In fact, no such order had been given and the main organisations in New York, Detroit, and Chicago had actually united. Annoyed, Lüdecke ordered the leader of the New York branch to cease all further public activities and then headed off to Washington, where he set up an office. Here, with credentials authorising him to represent the foreign political interests of the Nazi party in the USA, Canada, and Mexico, Lüdecke also presented himself as a representative of the National Socialist Press Service and received passes to the Capitol press gallery and to the White House.

However, trouble was looming: Strasser, Lüdecke's political patron within the NSDAP, resigned on 8 December 1932. Lüdecke continued to disseminate NSDAP material to the American press, but he received no directions from Hitler, Rosenberg, or Amann, the latter even forgetting to send his funds for January and February. Finally, on 30 January 1933, Hitler was appointed Chancellor. There was now no need for Lüdecke as a fund-raiser and his propaganda activities could be better undertaken by the embassy. Unsure of his position, and short of money, Lüdecke decided to return to Berlin, booking a passage for I March 1933 on the *Albert Ballin*. Before he sailed, Lüdecke spent a few days in New York, of which he makes an intriguing statement:

In New York I was the guest of a vice-consul at the German consulate-general whom I had known for some time as an able man and a secret member of the Nazi Party. On my way through New York the preceding October I had made an arrangement with him and had found him very useful. From his home, I now gave last instructions to the men I had organized in many places over a long period of time, for example employees of the various steamship lines.[33]

Here, Lüdecke seems to imply that he had been organising an espionage network. His journalistic cover would also have been useful for such activities, though his position as representative of the NSDAP would have made him rather conspicuous. Nevertheless, this and later events strongly suggest that Lüdecke was involved in intelligence gathering. Perhaps he was more successful at that than at fundraising.

Another whom Lüdecke met while in New York was Mrs Henry Loomis – aunt to Secretary of State Stimson and mother of Alfred – to whom he had been introduced earlier by White Russian connections, possibly in 1924. This lady not only provided generous support to the White Russians, but may also have provided funds to Hitler. Lüdecke writes of being entertained at her home in Tuxedo Park, New York – where Alfred would set up a radar research laboratory in 1940 – and receiving her wholehearted co-operation.[34] Whether this was financial is not clear; it seems to have involved setting up a lecture tour for Lüdecke in the USA in April 1933, with a reciprocal arrangement for Mrs Loomis in Germany later that same year. Neither event ever took place.

Arriving back in Germany, Lüdecke went to report to Hitler at the Reich Chancellery. After telling of the situation in America and Canada, and the effect which this might have on British politics, Lüdecke raised the ever troubling question of money:

I touched lightly on having been left in the lurch about money, whereupon he patted my shoulder, saying: "We've had our difficulties, believe me. From now on things will be different".[35]

They were certainly different for Lüdecke; they took a turn for the worse. Allegations about his mysterious career began to circulate:

Brückner [Hitler's adjutant] came running after me.
"Do you know a Dr. Somebody from California?" he asked. "He left just a minute ago. Hanfstaengl urged me to see him. I sent him flying back and told him not to pester me with gossip. The man had a letter from Dr. Nieland and said he was the representative of a certain person."
"Yes," I said, "I expect you mean 'G.'"
"That was it – 'G.' He drivelled about your having been in prison in America; he must warn me against you, and similar rubbish. But you ought to know about it. Chummy with Hess, and now he has an office with Goering in his Palais. So watch your step!"

134

Lüdecke makes no mention in his book of ever having been imprisoned in America, there is no mention of it in his FBI file, and since he was eligible for US citizenship, which he was later granted, it is most unlikely that he was ever convicted of a Federal offence. There is then the question of 'Dr. Somebody' and 'G'. The fact that Lüdecke, who was writing in America, under US law, suppresses the identity of 'G' suggests that 'G' may have been a US citizen whose name he could not reveal for risk of a libel action. There is, of course, no reason to suppose that that person's name even began with 'G'.

Shortly after this encounter, Lüdecke met with Rosenberg to discuss further plans for the development of Nazi interests in America. Among these was a rather fanciful scheme to purchase *The Washington Post*, at that time a rather mediocre journal. The scheme came to nothing and the *Post* was bought at auction on 1 June 1933 by Eugene Meyer, who is generally credited with making that paper the respected journal that it is today. Curiously, the scheme seems to have been supported by Rosenberg and his Foreign Bureau, rather than by Amann and the *Eher Verlag*. Perhaps that is a measure of how seriously Hitler took the idea.

Lüdecke now began to promote the idea of an international Nazi propaganda organisation, separate from both government and party so that its activities could not be in any way attributable. Now, propaganda was the responsibility of Goebbels, but Lüdecke does not seem to have consulted him; instead, Rosenberg, Lüdecke's new patron, took up the scheme and a luncheon for Nazi leaders and wealthy industrialists was called at the *Kaiserhof* to discuss financing. Lüdecke shows a rather low opinion of the people he expected to finance his latest scheme:

> *There they were – the élite of leading Gentiles in industry, commerce, finance, agriculture, shipping, and banking . . . I saw some fine, proud figures among these gold-blooded aristocrats. But for the most part I saw fat-bellied, money-making fatheads, and I saw too the irony of our readiness to mobilize the very forces against which the socialist aims of the Nazi revolution were to have been directed.*[36]

After Rosenberg, Lüdecke addressed the meeting, outlined the likely activities of the proposed organisation, and appealed for funds. A pledge list was circulated and a million marks were promised.

There is a problem with these assertions, which seem to refer to the first week of May 1933 (Lüdecke rarely gives dates in his account); that problem is the *Adolf Hitler Spende*, described in Chapter 13. Briefly, one of the principles of the *AH Spende*, as laid down by Krupp when he took over the fund in April 1933, was that a contribution to the fund would absolve contributors of the need to give to any other NSDAP funds. Most of Lüdecke's audience, who were unlikely to have much interest in propaganda, could easily have refused to contribute. Indeed, contributions to the *AH Spende* were intended to fund the very sorts of activity that Lüdecke was proposing. One must therefore view Lüdecke's claims of funding with some scepticism. Hard-headed businessmen rarely give when they have already 'given at the office'.

Still, according to Ludecke, he and Rosenberg did manage to translate those pledges into half a million marks in cash and proceeded to establish the offices of the *Aussenpolitische Amt* (APA – Foreign Policy Bureau) at Wilhelmstraße 70a, next to the British embassy. Here, Lüdecke was to learn the truth of the expression that there is no such thing as a free lunch, or, more accurately, that large contributions given at fund-raising luncheons often come with obligations. An IG Farben director, who had pledged RM 100,000, promised another RM 100,000 in support of Lüdecke's Washington office in exchange for promoting his company in the USA. That the executive should propose that Lüdecke collaborate with Ivy Lee, who had founded the first public relations company in New York in 1904, only added insult to injury. Somewhat naïvely, Lüdecke wrote:

> But it alarmed me to see our financial sponsors already beginning to spin their webs about us, with only half their subscriptions in our hands.[37]

The next day, Tuesday, 9 May 1933, Lüdecke was briefly arrested by the Gestapo, being released the following day. He then received another shock for which a little thought might have prepared him: Dr. Kurt Schmitt, Director General of Allianz, Germany's largest insurance company, withdrew his promised support for the *Aussenpolitische Amt*, having been told – presumably by Goebbels or one of his staff – that propaganda was the responsibility of the Propaganda Ministry.

Amongst many things which Lüdecke seems to have ignored at that time is the fact that he was technically employed by Amann who, after all, was paying him – when he remembered to do so – to represent the Nazi press in Washington. Amann could hardly have failed to notice that Lüdecke was occupied with his own projects in Berlin. Things became even more embarrassing when a German language newspaper in America, the *New Yorker Staats-Zeitung*, announced, in bold headlines: LÜDECKE ARRESTED FOR SWINDLE AND EXTORTION. Lüdecke decided to sue, and engaged a Berlin lawyer who in turn instructed a New York attorney. He also asked the Nazi party court, the *Uschla*, to review the circumstances of his 9 May arrest and to clear his name.

On 4 July, after much hedging, the head of the *Uschla* told Rosenberg that he was sending a statement that would clear Lüdecke of any charges. The following day, the Gestapo arrested Lüdecke for the second time. The story of Lüdecke's arrest, imprisonment, escape, and flight to America are of little direct interest to this story and are told in detail in his own book.[38]

What Lüdecke does not mention is the interest which the FBI took in his case. Apparently convinced that he was a German spy – one report even claims that he was 'in charge of Gestapo and espionage activities in the United States' – the FBI placed Lüdecke under surveillance.[39] This surveillance was intensified after June, 1940, when a neighbour appears to have reported Lüdecke for:

. . . behaviour which also applies to this author. Lüdecke was arrested by Federal agents at the Hotel Walton, Chicago, on 9 December 1941 – his third or fourth arrest on suspicion of espionage. On 9 February 1942, the US Attorney General recommended that Lüdecke be interned, having placed him in the category of 'individuals believed to be the most dangerous . . . '. Lüdecke was interned at Fort Sheridan, Illinois, about 35km from Chicago, where he seems to have excited attention by talking too much to the guards, later being transferred to Camp Forest, Tennessee, where he seems to have remained until the end of the war. He was ordered to be deported in 1946, lodged an unsuccessful appeal that was heard in 1948, and – if such a thing is possible for a goose – went home with his tail between his legs. He was never heard of again, though his FBI file intriguingly notes 'no information re subject since 1954', suggesting that the authorities continued to maintain an interest in the Golden Goose.

Notes

1 LÜDE38, p. 5.
2 LÜDE38, p. 6. As this chapter shows, Lüdecke's 'new life' in the USA was not the success he had hoped for when these words were written in 1938.
3 LÜDE38, p. 78.
4 LÜDE38, pp. 71-4.
5 LÜDE38, p. 108.
6 LÜDE38, p. 108.
7 LÜDE38, pp. 109-22; KERS98, p. 186.
8 LÜDE38, p. 125.
9 LÜDE38, p. 133. Lüdecke was apparently under surveillance by the German embassy in Rome during this visit – see e.g. DEUE62, pp. 543-7. The author of this document speculates as to whether Lüdecke is the same Lüdecke who was a Polish spy in Switzerland during the First World War!
10 LÜDE38, p. 137.
11 POOL78, p. 329.
12 POOL78, p. 330, citing Macartney, C.A. *October Fifteenth: A History of Modern Hungary, 1929-45.* Edinburgh 1957. Vol. I, p. 72.
13 LÜDE38, pp. 177-8.
14 LÜDE38, p. 176.
15 LÜDE38, p. 176.
16 LÜDE38, facing p. 176. The original German text reads: *Indem ich Ihnen zunächst für Ihre Vertreutung der Bewegung in Italien meinen herzlichsten Dank ausspreche, bitte ich Sie, für die Interessen der Deutschen Freiheitsbewegung in Nordamerika zu werben und besonders finanzielle Mittel hierfür zu sammeln. Ich bitte Sie, diese Mittel zunächst persönlich in Empfang zu nehmen und wenn*

möglich auch persönlich herüberzubringen. Indem ich Ihnen für Ihre Bemühungen schon im voraus aufs beste danke, grüße ich Sie herzlichst.

17 A photograph of the document is given in LÜDE38, facing p. 177. The middle lines of the text are badly mutilated by a fold in the document.

18 LÜDE38, p. 191.

19 LÜDE38, pp. 190-1.

20 LÜDE38, pp. 191-2.

21 LÜDE38, p. 192.

22 LÜDE38, pp. 193-6.

23 LÜDE38, p. 201.

24 LÜDE38, p. 201.

25 LÜDE38, p. 204.

26 LÜDE38, pp. 232-8.

27 LÜDE38, pp. 242-6.

28 LÜDE38, pp. 263-4. Ludecke frequently uses the term "folkic" as an equivalent to the Völkischer, as in *Völkischer Beobachter*. This term has no simple English equivalent but carries overtones of nationalism, racism, Pan-Germanism, Nordic mysticism and opposition to the terms of the Treaty of Versailles.

29 LÜDE38, p. 264.

30 LÜDE38, p. 366.

31 LÜDE38, p. 369.

32 LÜDE38, p. 459.

33 LÜDE38, p. 501.

34 LÜDE38, p. 502.

35 LÜDE38, p. 510.

36 LÜDE38, p. 551.

37 LÜDE38, p. 569.

38 LÜDE38, pp. 603-671.

39 FBI- Lüd. Report dated June 18, 1943, in Chicago File 65-1510.

40 Ibid. Report dated June 3, 1941, in Detroit File 65-291.

Chapter Nine

BIG BUSINESS

Nothing is illegal if one hundred well-placed businessmen decide to do it.
Andrew Young, quoted in Morris K. Udall,
Too Funny to be President.

The industrialists of German Big Business had three salient characteristics: they gave large amounts of money; they gave that money mainly to the NSDAP; and they gave in the name of an industrial concern, an industry, or an industry association.

Most writers are somewhat vague about who or what they class as 'big business', 'industry', or 'industrialists' when considering the financing of Hitler and the NSDAP; only Turner is careful to define what he means by 'big business'.[1] This can cause difficulties in interpreting what writers mean when they use these terms without referring to a specific organisation or individual. For example, Hanfstaengl credits Funk (see below) with having contacts to 'industrialists' who were willing to foot the bill at Berlin's *Kaiserhof* hotel for Hitler and his entourage.[2] It is not at all clear whether Hanfstaengl means several individuals or an organisation representing members of a particular industry.

German business was somewhat different from other countries, being far more organised than in, say, Britain or the USA.[3] Cartels – business groups who agreed on prices, wage rates, etc. – had a long history in Germany, were not illegal, and were considered to bring stability. Estimates of the number of such cartels in Germany in the mid nineteen-twenties, range from 1,500 to 2,500. Along with the cartels there were a very large number of trade associations – *Verbände* – which formed nation-wide networks. Through a suitable *Verband*, a manufacturer of, say, screws in Hamburg could come into contact with other manufacturers, distributors, and major users throughout Germany – to their mutual advantage. By the mid nineteen-twenties, such groups, and groups of groups known as *Spitzenverbände* (Peak Associations) – were powerful, well financed, with considerable influence on the government – to some extent dictating economic policy. They openly subsidised politicians and political parties and from this has come the legend that Big Business financed Adolf Hitler. As this chapter shows, prior to 1933 such financing was nowhere near as large or as extensive as many think.

The involvement of German industry with the extreme right dated back to the period immediately after the First World War, when law and order broke down and armed left-wing agitation was at its height. In such circumstances, businesses were happy to pay for protection by financing paramilitary groups such as the *Freikorps*. Such groups suppressed left-wing revolts and protected property in Berlin, the Ruhr, and in the less industrialised Bavaria. Many links between those who were later prominent in the NSDAP and sources of finance from business were forged at this time. By the mid nineteen-twenties, many industry groups had formed associations outside the *Verbände* for managing political funds. One of the earliest was the *Kuratorium für den Wiederaufbau des Deutschen Wirtschaftslebens* (roughly, Trust for the Rebuilding of German Economic Life), generally referred to simply as the *Kuratorium*. Formed in 1919, it acted on behalf of banks and industries in the Berlin area, but by 1930 the organisation was all but defunct.

More important was the *Kommission zur Sammlung, Verwaltung und Verwendung des Industriellen Wahlfonds* (roughly, Commission for the Collection, Management and Use of Industrial Election Funds). Set up before the First World War by coal, iron and steel interests in the Ruhr, it provided financial support to middle-class politicians and parties. During the inflationary period, the organisation lost much of its funding and effectiveness and after 1924 it split into two funds. Both were initially managed by Alfred Hugenberg. Collaboration resumed in 1928 with the creation of the *Ruhrlade*, a secret organisation described below.

In practice, Hitler and the NSDAP found great difficulty in getting any financial support from Big Business prior to 1930 and the reasons for this are simple: Hitler and the NSDAP were perceived as anti-business. As early as 1921, Paul Reusch, later to become founder and president of the *Ruhrlade*, summed up the attitude of business to the NSDAP in a response to a letter from Nazi party member Alexander Glaser soliciting funds:

> . . . *we have no reason to support our own gravediggers.* [4]

And that is what any business supporter would have been doing on the basis of the Twenty-five Points which Hitler declared, and declared to be unalterable, on 24 February 1920:

> *13. We demand nationalisation of all businesses which have been up to the present formed into companies (Trusts).*
>
> *14. We demand that the profits from wholesale trade shall be shared out. . . .*
>
> *16. We demand . . . immediate communalisation of wholesale business premises, and their lease at a cheap rate to small traders, and that extreme consideration shall be shown to all small purveyors to the State, district authorities and smaller localities.* [5]

In late 1922 or early 1923, Rosenberg issued a pamphlet explaining what Clause Thirteen 'really' meant: Clause Thirteen was not as radical as it seemed and merely indicated the Nazis' intention to break monopolies, especially those with international connections, which were undoubtedly controlled by the 'International Zionist Conspiracy'.[6] Few industrialists were convinced. Ironically, Hitler, aided by Amann, went on to create one of the largest monopolies in Germany: the Nazi press. On a smaller scale, the SA tried – and failed – to monopolise the cigarette industry.

Even those businessmen who were sympathetic to the aims of the NSDAP in the early twenties doubted that Hitler's party would ever amount to a serious political force and were therefore reluctant to support it. One such was Ludwig Roselius, heir to a fortune from the well known brand of decaffeinated coffee *Kaffee Hag* and an ardent nationalist. In 1933, Roselius publicly regretted that he had failed to take Hitler seriously when he approached him in 1922.[7] (It is curious how many early supporters of Hitler were connected with the coffee industry.)

Another factor must also be borne in mind when considering relationships between Hitler and Big Business: it was not in Hitler's interest to be <u>known</u> to be receiving funds from organisations he publicly decried. Indeed, Hitler fought, and won, several libel suits against journalists who accused him of receiving financial support from Big Business. Such accusations were especially common in 1923 and usually alleged that Hitler was receiving money from the industrialist Hugo Stinnes; they were almost certainly groundless. Funding from Fritz Thyssen at that time is more probable and is examined in detail below.

Nothing much of significance happened between Hitler and Big Business until 1926 and most funding prior to then came from the Patrons, described in Chapter 10. In mid-1926, Hitler began to court the industrialists of the Ruhr, beginning with a series of speeches in Essen.[8] In fact, few of those who attended the Essen meetings could be called 'big' businessmen, though one was, and his attendance at the 27 April 1927 meeting would have far-reaching consequences. That man was Emil Kirdorf, the eighty-year-old 'Bismarck of coal'.

From about 1926 onwards, as Hitler and the NSDAP became better known, many – e.g. Bechstein and Borsig – found themselves in trouble for their Nazi associations. Robert Ley – then a chemist with IG Farben, later head of the Reich Labour Front – was sacked for refusing to temper his political activities. Others, especially small businesses, suffered boycotts. It became increasingly common for those who owned businesses or held official positions to become secret members of the NSDAP and by 1929, this had become almost official policy. For those not desiring absolute secrecy, the NSDAP set up special postal accounts to which sympathisers could contribute, knowing that the party would thus have a clear record of their support, ready for the day when they could 'come out of the closet'.

By the end of 1927, Hitler temporarily abandoned his efforts to solicit the financial support of Big Business in the Ruhr, though he continued to court businessmen in other areas. The perception at the time was that Big Business was not interested in Hitler and that his attempts to enlist its aid were more in the nature of blackmail:

> The German economy did not raise up Hitler. He is no creature of money; to be sure, he did approach big capital — though as a blackmailer, not as a lackey. But in that springtime of self-confidence [i.e. the 'Roaring Twenties' of 1925-29] there was nothing to be had from capital by blackmail.[9]

Following the Nazis' spectacular successes in the 1930 election, Big Business began to court Hitler. One of the first to do so was Emil Georg von Stauss, a director of the *Deutsche Bank und Disconto-Gesellschaft*. It was Stauss who introduced Hjalmar Schacht, a former President of the Reichsbank who had been the subject of much abuse by the Nazis, to Göring, who then introduced him to Hitler. At their first meeting, on 5 January 1931, Schacht was impressed by Hitler and decided that he was a man with whom he could co-operate. To maintain secrecy of their relationship, the Nazi press continued to attack Schacht throughout much of 1931. However, Schacht's support soon became known in business circles and did much to persuade Big Business that Hitler was, at last, worth supporting.

In January of 1930, Hitler made an open attempt to influence the lower ranks of Big Business outside the Ruhr. Following local elections, Wilhelm Frick had been proposed as a member of the Thuringian state cabinet. Not surprisingly, there were objections to this, especially from local business leaders who feared the 'Socialist' aspects of the NSDAP programme. Around 10 January, Hitler went to Weimar, the state capital of Thuringia, and lunched with a group of about twenty prominent politicians and businessmen at the *Hotel zum Elephanten*. The meeting was a success and later that evening he addressed a much larger meeting. Two weeks later, the DVP members of the proposed coalition, who had earlier been opposed to Frick's membership of the cabinet, voted to allow his appointment as minister for the interior and for education. Hitler is said to have boasted that this about-face was the result of pressure applied to the DVP by local businessmen, especially the cement industry. These were swayed by Hitler's promises of cuts in state taxation and his repudiation of the 'Socialist' aspects of Nazism. Support from small businessmen followed rapidly, including one thermometer manufacturer who joined the NSDAP because he objected to the 'Marxist' regulation, imposed by the Republic, that clinical thermometers meet certain standards of accuracy.[10]

It is generally believed that Hitler set out to court Big Business seriously in 1931 and such theories are usually found to be based on the single source of Dietrich's 1934 memoirs:

> In the summer of 1931 the Führer suddenly decided to cultivate systematically the authoritative leaders of the economy who stood at the centre of resistance as well as the parties they supported so as to break them, stone for stone, out of the structure of the regime. . . . During the following months the Führer criss-crossed the whole of Germany in his supercharged Mercedes. He turned up everywhere for confidential conferences with leading figures. They were arranged everywhere, whether in the capital of the Reich or in the provinces, in the Kaiserhof Hotel or in an isolated woodland glade in God's free nature.

142

Confidentiality had to be preserved in order not to provide the press with material for agitation. The desired effect did not go unattained. [11]

Dietrich's post-war memoirs are somewhat different:

The authoritative men of business and the officials of the industry associations displayed a cool political reserve and awaited developments. Hitler "the drummer" had to rely in his propaganda endeavours on the financial sacrifices of his party comrades, on membership dues and entrance fees for rallies. [12]

Turner uses this statement as evidence that Dietrich's earlier account is exaggerated. However, it seems unlikely that the second passage refers to the events of 1931 because by then Hitler no longer saw himself as the 'drummer', beating the way for the leader of Germany who had yet to emerge. By 1931, Hitler was convinced that <u>he</u> was that leader. It seems more likely that Dietrich is here referring to the late nineteen-twenties. Be that as it may, Dietrich's 1955 memoirs are remarkably silent on the fund-raising attempts of 1931. It should also be remembered that the 1934 book was written as propaganda, by a propagandist. It is not, therefore, necessarily an accurate historical record. Nonetheless, it seems to have been accepted by many as fact. Turner makes a much stronger case against such overtures by Hitler when he notes the lack of correspondence on any such meetings in the extensive files of the industrialists involved.[13] Another story, which ran in the left-wing press in the first half of 1931, to the effect that the *Bergbauverein* coal syndicate had levied a 50 *pfennig* per tonne premium on coal to finance the NSDAP and the *Deutscher Nationale Volkspartei* (DNVP – German Nationalist Party) also does not stand up to scrutiny.[14] Particularly telling is the fact that at that time coal was selling at the pithead for 42 *pfennig* a tonne.

Another event which has often been taken as showing that Hitler gained the support of Big Business in early 1932 is the well-known January 26 meeting with the Düsseldorf Industry Club. Dietrich has left his usual propaganda-serving account of the meeting in his 1934 memoir and this has been oft repeated by other writers.[15] One sentence stands out:

The effect on the businessmen, so far as they deserved that name, was profound and became evident in the ensuing difficult months of struggle. [16]

Some writers have taken this to mean that Big Business began to give large sums of money to the NSDAP after that date, though Dietrich makes no mention of money. Hoffmann, however, is explicit on the sum collected at the meeting:

His appeal met with immediate response. Sixty-five thousand marks made a good foundation; the first step towards the assumption of power had been taken. [17]

Dietrich's 1955 memoir is, again, somewhat different:

Not until 1932, after Göring had established close relations with the Stahlhelm *leader Fritz Thyssen and the latter had openly spoken out for Hitler in the industrial gathering at Düsseldorf did the ice break and numerous sympathetic attitudes come to expression. On that occasion a collection was attempted at the door which produced some well-meaning but insignificant sums. Beyond that, one could not speak of any support worthy of mention, much less of a financing of Hitler's political struggle by die Wirtschaft or "heavy industry", although some more or less notable contributions may have reached local party organisations at their rallies from individually sympathetic businessmen of their regions. Hitler's great propaganda tours of 1932 financed themselves exclusively through the entrance fees for giant rallies, at which seats in the front rows often went for fantastic prices.[18]*

While this appears to tell the 'truth', in that it contradicts the blatant propaganda of 1934, it must be remembered that Dietrich's 1955 memoir was also propaganda, though with different objectives: to show Otto Dietrich in a good light and, possibly, to do the same for Big Business. It would be interesting to know whether Dietrich himself ever received the support of Big Business – before or after 1945. Thyssen seems to support Dietrich's 1934 statements:

The speech made a deep impression on the assembled industrialists, and in consequence of this a number of large contributions flowed from the resources of heavy-industry into the treasury of the National Socialist Party.[19]

There is no evidence to support Thyssen's claim. It may also be significant that at no time was any member of the NSDAP – with the possible exceptions of Keppler and Funk – formally allocated the task of soliciting and managing contributions from businesses of any size. Whatever Hitler and the NSDAP may have received from Big Business at that time – and it is increasingly doubtful that they received anything – the Düsseldorf meeting was a propaganda disaster, with the leftist press presenting it as confirmation that Hitler was a capitalist puppet.

The year leading up to Hitler's coming to power was marked by a lack of purpose and cohesion on the part of Big Business and the bourgeois political parties such as the DVP and the DNVP. Some industry organisations found themselves short of funds as a result of the weak economy. Others were reluctant to contribute to any party because their previous contributions had not influenced affairs to their liking. The situation was further confused when the moderate SPD backed Hindenburg, the incumbent president and a man of the right. This split Big Business, with some elements backing the SPD because it supported Hindenburg, while others backed the DVP and the DNVP because these were the parties they had traditionally supported. Despite Thyssen's endorsement, few were prepared to support Hitler and the NSDAP. Matters were made even worse by the fact that most Big Business regarded the presidential election as a foregone conclusion – a win for Hindenburg – and so directed their funds towards the state elections in April, where their influence could have more effect. When a run-off election had to be held between Hitler and Hindenburg, the latter was forced to finance his campaign by misappropriating state funds.

Although it is clear that Hitler and the NSDAP made no concerted attempt to gain the financial support of Big Business in 1932, many industrialists and industry concerns put out feelers towards Hitler, often hoping to influence Nazi economic policy. (A futile exercise, since the NSDAP did not have an economic policy worthy of the name.) One of the first to do so was Friedrich Flick, founder of the *Gelsenkirchen* iron and steel conglomerate.

Regarded as an outsider by the *Ruhrlade*, especially after his ailing company had been the subject of a controversial rescue operation by the Weimar government, Flick arranged to meet Hitler in late February of 1932, at the *Kaiserhof* in Berlin. Flick took along his friend and deputy Otto Steinbrinck, a submariner and hero of the First World War. The meeting started badly when Hitler mistook Flick for Steinbrinck and began to talk about naval matters. In his Nuremberg testimony, Flick maintained that Hitler had been unsuccessful in his appeal for funds to fight the impending presidential election and some measure of how badly the meeting went can be gauged from the RM 450,000 which Flick gave to Hindenburg's campaign.

However, Flick had been contributing to the Berlin SA since early 1931 and soon got the reputation of being a 'soft touch', giving, not always without reluctance, about RM 15,000 to the SA, RM 15,000 to Himmler's SS, and similar sums to Robert Ley, to support his Cologne newspaper the *Westdeutscher Beobachter*, and to several other Nazi papers. Flick and Steinbrinck kept no proper records of the monies disbursed in this fashion but, in post-war interrogations, Flick estimated that a total of RM 50,000 had been given to Nazi organisations prior to 1933; Steinbrinck's estimate was RM 40,000; both were certainly underestimates.[20] However, it seems unlikely that there was any conscious effort on the part of Flick and Steinbrinck to hide or minimise the sums – compared to what Flick gave to others, such as Hindenburg, they were small – and the underestimation simply reflects a lack of bookkeeping. None of the money ever came near Hitler's pockets except for RM 20,000 given to the NSDAP during the November 1932 elections, and that almost certainly went directly to Schwarz.

The next to approach Hitler was Paul Reusch, leader of the *Ruhrlade*, on 19 March 1932. Reusch hoped to influence Hitler's economic policies and to dampdown the attacks on Big Business which were a regular feature of the Nazi press. He also hoped to persuade Hitler to withdraw from the election run-off against Hindenburg. This, Reusch hoped, would prevent friction between the NSDAP and the Bavarian People's Party, leading to an eventual coalition. Hitler refused. However, the two did strike a deal whereby two newspapers in which Reusch had a financial interest, the *Münchener Neuste Nachrichten* and the Nuremberg-based *Fränkischer Kurier*, would drop their pro-Hindenburg stance and remain neutral during the campaign. In return, Hitler agreed to moderate anti-Big Business tirades in the Nazi-controlled press. Reusch stuck to his part of the bargain; Hitler did not. Reusch then became briefly entangled in the creation of the Keppler Circle, which some have seen as definite proof of a conspiracy involving Hitler and Big Business.

Hjalmar Schacht, who had been courting Hitler since the Bad Harzburg meeting of October 1931, contacted Reusch and proposed hiring a political linkman to work with the NSDAP and help it to generate a coherent economic policy favourable to Big Business. Reusch was enthusiastic about the idea and set about arranging the RM 15,000 a year thought necessary to cover salary and expenses. Schacht contacted Hitler and received what he thought was approval. However, unknown to Reusch and Schacht, Hitler had already charged Keppler with the same task. Keppler agreed, but insisted on being Hitler's personal economic adviser, rather than being a member of the NSDAP bureaucracy. This suggests, but does not prove, that Keppler was paid out of Hitler's pocket and it is unlikely that his salary and expenses were less than the RM 15,000 a year proposed by Reusch and Schacht.

Towards the end of April 1932, Keppler, having sounded out various persons in the business community, met with Hitler and formally proposed an economic council under his, Keppler's, leadership. Hitler accepted the idea and, in a typical piece of duplicity, suggested to Keppler that he might include Schacht in the council. On 14 May, Keppler met again with Hitler, who assured him that he could take an independent line and should not be concerned about the work of Wagener and the Economic Policy Section of the NSDAP. Schacht, of course, was horrified to be approached by Keppler to join an organisation which he thought he was supposed to create and lead. Schacht was reluctant to join Keppler's organisation and Keppler began to intrigue against him, undermining what little influence Schacht had. After Keppler had enticed away two of the financial contributors to Schacht's scheme, Schacht capitulated and, in late June, agreed to join Keppler's group. (After the war, Schacht would deny ever having any connection with the Keppler circle.)

The Keppler Circle was formally created in June 1932 and, apart from Schacht, it consisted mainly of business acquaintances of Keppler, himself no more than a small chemicals manufacturer, rather than members of Big Business. The Circle included Karl Helfferich, an unemployed former colonial plantation manager; two Hamburg merchants, Franz Heinrich Witthoeft and Karl Vincent Krogmann; Friedrich Reinhart, a director of the Commerz- und Privatbank of Berlin; Rudolf Bingel, a minor executive at Siemens; Count Gottfried von Bismarck, the group's agriculture expert; two major figures in the potash industry, August Rosterg and Ewald Hecker; the then minor banker Kurt von Schröder; and Emil Meyer, a lawyer and Keppler's cousin.

von Schröder is interesting in that before his membership of the Keppler Circle he was almost completely unknown; it was only because of his membership that he became a prominent figure in Hitler's rise to power. To describe Schröder as 'an internationally known financier well connected with industry' is a gross exaggeration (for 1932) and allegations that Schröder financed the NSDAP are baseless.[21]

The Keppler Circle held its first meeting at Berlin's *Kaiserhof* on 20 June 1932, where it was addressed by Hitler. After that promising start, the Circle began to experience difficulties: the Circle, as is the habit of committees, began to argue – mostly about just what it was supposed to do. Within four months the Circle was paralysed. Hitler, who was never interested in economics, lost interest. The circle influenced neither Big Business nor Hitler, who kept Wagener's NSDAP committee going as part of his policy of competition within the party. He never listened to that, either. Some of the members of the circle gave valuable political help to Hitler in the months before his coming to power, but as an instrument of economic influence the Keppler Circle had no discernible effect. Later, the group was hijacked by Himmler, becoming *Der Freundeskreis Himmler* (The Circle of Himmler Friends) in which capacity it served as a fundraising body for his crackpot notions. Stories that the Keppler Circle raised funds for Hitler and the NSDAP prior to 1933 are without foundation.

Another group which tried to influence Nazi economic policy was the Wagemann Circle, a group which revolved around Prof. Ernst Wagemann, head of the Reich Statistical Office and also a member of the *Institut für Konjunkturforschung* (Institute for Economic Situation Research). One member of the Circle was Max Ilgner, a young IG Farben high-flyer who headed the company's Berlin office, though his career was presumably not hindered by the fact that his uncle, Hermann Schmitz, was Farben's principal financial director. Another member was Wichard von Möllendorf, an advisor to the Farben board. The Circle included several other major Berlin business figures, some of them Jewish. In an attempt to clarify the Nazis' economic policies, the Circle sent Ilgner and Möllendorf to visit Funk. At least two meetings took place in early 1932 and Funk reported that Hitler approved of the Circle's ideas, though some dispute then took place between Funk and Möllendorf, as a result of which contact ceased. However, it seems that at their first meeting Funk had asked Ilgner for financial support for his office in Berlin and Ilgner arranged monthly payments of RM 300-500 from IG Farben funds.[22] According to Ilgner, another IG Farben executive, Heinrich Gattineau, was also subsidising Funk from company funds. Other IG Farben money went to the NSDAP through the *Kränzchen*, as described below. No evidence has been found for any funds flowing from IG Farben to Hitler before 1933.

By the time of the November 1932 election campaign, the Nazis had succeeded in alienating most of Big Business through their radicalism, their anti-capitalist rhetoric and the general lack of an economic policy. Contributions to the NSDAP from Big Business – such as they were – dried up; only Flick, ever the outsider, continued to provide support. When Hitler finally came to power at the end of January 1933, it was not with the aid of Big Business.

The Donors

As the preceding brief history of Hitler's relations with Big Business shows, far less was given before 1933 than popularly supposed. This section examines the details of those individuals and organisations alleged to have provided money to Hitler and the NSDAP.

The Bergbauverein

The *Bergbauverein* was an association of coal companies, predominantly in the Ruhr. Ernst Brandi, head of one of the four regional mining units of United Steel and noted for a strong antipathy towards organised labour, was elected chairman in 1927. The executive director was Hans von Löwenstein, a man who resembled Brandi in every respect, including the title of *Bergassessor*, a hard-won professional status in the mining industry. More reactionary than Brandi, von Löwenstein had publicly supported the *Kapp Putsch* in 1920, championed Mussolini in the twenties, and attended the Harzburg meeting in October of 1931. Shortly after, he met Hitler.

In the winter of 1930-31, the *Bergbauverein* can best be described as unhappy; unhappy at losing up to 32 *pfennigs* a tonne on coal; unhappy at the way the political funds it contributed to the *Ruhrlade* were being disbursed; and unhappy with their membership of the industrial *Reichsverband*, which was felt to be under-representing the interests of coal. All of which unhappiness led to a row between the *Bergbauverein* and just about everyone else in the Ruhr. Although the *Bergbauverein* eventually backed down in this confrontation, it had the effect of moving Brandi and von Löwenstein closer to the Nazis. The only Nazi that there is evidence that Brandi gave financial support to is Josef Terboven, who had earlier acted as a link between Kirdorf and Hitler. Brandi is said to have made regular payments to Funk and Strasser, beginning in early 1931, but the evidence suggests that these payments were not large. In 1934, after the Nazis came to power, Brandi began having problems with Terboven, who was then *Gauleiter* of Essen, and had to call on others to remind Terboven of the support he had earlier received. Brandi's contributions, whatever they were, do not seem to have earned him many 'brownie points'. In short, there is little evidence that the *Bergbauverein* gave much to individual Nazis and none at all that it gave anything to Hitler or the NSDAP prior to 1933.

Hugenberg

By the late nineteen-twenties, Alfred Hugenberg, a former Krupp director, then a media magnate in his own right, was leader of the DNVP. His initial fortune was made by shrewdly investing funds which he had been given to use for propa-

148

ganda purposes during the First World War and pocketing the dividends for himself.[23] In the aftermath of the First World War, he entered politics and was elected as representative for Posen, East Prussia. Hugenberg enjoyed only limited support from heavy industry – his own interests were mainly in publishing – and most of his support came from the *Junkers* of East Prussia and similar agricultural interests. He did, however, enjoy the support of two right-wing industrialists, Kirdorf and Thyssen.

A far-sighted entrepreneur in some respects, Hugenberg recognised the value of the media – then consisting of print, radio, and 'newsreel' cinema, – to a politician. During the Depression he began buying near-bankrupt newspapers and other media enterprises. Germany's press at that time consisted largely of local newspapers and only those in the major cities could afford to cover national and international events; Hugenberg therefore set up his own news agency, *Wirtschaftsstelle für die Provinzpresse* and his own wire service, *Telegraph Union*. He set up an advertising agency, selling space in his provincial presses, and a pair of finance companies, to provide them with capital. Every innovation by Hugenberg was later adopted and exploited by Hitler and Amann. Although radio, being under government control, was out of his reach, Hugenberg gained control of the film company *UFA*, and through it, chains of cinemas across the country. Not surprisingly, in view of his political activities, Hugenberg ensured that the media that he effectively controlled distributed all the news that was fit to print – fit, that is, in the mind of Hugenberg. All this empire was controlled through the *Ostdeutsche Privatbank* on whose board sat Hugenberg's backers, mostly Prussian landowners. By 1924, Hugenberg's level of control over the press was sufficient to worry the government and when the *Deutsche Allgemeine Zeitung* (DAZ) fell into difficulties following the death of its owner, Hugo Stinnes, the government quietly subsidised the paper to prevent it from falling into the hands of either Hugenberg or the Left.

In 1929, the Dawes Plan, under which Germany's war reparations payments would be restructured – but not reduced – in return for a loan to Germany of $200 million, was replaced by the Young Plan, which required Germany to pay reparations at the rate of RM 2,050 million a year until 1988. Opposition to the Young Plan was widespread, even amongst moderate industrialists. Hugenberg mounted a campaign against it and Hitler was persuaded to lend his party's support. A committee to push for a plebiscite on the Young Plan was formed, consisting of Hugenberg, Hitler, Seldte (leader of the *Stahlhelm* ex-servicemens' organisation), and Heinrich Claß (leader of the ultra-nationalist Pan-German League). The only industrialist on the organising committee was Fritz Thyssen and the two principal contributors of funds to the campaign are said to have been Thyssen and the *Reichslandbund*, an organisation of East Prussian landowners.[24] Hugenberg willingly accepted Hitler into the organisation, believing that he could control him, and through him the rest of the German far right. Hitler joined with no intention of being dominated by Hugenberg or anyone else, but recognising that it would do the NSDAP nothing but good to get favourable coverage by the Hugenberg-controlled media. Hitler probably expected access to Hugenberg's funds. In the end, the plebiscite was defeated: 21 million votes were needed; six million were cast.

The question which concerns this work is: Did any of Hugenberg's money, or that of the committee campaigning against the Young Plan, flow to Hitler or the NSDAP? It has been alleged that Hugenberg and the DNVP channelled funds to Hitler and the source for such stories seems to be Thyssen.[25] Lüdecke tends to confirm Thyssen's allegations, especially the part played by two of Hugenberg's behind-the-scenes associates, Claß and *Finanzrat* Dr. Bang who had acted as link man between Hitler and Hugenberg in the early days of their relationship.

Kirdorf

Kirdorf's nickname 'The Bismarck of Coal' derived from his success in uniting much of the German coal industry. By 1927, when he first heard Hitler speak, his financial holdings including the *Gelsenkirchen Bergwerks* (a coal mining company which he had helped found in the 1870s and which later expanded into iron and steel) and the *Rhenisch-Westfälisches Kohlensyndikat* (Rhine-Westphalia Coal Syndicate, a bituminous coal cartel). To many, Kirdorf exemplified the reactionary *Herr-im-Hause*[26]: ruling the workers with an iron rod, conservative, anti-union, anti-Socialist, patriotic, and nationalist. After the First World War, Germany's defeat, the abdication of the Kaiser, the loss of the old Imperial values, the Republic and its mildly socialist government, all turned Kirdorf into an embittered old man and he became involved in right-wing politics, initially supporting Hugenberg's DNVP.

By the time of the Essen meeting with Hitler, Kirdorf had become disillusioned with the DNVP, which he saw as too conciliatory towards Germany's enemies. Kirdorf, however, did not meet privately with Hitler until later that year, when they met at the instigation of either Otto Dietrich or Frau Bruckmann.[27] A meeting was arranged and took place on 4 July at the Bruckmanns' Munich home, lasting several hours. On 1 August, Kirdorf joined the NSDAP, receiving membership number 71,032 and thereby qualifying for the Gold Party Badge awarded to the first 100,000 members.[28] On 26 October, Kirdorf brought Hitler to a meeting at his home of fourteen 'leading industrialists'. The meeting was not a notable success, but neither was it a failure: Hitler made a fairly good impression as an intelligent speaker, but there was no rush to join the NSDAP or to offer financial assistance. At this time, Kirdorf's contributions to Hitler and the NSDAP were relatively small. However, even after he left the party in 1928, the links that he offered to Big Business were considered so important that he was guest of honour at the *Parteitag* in Nuremberg in 1929. Kirdorf recalled the July meeting in 1937, when he was 97 years old (he died in 1938):

The inexorable logic and clear conciseness of his train of thought filled me with such enthusiasm with what he said. I asked the Führer to write a pamphlet on the topics he had discussed with me. I then distributed this pamphlet in business and industrial circles. . . . Shortly after our Munich conversation and as a result of the pamphlet written by the Führer and distributed by me, several meetings took place between the Führer and leading industrial personalities. [29]

This is the first identified public mention of this pamphlet, which was entitled *Der Weg zum Wiederaufsteig* – the Road to Resurgence, and raises the question: What was in it and why was it apparently kept so secret? Some authors have made much of the 'secrecy' surrounding this document, basing this on the fact that only one copy is known to have survived. Intended for businessmen, the pamphlet, which has been the subject of a paper by Turner, is not, in fact, much good. [30] Its economic ideas are simplistic, muddled, and badly written and any businessman who was not a fanatical anti-Communist or extreme rightist would probably have consigned it to the waste-paper bin – probably the principal reason for its low survival rate.

Speer alleges, while admitting that Hitler's own statements on such matters were rarely reliable, that at the time Kirdorf joined the NSDAP, that organisation was close to bankruptcy and that Kirdorf immediately paid off the majority of the party's debts. Turner analyses this allegation in some detail and concludes that it is improbable. [31] The author is inclined to agree on the basis of the following points.

- There is no evidence that the NSDAP was closer to bankruptcy in 1927 than at any other time prior to 1930.
- Kirdorf no longer had access to any substantial corporate funds, so any money would have had to come from Kirdorf's own pocket.
- Kirdorf was notoriously frugal, even tight-fisted, so the likelihood of him giving any substantial sum is small.

Nonetheless, it is highly probable that Kirdorf made a donation on joining the NSDAP; it is equally probable that the donation was not large. In August 1928, infuriated by an attack on his *Rhenisch-Westfälisches Kohlensyndikat*, Kirdorf resigned from the NSDAP and quietly rejoined the DNVP. He did, however re-join the party after Hitler came to power in 1933 when, in a typical piece of Nazi book-fiddling, he was given his original membership number.

The Kränzchen

The chemical combine IG Farben, which, while only created in 1925, had three of its directors sitting in the *Reichstag* by 1930: one in the DDP, one in the Centre party, and one in the rightist DVP. Through a secret political fund managed by

Wilhelm Kalle, and known as the *Kalle Kreis* (Kalle Circle) or the *Kränzchen* (literally either Small Wreath or Hen Party, the latter in the sense of an all-female gathering), it provided about RM 300,000 annually to the DDP, the Centre, and the DVP, with the majority of the funds going to the latter.[32] Very secretive, the existence of the *Kränzchen* was unknown even to those Farben executives who were not members. According to various accounts, the *Kränzchen* disbursed between RM 200,000 and RM 300,000 to various political parties during the 1932 election campaign; of this, the NSDAP received something between RM 20,000 and RM 45,000.[33] The problem with this assertion, which has been oft repeated, is that it rests on the testimony of IG Farben personnel – Ilgner and Gattineau – who were not themselves members of the *Kränzchen* and so are unlikely to have known anything about its dealings. Kalle, the leader of the *Kränzchen*, subsequently denied that any money went to the NSDAP prior to 1933.[34] Turner offers convincing independent evidence to support Kalle's statements.[35] However, some of the *Kränzchen* money may have reached the NSDAP indirectly and without the knowledge of the *Kränzchen* itself. In late 1931, the *Kränzchen* provided RM 10,000 at the request of General Schleicher to support the army's paramilitary *Wehrsport* programme. There is evidence that Schleicher transferred some of this money to Count Helldorf, leader of the Berlin SA.[36]

Krupp

Contrary to rumour, Krupp gave nothing to Hitler prior to 1933. Indeed, he was opposed to Hitler and his policies. However, in January of 1933 he underwent a mysterious conversion to Nazism and subsequently managed the *AH Spende*, to which he contributed millions.

The Ruhrlade

The *Ruhrlade* (Ruhr Chest or Treasury) was extremely secretive but is thought to have been founded on 9 January 1928 at the instigation of Paul Reusch, a man deeply critical of Hugenberg. It represented only heavy industry and had twelve members: Gustav Krupp and Arthur Klotzbach (*Krupp*); Fritz Thyssen, Alfred Vögler and Ernst Poensgen (*Vereinigte Stahlwerke*); Paul Reusch (*Gutterhof Stahlwerk*); Erich Fickler (*Harpener A.G.* and chair of the bituminous coal cartel); Paul Silverberg (*Rheinisch A.G.* and chair of the Rhineland lignite cartel); Fritz Springorum (*Hoesch Eisen- und Stahlwerk*); Peter Klöckner (*Klöckner-Werke*, a Duisburg coal and steel company); Karl Haniel, (*Gutehoffnungshütte* conglomerate); and Fritz Winkhaus, (*Köln-Neuessener Bergwerksverein*).[37] The members of the *Ruhrlade* met once a month, assessed levies on their various industries, collected the money, and decided amongst themselves how it should be spent.

Rumours of its existence soon began to circulate, quickly followed by rumours that the *Ruhrlade* was financing Hitler and the NSDAP. This was far from the truth at the time, and the organisation's policies were nowhere near as far right as those of Hitler. In fact, there is plenty of evidence that the *Ruhrlade* brought stability to heavy industry at a time of great uncertainty, thereby ensuring continued employment for the workers.

According to the best estimates, in 1928-1930, the *Ruhrlade* disbursed between 1.2 and 1.5 million *marks*.[38] Most of the money went to the centre or right of centre 'bourgeois' parties. For the 1928 election campaign, there is nothing to indicate that the *Ruhrlade* gave any support to Hitler or the NSDAP, though they did provide RM 200,000 to Hugenberg's DNVP – an organisation that served the interests of landowners, rather than heavy industry. Following those elections, the DNVP and the DVP each received RM 5,000 a month. In the 1930 election campaign, the *Ruhrlade* gave nothing to Hitler or the NSDAP. Indeed, the *Ruhrlade* became increasingly contemptuous of Hitler after the failure of the plebiscite against the Young Plan and one of their conditions for funding Hugenberg's DNVP during the election campaign was that it sever relations with Hitler. After the Nazis' surprising gains in the election, the *Ruhrlade* made a swift about-face.

In the summer of 1931, the *Ruhrlade* passed RM 2,500 to Walther Funk (see below) for the NSDAP, allegedly on the recommendation of Thyssen.[39] No doubt the members of the *Ruhrlade* thought that Funk would exercise some influence in their favour with the NSDAP, against the more left-wing economic views of Feder and Strasser. However, it seems that the *Ruhrlade* was not entirely against Strasser – or at least thought that he could be bought – since records show RM 15,800 passing to Strasser between October 1931 and January 1932, somewhat more than was given to Funk, whose views were closer to those of its members.

Schröder

It is often alleged that Baron Kurt von Schröder gave extensive financial support to Hitler and the NSDAP, usually on the grounds that he was well rewarded after the Nazis came to power, so he must have done something to deserve it. There is some evidence that Schröder formed a syndicate after the November 1932 elections to guarantee the NSDAP's debts, rather than to pay them.[40] If such a syndicate were formed, it would have greatly assisted the NSDAP which had passed its financial peak. It is interesting to note that one of the former directors of the Schröder bank was Allen Dulles, later head of the Swiss operations for the American OSS.

Stauss

Emil Georg von Stauss – the title appears to have been granted by the state of Württemberg and was considered by some to be of dubious validity – was a director of the *Deutsche Bank und Disconto-Gesellschaft*, one of Germany's largest banks.[41] In the nineteen-twenties he joined the DVP and gave that party some financial support. In 1930 he was elected to the Reichstag, but once there he seems to have been closer to the NSDAP than to his own party; perhaps he saw himself as a bridge between the two. Göring and Stauss got on well together and moved in the same social circles and Göring introduced the banker to Hitler some time during the first half of 1931. According to Otto Wagener, who was present at the meeting, Stauss was impressed by Hitler's views and offered to quit the DVP in favour of the NSDAP. Hitler persuaded Stauss to remain with the DVP and use his influence there on the Nazis' behalf. Stauss did so and there is evidence that he remained a financial supporter of the DVP until the Nazis came to power in 1933. Stauss's Nazi connections quickly became well known and caused several major Jewish depositors to withdraw funds from the bank. For this, and other reasons, he resigned from the bank in 1932, though he remained on the supervisory board. Although he never became an NSDAP member, Stauss was appointed an honorary member of the Nazi-controlled Reichstag in 1933 and served as Vice-President.

There is no evidence that Stauss ever contributed financially <u>directly</u> to Hitler or the NSDAP. According to Wagener, Stauss told him that he had given money to Göring in 1931 and offered more should the need arise.[42] Stauss also guaranteed the financial status of the Essen-based *National Zeitung* and helped the journal out of financial difficulties when it was temporarily closed by the Prussian authorities. If this is true, it would amount to a virtual gift to Hitler since the paper was later absorbed into the *Eher Verlag*.

Thyssen

In his unreliable, ghost-written autobiography, Fritz Thyssen states:

> *I financed the National Socialist Party for a single definite reason: I financed it because I believed that the Young Plan spelled catastrophe for Germany.* [43]

Thyssen's role in the financing of Hitler and the NSDAP has been exaggerated, not only by himself, but also by such generally well-informed writers such as Heiden:

> *. . . Fritz Thyssen . . . the prototype of the National Socialist money-man, an adept at eight-figure bankruptcies. . . . The [Vereinigte Stahlwerke] gambled heavily on the coming Third Reich, a state whose gigantic armaments programme would require immense quantities of steel and steel products. Thyssen financed Hitler just as confidently as the foolish duchess who hoped to recover her lost throne.*[44]

The only problem with Heiden's thesis is that, as this chapter shows and Turner has shown in much greater detail, it is wrong. In mitigation, it must be said that

Heiden did not have access to the extensive documentary evidence that has become available to post-war writers.

In 1923, Fritz Thyssen was 50 years old, bored and frustrated. His father, who controlled the family steel business, refused to relinquish control to his son. The only outlet for young Thyssen's restless energy was politics. It is known that he visited Munich in October of 1923 and, by his own account, gave 100,000 gold marks to Ludendorff to finance the November *Putsch*. However, although Hitler played a prominent part in the *Putsch*, there is no concrete evidence that any of this money ever reached either Hitler or the NSDAP. Ludendorff had many organisations to support in connection with the attempted *Putsch*, of which Hitler and the NSDAP were a minor factor. There is also the question of the robbery, described in Chapter 3. Why, if the Nazis were getting substantial amounts of cash from Thyssen via Ludendorff, was there any need for the risky and distracting robbery which took place on the night of the *Putsch*?

Thyssen seems to have begun his relationship with Hitler during the 1929 campaign against the Young Plan, at which time he was a member of the DNVP. Following the Nazis' electoral successes of 1930, Thyssen stated, at his denazification trial in 1946, that he gave Göring three sums of RM 50,000 each for political and personal expenses. Thyssen also said that he chose to support Göring because he felt that he would be a counterweight to the left-wing elements of the party. He also said that he felt that Göring's lifestyle should better reflect his position within the leadership of the NSDAP.[45] Doubtless, Göring saw no reason to disagree. No mention is made of his having given any such sums to Hitler, but many authors have chosen to believe that he did, simply because they find it inconceivable that Thyssen would not give to Hitler what he had given to his deputy. What such believers forget is that Thyssen was much closer to the high-living Göring – they shared several interests in common, including fine food, fine wines, and fine cigars – than to the ascetic, cream-bun-stuffing Hitler.

It seems that some of Thyssen's contributions to the NSDAP were inflated by a little bullying by Göring. According to one eyewitness, it was the custom for those attending receptions in Hitler's honour to pledge a financial contribution – whether to the NSDAP or to Hitler personally is uncertain – on a list which was kept by the door. On one occasion, a group of industrialists, including Thyssen, agreed that no one was to pledge more than RM 20,000. Thyssen was the first to leave and pledged the agreed amount, at which point Göring appeared, gave Thyssen a hearty slap on the back, and loudly reminded him that he had 'agreed' to pledge RM 100,000; without protest or comment, Thyssen altered the pledge figure.[46] Some time after late 1928 – possibly as late as mid-1931 – Thyssen guaranteed a loan to the NSDAP for the rebuilding of the *Braunes Haus*; only a part of it was ever repaid.

Otto Wagener was a successful businessman, active in right-wing politics in the nineteen-twenties. His career and his importance are summarised by Turner.[47] In 1929, Hitler came to his attention and from 1930 to 1933 he was head of the Nazi party's Economic Policy Office. Forced out of Hitler's favour by the combined machinations of Göring, Funk and Feder, he survived the Blood Purge of 1934 and withdrew to his country estate. During the Second World War, he re-entered the Army with the rank of captain, ending the war on the island of Rhodes as a major-general. In 1946, Wagener was held in a British prisoner of war camp at Bridgend, Wales. There he occupied his time in making a record of his dealings with Hitler, 1930-33. It is this memoir which is one of the major sources for allegations that Göring provided personal funds to Hitler during this period, ostensibly from his wife's fortune, but actually from Ruhr industrialists. If this story could be corroborated, it would explain much.

Two problems arise with Wagener's memoir: firstly, it is written as a conversational narrative; secondly, Wagener is clearly biased in his opinions about Göring, a man he deeply despised. Wagener clearly uses the conversational narrative as a literary form and as long as one is not tempted to believe that these are accurate records of conversations, there is no problem. The second point is more problematic and requires Wagener's statements about Göring to be subjected to additional scrutiny.

By late 1930, Hitler was becoming concerned that anti-business articles in the Nazi press were alienating Big Business, whose support – moral and financial – he needed. To counteract this and to bring some uniformity to Nazi press statements on economic matters, Wagener founded the *Wirtschaftspolitischer Pressedienst* (Economic Policy News Service – WPD), a twice-weekly newsletter distributed to all Nazi newspapers, spokesmen, and to *Gau* offices. Wagener also proposed to set up a newspaper in Essen, at the heart of the Ruhr and German heavy industry, presenting Nazi ideas, but more subdued in tone than the *Völkischer Beobachter*. The events surrounding the founding of the *National-Zeitung* are described by Wagener; only one aspect is of importance to this story: the RM 50,000 which paid for the repairs to the paper's printing plant.[48]

As Wagener tells it, the first time he visited Göring in Berlin was towards the end of 1930; it was their first contact since the 1929 Party Rally. Received by a Göring wearing a red toga and red Turkish slippers, Wagener was disgusted by the effeminate opulence he saw around him and what he suspected was evidence of Göring's drug habit. In the course of their conversation, Göring brought up the question of the RM 50,000 that Wagener had received from 'the Ruhr industrialists' for repairs to the printing shop of the *Bergwerks-Zeitung* (literally 'Mine

Newspaper', suggesting that it was connected with the coal industry), which was to print the *National-Zeitung*. That money, Göring claimed, was rightfully his, since he enjoyed a monopoly on financial contributions from the Ruhr area. In Wagener's reported conversation, the angry Göring says:

"So the fifty thousand marks you were given for your newspaper had been earmarked for me. The money was already put aside. I was expecting it to be transferred. Now it will not be sent. Can you imagine the position you have put me in? I am renovating a house here on Bismarckstrasse, two floors, as a suitable residence for myself, where I can hold receptions and give parties. The architects are waiting for their money. For the fifty thousand marks! And now, the money will not be forthcoming.

"I believe that my representation of the rising new Germany is more important than another newspaper! Even though I admit that a great deal could be achieved, even for me, by a good, new newspaper in the Ruhr district!

"But I also use the money I receive from the Ruhr to finance Hitler — him personally, and occasionally the party as well."

And then it flashed through my [i.e. Wagener's] *mind! So* there *is the root of Göring's power position with Hitler!* That *is the reason for Göring's occasional flying visits to Munich and Hitler's to Berlin.* That *is the reason he was kept away from me? That is why any mention of Göring was avoided in conversation with me. And that is the basis for Göring's influence over Adolf Hitler!*

"I [i.e. Göring] *am speaking to you in confidence. No one else needs to know. Nor do I ever tell Hitler where the money comes from."*[49] [Emphases in the original.]

Just what is one to make of this passage? The fact that this was written sixteen years after the event, without any benefit of notes made at the time, is evidence that this is not a real record of a conversation. Wagener's dislike of Göring is no more strongly stated in this passage than it is elsewhere in his memoir, so it seems unlikely that Wagener is distorting these events for his own purposes. The major weakness in this account comes in the last paragraph: Why would Göring reveal these damaging facts to Wagener? In the light of later statements by Wagener, recounted below, I am inclined to believe that something like this was said and attribute the saying to Göring's habitual bluster and bravado. Since Wagener meets both of Spedding's criteria – did he/she say it first (yes, he did) and was he/she a witness (yes, he was there) – the evidence is strong, but far from conclusive.

Pressed by Göring, Wagener says that he admitted that he had received the disputed RM 50,000 through Hans von Löwenstein – manager of the *Bergbauverein* – and Ludwig Grauert – managing director of *Arbeitnordwest*, the employers' association for the ferrous metals industry in the Ruhr and a well-known Nazi sympathiser. Grauert admitted in his post-war testimony that he had arranged a loan to finance the *National-Zeitung*. Grauert was also involved in at least one other 'loan' to Heß, money which could also have gone to Hitler personally. Having made a note of these names, Wagener has Göring say:

157

"I'm glad," he repeated once more, "that we are in agreement. I will report it to Hitler as well, so that there is no need for you to speak to him about this matter. He, too, prefers and is obliged to take the view that he does not accept money from industry or businessmen. That is another reason I hold his finances in my hands."[50]

Following Göring's statement recorded above, Wagener writes:

As I left the room and the building, I felt as if someone had hit me over the head with a wooden mallet.

And well he might. If Göring's statements to Wagener contained the facts as Wagener reports them, this is the strongest evidence yet of money flowing from Big Business to Hitler's pockets.

This conversation with Göring clearly disturbed Wagener and it is important to understand why, for it has a bearing on Wagener's subsequent actions. Despite having been a successful businessman, Wagener was opposed to Big Business, especially to the *Verbände* and *Spitzenverbände* which he correctly perceived as anti-socialist. Wagener proposed that once the Nazis were in power, they should abolish such organisations – along with huge combines such as IG Farben – and replace them with companies organised around a complex system of worker and founder ownership. Wagener, like Lüdecke, decided that Göring and others were corrupting Hitler's 'pure' national socialist ideas. Money from Big Business to Hitler meant an obligation from Hitler, so Wagener had a vested interest in thwarting any influence which Big Business might have on Hitler.

According to Wagener, he decided to find out the truth, and a few days after the meeting with Göring he went to see the one man who ought to have known the truth about Hitler's personal finances: Schwarz, the NSDAP treasurer:

At first [Schwarz] refused to discuss the subject with me. Not, he said, because he had any secrets to keep, but because Hitler himself had always refused to discuss the question with Schwarz.

But then he did grow somewhat more communicative and told me that Hitler's only source of income consisted of the royalties from his book, Mein Kampf, the exact figures being, however, known only to the Eher publishing house, and there only to Amann himself.

"But surely that sum cannot suffice to cover rent, food, car, driver, escort, and then the constant hotel stays in addition," I demurred.[51]

And there Wagener puts his finger on the problem: the numbers do not add up. Wagener does not say whether Schwarz agreed with him on this point, but notes that Schwarz claimed he had tried to make Hitler accept a monthly allowance from NSDAP funds, but that this offer had been firmly rejected. A few days after the discussion with Schwarz, Wagener brought up the subject rather obliquely, asking Hitler about Göring's sources of income. Hitler first claimed that Göring's money came from his wife, Carin. Wagener became more insistent, asking Hitler whether it was true that Göring obtained funds from the Ruhr. In Wagener's words, Hitler replied:

"Yes, he was just telling me about that. It shows you what a position Göring has already gained among the most outstanding German businessmen that they ask his [emphasis in the original] *advice about supporting your Essen newspaper. In a way, you owe it to Göring that your newspaper got off the ground. And on that occasion, they also offered to put means at his disposal if the party requires anything."*[52]

Leaving aside what appears to be Göring's attempt to claim credit for arranging the finance for the *National-Zeitung*, it is noteworthy that Hitler refers to 'the party', rather than to Göring or to himself. Wagener does not seem to have attached any significance to this. To reinforce his point, he told Hitler straight that Göring had complained to him about losing the RM 50,000 which he felt was due to him. Pushing even harder, Wagener claims to have said:

"As I heard from Göring himself, he allows himself to be financed by the Ruhr industry. So it is a matter, not of a new offer made to him, but of an old custom. And if the party coffers – though I don't know if they do – or anyone else in the party receives money from Göring, then it is more likely to originate in those funds from the Ruhr industry than from Carin Göring's child-support payments!"

[Hitler replies.] *"And why shouldn't Göring also have received money from Ruhr industrialists? I don't ask any Gauleiter where he gets his funds, nor do I question Göring on the matter. But that his wife has access to millions, and that he* [emphasis in the original] *has the use of that money, even at a time when it is quite certain that he received nothing from the Ruhr – I know more about that."*[53]

At which point, Hitler ended the conversation. If Wagener's recollection is accurate, it implies that Hitler was happy to admit – at any rate, to Wagener – that he did not enquire too closely into Göring's sources and that he was content to believe that the money came from Carin. Note that at no time does Hitler deny receiving money from Göring. While Wagener kept on looking for evidence to discredit Göring, he seems to have abandoned further inquiries into Hitler's personal finances. However, on the afternoon of 4 February 1931, he was sitting with Hitler and others in Berlin's *Kaiserhof*, when:

Hardly had Goebbels left than Göring arrived. Rushed, as he always was, he immediately told Hitler that he had to speak to him alone briefly and would be leaving again at once. I knew what he wanted. This was always his way when he brought Hitler money – the money that ostensibly came from Carin Göring but in reality originated in the Ruhr.[54]

Unfortunately, this is opinion, rather than evidence. Even though he implies that this was a regular procedure, Wagener does not say that he saw Göring pass a fistful of notes to Hitler. Wagener continued to look for evidence that money from Big Business was flowing to Hitler and increasingly began to see this as a struggle between himself, in Munich, and Funk and Göring in Berlin:

Hitler was clearly torn between the influences of his Berlin advisers and myself. In this effort, the Berliners were in a stronger position. For they were at the same time the financial backers of financial agents for Hitler and could always mention that these sources of money would cease to flow if the revolutionary plans were stressed too strongly, and they could constantly introduce him to new people with famous names who would influence him further in this direction.[55]

Although he offers no further evidence, Wagener also believed that Himmler and Keppler were subsidised and influenced by Big Business. Some of Wagener's suspicions are partly corroborated by Funk.

Finally, Göring's income in 1940 was, apparently by his own estimate, about one million marks a year.[56] This at least provides a benchmark for Hitler's possible income.

Funk

Walther Funk was a financial journalist, rather than a businessman, but he has an important place in this narrative both for the links which he forged between Hitler and Big Business and for the fairly detailed testimony which he later gave at Nuremberg. In 1920 he was editor of the business section of the *Berliner Börsenzeitung*, one of the leading financial newspapers, and served as editor of the paper from 1922 to 1932 at a salary of RM 36,000 a year.[57] A fervent nationalist and anti-Communist, he met Hitler in 1931 and joined the NSDAP shortly afterwards. He rapidly became Hitler's economic adviser, supplanting Wagener. In March of 1933, Funk was appointed Reich Press Chief and Chairman of the Reich broadcasting company. In 1938 he supplanted Schacht as Minister of Economics, later replacing him as president of the Reichsbank and Plenipotentiary for the War Economy. In 1942 he became responsible for the notorious 'Max Heiliger' account, used by the Reichsbank to receive the assets of the victims of the extermination camps. For this and other crimes he was sentenced to life imprisonment at Nuremberg, but released on the grounds of ill health in 1957, dying in Düsseldorf on 31 May 1960.

At his Nuremberg trial, Funk freely admitted that he had been a contact between Hitler and certain industrialists and industry organisations. However, Funk claimed that it was the Ruhr businessmen who had persuaded <u>him</u> to join the NSDAP so that he could influence the party's economic policy. In his testimony, Funk named Vögler and Gustav Knepper, head of the coal mining division of the *Vereinigte Stahlwerke*, as the men who had urged him to join the NSDAP, subsequently adding Fritz Springorum to the list.

Funk claimed that contributions were passed on to Hitler – the implication is Hitler personally – by him or were given to groups within the NSDAP. He also claimed that Big Business channelled contributions to or through Göring and Strasser, and even through Röhm, which seems unlikely. This has been partly confirmed by the post-war testimony of Grauert and Heinrichsbauer.[58] Heinrichsbauer claims to have passed money from 'Ruhr industrialists' to both Funk (RM 2-3,000 a month) and Strasser (RM 10,000 a month) after early

1931. Heinrichsbauer named as the sources of the money: Ernst Brandi (*Vereinigte Stahlwerke* and the *Bergbauverein*); Herbert Kauert; Ernst Tengelmann; Fritz Springorum (*Hoesch*); and Albert Vögler (*Vereinigte Stahlwerke*). Further confirmation comes from the records of the *Ruhrlade* which show RM 2,500 paid to Funk in the summer of 1931 and RM 15,800 to Strasser between October 1931 and January 1932.[59] Not all requests met with success and Heinrichsbauer and Funk failed to obtain any funds from Big Business for the furnishing of the *Braunes Haus* in 1931 or for the setting up of an NSDAP training and indoctrination centre.

Funk also seems to have been considered a source of emergency funds. When rumours began to circulate, in late January 1931, of a possible Army coup to forestall the Nazi rise to power, Hitler made contingency plans to arm the SA. Wagener says that he suggested to Hitler that he contact Funk and seek funds from the business community, whose interests would hardly be served by a civil war.[60] Funk arranged a meeting with suitable people on 3 February 1931 at the *Kaiserhof* hotel.[61] The first two men whom Funk brought to meet Hitler were Kurt Schmitt, of the insurance company *Allianz und Stuttgarter Verein Versicherungs*, and August von Finck, chairman of the *Allianz*'s supervisory board. Certainly an insurance company would be interested in preventing civil strife, though they were to be disappointed by the wholesale destruction of *Kristallnacht* in 1938. Characteristically, Hitler subjected the two to a half-hour lecture, rather than engaging in a dialogue, but, after side discussions with Funk, they pledged RM 5 million. Hitler, according to Wagener, was astonished. Others came and went over the next few days, including August Diehn, Günther Quandt, and August Rosterg, all of whom were associated with the potash industry. Soon, RM 13 million had been promised and by the time the meetings ended, RM 25 million is said to have been pledged, though there is no confirmation of this amount which is based solely on Wagener's recollections.[62]

After he joined the NSDAP in 1931 and began to solicit full time for the Nazis, Funk set up an office in Berlin which he financed by selling subscriptions to the Nazis' fortnightly economic newsletter. Funk's line seems to have been to solicit money for himself, rather than the NSDAP, promising to distribute that money within the party where it would help to promote the interests of his patrons. No doubt some of the money stuck to Funk's fingers as it passed through his hands. Certainly his lifestyle did not deteriorate after he left the editorship of a major paper for quasi-employment by the NSDAP; there are even suggestions that it improved.[63]

It has often been assumed by the more sensationalist writers, especially those on the political left, that the chemical company IG Farben was a major contributor to the rise of the Nazis, simply because it was the largest company in Germany. There is no evidence of any *official* Farben contributions prior to 1933. There is, however, strong evidence that junior executives gave modest sums of money to Funk from their discretionary funds, particularly during 1932. Most of these were already supporters of right-wing organisations and, like junior executives everywhere, they had an eye on the main chance and could see every advantage in hitching a ride on the Nazi bandwagon.

Some time in early 1932, with the help of Thyssen, Funk arranged a meeting with Ludwig Grauert, who had earlier arranged a loan to finance the launching of the *National-Zeitung*. Funk asked Grauert for RM 100,000. Just what this was for is uncertain, though Turner implies that it was solicited on behalf of Heß, at that time still the principal manager of Hitler's personal finances.[64] There seems to have been some urgency and Grauert was unable to consult with Ernst Pönsgen, his superior at *Arbeitnordwest*, instead getting the approval of Ernst Borbet, deputy chairman of the organisation. Grauert handed over the money, which he took from a fund intended to support employers whose workers were on strike. When Pönsgen returned and learned what Grauert had done, he was furious. Gustav Krupp was equally incensed and demanded Grauert's dismissal. The situation was saved by the intervention of Thyssen, who told the *Arbeitnordwest* that he had merely asked Grauert for the loan of the money and immediately repaid the RM 100,000 in full.

All of which leads to the question: Did Thyssen's 100,000 marks go to Heß, for Hitler's personal use, or to the NSDAP? The NSDAP certainly needed money, as Goebbels' diary constantly records, and it has been estimated that the Nazis were spending RM 200,000 a week during the various election campaigns. Then there is the question of the urgency: Judging from Grauert's frantic actions, it seems that the money was needed in hours, rather than days. True, the NSDAP had a cash-flow problem, but the party was well able to raise short-term loans to cover such contingencies. There is another possibility: Hitler's first expansion of *Haus Wachenfeld*, later to become the *Berghof*, but this is only speculation.

Notes

1 TURN85b, pp. xi-xxi.
2 HANF57, p. 217.
3 An excellent description is given by Turner (TURN85b, pp. xi-xxi) on which the following brief account is based.
4 TURN85b, p. 52, citing a letter from Glaser to Reusch dated 18 April, 1921 and letters from Reusch to Glaser dated April 23, 1921 and May 8, 1921, copies in the historical archives of the *Gutehoffnungshütte*, Oberhausen, file reference 30019393/5.
5 Translation from LÜDE38, p. 701. This quotes 'the official English translation by E.T.S. Dugdale, published by Frz. Eher Nachf., Munich, 1932.' It is ironic to note that policies similar to the latter part of Point 16 with regard to small and minority businesses have since been adopted in most Western countries, most notably in the USA. Hitler was clearly ahead of his time.
6 Rosenberg, Alfred. *Wesen, Grundsätze und Zeile der Nationalsozialistischen Deutschen*

Arbeiterpartei. Munich, 1923. Though dated 1923, the pamphlet actually appeared in November of 1922.

7   TURN85b, p. 53, quoting from Roselius, *Briefe und Schriften zu Deutschlands Erneurung.* Oldenburg, 1933. The author has been unable to obtain a copy of this work but Turner is generally reliable.

8   TURN85b, pp. 83-87.

9   HEID44, p. 212.

10 TURN85b, pp. 194-5.

11 Dietrich, Otto. *Mit Hitler in die Macht.* Eher Verlag, Munich, 1934, pp. 45-6. The translation is adapted from TURN85b, p. 171.

12 Dietrich, Otto. *Zwölf Jahre mit Hitler.* Munich, 1955, p. 185. The English and US texts do not contain the 'drummer' statement.

13 TURN85b, p. 172.

14 TURN85b, pp. 172-4.

15 e.g. TURN85b, p. 215; BULL62, pp. 196-9; KERS99, pp. 358-359.

16 DIET34, p. 49. The translation is taken from TURN85b, pp. 215-6.

17 HOFF55, pp. 64-5.

18 DIET55, pp. 185-6. The translation is taken from TURN85b, p. 216. The text in the English translation (DIET57) differs slightly in details but is otherwise identical.

19 THYS41, p. 132.

20 Nuremberg Trials, Case 5, Vol. 15a, p. 4981 for Steinbrinck's testimony. Ibid, Vol. 10a, pp. 3171 ff. for Flick.

21 See e.g. Pool (POOL78, pp. 463-4) and Strasser's *Hitler and I*, p. 139. HEID44, p. 282. Higham (HIGH83) gives a dramatic account of Schröder and his activities, from which one might conclude that Schröder – rather than Hitler – was in charge of the Third Reich.

22 TURN85b, p. 262, citing pre-trial interrogations of Ilgner.

23 TURN85b, p. 25.

24 POOL78, p. 224; no source given.

25 THYS41, pp. 133-4. See Chapter 5 for Thyssen's comments about Hitler's January 1932 speech in Düsseldorf. The *Münchener Post* claimed as early as 1922 that Hitler was financed by Hugenberg, but such a claim seems far-fetched. See FRAN62, p. 187.

26 Perhaps best translated as 'The Lord in his Castle'.

27 See Chapter 5. Pool (POOL78, p. 141) quotes from an alleged letter from Frau Bruckmann to Kirdorf, but the reference given makes no mention of any such letter. Heiden (HEID44, p. 270) claims that the introduction was arranged by Otto Dietrich and his father-in-law, but there is no mention of this in Dietrich's 1957 memoir.

28 It should be noted that membership numbers bore little relationship to reality and the numbering system was revised several times. Hanfstaengl, for example, did not join the NSDAP until 1931, receiving membership number 62 or 63.

29 *Preussische Zeitung,* 3 January 1937. The extract and translation given here is from POOL78, p. 142, and may not be accurate.

30   Turner, H.A. *Hitler's Secret Pamphlet for Industrialists*, 1927. *The Journal of Modern History.* 40 (1968), pp. 348-72.

31   TURN85b, p. 91.

32   TURN85b, p. 23.

33   Statement prepared by Ilgner at Nuremberg, entitled 'Papers about various questions', dated 21 June 1945. Pre-trial interrogations of Gattineau at Nuremberg, dated 17 January 1947, 5 March 1947, and an affidavit dated 13 March 1947.

34   Kalle affidavit at Nuremberg, dated 8 September 1947.

35   TURN85b, p. 263.

36   TURN85b, pp. 263-4.

37   TURN85b, p. 369, note 21.

38   TURN85b, pp. 26-27.

39   POOL78, p. 278; no source given. Thyssen makes no mention in his memoirs. TURN85B, p. 149 and note 58, p. 403.

40   POOL78, pp. 463-5. The evidence offered is tenuous.

41   Much of the information on Stauss is taken from Turner (TURN85b) pp. 142–144 and readers are recommended to consult Turner's list of references for further details.

42   TURN85b, p. 148.

43   THYS41, p. 118.

44   HEID44, p. 270. The 'foolish duchess' is presumably a reference to the divorced Duchess Eduard von Sachsen-Anhalt; see Chapter 6.

45   THYS41, p. 131. Thyssen's memoirs give no sums.

46   FROM43, p. 145. Thyssen (THYS41) makes no mention of any such incident.

47   TURN85a, pp. ix-xxvi.

48   TURN85a, pp. 114-116.

49   TURN85a, pp. 122-123. Mosley (MOSL74, p. 231) claims that Göring was a shareholder in the *National-Zeitung* and that his shares were paid for by Thyssen.

50   TURN85a, p. 124.

51   TURN85a, p. 129.

52   TURN85a, p. 131.

53   TURN85a, pp. 131-2.

54   TURN85, p. 240.

55   TURN85a, p. 265.

56   MOSL74, p. 264. Unfortunately, Mosley gives no source for this figure.

57   SNYD76, pp. 106-7. However, Turner (TURN85b, p. 146) claims that Funk resigned his editorial post in 1930 and went to work for the NSDAP, despite not becoming a party member until June 1931.

58   Pre-trial interrogation of Grauert, 28 September 1946; US National Archives RG238. Pre-trial interrogation of Heinrichsbauer, 9 and 13 January, 20 November 1947. US National Archives RG238.

59   TURN85b, p. 149 and note 58, p. 403.

60   TURN85a, p. 236.

61   TURN85a, pp. 232, 236; TURN85b, p. 150. Turner claims that this was the first time Hitler stayed at the *Kaiserhof*, citing: Julius Karl von Engelbrechten and Hans Volz, *Wir wandern durch nationalsozialistische Berlin.* (Munich, 1937), pp. 16, 63.

However, Kershaw (KERS98, p. 338, citing Hanfstaengl, *15 Jahre*) implies that Hitler began staying there in 1930, though the Kaiserhof story does not appear in HANF57. Hitler (HITL53, p. 564, 6 July 1942) is, as usual, vague about the subject and anyway claims that he paid for the hotel suite out of his own pocket, which is probably true.

62 TURN85a, p. 238; TURN85a, p. 243.
63 TURN85b, pp. 151-152.
64 TURN85b, p. 264.

Chapter Ten

THE TANGLED WEB

Oh what a tangled web we weave,
When first we practise to deceive!
Sir Walter Scott (1771-1832)
Marmion, Canto vi. Stanza 17.

Previous chapters describe how, prior to 1933, Hitler acquired different sources of funding over time. However, time does not tell the whole story: the web of persons and organisations which supplied Hitler also existed in space, with many overlaps. This chapter, therefore, looks at how money is alleged to have flowed to Hitler from diverse sources, though not necessarily at the same time. As far as is known, no previous attempt has been made to summarise these apparently independent networks and the surprising links between them. Another purpose of this chapter is to dispel some common myths such as 'Hitler was funded by Henry Ford' or 'Hitler was funded by the Royal Dutch-Shell oil company'.

The Hitler Web

The Hitler Web is that network of individual sources and other webs which supplied Hitler with his personal funds. As Figure 10-1 shows, Hitler and the NSDAP received money from seven major webs, and, in the case of Hitler, from some 'other sources'. Each web is described in detail in this, or the previous chapters. For clarity, all funds have been shown passing directly to Hitler, but funds did pass directly to the NSDAP; this distinction is made in the diagrams for the individual webs. It is worth noting that although the *Eher Verlag* provided some money to the NSDAP, mostly for election campaigns prior to 1934, there was little or no flow of funds in the opposite direction.

The *Reichswehr* Web

The *Reichswehr*, that rump of the German armed forces permitted under the Treaty of Versailles, was the first organisation to provide Hitler with funds. However, as Chapter 3 shows, this was not just a matter of simply handing over money. Figure 10-2 shows the web through which funds were channelled from military sources to Hitler and the DAP, later the NSDAP. Those elements which appear in other webs have a shadowed outline; dotted lines represent suspected, but unproven channels; principal channels are shown as heavy lines.

Hitler began his career as a paid agent of the Army, with funds initially provided by Mayr, later by Röhm. Röhm, however, was more interested in paramilitary organisations than in politics and the flow of funds under his direction tended to be more toward the NSDAP, and through it to the SA, rather than to Hitler. Röhm also tended to provide support in the form of services, rather than in cash, and such services were of greater direct value to the NSDAP than to Hitler.

The most interesting aspect of the Reichswehr Web is the position of the German Navy. The *Thule Gesellschaft* (see Appendix 2) had its offices and held its meetings in Munich's opulent *Hotel des Vierjahreszeit*, in rooms rented from the Naval Officers Club. Consequently, relations between the Navy and the *Thule Gesellschaft* were close and several naval officers were members. One prominent member was the publisher J.F. Lehmann whose company issued many naval publications.

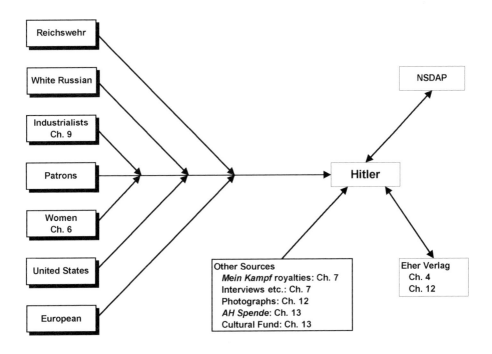

Figure 10-1: The Hitler Web

According to Sebottendorf, the German Navy channelled funds, via Lehmann and the *Thule Gesellschaft*, to Hitler and the NSDAP. Unfortunately, this allegation has not been corroborated. Neither has Sebottendorf's allegation that the Army and Navy each funded Hitler in a bid to control him, but for different, almost opposite reasons. One theory is that the Army funding, being via Bavarian elements, was an attempt to bring Hitler onto the side of the Bavarian separatist movement. The Pan-German *Thule Gesellschaft* was utterly opposed to any break-up of Germany, through Bavarian separatism or otherwise. The Navy probably did not care whether or not land-locked Bavaria separated from the rest of Germany. What the Navy probably did care about, as navies traditionally do, was keeping the Army in check. If the Army was funding and influencing Hitler, that was sufficient reason for the Navy to step in to try to gain control for itself.

Further evidence strengthens the naval connection. One of the principal

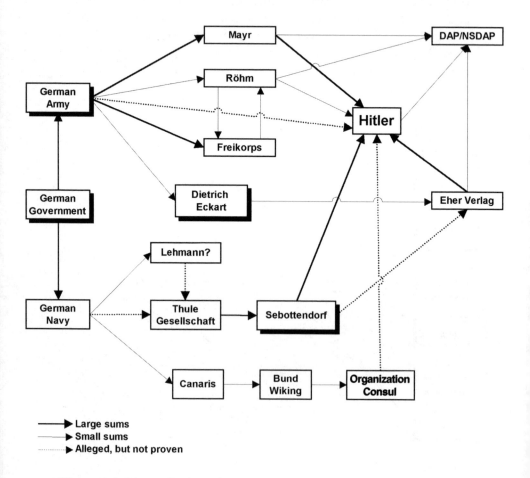

Figure 10-2: The *Reichswehr* Web

Freikorps elements involved in the abortive *Kapp Putsch* of March 1920 was the *Second Marine Brigade* under Ehrhardt, one of whose members, former Naval Lieutenant Hans Ulrich Klintzsch, was to become the first official leader of the SA in 1921. Following failure of the *Putsch*, Ehrhardt and his men, like the White Russian Biskupsky and many others, fled to Bavaria and re-formed under the name of the *Bund Wiking*. Lieutenant Commander (later Admiral) Wilhelm Canaris, then a member of naval intelligence, was instrumental in funding this organisation.[1] Ehrhardt also commanded a secret unit within the *Bund Wiking*, the *Organization Consul* which is said to have carried out assassinations and sabotage throughout Germany and to have been responsible for the murders of both Erzberger and Rathenau. According to Hanfstaengl, in the period leading up to the murders of Erzberger and Rathenau in June 1922, when Hitler was conducting a campaign against them in speeches and in the press, Hitler's office at the *Völkischer Beobachter* was guarded by men from the *Organization Consul* under the command of Klintzsch.[2] This could establish a link from Hitler, via *Organization Consul*, *Bund Wiking*, and Canaris to the naval staff, but any such link is extremely weak. For example, there is nothing significant about the bodyguard being commanded by Klintzsch; he was, after all, commander of the SA. Having men from the *Organization Consul* standing guard duty on an office might simply mean that they were considered fit only for static duty, and not for the roving mobs of the SA. Equally likely is that, as ex-soldiers, they were more used to mounting static guards – not one of the world's most fun-filled occupations – than the general SA riffraff. A further possibility, and like the others it is pure speculation, is that it is another manifestation of Hitler's policy of keeping the affairs of the *Völkischer Beobachter* – and the *Eher Verlag* – hidden from the eyes of the party. Nor is there any evidence that Canaris was funding the *Bund Wiking* at that time – 1922 – though he almost certainly did in 1920. Furthermore, if such a link existed, there is no evidence that any money flowed to Hitler or the NSDAP.

The White Russian Web

The White Russian Web supplied Hitler and the NSDAP with funds during the early nineteen-twenties. It is shown graphically in Figure 10-3; those elements which appear in other webs are again given a shadow outline.

Maximilian Erwin von Scheubner-Richter is the key to the White Russian Web, much of which was also tied to the *Thule Gesellschaft*. What the White Russians wanted was an end to Communist rule in Russia and the restoration of the monarchy. If these aims were to be achieved, they would require the support of a strong, re-armed Germany. The White Russians, therefore, would support any German political movement which was anti-Communist, for re-armament, and preferably anti-Semitic. In Hitler and the NSDAP they found a perfect match. Scheubner-Richter, though German, was well known and respected in

White Russian circles and it is not surprising that they should have heeded his recommendation to support Hitler. From Hitler's point of view, there could be no better channel for support than Scheubner-Richter; he knew everyone of any significance in right-wing circles and he was himself wealthy. He numbered many German industrialists among his contacts, such as Thyssen and Reusch, as well as Bavarian politicians such as the Catholic Cramer-Klett and Aman (not to be confused with Max Amann) of the Bavarian People's Party (BVP). As a former diplomat, he had useful contacts within the German Foreign Ministry.

An interesting, but little known figure, is Colonel Bauer, a former staff officer under Ludendorff, who later ran a private intelligence service which often handled 'deniable' jobs for the German government. Bauer is said to have discretely provided government funds to the White Russians, but it is impossible to determine whether any of this money found its way to Hitler.

General Vasili Biskupsky had been one of the youngest generals in the Russian Army and had commanded the Third Corps in Odessa, in the Ukraine. After the collapse of the White forces in the Ukraine, he fled to Berlin where he became friendly with General Max Hoffmann and through him with Sir Henri Deterding, chairman of Royal Dutch Shell. As Williams succinctly puts it:

> . . . undoubtedly one of the most disliked men of the Russian emigration. Biskupsky . . . arrived in Berlin in early 1919 where he quickly became embroiled with Colonel Vyrgolich against Avlov, with the British against the Germans, and with the Germans for money.[3]

Another friend of Biskupsky and Hoffmann from the Ukrainian adventure was Pavel Skoropadsky, himself linked to Otto Meissner, who was also briefly present in the Ukraine. Skoropadsky busied himself with trying to gain possession of some 400 million *marks* which was held by the Reichsbank on behalf of the Ukrainian government, without success. Biskupsky was involved in the 1920 *Kapp Putsch* – it is known that he received funds from both Kapp and Colonel Bauer – and had to flee Berlin, along with Skoropadsky and others, finding refuge in Munich, where he soon came into contact with Scheubner-Richter.[4] The latter introduced Biskupsky to Hitler and the two are said to have become friendly. Lang and von Schenck, in their commentary to Rosenberg's memoirs, claim:

> The most consistent financial assistance, however, was given the party by the White Russians, who wanted at any cost to have an outlet for their anti-Soviet propaganda. Thus, General Biskupsi [sic] became one of the principal financiers of the V.B. [Völkischer Beobachter] which, in return, published in each issue column after column of vituperations by White Russian authors.[5]

Biskupsky was certainly involved in financing the *Völkischer Beobachter* before Hitler took it over, but there is no evidence that his support continued after.

At this time, an argument was festering amongst the Russian émigrés as to who was the rightful heir to the Russian throne – Grand Duke Kyrill Vladimirovich or Grand Duke Nikolai. The details of this dispute are not relevant to this story, but the fact that Biskupsky pledged his support to Kyrill and was rewarded with the post of 'Prime Minister' most certainly is. In 1922, Kyrill, who was not a particularly forceful character, settled in Coburg, Germany, with his wife Grand Duchess Victoria, who was his divorced cousin and who more than made up for the strength of character that Kyrill lacked. At Coburg, where Victoria's family had its estates, they lived in seclusion when Kyrill was not acting the playboy.[6] It is said that Victoria collected for the NSDAP and that she and Mathilde, the wife

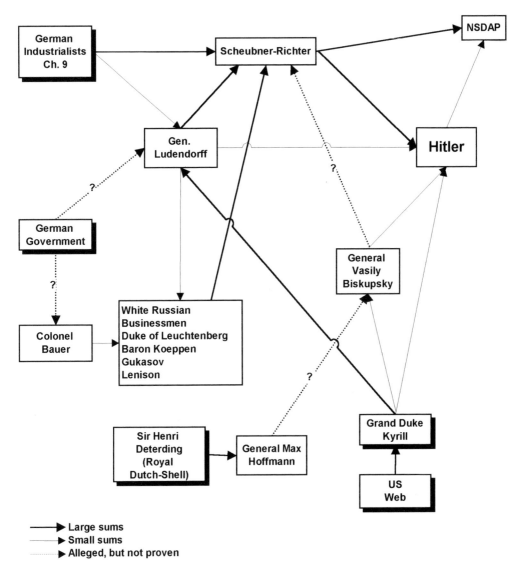

Figure 10-3: The White Russian Web

171

of Scheubner-Richter, used to watch the SA on parade in Munich. It is also said that, like many other women, she contributed jewellery to the Nazi cause. It is also possible that Grand Duke Kyrill received funding from Henry Ford, as described below in The US Web. What is known is that Kyrill, and other White Russians, were receiving support from the American YMCA in Berlin, the German government, and the American Aid Committee of Count Musin-Pushkin, which was largely financed by Princess Cantacuza-Grant in the USA – herself a relative of Elsa Bruckmann (see Patrons, below and Chapter 6.).[7]

Kyrill and Victoria did give money, if not to Hitler then to Ludendorff and possibly to Scheubner-Richter, and if they had no money to spare then the inference is that they passed on someone else's money.[8] Evidence for this comes in 1939 when General Biskupsky wrote to Arno Schickedanz, asking for the return of nearly half a million gold marks which he claimed Grand Duke Kyrill and his wife had given to Ludendorff in 1922-23.[9] Schickedanz was a Balt and an old and close friend of both Rosenberg and Scheubner-Richter; he was also close to Lüdecke, who describes him and his activities in some detail.[10] Biskupsky was unsuccessful in his claim. Could this have been money supplied by Ford? The evidence is minuscule, but the suspicion remains.

The Patrons Web

The Patrons have three distinguishing characteristics: They gave small or medium amounts of money; they gave that money mainly to Hitler; and they gave in their own name. The distinctions are fine ones, and there is necessarily some overlap between Big Business and Patrons. It should be noted that some Patrons were industrialists in the sense of being factory owners, but their donations were as individuals, rather than in the names of their various concerns. The Patrons and their contributions are summarised below, in alphabetical order.

Aristocracy

Many of the German aristocracy supported Hitler and the NSDAP whom they saw as both anti-Communist and in favour of the eventual restoration of some form of constitutional monarchy. While a few aristocrats such as Schaumburg-Lippe and Sachsen-Anhalt seem to have made significant contributions, either to Hitler or to the NSDAP, information on most is scanty.

Many of the Hohenzollern family, having renounced their claims to the throne, remained in Germany and several supported the Nazis in the hope that they might eventually restore the monarchy. Most prominent among these was the Kaiser's heir, Crown Prince August Wilhelm, popularly known as Auwi. While he certainly gave much moral support, including articles praising Hitler and the NSDAP in the foreign press, his financial contributions seem to have been small.

After the Nazis came to power in 1933, he is said to have been rewarded with a substantial annual allowance.

Otto Dietrich, in his post-war memoirs, both supports and contradicts these allegations. According to Dietrich, Hitler stated several times in 1932 that he intended to restore the Hohenzollern monarchy, making August Wilhelm's son Alexander the successor to Kaiser Wilhelm II. This, of course, never happened and Dietrich goes on to say:

> *After he came to power in 1933 he never mentioned the matter again. Thereafter his relationship with Prince August Wilhelm cooled, in fact became distinctly unfriendly. . . . He began making more and more spiteful remarks against the prince and the nobility as soon as he felt sure of the power he now held. Earlier he had not disdained the help of such people; as soon as he felt that he had won the peoples' favor, he grew cold toward the nobility.*[11]

If Hitler was as hostile as Dietrich portrays him, it seems surprising that he would have granted an allowance to the prince.

Among the minor aristocrats said to have given financial support are Prince Ratibor-Corvey, a wealthy Silesian land-owner who was said to be 'one of the best paying members of the party'.[12] Just what he gave, when, and to whom remains unknown. The Grand Duke of Hesse is said to have contributed to the NSDAP and most of his family were party members. The Duke of Coburg, an early supporter, joined the SA and gave financial support, probably to the latter rather than to the NSDAP, as this seems to have been the custom with SA members. Prince Friedrich Christian Fürst zu Schaumburg-Lippe, a young aristocrat and one of the first of the hereditary nobility to join the Nazis, presented himself in post-war interviews as a 'regular donor' to the NSDAP.[13] As recorded in Chapter 6, Hitler received RM 1,500 a month from the divorced Duchess of Sachsen-Anhalt – probably the only regular contribution he received from the aristocracy.

Aust & Kuhlo

Hermann Aust, the elderly chief executive of a Munich company which made a popular malt-coffee drink, first heard Hitler speak at the National Club, Berlin, in May of 1922 and invited Hitler to speak to the League of Bavarian Industrialists, of which he was chairman, at their Munich headquarters. Surprisingly, this was one of Hitler's first – if not the first – contacts with Bavarian industrialists. This quickly led to an invitation to address a meeting at Munich's exclusive *Herrenklub* and this was followed by a much larger meeting at the Merchants' Guild. In his testimony at Hitler's trial after the November *Putsch*, Aust described how, after the Merchants' Guild meeting, many of those present gave him small amounts of money, which he passed on to Hitler.[14] Dr. Kuhlo, director of the Association of Bavarian Industrialists and possibly Aust's son-in-law, was also present and was also accused of financing Hitler.[15] Certainly, as noted in Chapter 3, he was a Nazi sympathiser.

Bechstein

As patrons, Edwin Bechstein and his wife Hélène must be considered as a unit. Edwin, although he gave money to both Hitler and to the NSDAP, only came into contact with Hitler as a result of Hélène's interest in him.

Hitler first met the Bechsteins in Berlin, on a trip in 1921, and for a time their Berlin home was Hitler's *pied-à-terre* in the capital. Apart from gifts and the pledging of Frau Bechstein's jewellery against the loan from Frank (see below and Chapter 6), just what the Bechsteins contributed to Hitler is uncertain. It also seems that their financial aid did not last long, since by 1923 they were pleading poverty. At Hitler's 1924 trial, Frau Bechstein testified that Edwin had often given Hitler money to support the *Völkischer Beobachter*, but everyone claimed that.[16] Indeed, one is tempted to wonder whether Hitler did not use financial crises at the *Völkischer Beobachter* as an excuse to fill his own pockets. It would not have been out of character.

The only sum given by the Bechsteins for which there is documentary evidence relates for a bank loan of RM 45,000 which Hitler took from the Munich branch of the *Deutsche Hansabank* in 1924 and for which Edwin acted as guarantor.[17] By 1926 Bechstein was in trouble. Concerned by press reports of the close relationship which the Bechsteins enjoyed with Hitler, and that these would damage the company's sales, the Bechstein company formally expelled Edwin from its board. The Bechsteins income was now greatly reduced.

Borsig

Ernst von Borsig was head of the Berlin-based family business which had once been famous for its locomotives and heavy machinery, but whose fortunes were in decline by the early nineteen-twenties. When Hitler first spoke at Berlin's National Club in 1921, Borsig sent his private secretary along to observe and report. Favourably impressed, Borsig personally attended Hitler's second speech and subsequently arranged for a private meeting with Hitler, at which he asked what he could do to assist him and the NSDAP. Not surprisingly, Hitler wanted money. Borsig agreed, but wanted Hitler to open a branch headquarters in Berlin and to raise money for this, he enlisted the help of Karl Burhenne, a *Siemens und Halske* employee and a friend of Gansser.[18] Burhenne met Hitler, became converted, and joined Borsig in his fund-raising drive. They met with little success and Hitler was not to be represented in Berlin until 1925.

As with Bechstein, once rumours circulated in the press concerning his relations with Hitler, Borsig found himself in trouble. Fearful lest his already ailing company lose vital government contracts, Borsig issued a press statement admitting that he had met Hitler prior to 1924, but denying any subsequent contact. He also denied reports of his giving money to Hitler, but the denial was worded in such a way as to make it uncertain whether he was referring to pre-1924 or to the immediate past.

Did Borsig contribute to Hitler's personal needs? Probably not – or, at least, not deliberately – for he seems to have been a man more interested in causes and in groups, rather than in individuals. Nor was it likely that any contribution was large; Borsig's company was in financial difficulties and he habitually spread his contributions widely, and consequently thinly.

Bruckmann

Like the Bechsteins, Hugo and Elsa Bruckmann must be considered together. One of a well-known Munich family of publishers, Hugo Bruckmann set up his own company in 1917, but was forced to return to the family firm in 1930. Like Bechstein, he was relatively well-off compared to Hitler, but far from rich and the amounts of ready cash at his disposal were limited. While Bruckmann certainly gave small amounts to Hitler throughout the nineteen-twenties, the only detailed allegation is that Bruckmann guaranteed the rental payments on Hitler's Munich apartment.[19] Hitler rented this apartment from September 1929 until December 1938, when he bought the building outright. There have been allegations that Kirdorf paid for the apartment, but this cannot be substantiated.

Other than widening Hitler's social circle, perhaps the area where Hugo Bruckmann was of most benefit to the NSDAP, and so indirectly to Hitler, was through the *Kampfbund für Deutsche Kultur* (Activist Association for German Culture) which was founded in 1927 to combat 'alien' (i.e. Jewish) influences. The *Kampfbund* became a fertile recruiting ground for intellectuals to the NSDAP. Some insight into Bruckmann's financial affairs is given by correspondence which he had with Rosenberg, regretting his inability to put the *Kampfbund* on a firmer financial footing.[20]

Eckart, Dietrich

Although Dietrich Eckart was a prominent member of the NSDAP, he must also be numbered amongst one of its, and Hitler's, patrons. Though a somewhat bohemian drunk, Eckart was a successful journalist, poet and translator; his translation of *Peer Gynt* brought him substantial royalties and remains highly regarded. Eckart frequently subsidised Hitler and the party. Equally important, he had a wide circle of wealthy contacts in the far right community. It was to Eckart that Hitler turned to obtain the funds to buy the *Eher Verlag* in December of 1920. Of Eckart's contributions, Hitler later said:

The party was financed almost exclusively by my meetings. The membership dues stood in no relation to the money brought in by my speeches. To be sure, the party did have one big backer at that time; our unforgettable Dietrich Eckart. [21]

Eckart, Simon

Simon Eckart (no relation to Dietrich, with whom he is occasionally confused) was a farmer in Lower Bavaria. Wealthy to begin with, he married the equally wealthy daughter of a local brewer.[22] In 1920-1921, he guaranteed a loan which enabled the *Eher Verlag* to pay off the outstanding sum of RM 30,000 to the remaining original shareholders, Bierbaumer and Kunze. As far as has been established, this was the only time that he gave any financial assistance to Hitler or to the NSDAP.

Frank

Richard Frank was a Berlin coffee merchant who also sold a coffee substitute made from grain. This latter was often known by the nickname *Kornfrank* and may have given rise to Hitler's mistaken belief that Frank was a corn merchant. In September of 1923, using jewellery lent by Frau Bechstein as surety, Hitler was able to borrow 60,000 Swiss Francs from Frank. Just what use was made of this very large sum is not known, but Hitler implied that it was to tide over the *Völkischer Beobachter* during yet another financial crisis.

Gansser

Emil Gansser was a rather eccentric chemist and inventor who worked for the *Siemens und Halske* company until about 1919. After leaving *Siemens*, he became involved in rightist politics – especially anti-Catholic ones – and was a member of Berlin's National Club, where he introduced Hitler. Gansser also introduced Hitler to Admiral Schröder, former commander of the German marines, who was one of the first high-ranking officers to join the NSDAP and who had links to the *Thule Gesellschaft*. Gansser seems to have served as a source of emergency funds, particularly for the *Völkischer Beobachter* in its early days. For example, Eckart telegraphed Gansser on 28 November 1921 begging for money to keep the paper afloat.[23] Hitler again met Gansser in 1923 on a fund-raising expedition to Berlin, accompanied by Hanfstaengl. Partly for reasons of secrecy, partly as a result of Gansser's general eccentricity, they toured Berlin in a battered delivery van, with Hitler and Hanfstaengl squatting in the back. Hanfstaengl doubted whether the trip was financially successful, but, as described in Chapter 4, Hitler expressed gratitude for Gansser's financial support to the *Völkischer Beobachter*, so some money must have been forthcoming.

Gansser also introduced Hitler to *Justizrat* Claß and Dr. Burhenne, a director of Siemens, both of whom are said to have provided funds, though to what extent is unknown.[24] However, Gansser's fundraising, especially from Switzerland, was substantial and well documented, as described below under the European Web.

Grandel

Dr. Gottfried Grandel, an industrial chemist by training, was a spice merchant and manufacturer of cooking oil, based in Augsburg, Bavaria and a noted anti-Semite. He was one of the backers of Eckart's anti-Semitic weekly newspaper *Auf gut Deutsch* (In plain German), and in the early nineteen-twenties he either gave or loaned – possibly both – money to support the NSDAP. According to Kershaw, he paid for Eckart's and Hitler's flight to Berlin at the time of the *Kapp Putsch*.[25] In 1920-21, he was the co-guarantor, with Simon Eckart, of the RM 30,000 loan made to the *Eher Verlag* to pay off Bierbaumer and Kunze. In 1940, Grandel sued the *Eher Verlag* for the return of that guarantee, but there are suggestions that the loan was not repaid and Grandel had to make good the amount.[26]

Minor Contributors

Hanfstaengl's occasional financial support for Hitler is described in the early chapters of this book and his part in the purchase of the rotary press in Chapter 4. Similarly, Lüdecke's contributions are detailed in Chapter 8. There were also other minor contributors. Franz-Willing provides an extensive list of those alleged – mainly by the *Münchener Post* and the *Bayerische Kurier* – to have financed Hitler and the NSDAP.[27]

The United States Web

Concerning the United States Web – where it existed at all – there is much speculation and only a little documentary evidence. As noted in Chapter 5, in 1925 the *Teutonia Society* sent Hitler a cash gift for his birthday. It is unlikely to have been large, since *Teutonia*'s membership consisted mainly of manual workers.[28] In the case of *Teutonia*, there is evidence of contributions to the NSDAP (rather than to Hitler) up to 1932 and a contribution of 500 marks went towards the expenses of SA attending the *Parteitag* in 1929.[29] It is doubtful whether birthday gifts to Hitler could have been much larger.

Many such German clubs existed throughout the USA in the early twentieth century and their background, which has been well documented by Diamond, need not be repeated here.[30] What may be significant is that these clubs began life with close connections to German industry, notably Krupp, I.G. Farben and the Hamburg-Amerika shipping line.[31] However, as late as 1935, the clubs were receiving support from Germany, rather than providing funds to Hitler and the NSDAP.[32] 'Steel' alleges that a fundraising and espionage campaign run by Hjalmar Schacht raised 'almost a million dollars' for Hitler, but offers no concrete evidence.[33]

Since the beginnings of Hitler's rise to power there have been constant allegations that Hitler and the NSDAP were funded by Henry Ford. Although other writers have pointed out the lack of evidence for such claims, the allegations need to be examined in detail.[34] In 1918, convinced that the First World War had been orchestrated by 'Jewish bankers', Ford purchased a provincial newspaper, *The Dearborn Independent*, and turned it into a vehicle for his political views. The blatantly anti-Semitic journal did not sell well in America and many public libraries refused to carry it. Articles from the newspaper were collected into a four-volume set entitled *The International Jew*, published between 1920 and 1922. It was quickly translated into at least sixteen languages, including German under the title *The Eternal Jew*, a process which Ford expedited by giving away the copyright. The books had a great influence on Hitler and later on his own work, *Mein Kampf*, in which he refers to Henry Ford. Indeed, there are some who assert that Hitler plagiarised several passages from the German translation. Hanfstaengl writes that Ford was the only American figure Hitler had any time for, but makes no mention of any funding.[35] Heiden, in his 1938 biography of Hitler, wrote that Ford's funding of Hitler *has never been disputed*,[36] to which one must reply, "It has now". As noted in Chapter 5, Heiden claimed in his 1944 biography that there was evidence of Hitler receiving funds from Ford. Such concrete evidence has never been forthcoming, and *if* Henry Ford ever provided anything to Hitler and the NSDAP, such a flow of funds was long over by 1930.[37]

Upton Sinclair, better known as a novelist, wrote an historical biography of Henry Ford in which he asserted that the NSDAP received $40,000 to reprint German translations of Ford's anti-Semitic tracts and a further $300,000 was channelled 'to Hitler' (more probably to the NSDAP) through a grandson of the former Kaiser.[38]

Others who, in the nineteen-twenties, sought to draw attention to Ford's financing of Nazism included newspapers such as the *Manchester Guardian*, the *New York Times*, and the *Berliner Tageblatt*, and even a US Ambassador to Germany, William E. Dodd. Even in the nineteen-eighties, one author claimed, without providing any supporting evidence, that Ford sent Hitler RM 50,000 every year on his birthday.[39] According to Pool:

> Throughout the 1920s there were numerous leaks of information about Ford's financing of Hitler, but since then they have been suppressed and forgotten. [40]

Forgotten, maybe, but suppressed? By whom? By Ford? Certainly neither Ford nor Hitler would have wanted it widely known if Ford were providing funds to

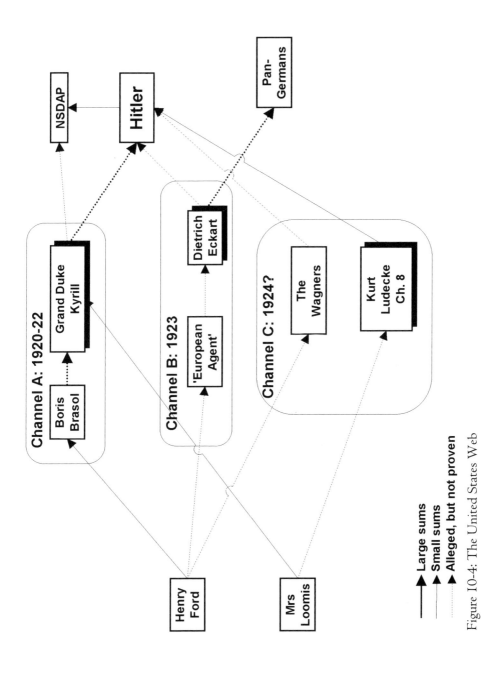

Figure 10-4: The United States Web

the NSDAP, or even to Hitler himself. Ford would have attracted the attention of the US State Department, which would not have been happy about a US national interfering in foreign politics. Indeed, it is surprising that his activities did not come to the State Department's notice; perhaps they did. Hitler had more to lose. Nothing would have been more damaging to Hitler's reputation as an independent politician than to have it revealed that he was in the pay of a foreign industrialist, one who represented the very epitome of capitalism. The natural consequence of this is that both men would have taken pains to ensure that any links between them were obscured, though neither refrained from expressing admiration for the other. It is also evident that if Ford did provide finance to Hitler, he did so over a number of years and through several different channels. These can conveniently be called, with great originality, Channel A (1920-22), Channel B (1923), and Channel C (1924-?). It is noteworthy that these channels form a chronological sequence, with little overlap in time.

Channel A: 1920-22

The first possible channel for funding was supplied by the White Russians, in particular by Boris Brasol and Count Cherep-Spiridovic. Brasol had a colourful career as a Tsarist agent, a US Government agent, a fanatical anti-Semite, and a bag-man between the Russian émigré communities in Europe and the USA. In 1920 he was hired as a consultant to Ford's paper, *The Dearborn Independent*. Cherep-Spiridovic also worked for the paper, selling subscriptions. One writer who investigated Ford, Brasol, and Cherep-Spiridovic was Norman Hapgood, later US ambassador to Denmark, who wrote a series of articles on the subject in the Hearst press, ironically an organisation sympathetic to Hitler's views.[41] In his articles, Hapgood claimed to have documentary proof that Brasol had received funds from Ford, though the precise nature of this 'proof' is not revealed. Hapgood's assertions are far from sufficient to establish a connection between Ford and Hitler, but they do suggest one to the White Russians: Brasol was the US representative of Grand Duke Kyrill – see The White Russian Web, above.

Channel B: 1923

The second possible channel for Ford's money is so direct and so obvious that it lacks credibility. In 1924, Erhard Auer, vice-president of the Bavarian parliament, sent a report to Reich President Ebert in connection with Hitler's trial, which reads, in part:

> *The Bavarian Diet has long had information that the Hitler movement was partly financed by an American anti-Semitic leader, Henry Ford. Mr Ford's interest in the Bavarian anti-Semitic movement*

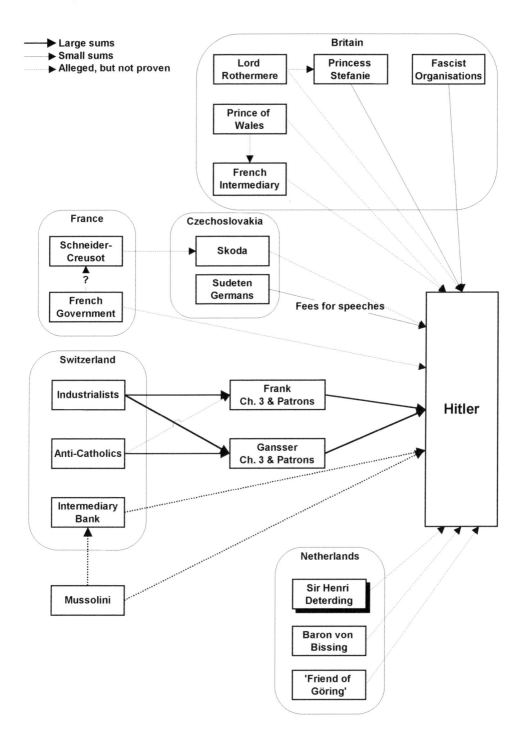

Figure 10-5: The European Web

began a year ago [i.e. in 1923] *when one of Mr. Ford's agents, seeking to sell tractors, came in contact with Diedrich Eichart the notorious Pan-German. Shortly after, Herr Eichart asked Mr. Ford's agent for financial aid. The agent returned to America and immediately Mr. Ford's money began coming to Munich. Herr Hitler openly boasts of Mr. Ford's support and praises Mr. Ford as a great individualist and a great anti-Semite.*[42]

It is generally assumed that 'Diedrich Eichart' is a misprint for Dietrich Eckart, something which seems unlikely, as Auer would certainly have been aware of Eckart and his activities. If it is, then why was Ford's agent trying to sell tractors to or with the help of Eckart, a drunken café-intellectual, with no known connection to farming? If it is indeed Eckart, then this suggests that the agent had no intention of selling tractors (in this instance) but was rather contacting Eckart for political reasons.

A second possibility is that the identities of Dietrich Eckart, the writer, and Simon Eckart, the farmer (see above under *Patrons*) somehow became confused. Certainly it would make more sense to approach a wealthy farmer with banking connections when attempting to sell tractors and Simon Eckart certainly had rightist leanings, but he was relatively unknown and it is stretching things to describe him as a 'notorious pan-German'.

The third possibility is that there really was a Diedrich Eichart, perhaps a farmer or agricultural equipment dealer, who was innocently contacted by Ford's agent in the course of his business and later confused by the Bavarian authorities with Dietrich Eckart. It would not be at all unreasonable for 'Eichart' – if he existed – to ask Ford for financial assistance in setting up a dealership. Extensive enquiries have so far failed to identify a credible candidate bearing this name.

However, some credibility to the idea that some of the Ford Company's European funds were channelled to Hitler is given by Ford's alleged remarks to Winifred Wagner, reported below.

Channel C: 1924-?

The third channel postulated for Ford funds runs through the Wagner family. On 28 January 1924, Siegfried and Winifred Wagner, son and daughter-in-law of the famous composer, arrived in New York on a mission to raise $200,000 with which to re-open the annual Wagner festival at the *Festspielhaus* in Bayreuth, Germany. Siegfried was booked on a tour of concert halls in major cities, where he would conduct his father's music; Winifred, who managed Siegfried's business affairs, was booked for a lecture tour of exclusive ladies' clubs. They were accompanied by Lüdecke.[43] This is not quite as surprising as it seems: Siegfried, like his father Richard, was an anti-Semitic German nationalist. The Wagners had been introduced to Hitler in 1920 or 1921 at the Bechsteins and he was thereafter a frequent guest at their home, *Haus Wahnfried*, in Bayreuth.

Lüdecke claims that he and the Wagners plotted how they could get to Henry Ford with the dual objective of raising funds for both the Bayreuth festival and for Hitler and the NSDAP.[44] They travelled to Detroit, arriving on 30 January, and checked into the Statler Hotel, where they found an invitation from Ford already awaiting them. The following day the Wagners travelled to the Ford estate outside Detroit; hardly surprisingly, the unknown Lüdecke was not included in the invitation. The meeting appears to have been a success and after dinner Winifred began to steer the conversation around to the question of finance for Hitler and the NSDAP. According to Pool, Ford forestalled her; he had, he said, already financed Hitler through the sale of vehicles exported to Germany.[45] If so, this would be consistent with the timing for Channel B, above. Winifred suggested that Hitler was now even more in need of finance and proposed that Ford meet with Lüdecke; Ford agreed and a meeting was arranged for the following day, 1 February.

Lüdecke and Ford talked for hours and found themselves in agreement on most matters but, according to Lüdecke, no financial support was forthcoming. Surprisingly, Lüdecke's account of his meeting with Ford makes no mention of the fact that Winifred Wagner had discussed finance for Hitler the previous day, nor does Ford ever rebuff Lüdecke with the claim that he had already financed Hitler. This tends to count against Pool's account. Lüdecke summarises the affair rather neatly:

Ford was deeply interested in what I had to tell, but he was not at all interested in what I had to ask.[46]

Lüdecke even tried bribery:

Diplomatically I conveyed that whoever helped us now would not fare badly from a business stand-point. If Ford lent us his concrete support — which was all we needed to grasp control of Germany — a binding agreement could be arranged whereby large concessions would be guaranteed there, and possibly elsewhere, from the moment of Hitler's rise to power.[47]

When bribery failed, Lüdecke became more direct:

He became immediately very wary when I pressed toward my goal with frank requests for money. The more I mentioned the word, the more Henry Ford cooled down from idealist to business man . . . at last, with utter finality, he said: "Well, that you talk over with Cameron."[48]

Cameron, whom Lüdecke had met in 1921, being the editor of the *Dearborn Independent*, Ford's anti-Semitic newspaper. Knowing that Cameron had little influence over Ford and was not himself in a position to dispense funds, Lüdecke wrote:

Ended was the pipe-dream of hurrying back to Munich with the promise of a million-dollar loan. Ended was the vision of Hitler's happy face when he heard the good news, ended my project of diverting a tithe of the sum to organize a foreign political bureau for the Party, with myself in charge.
. . . What a resounding syllable is a rich man's No![49]

The European Web

The European Web comprises Hitler's European sources of funding outside Germany. No evidence of any significant contributions prior to 1930 has been found from Belgium, Bulgaria, Denmark, Greece, Ireland, Liechtenstein, Norway, Portugal, Romania, Russia, Sweden, Turkey, Ukraine, or Yugoslavia. That does not, of course, mean that none existed. There is no evidence of any direct contributions from the Baltic States (Estonia, Latvia, or Lithuania), though several prominent Nazis, such as Rosenberg and Scheubner-Richter, were Balts by origin and Frau von Seidlitz certainly had connections to the region. Kurt Lüdecke, while his activities in Europe on behalf of Hitler attracted much attention, was largely ineffective; his activities are described in Chapter 8.

There is little hard evidence that Hitler or the NSDAP received any significant support from Britain, except possibly small sums from the British Union of Fascists (BUF) and small gifts from admirers, such as Unity Mitford. Indeed, they had little to give and the British Fascists (predecessor of the BUF), when formally wound up in 1935 following the death of its founder Miss Rotha Linton-Orman, had assets of £20 and debts of £1,706.[50] There is scant evidence of any attempts to solicit British contributions prior to the early nineteen-thirties and such evidence as there is suggests that the flow of money was in the opposite direction:

> There is no evidence that Hitler supported Mosley financially, though it seems highly likely, especially given his attachment to the Mitford girls. Some historians claim that Hitler funded the BU via a French banker named Armand Gregoire, who was later banker to Wallis Simpson.[51]

Cross, in his study of Fascism in Britain, produces strong evidence that the BUF received funds from Mussolini, but no evidence of funds flowing to or from Germany.[52] However, although Britons gave little in the way of money, some — especially anti-Semites — gave significant moral support. In 1924, Lüdecke visited Britain, where he met a few anti-Semitic cranks and came away empty handed. Lüdecke's words summarise the situation:

> In London, as in New York and Washington, all my interviews were sterile. The motto of the men who received me was 'My time is your time' — but time wasn't money.[53]

More effective than Lüdecke — probably because he did not come to Britain until the early nineteen-thirties, when Hitler and his policies were better known — was Dr. H. Thost, London correspondent for the *Völkischer Beobachter*.[54] The energetic Thost did much important work for the NSDAP as what today would be called an 'agent of influence'. He searched newspapers and magazines for articles by or references to persons who appeared to be sympathetic to Germany in general and Hitler's policies in particular. Once identified, he cultivated such people and, if they did turn out to be sympathetic to Hitler's aims, encouraged them to visit Germany and ensured that any such visits went smoothly. One area where Thost was particularly active was amongst the Baltic German exiles in Britain. Among these was Baron Wilhelm de Ropp, who had taken British citizenship around 1910 and fought in the British Army during the First World War. After the War, he worked as a freelance journalist and contributed articles from Berlin to *The Times*. Unknown to Thost, de Ropp had connections to British Intelligence through Major F.W. Winterbotham, then head of Air Intelligence and later to play a key role in *Ultra*.[55] In 1931, Winterbotham invited Rosenberg, who was relatively unknown in Britain, to London and de Ropp facilitated the meeting. Lüdecke was sceptical of Rosenberg's chances:

> *Rosenberg didn't understand English mentality. If you wanted to impress an Englishman to the extent of getting anything out of him, you had to show him a good fist and the prospect of a kick in the groin.*[56]

Presumably Lüdecke's opinions were the result of his 1924 experiences – or maybe the cause of them. Between them, Winterbotham and de Ropp introduced Rosenberg to several influential people, including Geoffrey Dawson, editor of *The Times*, and Montagu Norman, Governor of the Bank of England. Norman was pro-German, anti-French, and anti-Semitic, but there is no evidence that he was pro-Nazi. He was, however, on very friendly terms with Hjalmar Schacht and the two often met privately up to the outbreak of the Second World War. Norman was involved on many occasions with arranging loans to the German government. This is hardly surprising; it was, after all, part of his job, as it was for his colleagues in other countries, and the financial support of Germany was of concern to the British economy regardless of what government was in power. The question is: Did Norman arrange financing for Hitler or the NSDAP prior to 1933? The answer seems to be that he did, though only indirectly. Like any other political party, the NSDAP took out loans and the banks which granted those loans naturally took pains to ensure that such loans would be repaid. For a political party, questions of repayment are tied to its political prospects; will it keep its present membership and will that membership increase as predicted? One of many possible scenarios which worried the bankers was the possibility that, if Hitler and the NSDAP came to power, Britain might impose financial sanctions against Germany. Norman assured the bankers that this was unlikely; a moderately strong German economy was in Britain's interests. Whether such advice was ever given regarding personal loans to Hitler is not known; it seems unlikely.

It has been alleged that the British newspaper owner Lord Rothermere provided financial support to Hitler via Hanfstaengl, but Hanfstaengl himself makes no mention of this and the evidence is slender.[57] That Lord Rothermere was pro-Nazi and anti-Communist is without a doubt and he certainly ensured that the *Daily Mail*, his flagship publication, took a pro-Hitler line and Hitler favoured Rothermere's journalists when granting interviews and even contributed articles to the *Mail*. However, most of this took place after 1930, when Hitler had less need of financial aid from foreign sources. After 1934, even Rothermere's newspapers ceased their pro-Hitler line, possibly under pressure from Jewish advertisers.

Another who is alleged to have given financial support is the Prince of Wales, briefly King Edward VIII and, after his abdication, the Duke of Windsor. He was a man of pro-German sympathies but, despite visits to Germany and contacts with several shady characters close to Hitler, there is no evidence whatsoever of financial support from him and any gifts that were given, in whatever position he held, were given within the strict guidelines of diplomatic protocol.

In conclusion, it seems unlikely that Hitler received any support from Britain, except, perhaps, for the occasional gift from a fanatical admirer; a hand-knitted scarf with a swastika motif or a grubby ten shilling note enclosed in a tawdry birthday card.

There is some evidence that France provided indirect funding to the NSDAP, though there is nothing to suggest that Hitler gained personally from such funds. What little evidence there is, is weakened by French government policy at the time. France supported the idea of Bavarian separatism; a divided Germany would be a weakened Germany, and very much in France's interests. Hitler, however, was very much opposed to the Bavarian separatist movement and did all that he could to frustrate it. One must then ask: Why would the French government fund the NSDAP and its leader whose aims ran counter to those of France? Bracher suggests that it was out of gratitude for Hitler's decision not to actively oppose the French occupation of the Rheinland.[58] However, it is difficult to believe that Hitler allowed himself to be bought off by the French. To have done so would have left him open to blackmail. In 1920, a German magazine published 'documentary proof' of such funding, but the evidence connecting this to Hitler is slim.[59]

Allegations that he had received French money continued to dog Hitler, though never with any proof, and he won several libel actions against newspapers who published such allegations, including the Social-Democrat newspaper *Vorwarts* and Stephan Großmann, publisher of the Berlin magazine *Tagebuch der Zeit*. (It must be remembered that at that time left-wing newspapers such as *Vorwarts*, the *Münchener Post* and the *Bayerisches Wochenblatt* accused everyone, from the Bavarian government downwards, of being in the pay of the French; so did the NSDAP.[60]) Heiden offers something more specific, quoting a conversation alleged to have taken place between a British Member of Parliament, E.D. Morel, and von Kahr, in which Morel said he had been told by 'highly-placed Paris friends' that Hitler was receiving French money. Kahr, knowing Hitler to be against the separatist movement, is said to have refused to believe the allegation.[61] This is double hearsay. The Bavarian legation in Berlin had a subtly different story:

> In the light of various evidence, it seems probable that the Kampfbund has received money from France. The English Labour leader Morel asserted this during his latest visit to Munich and said he was convinced that the source of the money was not unknown to the recipient.[62]

186

The *Kampfbund* was very much in favour of Bavarian separatism. Lang and von Schenck, the editors of Rosenberg's memoirs, allege that the NSDAP received French money:

> From France, too, the NSDAP seems to have been getting money at that time. Again and again the name of a certain Colonel Richard pops up, a man who had once assisted the Bavarian separatists and who eventually got in touch with the Nazis.[63]

Lüdecke had ties to France – he had made his first fortune there – but his ready access to French currency brought him nothing but trouble. Even there, his 'important contacts' were mainly impoverished French anti-Semites and marginally less impoverished White Russian exiles. Lüdecke made two trips to France in 1924, but the only result was that Lüdecke – the alleged French *espion* – was arrested and interrogated by the *Sûreté*.[64]

'Steel' claims that, in February of 1932, Paul Faure, speaking in the *Chambre des Députés* (parliament), accused the French armaments company Schneider-Creusot of financing Hitler through Skoda, its Czech 'subsidiary'.[65]

As far as Hitler was concerned, Italy meant Mussolini and the Italian Fascist party and there are no records of any financial or other contacts with any other persons, except in the case of artworks, as described in Chapter 15. Nor does it seem as if Hitler ever considered Mussolini as a source of personal finance, but restricted his requests to funding for the NSDAP. Lüdecke was the first to make contact with Mussolini (see Chapter 8), in September of 1922 and at the end of August 1923. As usual, he failed to get any money, though the other objectives of his mission were largely achieved.

In November 1924, Göring, who was still recovering from a serious wound received during the attempted Munich *Putsch*, went to Venice to convalesce and attempted to negotiate a much needed loan of two million *lire* from Mussolini. Understandably, the Fascists were not impressed by the fiasco of the *Putsch* and Göring was forced into a humiliating and frustrating process of pleading by correspondence through Leo Negrelli, an agent of Mussolini. Göring had no stick with which to beat the Italian leader and the sole carrot that he could offer – apart from a promise that Hitler would come to meet Mussolini as soon as he had been released from prison – was NSDAP support for Italy's claim to the South Tyrol region of Austria, a policy that promised to lose Hitler much needed support in Bavaria. Mussolini remained noncommittal, failed to meet Göring, and there is no evidence that the two million lire ever materialised. Hitler was to make the same offer to Mussolini in 1938, this time with more concrete results.

Mussolini is known to have backed political and paramilitary groups in some countries, including the following: Hungarian nationalists; right-wing revolutionaries in Corsica, Malta, Macedonia and Croatia; the *Heimwehr*, an Austrian paramilitary group; and, of course, the right-wing forces during the Spanish Civil

War. On the basis of his support for the *Heimwehr* alone, it would be expected that Mussolini might spare a few lira to support Hitler and the NSDAP, who shared some political ideas with the Fascists, though they were by no means close enough to make the popular equation 'Fascism = Nazism'. However, there were two even stronger reasons for him to offer his support: Bavaria and the South Tyrol. France – Italy's political rival at the time – supported Bavarian separatism. The South Tyrol, once part of Austria, had been ceded to Italy after the First World War and many Germans and Austrians wanted it back. Hitler and the NSDAP were opposed to Bavarian separatism; more importantly, Hitler had made it plain that if he came to power he would make no claim for the restoration of the South Tyrol – the only German or Austrian politician to do so.

So much for Mussolini's reasons for supporting the NSDAP in the early nineteen-twenties, but what of proof? There is much anecdotal evidence for Mussolini's support, but, so far as the author is aware, no document has ever been discovered which confirms this. In March 1924, the Italian Ambassador to Germany, Alessandro de Bosdari, complained that Italian agents, carrying papers which identified them as representatives of the Fascist party, had been in contact with right-wing factions in Munich.[66] This may well be true, but it says nothing about money or Hitler or the NSDAP, and the date poses a problem: Hitler was in prison. Certainly such agents could have met with Amann, or Rosenberg, but there is no proof and Rosenberg, like Streicher, regularly attacked Mussolini in print, accusing him of being the tool of 'Jewish capital'.[67]

In 1929, several south German journalists published articles claiming that Hitler had received money from Mussolini to finance the Munich *Putsch*. Hitler sued in the Munich courts and won. However, the defendants appealed on the grounds that new evidence had come to light; articles written by a Berlin journalist Werner Abel in which he claimed to have been present when money had passed from the Italian Fascists to Hitler.[68] Abel claimed that in 1923 he introduced Hitler to a Captain Migliorati, on the staff of the Italian Embassy in Berlin, and that Migliorati later admitted that he had passed money to Hitler. The libel appeal was suspended until Migliorati could be found, which he was, in 1930, in New York. Migliorati swore a deposition that he had met Hitler, but denied ever passing money to him, and agreed to appear before the court in Munich. Hitler sued Abel for perjury. The case came before the court again in June of 1932. Migliorati did not appear, though his statement was read in court. The trial was a travesty, the court being biased in Hitler's favour; the libel was upheld and Abel received three years hard labour for perjury.

In a 1941 interview, Hermann Ullstein (of the eponymous publishing company) alleged that Otto Braun, Minister President of Prussia, had told him that he had proof that Hitler had received RM 18 million from Italy via a Swiss bank.[69] Such evidence, being second hand at best, is untrustworthy. Consequently, although one can conclude that the Italian Fascists probably gave some money to the NSDAP, it was never in large amounts and the likelihood of any money going to Hitler personally is remote.

The case for funding from Czechoslovakia is quite clear and hardly surprising: Hitler courted the Sudeten Germans and they responded with generous donations. Hitler also admitted receiving fees for speeches in Czechoslovakia and such fees certainly went into his own pocket. Bohemian industrialists von Duschnitz, von Asthaber, and various directors of the Skoda concern are also alleged to have provided funding to the NSDAP.[70]

Hanfstaengl writes of a Dutchman, a friend of Göring, who had 'channelled money to the party in his time' but gives no further details or supporting evidence.[71] Franz-Willing refers to a Dr. Baron von Bissing, though it is not known whether this is the same person.[72] One Dutchman who almost certainly provided support to Hitler and the NSDAP was Sir Henri Deterding, who was also connected with some of the White Russian Web.[73] Deterding was the first chairman of Royal Dutch Shell from its creation in 1907 until 1936, when he was forced to resign over his Nazi sympathies. Heiden implies that Deterding's contributions to Hitler may have begun as early as 1929.[74]

In May of 1933, Rosenberg made his second – and last – trip to Britain. This was no clandestine trip like the one in 1931; this trip was official and Rosenberg's anti-Semitic comments received much adverse publicity. One important meeting which took place during this trip was with Deterding, whom Rosenberg had met in 1931. Shortly after Rosenberg's visit, the *Daily Telegraph* reported that Deterding had granted Hitler future credits for the purchase of fuel, if, of course, there were any such credits. Or were they, in fact, credits to the NSDAP, allowing it to purchase fuel for its own transport? Other rumours followed thick and fast: Deterding gave Hitler four million Guilders; Deterding loaned Hitler £30 million – or was it £55 million? – in exchange for a promise of a petrol monopoly for his company; Deterding gave Hitler RM 10 million.[75]

The question of Deterding's contribution is further complicated by events which allegedly took place during the 'International London Inquiry' into the *Reichstag* fire of 27 February 1933. 'Steel' claims to have attended the Inquiry, though in what capacity he does not say:

> *A private meeting of the Inquiry Board was called and I pointed out to the meeting that there were certain well understood connections between Hitler and an international oil trust. I went into detail, citing the specific facts behind my allegations and telling the Inquiry Board where and how they might obtain documents to substantiate my points.*[76]

'Steel' does not mention Deterding by name, but a later paragraph suggests that the 'international oil trust' is almost certainly Royal Dutch-Shell and claims that his revelations – whatever they were – might embarrass the then British Foreign Secretary Sir John Simon. The whole statement raises more questions than it answers; it does, however, add to the rumours that Deterding provided funding to the NSDAP. Further evidence for Deterding's support comes in 1936, when he was forced to resign his post as Chairman of Shell on the grounds of his overt support for Hitler, though such overt support did not occur until after Hitler came to power in 1933. Shortly after his forced resignation, he divorced his wife, married a German woman, said to have been a Nazi supporter, and went to live on an estate in Mecklenburg. The property was alleged to have been tax exempt. There are thus strong grounds for believing that Deterding did give financial support to Hitler and the NSDAP, though whether any of that money was intended for Hitler's personal use is not known.

As noted in Chapter 3, Hitler certainly received some funding from Swiss sources, though to what extent is far from certain. In statements made to the police following the November 1923 *Putsch*, Schreck, Hitler's chauffeur and an SA leader, said that SA leaders received their funds in Swiss francs, but refused to say where from.[77] The Chief of Staff of the SA, *Kapitänleutnant* Hoffmann, confirmed Schreck's statements, as did a Major Streck, who also admitted to receiving Czech koruna and cash directly from Hitler.

This evidence naturally excited the authorities and an extensive investigation took place on both the German and Swiss sides. The conclusion was that 33,000 Swiss francs had been raised, mostly by Gansser's efforts.[78] There are suggestions that Frank may have done the same.[79] Gansser made at least six trips to Switzerland between April and December of 1923 and Hitler is said to have accompanied him on three occasions, in 1921, 1922 and 1923. The 1923 trip, at least, has been corroborated by Lüdecke, Hanfstaengl, and the police report, though Hitler denied it.

Notes

1   GORD72, pp. 72, 105.
2   HANF57, p. 76. Pool (POOL76, p. 74, note 86) has the SA bodyguard being replaced by men of the *Organization Consul*, citing Hanfstaengl as the source. But that is not what Hanfstaengl says: he merely notes that at the time he started visiting the *Völkischer Beobachter* offices, Hitler's office was guarded by men of the *Organization Consul*. This is not the same as Hitler's regular bodyguard. Furthermore, Hanfstaengl (HANF57, p. 93) has them still on guard prior to the November *Putsch* of 1923.
3   WILL72, p. 93.
4   Ibid., pp. 99-100. Williams suggests (p. 166) that Gertrud von Seidlitz (whose name he misspells "Gertrude von Seydlitz") was an intermediary between the White Russians and Hitler.
5   ROSE49, p. 63.
6   WILL72, pp. 22, 213-216.
7   WILL72, pp. 119-120.
8   For the Scheubner-Richter connection, see FRAN62, p. 191.

9   WILL72, pp. 348-50.

10   LÜDE38, pp. 261-2; 300; 340; 381; 554.

11   DIET57, p. 231.

12   FROM43, p. 92.

13   POOL78, p. 420, citing his own 1977 interview with Schaumburg-Lippe. Pool does not record what these regular payments were.

14   ROSE49, p. 63; FRAN62, p. 193.

15   FRAN62, p. 188, citing a *Münchener Post* article of 15 December 1922.

16   TURN85B, p. 379, citing SPD *Landesausschuss* Bayern, *Hitler und Kahr*, II, p. 102.

17   Statement made by Karl Rosenhauer, a director of the Deutsche Hansabank to the *Amtsgericht* München, dated 14 January 1929. In NSDAP HA 69/1507.

18   TURN85B, p. 51.

19   TURN85B, pp. 57-58.

20   Bruckmann correspondence with Rosenberg, US National Archives, RG 242, Microcopy T-454, 71/1402-11.

21   HEID44, p. 96; no source is given for the statement.

22   Eckart's obituary in the *Völkischer Beobachter*, Bavarian Edition, 23 April 1936 and a letter from Bernhard Schick, a former director of the Hansa Bank, dated 6 June 1935, now in the Bundesarchiv, Koblenz, Ref. NS 26/1218.

23   FRAN62, pp. 184-5, quoting from a later letter from Eckart to Gansser.

24   FRAN62, p. 185.

25   KERS98, p. 155.

26   TURN85B, p. 378, citing a letter from Grandel to Hitler, dated 27 October 1920, now in the US National Archives, RG 242, Microcopy T-84, 5/4337-38. Letter from Grandel to the Nazi *Hauptarchiv*, dated 22 October 1941, in NSDAP HA 26/514.

27   FRAN62, pp. 188-9.

28   DIAM74, p. 96.

29   Ibid., p. 97. *Teutonia* was dissolved in 1932.

30   Ibid., pp. 35-54.

31   Ibid., p. 43.

32   Ibid., p. 158, citing the evidence of the McCormack-Dickstein Committee which inquired into Nazi subversion in the USA.

33   STEE37, pp. 138-9. 'Steel' clearly disliked Schacht, whom he claims to have known, and does his best to blacken Schacht's reputation – which needed little blackening – by claiming Schacht's involvement in the most unlikely schemes.

34   DIAM74, pp. 96-97. Diamond manages to dismiss the allegations quite succinctly in a footnote. 'Steel' (STEE37, p. 140) makes similar allegations to Sinclair, but without mentioning a specific sum. 'Steel's book and Sinclair's book were published in the same year.

35   HANF57, p. 41.

36   HEID36, p. 236.

37   'Steel', however, (STEE37, p. 140) claims that in 1932 relations between Hitler and Ford were 'at their peak', but offers no evidence.

38   Sinclair, Upton. *The Flivver King: The Story of Ford America*, Pasadena, 1937, p. 109.

39 HIGH83, p. 156. Higham provides no source for this allegation. However, it is quite possible that the Ford Motor Company plant in Germany paid such a sum yearly – as other companies were required to do – to the AH Spende.

40 POOL78, p. 111.

41 Hapgood, Norman. *The inside story of Henry Ford's Jew-mania*. A six-part series. Hearst's International, June-November 1922.

42 POOL78, pp. 116-7 but the reference is unclear. The report is also referred to by Heiden (HEID44, p. 96) and seems to have been well known. Higham (HIGH83, p. 155) repeats the story and apparently accepts it as fact. Some writers seem to think that Ford's 'agent' was Warren C. Anderson, the Ford company's European manager, but he was recalled to the USA in late 1920 or early 1921 and fired in February of 1921.

43 Their visit to Ford is described in great detail: LÜDE38, pp. 181-90.

44 LÜDE38, pp. 181-3.

45 Pool (POOL78, p. 126) citing his interview with Frau Wagner in October 1977.

46 LÜDE38, p. 187.

47 LÜDE38, p. 188. The author, an engineer by training and blessed with an over-developed Surrealism node in his imagination, is captivated by the image of Hitler grasping Germany with a concrete support, itself an appropriate tool for a would-be architect.

48 LÜDE38, p. 189.

49 LÜDE38, p. 190.

50 CROS61, p. 62. The organisation's annual income from subscriptions declined rapidly from a high of £6,848 in 1925 to about £400 by 1929 and practically disap-peared after the founding of the BUF in 1932.

51 Newman, Kim & Eugene Byrne. *The Matter of Britain Series: British Fascist movements up to 1940*. http://www.angelfire.com/ak2/newmanbyrne/matter.html

52 CROS61, pp. 90-93.

53 LÜDE38, p. 201.

54 CECI72, pp. 169-70 and 175-6.

55 Cecil (CECI72, p. 170) claims that Schickedanz, not Thost, made the first approaches to de Ropp, but Lüdecke and most other writers claim that it was Thost. The question is academic: de Ropp was a British agent and was certainly under orders to develop links with the *Völkischer Beobachter* and, through it, to the NSDAP.

56 LÜDE38, p. 418.

57 POOL78, pp. 314-317. Higham (HIGH83, p. 190) claims, with no source indi-cated, that Rothermere gave 'Princess Stefanie Hohenlohe' $5 million in cash 'in the early nineteen-thirties' to assist Hitler in his rise to power.

58 BRAC70, p. 108.

59 *Neues Volk*, No. 14, 2 November 1920.

60 GORD72, pp. 34-5. The *Münchener Post* was rather fond of asking questions such as: 'Is it true that two weeks ago the NSDAP received 30-40 million marks from French sources?' – and then failing to answer the question. See FRAN62, p. 187.

61 HEID36, p. 238.

62 Document 217; in DEUE62, p. 560. *Das Staatsministerium des Äußern an die Bayerische Gesandtschaft Berlin. München, 4. 1. 1924* Translation by the author and M. Rosvall.

63 ROSE49, p. 63.

64 LÜDE38, pp. 232-8.

65 STEE37, pp. 120-21. The pseudonymous 'Steel' goes on to make a 'Merchants of Death' accusation against Schneider-Creusot, citing a conversation with an un-named Schneider-Creusot executive.

66 CASS70, p. 174, quoting from Anfuso, Filippo. *Da Palazzo Venezia al Lago di Gardia.* Rocca San Casciano, 1957. p. 34.

67 HEID44, p. 221. Not that this means much – such attacks were solely for the reader's benefit.

68 CASS70, pp. 170-2. *Berliner Tageblatt*, May 7, 8, 14 1929 and February 4, 5, 6 1930; Salvemini, Gaetano. *Prelude to World War II*, London, 1953, Victor Gollancz Ltd. pp. 44-5.

69 *Saturday Evening Post*, 13 July 1941. Salvemini (p. 45) also uses this story as evidence. Although the sum sounds enormous, it rather depends upon when it was given. At the time of the 1923 *Putsch*, the sum would have purchased 1/25 of a page of the *Völkischer Beobachter!*

70 FRAN62, p. 189, citing the *Bayerische Kurier und Münchner Fremdenblatt*, 5 January 1928.

71 HANF57, p. 186.

72 FRAN62, p. 189, citing the *Bayerische Kurier und Münchner Fremdenblatt*, 5 January 1928.

73 It has never been reliably established whether Deterding ever took British citizenship; nor has it ever been found whether he renounced his Dutch citizenship. The author has chosen to consider him Dutch.

74 HEID36, p. 240.

75 Many of these rumoured figures come from Roberts, Glyn. *The Most Powerful Man in the World: The Life of Sir Henri Deterding.* New York, 1938, Covici Friede. E.g. pp. 305, 319 and 322. Roberts, however, is clearly pursuing an anti-capitalist agenda and is rather selective in his sources.

76 STEE37, p. 191.

77 FRAN62, p. 196, quoting from Munich police documents. Subsequent statements are from the same source.

78 FRAN62, p. 196, citing *Hitlerputsch der Bayerisch Staatskanzlei, Aktennotiz von 6. 8. 1925.*

79 FRAN62, p. 184, citing a letter from Eckart to Gansser.

Chapter Eleven

THE YEARS OF PLENTY

[The rich] are indeed rather possessed by their money than possessors.
Robert Burton (1577-1640)
Anatomy of Melancholy,
Part i. Sect. 2, Member 3, Subsection 12.

The years 1933-45 were certainly years of plenty for Adolf Hitler. His personal income from the *Eher Verlag* (including his royalties from *Mein Kampf*) increased rapidly, as did his income from the books and pictures published by Hoffmann. To these were added the funds of the *Adolf Hitler Spende* and the Cultural Fund. Hitler began to spend accordingly.

Hitler was also showered with gifts from grateful admirers, at home and abroad. Officially, he refused all gifts. In practice, he accepted whatever was interesting or valuable enough to take his fancy – especially artworks. In at least one instance, as this chapter records, an eccentric gift to 'S.E. Herr Hitler, President, Republique Grand Allemagne, Hamburg' led to an episode of high farce.

On 1 January 1933, in a special edition entitled *Ein Jahr Deutscher Politik* (A year in German politics), the influential *Frankfurther Zeitung* announced the end of National Socialism. On the same day, the satirical magazine *Simplicissimus* published its annual poem, reviewing the year, which contained the following lines:[1]

Eins nur lässt sich sicher sagen,	One thing is sure for all of us,
Und das freut uns rund herum,	And we're delighted every one,
Hitler geht es an den Kragen.	Hitler gets it in the puss,
Dieses "Führers" Zeit ist um.	This "Führer's" time is done.

Thirty days later, on Monday, 30 January, Adolf Hitler was appointed Chancellor of the German Reich at an initial combined salary and expenses of RM 47,200 per year.

On 15 January, an election took place in the state of Lippe-Detmold. The Nazis regained the seats they had lost in November, but there is clear evidence that the party was in financial difficulties. During the election campaign the previous December, Otto Dietrich recounts:

> *Hitler's large-scale propaganda tours in the decisive year of 1932 were financed solely by the entrance fees at the gigantic mass demonstrations at which fantastic prices were often paid for seats in the first rows. Assertions have often been made that Hitler came to power on money from heavy industry. On this question I can contribute the following personal details.*
>
> *. . . The true facts emerge even more clearly from a small incident that took place during the election campaign in Lippe in December 1932. At that time I accompanied Hitler as press reporter to the public meetings and could therefore watch the process by which, from one meeting to the next, he literally scraped up the money to cover his travelling expenses. Just seven weeks before he came to power Hitler was spending the night at the Grevenburg near Detmold when his chief adjutant came to me and in great embarrassment asked whether I could advance him 2,000 marks since Hitler had not got another pfennig and the local Party organisation had been unable to pay the rental for the hall where the next day's demonstration was slated to be held. How could such a financial predicament at such a decisive moment be conceivable if Hitler had been receiving money from industry?[2]*

The 'chief adjutant' was presumably Schaub, since other sources indicate that he was the bag-man on such occasions.[3] On another occasion, a bailiff, acting on behalf of creditors, seized the admission receipts at a party rally.[4] One author claims, without any supporting figures, that the NSDAP owed RM 90 million by this time.[5] According to Heiden, a group of businessmen, led by Otto Wolff and including Thyssen, underwrote the NSDAP finances and thus saved Hitler, who had personally guaranteed loans for the party, from bankruptcy.[6] Thyssen, however, refers to no such underwriting and his memoirs make no mention of Wolff.

At his first cabinet meeting, on 1 February, Hitler stage-managed events to provoke yet another election. Goebbels wrote in his diary:

> *Now it is easy to carry on the fight, for we can call on all the State's means. . . . And this time of course there is no lack of money.*

Indeed, there was not, but at the second cabinet meeting, on 2 February, Schwerin von Krosigk, now Finance Minister, refused a request for one million *marks* for the Nazis' election campaign expenses. Hitler was unperturbed; a million *marks* was chicken-feed. On 20 February, Göring summoned twenty or so leading industrialists to a meeting, chaired by Hjalmar Schacht and held at Göring's official residence as leader of the *Reichstag*. Among those present were Krupp, Vögler, and Schnitzler and Bosch of IG Farben. Ostensibly, the meeting was called for Hitler to brief the industrialists on his future economic policy. What they got was a typical piece of Nazi political theatre. First the businessmen had to wait for Göring to arrive. Next they had to wait further for Hitler to arrive. When he did so, he subjected his guests to a ninety-minute political harangue in which economics was barely mentioned and the main theme was the need to destroy Communism – by force, if necessary. For this, another election was required to consolidate Hitler's power. Forced to abandon his carefully prepared speech, Krupp murmured a few words of thanks and Hitler left. Göring then took the floor, further stressing the need for yet another election if German Bolshevism were to be finally crushed. He did, however, reassure his listeners that the Nazis planned no rash economic experiments. The real purpose of the meeting became clear when Göring stated that those not in the forefront of the political battle had a responsibility to make financial sacrifices, noting, '. . . the elections will certainly be the last for the next ten years, probably for the next hundred years.'[7] Schacht took Göring's place and repeated the same message: give us your money – three million *marks* of it. The business leaders simply gave in: Krupp is said to have pledged RM 1,000,000; Schnitzler RM 400,000; and the rest some RM 3,000,000 between them.[8] Over the following weeks, three million marks was delivered to Schacht who acted as administrator of the fund, which he called the *Nationale Treuhand*. It would eventually become the *Adolf Hitler Spende*. On 5 March 1933, Germans went to the polls in the last free parliamentary elections for sixteen years.

One thing of great significance may be deduced from this meeting: there had been no great flow of funds from Big Business in the last months of 1932. For, if Big Business had been freely contributing to Hitler and the NSDAP there would have been no need for the meeting to take place and no reason to inveigle the industrialists into attending. It is thus reasonable to assume that this was the first major contribution by Big Business; it would not be the last.

Even though Hitler had been appointed Chancellor, he was still in financial difficulties: he owed RM400,000 in unpaid income tax and he had a substantial unpaid hotel bill at Berlin's *Kaiserhof*.[9] Somehow, this problem had to be solved. Fortunately, the first of the necessary solutions appeared almost immediately in the shape of Gustav Krupp. Krupp's interests would best be served by a Chancellor who would curb the power of the trade unions and pursue a policy of re-armament, both of which Hitler promised to do. However, Krupp was hesitant; among his colleagues he privately doubted whether Hitler would stay long in power. A few days prior to passage of the Enabling Act, which effectively gave Hitler absolute power, Krupp met with a group of top army officers and learned that they supported Hitler. The Enabling Act removed Krupp's last doubts. Krupp was now convinced that Hitler was the man for the job and immediately became an outspoken supporter; it is doubtful, though not impossible, that such a conversion took place as rapidly as it has been portrayed. On 1 April, Krupp met with Hitler and agreed a deal: if Hitler supported Krupp as leader of German industry, he would ensure that Hitler received financial support. Thus it was that the *Adolf Hitler Spende* came into being. Officially, the fund was intended to finance the NSDAP and its affiliates such as the SA; for a short time, it did, but the fund quickly became one of the main sources of Hitler's personal fortune.

On 1 May, the day traditionally dedicated to organised labour in Europe,

Hitler took over the trade unions, replacing them by the *Deutsche Arbeitsfront* (DAF – German Work Front) into which their assets were absorbed. These assets were considerable; the unions had built up substantial strike funds and also owned banks, newspapers, workers' hostels, co-operative stores, other businesses, and property. All these now came under the control of Robert Ley and, while they probably did not provide anything to Hitler directly, they solved the problems of paying for the NSDAP and its affiliates and freed the *Adolf Hitler Spende* for a more 'worthy' cause: Adolf Hitler himself. With four million members, the unions had an annual turnover of RM 184 million.[10] There is evidence that some of this money was used to purchase paintings for the Linz Collection, though not for Hitler's Personal Collection.

Another significant event of May 1933 was the ban, imposed by Goebbels, on the unauthorised use of Hitler's name or image on commercial products; Adolf Hitler was now copyright. Hitler, naturally, had no objection to the use of his name for non-commercial purposes; anything was permissible if it strengthened the cult of the *Führer*. Hitler Oaks and other trees of pagan significance were ceremonially dedicated across Germany. Streets, squares, and buildings were renamed. Only in the case of long-standing historic names was any objection raised. Hitler refused to sanction the re-naming of the 700-year-old *Marktplatz* in Strausberg (to the east of Berlin), but allowed Nuremberg's *Hauptmarkt* to become *Adolf Hitler Platz*. The village of Sutzken, in East Prussia, was allowed to become Hitlershöhe and a lake in Upper Silesia became Hitlersee. However, the mayor of Bad Godesberg, where Hitler would later confer with British Prime Minister Neville Chamberlain, was prohibited from advertising the town as 'the favourite place to stay of the Reich Chancellor Adolf Hitler'.[11] Even close acquaintances were not exempt from the ban. The owner of the *Pension Moritz*, once Hitler's favourite hotel in the Obersalzberg, was forced to change the letterhead of his hotel's writing paper from *Lieblings-Aufenthalt und Wohnsitz Adolf Hitlers* (Favourite haunt and residence of Adolf Hitler) to *Lieblings-Aufenthalt und Adolf Hitlers*.[12] The Führer image was protected; now it could be exploited.

Bormann seized upon this as one solution to Hitler's financial problems. He and Hoffmann approached Ohnesorge, the Minister of Posts and a long-time Nazi, and pointed out that their master was due a royalty each time his image was used – such as on postage stamps. The royalty was tiny, but multiplied by the numbers – millions of postage stamps sold – it became a substantial source of income. Initially the practice was confined to special issue stamps, whose royalties were advertised as going to the Adolf Hitler Cultural Fund; it was only after 1941 that the majority of stamps carried Hitler's portrait. The German public, however, was encouraged to believe that it was only the special issues which contributed to the fund.

The copyright was equally lucrative for Hoffmann who enjoyed a monopoly on Hitler's photographs and published numerous 'coffee table' books. It was the beginning of Bormann's campaign – largely successful, except for the profits from the *Eher Verlag* – to take control of Hitler's financial affairs, which were then in the hands of Heß.

June of 1933 brought a new financial problem: the impending bankruptcy of the Jewish-owned *Teitz* chain of department stores. In 1932, *Teitz* had borrowed over RM 100 million from the government; now a new government was in power and *Teitz*, which employed over 14,000 people, was still in trouble and needed further funds. Clearly, a request for help from a Jewish owned department store chain stood little chance with a Nazi government, even after an appeal by the 14,000 employees, many of whom were NSDAP members. Hitler was ready to turn down the request until it was pointed out that if *Teitz* went bankrupt so would many of its suppliers – and their banks, several of whom were contributors to the *Adolf Hitler Spende*. Hitler changed his mind; *Teitz* received a further loan.

With few exceptions, the foreign press was undecided as to what attitude to take to Hitler; should he be portrayed as a monster or a buffoon? Cartoonists, of course, could portray him as both and in the nineteen-thirties, when newspapers were at the height of their influence, they could afford to employ some brilliant cartoonists, such as Britain's 'Vicky' and David Low. Hanfstaengl, who was notably more sophisticated than the average Nazi, had a brilliant idea: to publish a book exploiting the foreign cartoonists and playing their portrayals back at them. The result was *Tat gegen Tinte* (Facts versus Ink). In his foreword to the book – which was published in July 1933 – Hanfstaengl explained that the book's objective was to distinguish between the real and the cartoon Hitler. Happily, most foreign readers easily penetrated the fog of propaganda. Whether Hitler received any money from the proceeds – he endorsed the book with a rare, laughing image of himself – is not known.

Hitler's tax return for 1933 – his last – gives his income as RM 1,232,335, of which RM 861,146 was royalties from *Mein Kampf* which sold a staggering 854,127 copies. Other income was not itemised. He claimed deductions of RM 616,167 all which was allowed, leaving a theoretical net income of RM 616,618. He was assessed for RM 297,005 of taxes and penalties; this was to have interesting repercussions.

Shortly after Hitler's assumption of power, Schaub assumed responsibility for his master's tax affairs and, so it appears, for most of his personal papers and major possessions. On 7 February, the *Völkischer Beobachter* announced that Hitler, since he earned his living as a writer, proposed to donate his salary as Chancellor to the *Hilfskasse* (Relief Fund), a fund for the dependants of SS and SA members and of police who had been killed during the previous years' riots.[13] Schaub immediately set about putting Hitler's tax affairs in order. Fritz Reinhardt, a long-time Nazi and a former teacher of bookkeeping from Thuringia, had been appointed Secretary of State to the Reich Ministry of Finance. Schaub contacted Reinhardt and from Reinhardt the message filtered down to the Finance Office in Munich, where they first addressed themselves to the question of Hitler's charitable disposition of his salary. On 31 March, Tax Inspector Vogl, who handled Hitler's affairs, wrote from Munich to the State Finance Office:

The question now arises whether the Reich Chancellor is taxable for his salary in addition to his other income. The increase in the total income will give rise, as a result of the higher bracket, to a considerable rise in the income tax assessment, which would impose an unjust hardship since the Chancellor has designated his salary, in a magnanimous manner, for charitable purposes.[14]

Meanwhile, in Berlin, State Secretary Lammers, head of the Reich Chancellery, wrote to Schwerin von Krosigk, Reich Minister of Finance, of Hitler's decision to donate his salary to charity. On 15 March, Krosigk wrote to Lammers saying that he had decided that Hitler's salary would not be subject to tax. By an oversight on Krosigk's part, this had the unfortunate result that Hitler's quarterly advance tax payments for 1933 were calculated on the basis of his 1932 returns, greatly increasing his overall tax liability for 1933. However, this problem was not long in being rectified.

Between 1 and 10 January 1934, Hitler published a series of 'thank-you notes' in the *Völkischer Beobachter*. Some idea of a person's standing in the party, or in Hitler's favour, can be gained from their order of appearance: 1 January: Heß; Schwarz; Amann; Himmler; Röhm; Goebbels; Rosenberg. 3 January: Göring; Ley; Schirach; Buch; Seldte. 10 January: Darré. It is a measure of their importance that Schwarz and Amann – the one responsible for the party's finances, the other, at that time, for Hitler's – are second only to Heß, the Deputy Führer. Bormann is not even mentioned.

Early in 1934, Schaub again approached Reinhardt about Hitler's tax liabilities in compiling his returns for 1933. On 30 January, Reinhardt replied:

With reference to the extraordinary expenditures incurred by you in your capacity as leader of the German Nation, I declare myself in agreement with your deduction of fifty percent of gross income for professional expenditures in the tax period 1933.[15]

Curiously, this decision was not communicated to the Munich Finance Office until 29 March. On 22 March, Hitler filed his 1933 return. This still left Hitler with a substantial bill for taxes, arrears, and penalties. In accordance with standard Finance Office procedures, a final tax liability notice was sent to Hitler at the end of August, with the due date for payment set at the end of September. In accordance with standard Hitler Office procedures, nothing was done. The Finance Office sent a reminder at the end of October. According to an internal memorandum of mid-November from Dr Lizius, chief of the Finance Office Munich-East, Tax Inspector Vogl tried to contact Schaub by telephone on 7, 8, 9, and 10 November – without success.

The bureaucrats in Munich began to get nervous. On the one hand, as state officials, they had to uphold the law; on the other hand, they were dealing with a new regime, headed by a man wielding absolute powers and with a reputation for ruthlessness and a proven disregard for legal niceties. Like bureaucrats the world over, they decided to cover themselves against all possibilities. On 20 October, the Finance Office prepared a statement of delinquent taxes for 1933/34, revealing that Hitler was behind in his payments to the extent of RM 405,494. A formal tax delinquency notice was prepared, but not sent. On 13 November, Schaub wrote to Vogl:

> With regard to the Reich Chancellor's tax affairs, I wish to inform you that as soon as State Secretary Reinhardt returns from sick leave you will have further information. Until then I beg you to be patient.[16]

Covering himself, Schaub also wrote to the Ministry of Finance. From there, *Oberregierungsrat* Herting, a member of Reinhardt's secretariat, wrote on 27 November to Dr Lizius:

> [I understand that] with regard to the Führer's tax affairs some kind of decisions are to be taken or payments made . . . I would be grateful to you if postponable decisions could be delayed until then.[17]

Herting repeated Schaub's assurances that he was anxious to discuss the matter with Reinhardt as soon as the latter returned from sick leave. Lizius executed a series of covering manoeuvres. First he passed the problem up to his superior, Dr Ludwig Mirre, President of the State Finance Office, Munich. Lizius also wrote a 'memorandum to file', detailing all that had been done so far. On 19 December, Mirre replied:

> I have discussed the Führer's tax affairs informally with the State Secretary [Reinhardt]. We were agreed that in view of the Führer's constitutional position he is not liable to taxation and that it is a constitutional question whether and to what extent the Führer is on the same footing with a person liable to taxation. Moreover, the preparation and serving of a tax assessment notice would not in and of itself establish a legal tax obligation. All tax notices, so far as they would establish an obligation for the Führer, are without legal effect. I therefore request that until further notice nothing be undertaken in the matter, but that care be exercised to keep the records under lock and key and that the estimated taxes not be indicated as delinquent.[18]

Thus, on an appropriately conspiratorial note, ended the saga of Adolf Hitler's tax affairs. It must be presumed that the Munich tax office breathed a sigh of relief. Ever conscientious, Lizius covered himself with yet another 'memorandum to file', dated 25 February 1935, which ends:

> The order to declare the Führer tax-exempt was therefore final. Thereupon I withdrew all the Führer's records, including the tax cards, from official circulation and placed them under lock and key.[19]

. . . where they were discovered in 1945. However, in conformance with the 'cock-up' – rather than the 'conspiracy' – theory of history, there was one more act to play. Through an oversight, a tax declaration form was sent to Hitler's private office in January of 1935. Down from on high came a cold, but polite request as to why this had been done when the *Führer* was tax-exempt? Lizius' investigation was thorough and is documented in a series of memoranda, beginning in March. With a sigh of relief, Lizius was able to report that the notices had been prepared before his *Führer's* tax status had been determined. To prevent any possible future accidents, on 12 March Hitler's mailing address plates and his tax card were withdrawn from the files and added to the locked dossier. For tax purposes, Adolf Hitler no longer existed.

In the final ironic twist, Dr Ludwig Mirre, President of the State Finance Office in Munich who, by his own, probably illegal, action had given Hitler tax-exempt status, received an appropriate reward. In 1943, he was appointed President of the *Reichsfinanzhof*, the highest appellate court for taxation disputes.[20]

In 1935 Hitler quietly resumed collecting his salary as Chancellor (now raised to RM 60,000 a year) that he had given up with so much fanfare in 1933. In addition he continued to receive – and declare, though not pay any tax on – royalties for new and re-printed articles 'written' by him and fees for interviews. The NSDAP too had no real financial worries, despite Schwarz's claims that it operated in the red until 1940, since it was now receiving state subsidies: RM 5.96 million in 1935; RM 88.56 million in 1940.[21] With such generous subsidies, the NSDAP had no need of any help from the *Eher Verlag* whose profits now became available to Hitler and Amann.

In the summer of 1935, Hitler decided to expand the *Berghof* into something much grander, as described in Chapter 14. On 9 August 1935, Eva Braun and her younger sister Gretl moved into a rented three-room apartment in Munich's Bogenhausen district, a short walk from Hitler's own Munich residence. In March 1936, following one of her several suicide attempts, Hitler bought Eva a house and opened a bank account for her into which he paid a monthly allowance. The house and its contents are described in detail in Chapter 14. With the house, Eva received a 3.2 litre Mercedes cabriolet, originally a gift from the Mercedes company to Hitler.

On 30 January 1937, Speer was appointed a State Secretary of the Reich government.[22] From this point on, Speer began to dine regularly with Hitler in Berlin – though he had long since done so in Munich. It was at these meals that the steward Kannenberg once served black caviar. Hitler, who had never tasted caviar before, praised the taste and ate it by the spoonful for several weeks – until he learned the price. Then, for several more weeks he ordered that he be served the cheaper red caviar, finally giving that up when he decided that the idea of a caviar-guzzling *Führer* was politically incorrect. Following a performance of *Madame Butterfly* at the *Berlin Volksoper*, Hitler was so enraptured by the opera that he donated RM 100,000 a year to the company – probably from the Cultural Fund. Indeed, it was on 25 March 1937 that Hitler's portrait first appeared on a stamp – a special six *pfennig* issue, in sets of four. However, it was not until 1941 that his portrait appeared on all regular stamps.

On 4 February 1938, Hitler appointed General Walther von Brauchitsch as Commander-in-Chief of the Army. The appointment involved a curious incident. von Brauchitsch was in the middle of divorce proceedings and his wife was demanding a considerable settlement, which von Brauchitsch could not afford. Therefore, he told Hitler, he would be unable to accept the position unless some means were found to satisfy his wife's financial demands. Hitler seized the opportunity; a General who was financially indebted, as well as morally, was more than he had dared to hope for. Hitler persuaded von Brauchitsch's wife to accept a settlement of RM 80,000 and paid it.

On 8 April 1938, following the *Anschluss* with Austria, Hitler journeyed to Linz and on the following day lunched with his childhood friend Kubizek. In the course of their conversation, Kubizek said that his own musical ambitions had been shattered by the First World War, but that his three sons were musically gifted and he hoped they would be able to study at the Bruckner Conservatory. Hitler immediately arranged to pay their fees and one, Augustin, became a well-known composer and conductor. Hitler also purchased his father's former estate at Leonding, five kilometres from Linz, and turned it into his 'official' ancestral home and a place of pilgrimage.[23]

On 2 May 1938, Hitler set out for Rome on a visit to Mussolini. Concerned about his health, he spent several hours on the train dictating his will, having already dictated a political testament on November 5, 1937. Speer implies that these were substantially the documents witnessed in the Chancellery bunker in April of 1945, but the surviving wills differ greatly in details. The 1938 will, which was deposited with *Reichsminister* Lammers, was fairly straightforward; everything went to the NSDAP, with the proviso that the party then execute certain legacies. RM 1,000 a month for life was to be given to Eva Braun (a rather niggardly sum, slightly more than twice her monthly salary as Hoffmann's 'secretary'), with similar sums going to Hitler's sisters – Angela and Paula – and to Eva's two sisters. Hitler's half-brother, Alois junior, received a lump sum of RM 60,000. There were other bequests to his housekeeper, Frau Winter, his valets, and to relatives in Spital. The NSDAP was also ordered to take care of Hitler's adjutants, Brückner and Wiedemann, for life. The will also stipulated that Hitler's half-sister Angela should receive all the furniture, clothes and other effects of her late daughter Geli, together with Adolf Ziegler's portrait of her.[24]

In July 1938, Hitler honoured a man who is alleged to have given financial support to himself and the NSDAP: Henry Ford. At Ford's birthday dinner on 30 July, Karl Kapp, German Consul in Cleveland, and Fritz Hailer, German Consul in Detroit, invested Ford with the Grand Cross of the Supreme Order of the German Eagle – the highest award offered for non-Germans – 'in recognition of [Ford's] pioneering in making motor cars available for the masses'. The award was violently attacked in the American press, though not by *The Dearborn Independent*.

Early in 1939 – the date is uncertain – Eva Braun received her own apartment in the Chancellery building: Hindenburg's old bedroom. The curtains were kept closed, she took her meals alone in her room, and, in keeping with the fiction that she was merely a secretary, she had to use the servants' entrance. What is of certain date, since it was a present for her twenty-seventh birthday on 6 February, is that Eva received one of the first prototype Volkswagens. However, since the vehicle was so conspicuous, she could rarely drive it and it spent the war in a garage at the *Berghof*. Eva's 1945 will bequeathed the car to her sister Ilse, the Mercedes to her father.

In March, following the complete take-over of Czechoslovakia, Hitler spent a night in Prague's Hradcany Castle and is said to have personally looted several tapestries, stuffing them into the boot of his car.[25] Writing of this period in their friendship, Speer gives some details of Hitler's love of operettas such as *Die Fledermaus* and *The Merry Widow*, though he claims that Hitler was equally happy – if not happier – attending simple variety shows.[26] Speer claims that Hitler would pay from the *AH Spende* to have these operettas performed in especially lavish style, though he gives no details of the sums spent.[27] On 20 April, Hitler's fiftieth birthday, Speer gives a glimpse of the sort of birthday presents Hitler was receiving at the height of his power:

[In the former cabinet room where Bismarck had presided over the Congress of Berlin in 1878] *Hitler's birthday presents were heaped up on long tables – pretty much a collection of kitsch sent by his Reichsleiters and Gauleiters: white marble nudes, small bronze casts of such well-known works as the Roman boy extracting a thorn from his foot, and oil paintings whose level matched the stuff exhibited in the House of Art. Hitler spoke well of some of the presents, made fun of others, but there was in fact not much difference between them.*[28]

Clearly they had only increased in number and cost – rather than quality – since Hanfstaengl had had similar experiences in 1923 and 1924, and made similar comments, as did Hoffmann. Speer presented Hitler with his favourite gift: a four metre high model of the gigantic triumphal arch that was planned to dominate a rebuilt Berlin. Eva Braun's present was not only original, it was provocative: a set of gold and diamond cufflinks depicting a swastika superimposed on the arms of the Polish city of Danzig. Hitler is said to have worn them to the end of his life.[29]

At the outbreak of war, the British Government set up a 'Contraband Control' whereby the Royal Navy intercepted and searched cargo ships passing the British Isles, possibly en route for Germany. If any 'strategic materials' (e.g. rubber) were found to be destined for Germany, they were confiscated. At this stage, during what came to be known as the Phoney War, these operations were very gentlemanly affairs, not without their humour. For example, the captain of, say, a neutral Swedish ship en route to Hamburg with a cargo of one hundred tons of natural rubber would invariably maintain that the material was of no strategic value as it was of a grade only suitable for the manufacture of contraceptives.

Almost immediately, a difficult situation occurred: the Royal Navy seized 2,080 kilograms of coffee beans, in twenty bags, a gift from the Imam of Yemen, addressed to 'S.E. Herr Hitler, President, Republique Grand Allemagne, Hamburg'. The cargo was seized from the Danish vessel *Danmark*, Captain E.H. Christensen. Unfortunately, in this case, the Royal Navy was insufficiently sensitive to the nuances of middle-eastern politics. Yemen was nominally independent, but under British protection because of the vital naval base in the port of Aden. Relations between Britain and the Imam were especially sensitive: the Imam wanted the British out of Aden, but also wanted his country protected. The British were determined to keep Aden, but were loath to expend resources on defending anything except the port itself. Once it became known to the British government that the coffee had been seized, they were all – Foreign Office, Colonial Office, War Office, and Ministry of Economic Warfare – agreed that the coffee should be allowed to proceed to its intended destination with the minimum of fuss, so as not to offend the Imam, whose sensitivities were of more strategic importance than Hitler's enjoying a morning cup of Java. Unfortunately, the Ministry of Information chose just the wrong moment to hold a press day at Contraband Control and an alert *Times* journalist spotted the twenty bags. The cat was out of the bag or, in this case, the beans were well and truly spilled. Memos began to circulate in Whitehall. On 26 September, an anonymous Foreign Office official with appalling hand-writing noted:

> *Major Fox rang up to say that the W.O.* [War Office] *were rather* [the word looks like 'aptalid' but is probably 'appalled'] *by the impounding of this coffee and the publicity given to it. They were afraid that it would very much indispose the Imam.*
>
> *I told Major Fox what the position was and he said that he hoped that if we did release the coffee, equal publicity would be given to our action.*
>
> *I suspect the Imam will have the sense to realise that contraband is contraband, even if it is a present for Herr Hitler. He will probably ask us to pay for what we have seized.* [30]

The various ministries continued to argue about a possible course of action until, on 2 October, someone noticed that the cargo manifest only listed who the coffee was going to, not whom it was coming from. Therefore, although the Foreign Office knew from intelligence reports that the coffee was from the Imam, it did not <u>officially</u> know. It was thus proposed to do nothing and to let the Imam learn of the seizure from newspaper reports. In a lengthy Foreign Office minute of 2 October, one official commented:

> *I have drafted a letter to Mr. Loxley, who told me that the reason why the publicity people are so keen on the coffee was that they are "looking for a laugh" out of the contraband service.* [31]

Little did they suspect that over sixty years later their wish would be granted. Sir S. Gaselee, however, was not amused. In his hand-written comment to the previous comment he wrote:

A deplorable affair throughout. We should either have taken the coffee and said nothing, or let it go forward to its addressee, loudly patting ourselves on the back for our magnanimity and consideration for the ruler of the Yemen.

I venture to think that it would be a great mistake to return it to him: an Eastern potentate does not like such a treatment of a gift. I would now veil the whole business in as much obscurity as possible.

The question of the return of the coffee became further complicated by the question of who would pay the freight charges. The Ministry of Economic Warfare thought that the Foreign Office should pay, and vice-versa. Mr. Baggalay of the Foreign Office outlined the position to Mr. P.N. Loxley of the Ministry of Economic Warfare in a letter of 7 October in which he noted:

. . . the only question which remains is whether or not any further references to the subject should be allowed in the press or in films. On full reflection we think that it would be much better that nothing further should be published and no films made of the bags of coffee themselves (as is, I believe, proposed). This may seem slightly redolent of shutting the stable door after the horse has fled, but at present the lengths to which publicity has gone are not very serious, and if a halt is made now, no great harm may be done. In particular, no attempt has yet been made to "get a laugh" out of the seizure, and, as I told you on the telephone, while we are all the better for laughing when we can at Hitler's expense, it would be fatal to try to be humourous [sic] at the expense of the King of the Yemen. . . . [32]

The Foreign Office began to make enquiries with shipping agents Gellatly Hankey and Company about the possible costs and procedures for returning the coffee to the Imam, or if not to he, then to the Yemeni Ministry of Foreign Affairs. Another minute was circulated on 16 November, wondering, amongst other things, how long the coffee could be kept in the contraband stores, which were under the control of the Procurator General. As P.M. Ayres commented on 23 November:

I have spoken to someone at the Procurator General's office. There seems to be no objection to leaving the coffee as long as we like, though it is suggested that the coffee will not improve with keeping. [33]

Mr. Rule, of Gellatly Hankey and Co., gave his own suggestions to the minute, as recorded by Mr. Baggallay, which were somewhat more practical than those of the professional diplomatists:

Mr. Rule said he quite saw that it would not be possible to forward the coffee to Germany, but he wondered whether it was wise to return it to the Yemen, seeing that the Yemen was already full of coffee.

. . . Mr. Rule also asked whether it would be possible to send the Imam some sort of present in return for the coffee. I said that admittedly we did not send him many presents, not at any rate to the extent that the Italians did, but that all the same I thought it would be difficult to do that in this case. If, as a result of any message we might send to the Yemen, the Imam asked us to keep the coffee, then we would certainly have to send some sort of return present.

(I may add that Mr. Rule referred to the question of presents on the strength of a letter from their

agent at Hodeida, Mr. Perkins, who had apparently remarked on the comparative absence of civilities of this kind on our part compared to the constant attentions of the Italians and the Germans — all of which I fear is very true.)[34]

By all accounts Adolf Hitler drank very little coffee; it upset his stomach. The Imam, it seems, had not done his research. Eventually, a solution was found: the Imam was given a rather well-used Bofors anti-aircraft gun and the coffee was given to the King of England — or was it? In his post-war memoirs, Otto Dietrich makes the tantalising statement:

> *One Christmas during the war years Hitler gave each person on his* [Christmas present] *list a package of coffee from a shipload that a Near Eastern shah had sent to him as a personal present.*[35]

Which leaves open the possibilities that either the Foreign Office changed its mind or there was another consignment of coffee sent to 'S.E. Herr Hitler, President, Republique Grand Allemagne, Hamburg'.

On 20 April 1941, his fifty-second birthday, Hitler received the usual mountain of presents, including:

> *. . . four hundred pounds of coffee, three hundred of tea, fifty of cocoa, some of them announced as coming from the United States. That meant that many Germans had sacrificed their own small allotments of coffee, tea and cocoa to give Der Fuehrer, who could get all he wanted.*[36]

On 10 May, Rudolph Heß, nominally Hitler's deputy, flew to Britain on a mission which remains mysterious and controversial to this day. The departure of Heß, though it had little effect on the war, had far reaching consequences for Hitler's financial affairs: it led to Bormann becoming Hitler's personal secretary.

At a 1941 dinner in honour of Himmler, Hitler is recorded as saying:

> *As far as my own private existence is concerned, I shall always live simply — but in my capacity of Führer and Head of the State, I am obliged to stand out clearly from amongst all the people around me. If my close associates glitter with decorations, I can distinguish myself from them only by wearing none at all.* [37]

This, as we have seen, is a gross distortion. Hitler certainly distinguished himself from Göring by the drabness of his uniform, but his lifestyle, with fifty servants at the Berghof alone, can hardly be called 'simple'.

On 4 July 1942, having become obsessed with his own mortality, Hitler is said to have remarked that, 'since he could take nothing with him into the grave, he might as well pay his headquarters expenses out of his own pocket'.[38] It is unclear from the context whether 'headquarters' refers to the *Wolfsschanze*, in East Prussia, where this statement is alleged to have been made, or to the *Berghof*. At the *Wolfsschanze* in the summer of 1942, Hitler once again demonstrated needless extravagance. The headquarters was situated in the Masurian lakes, a damp location, infested in summertime with mosquitoes and lusty bullfrogs. In an effort to control the mosquitoes, the staff poured kerosene onto the lakes. Unfortunately, this also killed the bullfrogs. Hitler was incensed. The frogs, he said, serenaded him to sleep. Fresh frogs were imported from elsewhere.[39]

From here on, with the war beginning to go badly, Hitler's income and expenditure patterns changed. Increasingly, his financial affairs became dominated by Bormann (though Amann seems to have remained in charge of income from the *Eher Verlag*) and Hitler was less in direct control of his own expenditures. Hitler's Fortune must now be judged on the basis of those who managed it and the assets it purchased.

Notes

1 Words and translation from DAVI77, p. 339.
2 DIET57, pp. 171-2.
3 von Lang (LANG79, p. 89) claims that it was Brückner who asked for the money; I have chosen to believe it was Schaub since he was known to have been responsible for similar tasks on other occasions.
4 TURN85B, p. 318.
5 POOL78, p. 385.
6 HEID44, p. 410.
7 KERS98, p. 448, citing Turner; TOLA76, p. 303.
8 POOL97, p. 32; TOLA76, p. 304; MOSL74, p. 153.
9 DAVI77, p. 346.
10 FRA46, p. 113. Pool, (POOL97, p. 57) seems to think that these were the total assets.
11 KERS98, p. 484.
12 CHAU01, p. 38 which shows facsimiles letters written on different dates. The first is undated; the second dated 9 October 1933; and the third, to which a swastika logo has now been added and all references to Hitler removed, is dated 24 January 1934.
13 HEID44, p. 434. Heiden has people bursting into tears of joy when they heard the news on the radio – though not in his 1936 book. Domarus (DOMA62a, p. 242) has the text of a wire from the *Wolffs Telegraphisches Büro* (presumably intended for foreign consumption) which makes no mention of the salary being donated to charity.
14 HALE64, p. 838.
15 HALE64, p. 839.
16 HALE64, p. 840.
17 HALE64, p. 840.
18 HALE64, p. 840.
19 HALE64, pp. 840-841.
20 HALE64, p. 841.
21 ORLO73, p. 149 and associated footnote 206.
22 SPEE70, p. 76.
23 SCHW89, p. 10.

24 SPEE70, p. 106; MASE73, p. 213. GUN68, p. 169, has the date as 8 May.

25 Roxan, David, and K. Wanstall. *The Jackdaw of Linz*, 1964, p. 37.

26 SPEE70, p. 130.

27 Spotts also refers to the financing of The Merry Widow [SPOT03, p. 273]. To this author, it seems more likely that such productions were financed from the Cultural Fund, rather than from the *AH Spende*.

28 SPEE70, p. 149. Additional details are given in the *Völkischer Beobachter* of 21 April 1939.

29 GUN68, p. 180.

30 Foreign Office minute dated 26 September 1939, from Mr. E. Baggallay, reference E 6678/6678/91. In File FO371/23189, Public Record Office, Kew, England.

31 Foreign Office minute dated 2 October 1939, from Mr. E. Baggallay, reference E 6764/6678/91. In File FO371/23189, Public Record Office, Kew, England.

32 Foreign Office letter dated 7 October 1939, from Mr. E. Baggallay, reference E 6764/6678/91. In File FO371/23189, Public Record Office, Kew, England.

33 Foreign Office minute dated 16 November 1939, from Mr. E. Baggallay, reference E 7549/6678/91. In File FO371/23189, Public Record Office, Kew, England.

34 Ibid.

35 DIET57, p. 182.

36 Flannery, Harry ,W. *Assignment to Berlin*. 1942. Extract quoted from the US Office of Strategic Services Hitler Source Book.

37 HITL53, p. 102. Night of 21-22 October, 1941.

38 MASE73, p. 217. Maser claims that this statement was made on 4 July 1942; however the author can find no corresponding statement in HITL53.

39 ODON78, p. 52.

Chapter Twelve

BUSINESS-LIKE DWARFS

William sighed. 'My father used to say that gold is all dwarfs think about.'
'Pretty much.' The dwarf took another pinch of snuff.
Terry Pratchett, 1947–
The Truth, pp. 182-3

Two men dominated Hitler's personal business affairs prior to 1934: Max Amann and Heinrich Hoffmann. Neither was particularly tall and Oron Hale, the historian who first researched the financial affairs of the *Eher Verlag* and Hitler's tax records, used the phrase 'Hitler's Business Dwarfs' as a chapter heading in his book *The Captive Press in the Third Reich*. In fact, it was Heiden who first referred to '*Max Amann and Heinrich Hoffmann . . . two business-like dwarfs*'.[1] Amann greatly enriched Hitler – and himself – through his astute management of the *Eher Verlag*; Hoffmann did likewise through his management and copyrighting of Hitler's image. Adolf Müller, the printer, contributed directly to Amann's personal wealth and indirectly to Hitler's.

Few of those close to Hitler who have written memoirs, or who testified at the Nuremberg trials or at later denazification courts have had much to say about the management of his personal finances. The one exception is Otto Dietrich, in his post-war memoirs. Dietrich, however, was never as close to Hitler as he sometimes likes to claim; nonetheless, his observations, remote or second-hand though they may be, are worth examining in some detail:

> *Hitler paid for the* Berghof *out of the income from his book,* Mein Kampf. *This raises the question of his habits and ideas with regard to money, capital and private property – a subject that has been much discussed.*[2]

Hitler needed far more than the profits from *Mein Kampf* to finance the *Berghof*. That his finances should be 'much discussed' comes as no surprise, but such discussion as there was must necessarily have been in private; as Wagener noted (see Chapter 9), such discussion was actively discouraged. Dietrich continues:

Actually it may be said that money meant nothing to Hitler. He never had a bank account. He did not use a wallet. Whenever he needed ready cash for contributions to the Winter Relief or for some similar purpose, it was slipped to him by his adjutant, or else he reached for loose change in his trousers pocket.[3]

It is certainly untrue that Hitler never had a bank account; throughout the nineteen-twenties his notepaper carried the number of his personal account and two bank accounts in his name were seized by the State of Bavaria in 1948. The adjutant was generally Schaub, whose story is recounted in the next chapter. Dietrich, however, clearly understood the importance of Amann and he seems to link Hitler directly through Amann to the *Eher Verlag*. Dietrich also notes:

In financial matters Hitler was ignorant, but generous. As a private person he did not know how to handle his own money, and as head of state he could not manage the government budget.[4]

Max Amann

Max Amann is one of those figures who is always mentioned in histories of the Nazi period – especially in biographies of Hitler – but who seems peripheral. A loyal party man, an old wartime comrade of Hitler, and the general manager of the *Eher Verlag*. A technocrat – and an effective one – but one operating in a field which had little direct impact on either the Nazis or the subsequent war. All of this is true – as far as it goes – but it misses the most important point of all: Max Amann was one of Hitler's bankers. Without Amann, Hitler would never have been able to propagate his ideas so effectively; *Mein Kampf* would probably never have been published at all, let alone become a best seller; and Hitler would never have become one of the richest men in Europe. So who was Max Amann?

Only one other author has previously studied Max Amann in depth and that is Professor Oron Hale who, as a Lieutenant-Colonel in the US Army and head of the Foreign Press Section, War Department General Staff, interviewed Amann at Nuremberg in 1945 and later in 1950-52. Hale's account is invaluable to the historian, but suffers from a tendency to be as brutal as possible towards his subject.[5] This is understandable; Hale saw at first hand the havoc that Hitler, aided by Amann and his associates, had wrought over Europe. Hale was also no doubt aware of the various scandals in Amann's life; he is said, like Müller, to have had several illegitimate children and his wife had tried, unsuccessfully, to drown herself because of her husband's infidelities.[6] It is not the purpose of this work to rehabilitate Amann; what is suggested is that he was a man ahead of his time; Amann's business practices, reprehensible though they were to a man of Hale's generation, appear tame when compared to those of some of his present-day equivalents. Two contrary opinions of Amann's abilities are often quoted:

As regards Amann, I can say positively that he's a genius. He is the greatest newspaper proprietor in the world![7]

Max Amann — Hitler's business dwarf.[8]

Lüdecke, who knew Amann well and may have had good reasons to dislike him, was even more emphatic, even prophetic:

The whole secret of the Eher Verlag *probably never will be known. Certain it is that Hitler's extraordinary rise from an obscure nobody to a national leader and Mikado over sixty million Germans could never have taken place without Amann's aid.*[9]

As usual, the truth lies somewhere in between. Max Amann was born in Munich on 24 November 1891, and died there, in extreme poverty, on 31 March 1957. He attended some form of business school — probably at technical high-school level — and served an office apprenticeship with a Munich law firm. Called up on the outbreak of war in 1914, he served in the front line and rose to the rank of sergeant. From 1915 to 1918 he was Hitler's company sergeant.[10] Discharged from the army in 1919, Amann married, fathered two children, and took a job with a mortgage bank where he was working in 1920 when he somehow resumed contact with Hitler. As with so many things concerned with Nazi Germany, there are two versions of this encounter: one disseminated before 1945, the other after.

According to Amann's pre-1945 story, in early 1920 he met Hitler by chance in the street and was invited to attend an NSDAP meeting, as a result of which he joined the party in February of that year. (His NSDAP membership number was 3, leading some ill-informed persons to think that he was number three in the party hierarchy.) In the summer of 1921, following his take-over of the party apparatus, Hitler offered Amann the full-time position of business manager to the NSDAP. Amann was reluctant to accept the post as he had a secure job with good pension prospects; what, he asked, could the NSDAP offer that was better? According to Amann, Hitler then proceeded to give him a two hour lecture on the perils of Bolshevism, adding, 'What good will your pension rights do you if some day the Bolsheviks string you up from a lamp post?'[11] Amann took three days to think over Hitler's offer before accepting.

The version after 1945 was somewhat different.[12] Amann posed as a simple businessman whose only interest was in publishing and who had had no more involvement with the Nazi party than the minimum necessary for his business activities. As the records show, this was far from the truth. However, as the records also show, Amann had every reason to lie; he had several hundred million *marks* to lose. Just how he got to that enviable position is best examined chronologically.

From the start, Amann and Hitler seem to have been close friends. Hanfstaengl describes how Hitler would pass by Amann's office each morning for coffee and a chat.[13] At some point (perhaps in 1922, but the date is uncertain), Amann was appointed business manager of the NSDAP, replacing Rudolf Schüßler – ironically, manager of the Jewish-owned Aufhäuser bank in Munich.

In 1923, Amann played a minor role in the *Putsch*, for which he was jailed for 23 days on a charge of 'aiding and abetting high treason'. At his trial, on 15 April 1924, he fudged his part in events – which was anyway minor – and was let off with a fine of 100 gold *marks* or ten days' imprisonment on the lesser count of 'illegal assumption of official authority'. The court was, in any case, biased towards the conspirators.

The police were naturally interested in the funding of the Nazi party and on 2 June 1924 Amann was interrogated. Amann stoutly maintained that, as business manager of the NSDAP, he was only responsible for membership dues and contributions. He admitted to passing funds to Göring for support of the SA and further disclosed that the NSDAP bank account was with the Hansabank. Amann also admitted that admirers made substantial gifts to Hitler, but refused to disclose either the amounts or the sources. He denied that these gifts passed through his hands – which was untrue – claiming that they were given to Hitler personally and used by him for party propaganda.

When the NSDAP was re-founded on 16 February 1925, Franz Xaver Schwarz took on the duties of party treasurer, relieving Amann as business manager. As part of this reorganisation, Hitler insisted that the *Eher Verlag* remained independent of Schwarz's financial oversight.[14] Amann, as general manager, would report directly to Hitler, as leader of the party. Amann was a good, if rather forceful, manager, very much in the modern 'tabloid' mould, if the following anecdote from Heiden is to be believed:

> *The paper must be sensational, Amann demanded; it must politically educate our members, said Rosenberg, whom God had not created to be a newspaperman. 'I spit on the members; business comes first', Amann cried back; and he said the same thing to his leader, Hitler.*[15]

Amann – together with Streicher and Esser – was the source of much friction at this time between the NSDAP in north Germany and its counterpart in Bavaria.[16] The north – probably rightly – saw this trio dominating the NSDAP to the detriment of northern interests. It may well be that Hitler moved Amann to the less prominent, though potentially more important, post of general manager at the *Eher Verlag* as a means of placating the northern factions. Lüdecke writes, of Amann and Streicher:

> *. . . it is only fair to say that their attitude was dictated not by petty, selfish ambition, but by fanatic devotion to Hitler, whom both regarded as the only true prophet. This fervent conviction and their limitations of experience, made them unbearable fellows at times and created very unpleasant situations. Yet Amann's position as holder of the money-bag and as Hitler's most intimate confidant in financial matters was unassailable . . .*[17]

The implication is that the 'money bag' was Hitler's rather than that of the

NSDAP, since Schwarz had replaced Amann as party treasurer. From their earliest association, Hitler put great trust in Amann. It is a measure of that trust that only two people were permitted to escort Geli Raubal alone to the theatre and to restaurants: the two 'business-like dwarfs', Amann and Hoffmann. That trust extended to financial matters. Much has been made of Amann's violent nature and there is plenty of evidence for it. Even so, the image of Amann and Rosenberg hurling ink pots at each other is not without a certain humour, as is the story of Amann bullying Josef Berchtold:

> Berchtold was not only SS leader, but also an editor of the Völkischer Beobachter, letting himself be bullied into the most humiliating services by the efficient and violent Amann. Consequently, Berchtold had to instruct his troop 'to recruit readers and advertisers for the Völkischer Beobachter'. [18]

Lüdecke describes Amann in 1932:

> I hadn't seen him for seven years. He was the same little man, strong and active looking, with a heavy head on a short neck almost lost between his shoulders. I was aware again of his prominent nose and small, peculiarly brilliant blue eyes, which constantly wandered about as if roving for game. [19]

Amann was a keen hunter, sharing the passion for the chase with Göring and many other Nazis. Some time in 1931, while hunting with his old friend Ritter von Epp – source of part of the money originally used to purchase the *Eher Verlag* – Amann lost his left arm in a firearms accident. Just what effect this accident had on Amann, and whether it affected his behaviour, if at all, is not clear. Certainly, he carried on hunting.

Shortly after the January 1933 elections, on 13 March, Goebbels was appointed *Reichsminister für Volkserklärung und Propaganda* (Reich Minister for Public Enlightenment and Propaganda), which nominally put him in overall charge of the German press. However, in keeping with the Hitlerian principles of 'divide and rule', Amann was appointed head of Reich Press Chamber and Otto Dietrich "Press Chief of the Reich Government". Both Amann and Dietrich were nominally under Goebbels, a situation which Dietrich seems to have accepted but which Amann merely ignored.

In early 1933, the Nazi leadership began to put pressure on the Ullstein publishing company, Germany's largest. Jewish-owned and -managed, Ullstein not only published books, for which it was world famous, but also newspapers, weeklies, magazines, and trade publications. Politically liberal, among its publications were the daily *Berliner Morgenpost* (circulation about 500,000); the daily *B-Z am Mittag* (200,000); and the weeklies *Montagspost* (500,000+); *Berliner Illustrierte* (2 million); and *Grüne Post*, a family magazine (1 million). [20] With such circulation and its liberal traditions, the Ullstein empire offered serious competition not only to the *Eher Verlag* but also to the ideas and ideals of the NSDAP. After January 1933, the Ullstein company was doomed, despite the efforts of the owners which included a complete reorganisation, with a non-Jewish board and senior managers.

An attempt to enlist the support of Heß, through the intermediary of Karl Haushofer, failed completely.

In January of 1934, the Ullstein affair came to a head. Goebbels, in overall charge of the German press, had closed down the *Grüne Post* – an inoffensive 'family' paper – for three months for alleged infractions of the press laws. Amann, ever the businessman, smelled trouble; if such closures continued, or even increased – and there were signs that they would – the Ullstein companies would be in danger of bankruptcy. And a bankrupt company would be worthless to Amann and the *Eher Verlag*, and thus to Hitler. To make matters worse, Goebbels, who owned his own publishing house in Berlin, was showing signs of wanting to take over Ullstein – bankrupt or not. The problem was, the *Eher Verlag* did not have the money to purchase Ullstein, and neither did Goebbels, unless it were forced into a sale at an unrealistically low price. At that time, Ullstein was just too big and too powerful for the usual intimidation tactics to work. Something else would have to be done.

At this point, a new and interesting character entered the story: Dr. h.c. Max Winkler.[21] In 1923, Winkler was a government-appointed trustee, handling businesses in that part of Poland that had previously been part of West Prussia. It was a difficult and responsible job and Winkler, who was largely self-educated, did it well. In 1929, as part of his legitimate business on behalf of the government, Winkler formed a company called Cautio GmbH, of which he was the sole director and shareholder. One of the tasks which he performed for the German government was the setting up and operation of newspapers to serve the German minorities in Poland, and for this he set up another company, *Cura Treuhand und Prüfung GmbH* (Cura Trustee and Auditing Company).

After the Nazi victory in the 1933 elections, Winkler, who had previously been an active fund-raiser for the Social Democrats, moved rapidly to the right and brought himself to the favourable notice of Amann, Goebbels, Funk, Lammers, and Reinhardt – thus ensuring his continued employment as Reich trustee for the German press in Poland. With his knowledge of the newspaper industry and his good business sense, he soon began working as an agent of Goebbels, for whom he purchased the *Telegraph Union* from Hugenberg, later merging it with the *Wolff Telegraph Bureau* to form DNB, a news agency entirely subservient to Goebbels' Ministry of Propaganda.

By early 1934, the Ullstein family was ready to sell. Frau Ullstein dropped a hint to Winkler, who passed the news on to Goebbels. Goebbels then authorised Winkler to make the Ullstein family an offer: the business was valued at between fifty and sixty million marks; Winkler offered twelve. After further negotiations, the Ullsteins bowed to the inevitable and accepted, thinking that they were selling to the Reich Propaganda ministry.

Meanwhile, probably prompted by Amann, Hitler intervened. Since the *Eher Verlag* did not have the necessary funds, a loan of RM 30 million was arranged from the seized assets of the trade-union run *Bank Deutscher Arbeit*. When Winkler requested the first payment, it was not the finance ministry but the private concern of *Eher Verlag* which paid, and which received title to Ullstein. As Amann is said to have remarked: *Now we have bought the largest German publishing house and it has not cost us as much as a pencil.*[22] These moves did not pass unnoticed. In his introduction to Bella Fromm's *Blood and Banquets*, Frederick T. Birchall, chief European correspondent of *The New York Times* from 1932-39 writes:

> *The great House of Ullstein . . . was "Aryanized" and taken over by the Nazis. Its ownership, long afterwards, was revealed as resting with the publishers of Hitler's* Mein Kampf, *with little doubt that the profits went to the Fuehrer himself. No wonder that he could forego his salary as Chancellor.*[23]

Birchall was closer to the truth than he realised. Not only was Amann adept at acquiring profitable businesses, he was equally adept at disposing of unprofitable ones, as Hitler remarks:

> [Amann is] *likewise very clever when it's a matter of handing over to others businesses that are not showing a profit. That's what happened when he gave Sauckel a newspaper. It had belonged to Dinter, and Amann had taken it over for political reasons. A short time afterwards, I happened to ask Sauckel what Amann's present had brought him in. "Up to date it has cost me twenty thousand marks," he replied.*[24]

On 30 January 1936, Amann was appointed *SS Obergruppenführer*, probably as an *Ehrenführer*, an honorary position bestowed by Himmler.[25] Such appointments were a form of flattery by Himmler; most honorary SS members did not parade such titles because they were not as important as their own. The 1942 *Dienstalterliste* of the SS shows Amann as being attached to the *Stab des Reichsführers SS*, as most honorary members were. Such attachment was purely symbolic. In 1938 (or possibly 1936), Amann was also given 'plenipotentiary powers' by Hitler.[26] The nature of these powers remains unclear. In diplomacy, a plenipotentiary is someone with powers to act on behalf of a government; did Amann mean that he was given the power to act on Hitler's behalf? If so, the most likely areas in which Amann could exercise such powers are the management of the *Eher Verlag*, where he was already general manager, the management of Hitler's royalties from *Mein Kampf*, and the overall control of the German press. In the case of *Mein Kampf*, the evidence strongly suggests that Amann had been managing Hitler's royalties since it was first published. For the German press, Goebbels, through the Propaganda Ministry, was in control of content and, as can be seen from the history of take-overs, the *Eher Verlag* was rapidly <u>becoming</u> the German press. Which leads back to Amann acting as plenipotentiary for Hitler with regard to the *Eher Verlag*. If this reasoning is correct – and the author freely admits that it is somewhat tenuous – it is further evidence of Hitler's personal interest in the *Eher Verlag*.

Throughout his so-called 'Secret Conversations', Hitler has much to say about Amann:

> *Amann is one of the oldest of my companions. He was infinitely valuable to me, for I had no notion of what double entry book-keeping was.... As regards Amann, I can say positively that he's a genius. He's the greatest newspaper proprietor in the world. Despite his great discretion, which explains why it's not generally known, I declare that Rothermere and Beaverbrook are mere dwarfs compared to him. Today, the Zentral Verlag owns from 70 percent to 90 percent of the German press.*[27]

Since Amann was sometimes referred to by Hitler as 'that dwarf', the comparison with Rothermere and Beaverbrook is somewhat ironic. Again:

> *Amann's great idea was to guarantee the financial existence of the newspaper by the profits realised on the Party editions. These profits accumulated so quickly that the newspaper quickly stopped being exposed to any risks.*[28]

Is Hitler here implying that it was the profits from the obligatory purchase of copies of the *Völkischer Beobachter* that kept the paper financially sound, rather than random street sales and non-party subscriptions? If so, then the implication is that the NSDAP was indirectly contributing to the income of both Hitler and Amann. Hitler goes on to shed some light on the ownership of the *Völkischer Beobachter*:

> *Amann realised what a tour de force it was to maintain the house of publication during my incarceration in Landsberg. For once, the juggleries* [sic] *of the lawyers were useful to us. The publishing house was a limited company, and the law required the unanimous agreement of its members for its dissolution. By chance, one of the members, Herr von Sebottendorf, was always abroad (in Turkey, I think), and of course Amann could never succeed in getting hold of him. ...*
>
> *Very intelligently, for reasons of camouflage, Amann created on the side the Hoheneichen* [Verlag] *whose name covered certain publications. And he left the press to Adolf Müller so as not to have to bring action against Party comrades for payment of their bills.*
>
> *The fact that I was able to keep the* Völkischer Beobachter *on its feet throughout the period of our struggle— and in spite of the three failures it had suffered before I took it over—I owe first and foremost to the collaboration of* Reichsleiter Amann. *He, as an intelligent business man, refused to accept responsibility for an enterprise if it did not possess the economic prerequisites of potential success. Thanks to this rule of his, the publishing firm of Eher, the proprietors of the* Völkischer Beobachter, *developed into one of the most powerful newspaper trusts in the world, beside which the American Press Lords appeared like pigmies.*[29]

Hitler talks of Amann's discretion over money matters:

> *If the* Völkischer Beobachter, *which originally had merely a few thousand subscribers, has now become a gigantic enterprise, in which reckoning is by the million, we owe it first and foremost to the exemplary industry of Reichsleiter Amann. Thanks to a quite military discipline, he has succeeded in getting the very best out of his colleagues, suppressing particularly all contact between the editorial and the administrative staffs. I don't know how often Amann, when telling me of the great financial development of the newspaper, begged me to make no mention of the fact in front of Rosenberg, the editor in chief, or the other members of the editorial staff. Otherwise, he used to say, they would plague him for higher salaries.*[30]

Could it be that another reason for Amann's reticence was the profit that the paper was making for himself and for Hitler?

Amann was taken prisoner in early May, 1945, at his summer home on the Tegernsee by security troops of the US 141st Infantry, on a SHAEF warrant, charging him with war crimes. Even at the end of the war, Amann's importance was completely misunderstood. In 1945, US General George S. Patton presented the Huntington Library in Pasadena, California, with the original draft of the notorious Nuremberg Laws and a limited edition of *Mein Kampf*, about which he said:

> *That book was alleged by a talkative German to be one of a limited edition of the unexpurgated text. There were alleged to have been 100 copies. It was published by a man named Emman [sic]. He is the No 3 bad man in Germany. I have him in jail now. We'll stretch him pretty quick!* [31]

Patton was wrong. Amann did testify at Nuremberg, and his testimony was true only in so far as it went: he was only obeying orders.[32]

In 1948 Amann, like all Germans of any significance to the Nazi cause, underwent a 'denazification trial' – in this case, a trial initiated by the German authorities, rather than by the occupying powers. Well reported, the transcript has been used to portray Amann as a brutal, two-fisted roughneck. During the trial, eleven instances of violence were alleged, though few, if any, were judicially proven. In his summing-up of the trial, the general prosecutor said that, 'in his entire life Amann was never anything more than a brutal sergeant'.[33] The prosecutor declared Amann to be 'a major offender' and sentenced him to ten years' hard labour, confiscation of all but DM 5,000 of his property, and 'loss of civil rights'.

There seems little doubt that Amann was a blusterer and a verbal bully, but there seems little hard evidence of physical violence. Yet his blustering and business practices seem little different from those of many businessmen today. That he was an anti-Semite and an active Nazi is beyond question. There is also no doubt that without Max Amann neither the Nazis nor Hitler would have had the funds that they did. Nor would Amann himself.

One of the things which a denazification court looked for was evidence of unusual growth in income after 1933. As Table 12-1 and Figure 12-1 show, in Amann's case the evidence was damning. Of course, not all of this was income from the *Eher Verlag*; some must have come from his shares in *Müller u. Sohn*, the printers. According to Hale, Amann received five percent of the profits of the *Eher Verlag* in addition to his salary. How much of his income came from his one third share in *Müller u. Sohn* is not known, but a reasonable guess might be between ten and fifty percent. If these assumptions are correct, then the evidence of Amann's denazification trial gives a back door route to an estimate of the *Eher Verlag's* profits – and thus to Hitler's possible income from that source. Hale also gives Amann's 1944 income as RM 3,800,000 which is consistent with the denazification trial data, but is not included in that source. Using these data, and for simplicity, neglecting Amann's salary, minimum and maximum estimates of *the Eher Verlag's* profits are given in Table 12-2. It is clear that Amann did very well out of his five percent. In the 1950 confiscation order for his property, his assets are listed as[34]:

1   Property at St Quirin, valued at DM 420,000
2   Interior furnishings of the St Quirin property, valued at DM 800,000
3   Property in Munich, Wasserburger Straße 6, valued at DM 112,000
4   Interior furnishings of the Munich property, valued at DM 100,000
5   Shares in the printing company of *Müller u. Sohn*, valued at RM 1,600,000
6   Reich treasury notes to the value of RM 4,885,000
7   Bonds of value RM 187,000 equivalent to DM 13,390
8   Bank account containing DM 3,000
9   Bank account containing DM 13,571

These assets total RM 26.9 million. Interpolating Amann's income for those years for which no records are quoted, gives his total income between 1934 and 1944 as RM 24.4 million. The small difference between asset value and total income is insignificant and can be accounted for by the usual appreciation of property values. There is clearly no discrepancy between Amann's income and assets.

It is interesting to note that this list of assets makes no mention of the *Eher*

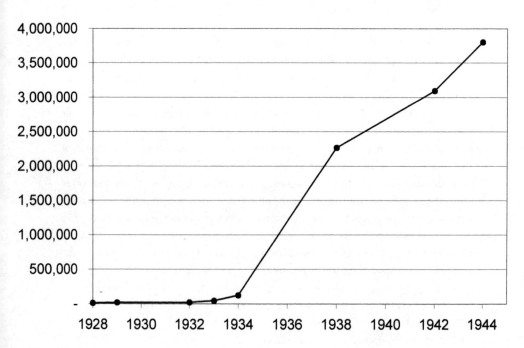

Figure 12-1: Max Amann's Income (RM)

Table 12-1: Amann's income, 1928-42

Year	Income (RM)
1928	11,541
1929	18,095
1932	21,830
1933	44,477
1934	122,403
1938	2,266,108
1942	3,092,705

Table 12-2: Eher Verlag, estimated profits 1933-44

		From Muller u. Sohn		5% of Eher Verlag		Eher Verlag profits	
Year	Income	Min	Max	Min	Max	Min	Max
1933	44,477	4,448	22,239	22,239	40,029	444,770	800,586
1934	122,703	12,270	61,352	61,352	110,433	1,227,030	2,208,654
1938	2,266,108	226,611	1,133,054	1,133,054	2,039,497	22,661,080	40,789,944
1942	3,092,705	309,271	1,546,353	1,546,353	2,783,435	30,927,050	55,668,690
1944	3,800,000	380,000	1,900,000	1,900,000	3,420,000	38,000,000	68,400,000

Verlag, suggesting that Amann owned no shares in that business, even though he received a portion of the profits. However, Hale claims that in 1943 Amann's business assets were assessed for tax purposes at ten million marks. This is not consistent with the assets listed at his denazification trial, of which only the shares in Müller u. Sohn seem to fit the criterion of 'business asset'. Even if the Reich Treasury notes and the bonds are counted as business assets, this still leaves RM 3.3 million unaccounted for. The discrepancy could be accounted for by assuming that Amann did hold shares in the Eher Verlag, but there is no other supporting evidence for this.

Heinrich Hoffmann

Hoffmann is far better known than Amann, simply because he was Hitler's official photographer. This in itself would not be sufficient to warrant his inclusion in this story but, as Snyder, one of the few writers to group the two men together, notes:

Court photographer to Hitler and the National Socialist Party and, with Max Amann, the man responsible for the Fuehrer's wealth.[35]

Heinrich Hoffmann was born on 12 September, 1885, at Fürth, and died 16 December 1957, in Munich. The son of a successful photographer, he learned his craft in his father's business. He served as a photographer in the Bavarian Army in WWI and published his first book of photographs, *Ein Jahr Bayerische Revolution im Bilde* (*A Year of Bavarian Revolution in Photographs*), in 1919.[36] This book, which had nothing to do with Hitler, became a best-seller and by 1925 had brought him a net profit of half a million marks.[37] In 1923, he became Hitler's personal photographer, and for a long time was the only person allowed to photograph him. Otto Dietrich, in his post-war memoirs, claims that Hoffmann and his family were the only people Hitler regularly associated with in Munich, but this is clearly at odds with the other evidence. However, Dietrich is correct when he notes that Hitler admired Hoffmann's conversational gifts and his knowledge of painting.

Hoffmann encouraged Hitler in his art collecting, introduced him to his later mistress and wife, Eva Braun, and also introduced him to Morell, who became his personal physician. He published a series of picture books, with titles such as *Germany Awakened*, *The Brown House*, and *Hitler Unknown*, all of which had huge sales and made Hoffmann a fortune, though Gun rather mysteriously remarks:

. . . he managed to amass millions and would have pocketed much more had Martin Bormann not been "breathing down his neck."[38]

He held the title deeds to Eva Braun's Munich apartment on Hitler's behalf and also controlled profits from a book of photographs taken by her and her sister, Gretl. He was elected to the *Reichstag* in 1933 and given an honorary professorship, a title highly valued in Germany and not necessarily associated with an academic appointment, in 1938. Hoffmann, like Hanfstaengl, had a reputation as something of a 'court jester', as Lüdecke notes:

. . . Hoffmann was an ideal companion, humorous and amusing, a good story-teller, with plenty of what the Germans call 'mother-wit'. At Haus Wachenfeld, Kannenberg with his accordion and Hoffmann are said to be a team that can make Hitler laugh himself sick. I found plenty of horse-sense behind his jester's mask, however, and we had a rollicking time.[39]

Hoffmann was tried as a war profiteer before a German court in 1947. Sentenced to ten years' imprisonment, all his fortune, except DM 3,000, was confiscated, and his title of professor was annulled. In 1948, his sentence was reduced to three years, then raised to five years in 1950. Somehow, he persuaded the authorities to return to him his extensive collection of glass-plate photographic negatives of

Hitler, which was later purchased from Hoffmann's son by Gerd Heidemann, one of the parties to the notorious 'Hitler Diaries' fraud of the nineteen-eighties.

Müller

In its early days, the *Eher Verlag* owned no printing plant; instead, all printing was sub-contracted to the firm of *M. Müller u. Sohn* whose plant was at Schellingstraße 39, on the corner with Barerstraße, in the district of Alte Pinakothek – close to the editorial offices of the *Völkischer Beobachter* and about 20 minutes walk from the *Eher Verlag* offices. It was also opposite the photographic studios of Heinrich Hoffmann. The son, Adolf Müller, was a Nazi party supporter from the earliest days, though not a party member but rather a member of the Bavarian People's Party. He was also an astute – and lucky – businessman. With Amann's help, the company prospered. By 1933 his company was the exclusive printer of all official Nazi party material, including books and the *Völkischer Beobachter*, and Müller was a very wealthy man; as early as 1928, he had a luxurious house at St Quirin, on the shores of the Tegernsee about 50km south of Munich. Amann, too, built a palatial summer home there. Heiden describes him:

> . . . a short stout man, who was unknown to most of the Party-comrades. On this stranger, however, the whole re-organisation of the Party was based. He was Adolf Müller, the almost stone-deaf printing-press proprietor, and owner of the rotary machine of the Völkischer Beobachter.[40]

Max Amann was also a shareholder in M. Müller und Söhn and retained his holding even after such investments by party members were banned in 1934, receiving a generous percentage of the profits.

Adolf Müller appears to have been close to Hitler in the early twenties, even teaching Hitler to drive – and refusing to be driven by him in consequence! His large house on the Tegernsee, near Munich, was often used by Hitler and the leaders of the NSDAP for conferences.[41] When Geli Raubal died in 1931, it was to Müller's home that Hitler retired in a state of near-hysterical despair.[42] Of Müller, Lüdecke wrote:

> Though Mueller was a member of the Bavarian People's party, he was first of all a business man, and he had done the printing for the Party since the acquisition of the Beobachter. Until the putsch in 1923, business had been good and the two Adolfs had become friends. This friendship was to prove valuable. In the critical time after Hitler's release from Landsberg, it was Adolf Mueller who advanced cash and printed the paper on credit until it was afloat again. Herr Mueller, who is stout and almost deaf, must have an excellent nose, for he became a millionaire.[43]

Müller was always fairly tolerant of late payments by both the NSDAP and the *Eher Verlag*, though occasionally he would threaten not to print the *Völkischer Beobachter* until he received at least some of the money due. On such occasions, Hitler would launch into one of his screaming tirades, but since Müller was profoundly deaf he easily ignored them. Some money was usually paid and normal relations restored. Hitler has much to say about Müller:

> It was through Dietrich Eckart that I got to know Müller. Our first encounter was not favourable, and I was astonished that Eckart should have put me in touch with such an individual . . .
>
> That happened well before I had the VB. Müller was wedged in his arm-chair with the self assurance of a plutocrat. His first words were: "To prevent any misunderstanding from arising, let it be clearly understood that, where there's no payment, there's no printing either."
>
> When one visited him, Müller never ceased to groan. Nevertheless, he grew fatter and fatter. He printed more and more. He constantly bought new machines, but his leitmotiv was: "I can't get along on these rates. I'm ruining myself." "To see you so fat, one wouldn't believe it." "I've so many worries that I drink a little to drown them, and that swells you up!" His press is equipped in the most modern style. He's a real genius in the Party. Cunning, nobody could be more so, but he was an employer with a sense of social responsibility. He paid his workers well, and when he took them for an outing, he paid no attention to expense. For a firm of that size, in any case, that meant less than nothing. And the VB was always there to cough up!
>
> I never made a journey with Müller without his having to pay a visit to some woman by whom he had a child. At the birth of each of his bastards, he would open an account for them at the Savings Bank, with first payment of five thousand marks. I actually know four illegitimate children of his. I wonder how such an ugly man manages to have such lovely children! I must add that Müller adores children.
>
> Every week he spends two days with Ida on the Tegernsee, although he's divorced from her. He had married her simply so that his children should have a respectable name. He likewise spends two days with his legitimate wife, at Munich, and lastly two days at his business. The rest of the time he devotes to shooting.
>
> That Müller's really quite a fellow. [44]

Again:

> For all our propaganda tours, the Party-owned presses had to print all the pamphlets without any guarantee of expenses. A man like Müller, who ran the printing presses for the Völkischer Beobachter in his own name, and for his own profit, was never victimised in this way. He would only accept orders for pamphlets against cash payment, and he always refused any dubious orders by saying that his workmen fed themselves not on political convictions, but on the pay he gave them. Our local chiefs, on the other hand, went on the theory that idealism should replace payment as far as the Party printing-presses were concerned— a theory so economically unsound that it threatened to ruin the presses in question. [45]

Notes

1   HEID44, p. 234.
2   DIET57, p. 195.
3   DIET57, pp. 195-6.
4   Ibid., p. 196.
5   HALE64.

6 LANG79, p. 277.

7 HITL53, p. 319. The evening of 22 February 1942.

8 HALE64, p. 21.

9 LÜDE38, p. 367.

10 KERS98, p. 91.

11 *Max Amann: Ein Leben für Führer und Volk.* pp. 9-10. Munich, 1941, Eher Verlag.

12 HALE64, p. 23. Hale quotes from interview notes with Amann, dated 23 August 1945. Whether these are Hales' personal notes – he interviewed Amann on several occasions – or notes made by an arresting officer is not clear.

13 HANF57, p. 44.

14 HALE64, p. 26. Quoting an un-referenced statement by Schwarz, dated 15 May 1945.

15 HEID44, p. 226.

16 KERS98, p. 270.

17 LÜDE38, p. 225.

18 HEID44, p. 243. Berchtold led the *Stosstrupp Adolf Hitler* when it was initially founded in 1923. Following Röhm's departure to Bolivia and the virtual collapse of the SA in 1925, the SS was created with Berchtold as its leader. However, the elite nature of the SS was incompatible with Berchtold's socialist principles and he resigned the leadership around 1928.

19 LÜDE38, p. 368.

20 All figures from HALE64, p. 131.

21 h.c.: *honoris causa*, indicating an honorary doctorate.

22 HALE64, p. 137, citing statements by Winkler and Wilhelm Baur.

23 FROM43, p. 9.

24 HITL53, p. 319. Evening of 22 February 1942. The Sauckel referred to is presumably Fritz Sauckel, Governor of Thuringia. Plenipotentiary for Labour Allocation during the Second World War, Sauckel was responsible for slave labour, for which he was tried and found guilty at Nuremberg and executed on 16 October 1946.

25 Information from the *Dienstalterliste* and subsequent comments kindly provided by Jason Leech in a personal message to the author. Other recipients included Ribbentrop, Bormann, Lammers, Schwartz, Dietrich etc.

26 HALE64, p. 27. Quoting notes of an interview with Amann on 22 August 1945. At that time, Amann said he had been given those powers in 1936, but he signed the 1943 auditors' report *Auf Grund der Vollmacht des Führers vom 10.XI.38* – By reason of the Führer's authority of 10 November 1938.

27 HITL53, pp. 317-9. Evening of 22 February 1942.

28 HITL53, pp. 333-4. Night of 27-28 February 1942.

29 HITL53, p. 437. 6 May 1942.

30 HITL53, p. 451. Dinner on 14 May 1942.

31 Kuntz, Tom. *On Display in Los Angeles: Legal Foreshadowing of Nazi Horror.* The New York Times. Sunday July 4, 1999.

32 A copy of Amann's statement can be viewed in the Shofar FTP Archive Files imt/nca/nca-05/nca-05-3016-ps

33 *Süddeutsche Zeitung,* 7 December 1948.

34 AMAN50.

35 SNYD76, p. 167.

36 Hoffmann had his own publishing company, *Photobericht Hoffmann.* The book's text was by Emil Herols.

37 HOFF55, p. 63.

38 GUN68, p. 47.

39 LÜDE38, p. 463.

40 HEID36, pp. 199-200.

41 HANF57, p. 130 and others.

42 HANF57, p. 165.

43 LÜDE38, p. 367.

44 HITL53, pp. 336-7. Luncheon on 1 March 1942.

45 HITL53, p. 437. 6 May 1942.

Chapter Thirteen

THE *ADOLF HITLER SPENDE*
(AND OTHER MAJOR SOURCES)

Ah, make the most of what we yet may spend,
Before we too into the Dust descend;
Dust into Dust, and under Dust to lie . . .
Edward Fitzgerald, 1809-1883
The Rubáiyát of Omar Khayyám (1859), 23

The actual origin of the *Adolf Hitler Spende der Deutschen Wirtschaft* (Adolf Hitler Fund of German Business — for convenience, this is referred to hereafter as the *AH Spende*) is somewhat uncertain. What is without doubt is that it was the major source of his personal fortune. Beside the *AH Spende*, even the royalties from *Mein Kampf* and the considerable income from the *Eher Verlag* lost their significance.

The origins of the *AH Spende* are thought to be the *National Treuhand* (roughly translatable as National Trust), which was founded on 20 February 1933 at a meeting at Göring's house. Schacht is the principal witness:

> *The amounts contributed by the participants in the meeting of 20 February 1933 at Göring's house were paid by them to the bankers. Delbruck, Schickler & Co., Berlin, to the credit of an account National Treuhand . . . It was arranged that I was entitled to dispose of this account, which I administered as a trustee, and that in case of my death, or that in case the trusteeship should be terminated in any other way, Rudolf Heß should be entitled to dispose of the account.*
>
> *I disposed of the amounts of this account by writing out checks to Mr. Heß. I do not know what Mr. Heß actually did with the money.*
>
> *On 4 April 1933, I closed the account with Delbruck, Schickler & Co. and had the balance transferred to the 'Account Ic' with the Reichsbank which was in my name. Later on I was ordered directly by Hitler, who was authorized by the assembly of 20 February 1933 to dispose of the amounts collected, or through Heß, his deputy, to pay the balance of about 600,000 marks to Ribbentrop.*[1]

A copy of what purports to be a translation of the balance sheet for the *National Treuhand* has been provided to the author by someone who wishes to remain anonymous. Although its provenance is somewhat dubious, it has been included as Table 13-I because it tallies to some extent with Schacht's Nuremberg testimony. If it is a forgery, it is difficult to see what purpose it serves. It is clear from Schacht's account that the majority of the money was transferred to Heß – RM 1,150,000, according to the 'balance sheet'. The organisations donating to the fund – if they are genuine – speak for themselves; many remain household names today. The transfer on 27 February to the *Eher Verlag* is interesting since the immediate suspicion is that the fund was being used to support the company. However, it must be remembered that the *National Treuhand* was set up specifically to cover the NSDAP's election expenses – which accounts for its rather short life – and the *Eher Verlag* published most of the party's propaganda. Why Schacht should have handed the balance of the account to Ribbentrop, and what the latter did with the money, is a mystery.

In 1933, following his sudden conversion to Nazism, the industrialist Gustav Krupp von Bohlen und Halbach agreed to raise funds for Hitler and began what became the *AH Spende*. However, according to one source, the *AH Spende*'s stated purpose was '. . . *to support the SA, the SS, Hitler Youth, and political organisation of the Nazi party*.'[2] Krupp took up his post in April and immediately approached the major leaders of German industry for contributions, stressing the urgency of the situation with the phrase '*whoever helps quickly, helps doubly*.'

One inducement to contribute to the *AH Spende* that Krupp offered to his colleagues was immunity from further solicitations. Contribute to the *AH Spende* now, and no other contributions would be solicited by the NSDAP or its affiliates. Even in 1933, this was a serious problem as the number of Nazi organisations was large.[3] Krupp proposed to eliminate sporadic contributions to individual bodies in favour of a single monthly contribution, initially equal to one half percent of a company's wage and salary bill in 1932.

Over RM 30 million were contributed to the *AH Spende* in 1932 and Krupp himself is said to have given RM 6 million over several years.[4] Krupp served as the first chairman of the *AH Spende*, the office later passing to his son, Alfried. In accepting the fund, Hitler is said to have announced that he would use the money for cultural affairs and to provide charitable relief to distressed old comrades. In fact, in 1933 and 1934, most of the monies in the fund were spent on political projects.

One source claims that the *AH Spende* provided Hitler with RM 100 million per year.[5] Others put the total received at between 300 million and one billion.[6] Who could be trusted to manage such vast sums? Hitler turned to Heß, who already managed his financial affairs, and Heß delegated the task to his more experienced deputy, Bormann.

Although the *AH Spende* was supposed to be to help support the political organisations of the NSDAP, after 1935 it became more and more Hitler's personal treasure chest. This was acknowledged by Krupp, the administrator of the *AH Spende* (if not by the contributors), when he wrote to Schacht that the purpose of

Table 13-1: National Treuhand balance sheet

			Out	In
Feb.	23	Verein für die bergbaulichen Interessen, Essen		200,000.00
	24	Rudolf Heß, Berlin	100,000.00	
	24	Karl Herrmann, Automobile Exhibition, Berlin		150,000.00
				100,000.00
	25	Director A. Steinke		200,000.00
	25	Demag A.G., Duisburg		50,000.00
	27	Telefunken Gesellschaft		85,000.00
		Osram G.m.b.H., Berlin		40,000.00
	27	Eher Verlag. Bayerische Hypotheken-und Wechselbank, Munich.	100,000.00	
	27	Rudolf Heß, Berlin	100,000.00	
	28	I.G. Farbenindustrie A.G. Frankfurt/M		400,000.00
	28	Telegraph expenses for transfer to Munich	8.00	
Mar.	1	Your Payment		125,000.00
	2	Bayerische Hypotheken-und Wechselbank, Munich. Account of Josef Jung	400,000.00	
		Telegraph transfer expenses	23.00	
		Rudolf Heß	300,000.00	
	2	Director Karl Lange, Berlin		30,000.00
	3	Dir. Karl Lange, 'Maschinen-industrie' Account		20,000.00
		Verein ruer die bergbaulichen Interessen, Essen		100,000.00
		Karl Herrmann, Berlin, Dessauerstraße 28/9		150,000.00
		Allgemeine Elektrizitaetsgesellschaft, Berlin		60,000.00
	7	General-direktor Dr. F. Springorum, Dortmund		36,000.00
	8	Bayerische Hypotheken-und Wechselbank, Munich.	100,000.00	
Mar.	8	Bayerische Hypotheken-und Wechselbank, Munich.	100,000.00	
		Rudolf Heß	250,000.00	
	10	Accumulatoren-Fabrik A.G. Berlin		25,000.00
	13	Verein f.d. bergbaulichen Interessen, Essen		300,000.00
	14	Rudolf Heß	200,000.00	
	29	Rudolf Heß	200,000.00	
April	4	Commerz-und Privatbank Dep. Kasse N. Berlin W.9 Potsdamerstr. 1 f. Special		
		Account S 29	99,000.00	
	5	Interests according to list 1 percent		404.50
		Phone bills	1.00	
		Postage	2.50	
		Balance	<u>72,370.00</u>	
		Balance carried over	<u>2,021,404.50</u>	<u>2,021,404.50</u>
				72,370.00

227

the *AH Spende* was 'to represent a token of gratitude to the leader of the nation'. Also after 1935, Bormann began to expand the fund; *Gauleiters* were reminded that any legacies left to Hitler were to be forwarded to the *AH Spende* and levies were imposed upon members of the *Reichskulturkammer*. After all, reasoned Bormann, if the *AH Spende* was generous enough to provide places of employment for actors and musicians, it was only right that they, too, should show their appreciation in the way the *Führer* appreciated most – with money.

Otto Dietrich gives his account of the *AH Spende* in his post-war memoirs:

> In 1934 I heard that "business" had voluntarily donated to Hitler – in gratitude, so to speak, for the boost he had given to the economy – a fund of several million marks annually which was to be at his personal disposal, to use as he saw fit. Hitler himself in no way requested these funds and so far as I know never himself directed the spending of them. Under the name of the Adolf Hitler Industrial Fund the sum was administered by Rudolf Hess, then chief of staff, and later Party secretary Martin Bormann. Bormann, acting as trustee, used the money for Hitler's personal projects. [7]

It must be remembered – and it seems clear from his use of the expression 'I heard' – that Dietrich was not in a position to know much about Hitler's personal finances. He was, however, able to observe Bormann and his activities:

> Other funds were used to extend Hitler's private domain on the Obersalzberg beyond the actual Berghof property . . . This work was tied up with Martin Bormann's rise to the point of becoming one of Hitler's closest intimates. I have mentioned earlier that as chief of staff for Rudolf Hess, Bormann was in charge of the Adolf Hitler Industrial Fund. Bormann had formerly been administrator of the SA Relief Fund. Using the millions of the Industrial Fund to enlarge Hitler's private holdings around the Berghof, Bormann skilfully wheedled his way into Hitler's favor . . . [8]

Bormann also became involved in the daily running of the Berghof:

> Bormann then assumed economic and financial direction of the entire "household of the Fuehrer." He was especially attentive to the lady of the house, anticipating her every wish and skilfully helping her with the often rather complicated arrangements for social and state functions. This was all the more necessary since she herself tactfully kept in the background as much as possible. Bormann's adroitness in this manner undoubtedly strengthened his unassailable position of trust with Hitler, who was extraordinarily sensitive about Eva Braun. [9]

Despite his attentions, Eva Braun loathed Bormann, whom she described as 'an oversexed toad'. [10] According to O'Donnell, the *AH Spende* was used to pay for the bunker beneath the Reich Chancellery in Berlin, where Hitler finally committed suicide, but this seems most unlikely. [11] Why would Hitler's personal funds be necessary for a legitimate expense of government?

Closed Shops

At around the same time that the *AH Spende* was being organised, Rosenberg organised the 'Fighting League for German Culture'. This organisation spawned unions for professionals, such as lawyers, physicians and teachers, for whom membership was compulsory: no membership, no job.

A law of 22 September 1933 created the *Reichskulturkammer* (RKK – Reich Chamber of Culture) to which anyone wanting to work in one of its seven chambers – literature, music, film, theatre, radio, fine arts, and press – had to belong. Again, no membership, no job. The RKK was directed by Goebbels and was closely connected to his *Reichsministerium für Volksaufklärung und Propaganda* (Ministry for Public Enlightenment and Propaganda). In parallel with this, according to the usual Nazi principle of divide and rule, Ley controlled the artists' professional associations. Although the primary purpose of these organisations was to ensure that nothing reached the public that did not conform to the Nazi party line, a portion of the dues they collected also helped swell the funds of the *AH Spende*.

How much?

Estimating the amounts of the *AH Spende* is extraordinarily difficult, since documentation is lacking. The lowest estimate is Spott's, of 300 million over 13 years (Ref. A in Table 13-2); the highest is his upper estimate of 1,000 million (Ref. D in the table).[12] The closest thing to hard evidence is Krupp's claim that over 30 million *marks* (some sources give 32 million) were given in 1932 – the year before Hitler came to power (Ref. B assumes that this remained constant). Assuming that RM 32 million is correct, it would not be unreasonable for it to double after Hitler became Chancellor and thereafter to grow at a reasonable rate – say five percent per annum. It would also be reasonable to assume that income topped-out in say, 1943, as Allied bombing began to affect German industry. This is shown as Ref. C in Table 13-2. Quite remarkably – and the author did not juggle the figures to make it that way – these assumptions lead to an aggregate of a little over 1,000 million *marks*.

Table 13-2: Income from the AH Spende (million RM)

Year	1932	1933	1934	1935	1936	1937	1938	1939	1940	1941	1942	1943	1944	Total
Ref. A	23	23	23	23	23	23	23	23	23	23	23	23	23	299
Ref. B	32	32	32	32	32	32	32	32	32	32	32	32	32	416
Ref. C	32	64	67	71	74	78	82	86	90	95	99	99	99	1035
Ref. D	77	77	77	77	77	77	77	77	77	77	77	77	77	1001

Images

Encouraged by the Munich photographer Heinrich Hoffmann, Hitler profited greatly from royalties from the reproduction of his image, in particular photographs and illustrated books produced by Hoffmann and, after 1937 and in a different way, the use of Hitler's image on postage stamps.

Photographs and illustrated books

Hitler gave Hoffmann a monopoly on photographs of himself in exchange for a share of the profits, which would become large. So jealous was Hoffmann of his monopoly that when the American correspondent Hubert R. Knickerbocker brought along the renowned photographer James Edward Abbé to an interview with Hitler in November 1931, and Abbé succeeded in shooting several portraits of Hitler, Hoffmann was incensed.

Several copies of paintings made by Hitler were also published, including a limited edition portfolio of seven wartime works (published by Hoffmann in 1935), a similar portfolio for the *Hitlerjugend*, a 1936 propaganda publication entitled *Adolf Hitler: Pictures from the Life of the Führer, 1931-35* which included five works, and some images published in the American magazines *Esquire* (1936) and *Colliers* (1938).[13] Whether Hitler personally profited from these publications is not known.

Postage stamps

After 1937, Hitler received substantial sums for the use of his copyright image on postage stamps. According to Otto Dietrich, in his post-war memoir:

> Hitler was able to extend such generous patronage to German art and artists by means of a "cultural fund" which Postal Minister Ohnesorge had on his own initiative set up. With Hitler's permission Ohnesorge had printed a special stamp for collectors bearing a picture of Hitler. This stamp could be bought at all post offices in the Reich; the sale of it yielded several million marks which Ohnesorge turned over to Hitler for his own use every year.[14]

Hoffmann adds further weight to this story when he writes:

> The picture was accordingly earmarked for the Linz Gallery, and the funds for its purchase came from the Reich Postal Service, from the money acquired from the sales of a special issue of 'Hitler-stamps', which brought in many millions of marks. I myself was once present when Ohnesorge, the Postmaster General, handed Hitler a cheque for fifty million marks derived from this source.[15]

(The sum sounds incredible, but it was not.) Monies derived from this source were known as the Cultural Fund. Most writers present the Cultural Fund as if, like the *AH Spende*, it was some sort of undercover, quasi-fraudulent operation. It does not seem to have been. Indeed, Backes refers to 'its legal foundation in May 1937'.[16] Nor was there anything covert about it; special issue stamps were advertised as benefiting the fund and events were publicised as being supported by the fund. The German public knew that it was contributing, though it is doubtful if it could imagine how much. Despite the fund's legality, it was Hitler who decided how the funds were spent; it can therefore be included as part of Hitler's Fortune, though there is little evidence that any of it went to finance his personal possessions. Indeed, most of it went to finance performing arts, artists, and the purchase of paintings for the Linz Collection. Not all of this money came from postage stamps; the Cultural Fund also received contributions, arranged by Goebbels, from the film industry.

Between 1937 and 1941, all the stamps were special issues, typically promoting some charity; after 1942, the majority of stamps, except some special issues, bore his likeness.[17] The stamps were sold in 'German' territory, which included not only Germany and Austria, but also annexed territory, such as the Sudetenland and eastern Poland, and the Protectorate of Bohemia and Moravia as well as the Polish *Generalgouvernement*.

How much?

Because the fund was public knowledge, many of its records have survived (unlike those of the *AH Spende*) and Backes has provided a well-researched analysis and, on the basis of official documents, says that RM 40,777,380 flowed to the culture fund from 1937 to 20 April 1943.[18] This seems to refer to funds directly from the German Post Office because Backes notes that in addition Frank, the Minister of State for Bohemia and Moravia, transferred approximately eight million marks from the sales from special stamps in August 1943; RM 1,755,000 in April 1944 and RM 9,400,000 RM in November 1944. These figures are clearly incomplete, but at least offer a minimum estimate of the fund's income. Using these and other figures taken from Backes, and making reasonable assumptions about interest, growth of income over time and so on, it is a simple matter to estimate total income of the fund. As shown in Table 13-3, this was somewhere between

Table 13-3: Income from the Cultural Fund (million RM)

Year	1937	1938	1939	1940	1941	1942	1943	1944	Totals
Minimum	24.8	24.8	24.8	30.5	37.8	55.8	35.0	35.2	**268.6**
Probable	25.5	25.5	25.5	30.5	38.5	56.5	35.8	36.2	**273.7**
Maximum	25.5	25.5	25.5	32.5	42.8	65.5	53.2	52.2	**322.6**

RM 268 million and RM 323 million. Ohnesorge's fifty million mark cheque no longer seems so ridiculous.

The Controllers

Before looking at what Hitler spent, it is useful to summarise who controlled his money and when. Between 1920 and 1945, several people handled Hitler's personal money, managing his funds as well as receiving contributions, collecting fees and 'expenses', and paying for the day-to-day cash needs of his personal court. Because their duties certainly overlapped in time and space, they are treated below in alphabetical order.

Amann

As far as is known, Max Amann (described in detail in the previous chapter) only controlled the profits from the *Eher Verlag* and Hitler's royalties on sales of *Mein Kampf*, the latter including both domestic and foreign sales. In 1935, Hitler remarked to Speer:

> *I've absolutely used up the income from my book, although Amann's given me a further advance of several hundred thousand. Even so, there's not enough money.*[19]

It seems probable that Bormann had not yet taken control of Hitler's finances in 1935, but the question is: How did Amann handle the money? Did he give it to Hitler personally? Did he transfer it to a central fund? Or did he simply pay bills on Hitler's behalf? Given Hitler's 'divide and rule' habits and his secrecy about money, the latter seems most probable since it avoids anyone but he and Amann knowing the details.

There is strong evidence that Amann controlled at least some of Hitler's 'offshore' funds, notably an account in Switzerland which probably received foreign royalty payments for *Mein Kampf*. There is no evidence as to what this account was used for, but it would certainly have been useful to Hitler for buying paintings on the Swiss market, something he and his agents certainly did.

Bormann

Bormann's life has been well chronicled by von Lang; what is given here is merely a summary of material relevant to Hitler's finances.[20] Bormann joined the NSDAP and the SA in 1926.[21] Having learned bookkeeping as a farm estate manager, Bormann became financial manager and general factotum for the weekly newsletter *Der Nationalsozialist*. He appears to have been a successful manager and came to the notice of several senior NSDAP figures, including

Pfeffer von Salomon, then head of the SA. Needing a reliable manager for the SA Insurance Office, Salomon chose Bormann.[22] Almost immediately, Bormann re-negotiated the contract with an insurance company, greatly reducing the *per capita* monthly payment to the company – and the scope of cover – while keeping party members' monthly contributions unchanged. This 'nice little earner' for the NSDAP did not pass unnoticed. When the insurance company subsequently cancelled the contract in 1930, Bormann set up the *Hilfskasse* relief fund and increased members contributions by fifty percent to thirty *pfennigs*. Payment of dues was compulsory; payment of benefits was at the discretion of Bormann. The arithmetic was simple: 390,000 NSDAP members at the end of 1930, paying 30 *pfennig* a month, generated over 1.4 million *marks* a year. Hitler was delighted and acknowledged Bormann as a financial wizard. The fund was moved from the SA into the party organisation proper and Bormann moved with it. In 1931, Bormann brought in his younger brother, Albert, as head of the Property Damage section at the *Hilfskasse*. Albert, whose personality was much more attractive than that of his brother, did not stay long, transferring within six months to the Führer Chancellery under the shadowy Philipp Bouhler.

By 1932, Bormann was in the *Braunes Haus*, managing the *Hilfskasse* with an estimated income of over three million *marks* per annum. By 1933, it was becoming clear that Bormann had his eye on the position of Party Treasurer, a post then, and thereafter, occupied by Xaver Schwarz. Schwarz had no intention of quitting and seems to have set about trying to curb Bormann and the *Hilfskasse*. Unfortunately, events moved too quickly for whatever Schwarz had planned: Bormann resigned from the *Hilfskasse* and moved under Heß's wing as *Stabsleiter, Amt Heß* (Chief of Staff, Heß Bureau), taking up his appointment on 3 July 1933. Bormann had moved closer to the seat of power. On 10 October 1933, Bormann was appointed to the rank of *Reichsleiter*; only Hitler, Göring and Heß ranked higher.[23] Bormann began to expand his empire, circumventing Schwarz, who had financial control over all party appointments, by giving his staff vacant positions in the civil service.

As 1934 progressed, Bormann tried, unsuccessfully, to ingratiate himself with the men of the *vom dem Berg*: the adjutants, Wiedemann, Schaub and Brückner; Hoffmann; and Schreck, Hitler's principal chauffeur. Rebuffed, he began to intrigue against them but, by all appearances, failed and only Wiedemann left the group.

It is generally accepted that by mid-1935, Bormann had largely assumed control of Hitler's finances, though still nominally under the control of Heß. After the departure of Heß in May of 1941, he was in full control except, possibly, of those funds managed by Amann. The following announcement was made in the party press:

Bormann's power was now assured.

Bormann's rise to the control of Hitler's finances was greatly aided by his being placed in charge of the rebuilding and expansion of the *Berghof*, which began in the summer of 1936 and continued up to the end of the Third Reich in 1945. It was not just Bormann's involvement in project management that brought him to this position, which naturally required him to spend much of his time 'on site', but the fact that Hitler, too, spent increasing amounts of his time at the *Berghof*, leaving Heß holding the fort in Berlin. More and more Bormann became Hitler's private secretary in fact, if not in name, only assuming the formal title on 12 April 1943.

However, as early as 1942, Bormann had taken control of Hitler's appointments calendar, with the exception of military matters. Whether this control extended to Amann is not known; probably it did. Not surprisingly, this power exercised by Bormann caused much resentment – even amongst those such as Speer, whose access to Hitler was virtually unlimited – and Speer, Sauckel, Lammers and Milch plotted Bormann's downfall with, they thought, the assistance of Göring. It was not to be. Bormann made Göring a gift of six million *marks* from the *AH Spende* and the portly *Reichsmarschall's* support evaporated. In July of 1943, following his formal appointment as Secretary to the Führer, Bormann made and circulated a list of five points defining his responsibilities. Point number one was 'to manage the Führer's numerous personal affairs'.

One little-known figure is Bormann's assistant, Helmut von Hummel. von Hummel, whom Plaut described as 'a particularly vicious Nazi', was in charge of Hitler's private funds, the administration of *Sonderauftrag Linz* (see Chapter 15), several farms in Mecklenburg, and the Obersalzberg compound.[25] He was also responsible for negotiating with Speer for manpower and materials. Hummel survived the war and was arrested in Salzburg, Austria, in mid-May, 1946. Despite being in a position to reveal much about Hitler's finances, he was never interrogated in depth or called as a witness at the Nuremberg trials.

Bouhler

Philipp Bouhler was head of Hitler's personal Chancellery and, as such, would have been the logical choice to manage his personal finances. No evidence has ever been found that he did. An efficient administrator, Bouhler had set up the NSDAP administration after the party was re-founded in 1925. Partially crippled by injuries from the First World War, he was a bespectacled, mild-mannered, introvert within whom burned an intense ideological flame. A born empire builder, he took full advantage of the opportunities offered by the vagueness of Hitler's directives. In 1933, the *Führerkanzlei* had 26 employees; when it moved into its new home near the *Reichkanzlei* in 1936, it had six departments and about fifty employees; by 1942, the number of employees was near 250.

Heß

According to Schwarz, Hitler left the day-to-day management of his money to Heß. This is partly corroborated by Heß's employment, from 1925 onwards, as Hitler's secretary and by Heß's signature appearing on some of Hitler's letters to the tax authorities. However, Heß could clearly have played no part in Hitler's financial affairs after his flight to England on 10 May 1941. Even before that date, Bormann had begun to take over many of Heß's functions, including the general management of Hitler's money, and especially that of the *AH Spende*.

On 21 April 1933, Hitler appointed Heß to the post of *Stellvertreter des Führers* – Deputy Führer, usually abbreviated to StdF – by which name the office was also generally known. Like most things in the Nazi organisation, the functions of the StdF were not well defined (and the powers it evolved are of no relevance to Hitler's finances) and the only thing which Hitler made absolutely clear from its inception was that the post had no authority over Schwarz and the party treasury. Heß, whose administrative abilities were negligible, chose Bormann, an administrator of proven ability, as his *Stabsleiter* or Chief of Staff.

One area where Heß acted for Hitler in the nineteen-twenties and -thirties was in soliciting financial assistance, notably when approaching Thyssen to guarantee the loan for refurbishing the *Braunes Haus* and Funk for pledges should it have been necessary to arm the SA in 1931. However, such assistance was probably in the name of the NSDAP, rather than Hitler personally.

Keppler (see Chapter 9) was brought into the StdF in July of 1933 and it was ordered that while Heß was in charge of political affairs, Keppler was in charge of economic matters. Since the StdF was specifically excluded from any involvement with party finances, controlled by Schwarz, there seems to be a conflict of interest in some areas, especially in the development of businesses to provide local finance at the *Kreis* and *Gau* level. Just where Keppler and Bormann stood in relation to each other while Heß remained deputy Führer is a matter for conjecture. The significance is, of course, that this move brought together a man who had done much to establish fundraising sources prior to 1933 – Keppler – and the one who would largely control them after 1933 – Bormann. It thus seems almost certain that either Keppler and Bormann collaborated or, more likely, that Bormann took over Keppler's sources and quietly eased him out of the way.

Ohnesorge

Ohnesorge, who was largely responsible for collecting revenues for the Cultural Fund, had been a friend of Hitler's since 1920 and they remained on good terms to the end, though they were estranged from the late twenties to 1931 after Hitler allegedly made advances to one of Ohnesorge's daughters. According to Hanfstaengl, he went down on his knees and stated that although a man in his position could not marry, he begged her to come and live with him in Munich[26]. Ohnesorge was furious and broke off relations with Hitler, only resuming them once all his daughters were safely married.

Schaub

Julius Schaub was Hitler's travelling adjutant and general gofer, often dubbed the *Reisemarschall* (Travel Marshal, a play on *Reichsmarschall*) since he took care of all Hitler's travel arrangements. Like many of those close to Hitler, he had served time in Landsberg prison for his part in the *Putsch*. As Wagener puts it:

> *Almost always* [Hitler] *took his breakfast in his room between nine and ten o'clock in the morning, and Schaub was always on hand to run errands, make telephone calls, and finally, to pack for Hitler. That is why, whenever Heß was absent, everyone turned to Schaub if we wished to be announced to Hitler or if we needed something from him.*
>
> *Schaub was his master's loyal servant. Deep down, he had a decent nature and was not at all interested in politics and science. If one wanted to make certain that Hitler would read a particular item, one gave or sent it to Schaub.*[27]

Schaub also took care of Hitler's day-to-day monetary needs. One can imagine that for this purpose he drew money from the office petty cash, but which office? Equally important to this story, Schaub was the guardian of his private papers.

Paying money was not Schaub's only responsibility; prior to 1933 he also collected it. When Hitler gave a speech – whether at an NSDAP-organised function or to some private body such as a businessmens' club – Schaub negotiated the fee or percentage. No records of these amounts exists, and they were never declared on Hitler's tax returns, so it is possible that the money simply entered a cash box kept by Schaub. The money almost certainly never went into a bank account – at least, prior to 1933 – since that would have left a record. If Schaub's memoirs, which he is known to have written, ever see the light of day we would know much more about Hitler's financial affairs.

Schreck

Julius Schreck, who bore a close resemblance to Adolf Hitler, was Hitler's chauffeur from 1931 until his rather mysterious death in 1936.[28] There is some evidence that Schreck duplicated Schaub's functions, especially when travelling. When, during the 1932 election campaign, Erich Kempka became Hitler's second chauffeur, he may have duplicated Schreck's duties as bag-man, though it is probable that either Heß or Schaub had primary responsibility.

Notes

1   Prosecution Exhibit 55. Trials of War Criminals before the Nuremberg Military Tribunals under Control Council Law No. 10, Nuremberg, October 1946-April 1949, Volume VII, I.G. Farben, (Washington: US Government Printing Office, 1952).

2   POOL97, p. 52; no source given for this apparent quotation.

3   The *Fragenbogen*, which was drawn up in 1946 and had to be completed as part of denazification procedures, lists 56 major organisations, not including those of the SS.

4   POOL97, p. 53; citing Lochner, *Tycoons and Tyrants*, pp. 122-23 and MANC70, p. 369.

5   LANG79, p. 89; POOL97, p.151, seems to echo the same sum; neither gives any evidence to substantiate it.

6   BACK88, p. 89. Schwarzwäller, pp. 197-8, the latter ref. being to the original German version.

7   DIET57, pp. 172-3.

8   DIET57, pp. 196-7.

9   DIET57, pp. 201-2.

10 ODON78, p. 107.

11 Ibid., p. 106.

12 SPOT03, p. 82.

13 SPOT03, p. 140.

14 DIET57, p. 180.

15 HOFF55, pp. 182-3. The picture referred to is Vermeer's *The Artist in his Studio*.

16 BACK88, p. 89.

17 See e.g. *Stanley Gibbons Simplified Catalogue: Stamps of the World*, Vol. 2, pp. 273-5. Ringwood, 2002. ISBN 085259-537-9.

18 BACK88, p. 89.

19 SPEE70, p. 86.

20 LANG79, passim.

21 LANG79, p. 40; von Lang provides convincing proof that Bormann joined the NSDAP up to eight months earlier than he later claimed.

22 The office was set up to provide insurance for SA men injured in street fighting and the families of those killed. A new manager was urgently needed because the previous one had absconded with RM 2,000. LANG79, p. 44.

23 The intervening manoeuvres are described by von Lang. LANG79, pp. 68-9.

24 LANG79, p. 138.

25 PLAU46b.

26   HANF57, p. 137.
27   TURN85a, p. 86.
28   Hoffmann (HOFF55, pp. 201 and 219) implies that Schreck died as a result of an attempt to poison Hitler. Some writers have referred to Schreck's death as the result of an 'assassination attempt' – which would certainly include poisoning – while others suggest an automobile accident. Domarus says it was simply meningitis.

Chapter Fourteen

THE BERGHOF
(AND OTHER REAL ESTATE)

*[Hitler] gave orders that in the future the important buildings of his Reich were to be
erected inkeeping with this [Theory of Ruin Value].*
Albert Speer (1905-81)
Inside the Third Reich, p. 56

The *Berghof* – here used to describe the whole complex of real estate in the Bavarian
Alps, on the German-Austrian border – was probably Hitler's most valuable
possession. As will be seen, not only did the place figure largely in Nazi mythology
(not for nothing did some of Hitler's inner circle refer to themselves as the *vom
dem Berg* – the people from the mountain), but it became an extension of Hitler's
personality – a luxurious showcase for a mighty leader and his trophies, paid for
by grateful admirers. It did not start out that way.

Berchtesgaden is a small town at the foot of a range of mountains which look
as if they were Hollywood's idea of a set for Wagner's *Ring* – which, if Hitler's
Wagnerian view of himself and the Third Reich is accepted, they were. About
ten kilometres from Berchtesgaden, on a mountain called the Hoher Goll, lies the
small village of Obersalzberg. It was here that Hitler created his mountain retreat.
Even before Hitler set eyes on the place, the area had long been a retreat for the
rich; attracted by its thermal springs, beauty, and isolation, Bavaria's kings chose
the land at the foot of Mount Watzmann as their summer residence. By 1923,
when Hitler first visited, it had become the favourite location for the summer
homes of wealthy industrialists such as Bechstein and Winter, from whose widow
Hitler bought his first property.

In 1923, following his abortive attempt to confront the Bavarian government
during the May Day celebrations, Hitler retreated to the *Pension Moritz*, a modest
guest house on the slopes of the Obersalzberg, in the company of Dietrich Eckart
and others.[1] As was his habit, he registered under the pseudonym of Herr Wolf.
The owners of the guest house, a couple named Büchner, were early supporters
of the Nazi party. Snapping a dog whip around the room, he lectured Frau
Büchner on the iniquities of Berlin and compared himself to Jesus Christ,

cleansing the Temple, a touch of bombast that was not lost on Eckart and Hanfstaengl.[2]

In the spring and summer of 1925, Hitler again stayed at the *Pension Moritz*, this time occupying a small cottage above the main building.[3] Here he finished the first volume of *Mein Kampf*. Rebuilt, and greatly enlarged, *Pension Moritz* later became known as the *Platterhof*. In July 1926, at the suggestion of the Bechsteins, he joined them at the *Marienheim*, higher up the mountain. Finding the atmosphere too formal for his taste, Hitler abandoned the mountainside completely and moved down to the *Deutsches Haus*, in the town of Berchtesgaden itself.[4] Here, in the company of Heß, Emil Maurice, Heinrich Hoffmann and Gregor Strasser, he relaxed and finished the second volume of *Mein Kampf*.

After the elections of 20 May 1928, Hitler again returned to Berchtesgaden, this time to *Haus Wachenfeld*, the property that would eventually be transformed into the *Berghof*.[5] Hitler initially rented the villa for a hundred *marks* a month from the widow of an industrialist from Buxtehude called Winter and a Nazi party member (Wachenfeld was his wife's maiden name.) Heiden, however, says that the house was rented only in Angela's name.[6] In 1942, Hitler recalled the events leading up to the purchase in some detail:

> *I went once to Buxtehude. Since I'd invested a lot of money in the house, I wanted a price, against the event of a sale, to be fixed before a lawyer. The most agreeable thing for me would have been to buy at once, but Frau Winter couldn't make up her mind to sell the house, which she had from her late husband. We had arrived by car from Hamburg. When I asked where was the Winter factory, I was told it had burned down precisely the night before. I told myself that I'd come at the proper moment.*
>
> *I visited Frau Winter in her house. I was received at first by her daughter. The mother came, beaming: "What a coincidence!" she said. "You arrive, and the factory was burnt down last night. Two pieces of luck!" The fact was that during the inflation two Jews had bought the factory for nothing, profiting by a widow's weakness. She added: "This is such a good day for me that I agree to sell you the house."*
>
> *. . . I went for a short walk with the old lady, and learnt that she had the right to dwell only in the house belonging to the factory. By good luck, although the lightning had struck the factory, the living house had been spared!*
>
> *That's how I became a property owner at Obersalzberg.*[7]

Some writers claim that Hitler was offered the property at an advantageous price because Frau Winter was in financial difficulties; Hitler's account, if it is to be believed, does not support this.

The house was a simple affair of five rooms, built in 1916 or 17 in the local style with a ground floor of stone and an upper floor of wood, surrounded by a veranda and with the roof weighted with rocks against winter storms.[8] Photographs of *Haus Wachenfeld* in its original state, and after the 1932 expansion, appear in the illustrations. Hitler added several rooms and a stone patio shortly after he purchased the house. Even at this early stage, when the house was still no more than a large cabin, Hitler seems to have been determined to fill it with art works, of whatever quality:

> ... I remember bringing up from Berchtesgaden in a basket, a bust acquired by the Baroness [Abegg, a friend of Gansser] that everybody attributed to Donatello. I regretted the sweat it cost me all the more since, when I dragged it from the basket, it proved to be a bad copy in clay.[9]

Not for the first time had Hitler acquired a fake.

The *Haus Wachenfeld* saw many strange scenes, not least when, after the less than successful 1932 election, the astrologer Erik Jan Hanussen announced that, although Hitler's horoscope favoured his political success, several obstacles remained. However, said Hanussen, these could be removed by procuring a mandrake root from a butcher's yard in Braunau-am-Inn, by the light of the full moon. This he did, presenting the root to Hitler, with due ceremony, on New Year's Day, 1933. Presumably Hanussen harvested the root on 13 December, the previous full moon, but a lapse of eighteen days must surely have detracted from the root's freshness.[10]

Following his appointment as Chancellor, Hitler spent the summer of 1933 at *Haus Wachenfeld*, accompanied by Hélène Hanfstaengl and her son, Egon. It appears to have been their first visit and we owe one of the few descriptions of the interior of the house, before its extensive rebuilding after 1935, to Egon, as recorded by Toland:

> His room on the first floor, which faced directly toward Salzburg, was modest, in keeping with the rest of the villa. "He had a small writing table, and a number of simple 'bookshelves,'" recalled Egon. "I especially looked to see what kind of literature the Führer had chosen for his relaxation." Surprisingly, the majority of the books were the Wild West novels of Karl May, more suitable for Egon himself than a Chancellor.
>
> ... They all had meals together in the pleasant but modest dining room downstairs. Egon couldn't stand the Austrian cooking that was prepared by Angela Raubal, particularly string beans served in a sauce made of milk, flour and quantities of sugar, but he was fascinated by the free and easy table conversation. "... But here in his 'Landhaus' he frequently appeared wholly in the becoming guise of an ordinary host, an average man. He talked a lot about motorcars, engines, the size and performance of different ships, and technical things of that sort."[11]

Here, seen through the eyes of a twelve-year-old boy (though recalled at age 50) is the picture of Hitler, 'an average man', in his modest villa. Other reminiscences support the young Hanfstaengl's recollection. The cowboy books are a typical touch; Hitler had long been a fan of Karl May and praised him highly. Between 1933 and 1934, Hitler re-read all of May's sixty plus books and held them in such high esteem that he presented his nephew, Heinz Hitler, with a copy of the collected works while the youth was studying at the National-Political Education Centre.[12] May, it should be noted, while being a successful writer of westerns in the Fenimore Cooper tradition, never actually visited America.

It is significant that the young Hanfstaengl refers to *Haus Wachenfeld* as Hitler's

Landhaus, a term which can be translated as 'Country Cottage'. Such weekend or summertime retreats were, and are, quite common in Northern Europe. They range from the small, though often highly decorated, one-room huts on allotment gardens, to be seen in the working-class suburbs of major cities, to the hundred room 'hunting lodges' of the wealthy. The vast majority are two- or three-roomed cabins in the woods. Today, many are owned on a 'time-share' basis. Culturally, they are the working person's retreat from business life, where a weekend can be spent in isolation, away from the telephone and the distractions of the city. As such, reading matter tends to be simple and uncomplicated; Hitler's choice of cowboy novels (a taste he shared with General Dwight D. Eisenhower) was far from unusual and one that remains popular in weekend cottages to this day.[13]

This, then, can be taken as a benchmark of Hitler's projected image in 1933; the simple, ex-soldier made good, spending a few days in his modest *Landhaus*, relaxing with a good western. This should not be taken to imply that the image is an accurate reflection of his private life, but it is certainly the image he tried to present. Hitler did not publicise his private life – far from it – he rather created a fictitious private life to fit his public image. It was an image that was soon to change.

Around this time, the house was expanded under the direction of Alois Degano, an architect from Tegernsee, who was instructed to change the outward appearance as little as possible. By the summer of 1933, *Haus Wachenfeld* had become a place of pilgrimage, and the crowds were becoming such a nuisance that action had to be taken. On 19 August, Himmler, as Commander of the Bavarian Political Police, ordered special traffic restrictions for the area, and warned against the use of field glasses by those attempting to observe Hitler's every move.[14] The mountain was beginning its transition from paradise to fortress.

As early as January 1935, Hitler was buying up property in the area and beginning a wholesale reconstruction of his *Landhaus*, moving it upscale from the common man's retreat to the plutocrat's summer palace. Not everything went smoothly, as Toland records:

> He mused in the same melancholy vein to his sister Angela as they sat on the porch looking out towards Salzburg. He was upset over a story that he had cheated a neighbouring farmer of a thousand marks on the sale of a piece of property. "Look, Adolf, it is not that bad," she said. "A thousand marks more or less won't seem so important when you become 'The Old Man of the Obersalzberg' in a few decades!" Hitler was silent, then put an arm around her shoulder. "First of all, a thousand marks more or less *is* the point and secondly, dear Angela, I shall never become the Old Man of the Obersalzberg. I have so little time."[15]

Shortly after this alleged conversation, in the autumn of 1936, Hitler's relationship with his half-sister began to deteriorate, mostly over Angela's dislike of Eva Braun, but also because of Angela's intention to marry Professor Martin Hammitsch, director of the State School of Building Construction in Dresden. A third factor is said to have been Angela's liking for publicity; she saw herself more as *chatelaine* than housekeeper.[16] Whatever the reasons – and there seems no truth in the rumour that Hitler dismissed her – Angela left and Eva Braun slid smoothly into her place.

It seems that a decision had been taken around this time that *Haus Wachenfeld* should become Hitler's official summer residence, rather than his personal retreat. Consequently, the place needed to be enlarged to accommodate visitors. There would need to be accommodation not only for Chancellery staff, but also for the staffs of the visitors. All this would need a larger staff – cooks, maids, security guards, maintenance personnel – to run it, and they would need to be accommodated. Eva Braun had to be accommodated (previously, Angela had always managed to manoeuvre the accommodation arrangements so that Eva had been forced to stay in a nearby hotel), so the plans included a bedroom, boudoir, and bathroom with discreet access to Hitler's own quarters. In this major reconstruction, *Haus Wachenfeld* would lose its name and *Landhaus* status, with all its implied charm, and assume the Wagnerian title of *Berghof* – Mountain Court. Supervision of the project was entrusted to Martin Bormann.

The choice of Bormann cannot easily be explained. A competent administrator, Bormann had no experience of construction projects and was more at home in the corridors of power than on a building site. Speer would have been the obvious choice, but he was heavily involved in other construction projects; the most likely explanation is that Bormann pushed himself into the job, adding another spoke to the wheel of his growing empire. Bormann's lack of experience in construction led to cost overruns and technical blunders. Dietrich, like many in Hitler's entourage, was unhappy with Bormann's wholesale destruction of the local landscape:

> In 1936 Bormann came to Berchtesgaden armed with money from the Industrial Fund [i.e. the AH Spende.] He bought parcel after parcel of land around Hitler's house and began literally to bore holes into the mountain. Hitler watched these proceedings with some initial doubts, but after a while he let Bormann have his head. He would often pun on the name, saying Bormann was certainly a man for boring. . . . The peace of the remote mountain was replaced by noisy bustle. . . . The silence of the mountainside was shattered by the rumble of dynamite explosions. After a while Hitler directed Bormann not to undertake any blasting before noon, so that he would not be awakened from his sleep.[17]

Dietrich also offers a few insights into the scale of the construction work, claiming that five thousand workers, most of them foreign labourers, were employed on the project well into the war years.[18]

It is said that Hitler drew up the plans himself, and this would certainly have been in character. Speer comments on the fact that the famous picture window in the great hall, which could be raised and lowered electrically, was sited over the garage, allowing exhaust fumes to enter when the window was down.[19] A properly trained architect, notes Speer, would never have made such an elementary mistake.

A Munich architect Professor Roderich Fick supervised the construction and the detailed work – laying out the wiring, the water pipes, designing foundations, calculating stresses, sizing the beams – that Hitler had not the time, the experience, or the inclination to do.[20] The *Berghof* was formally opened on 5 July 1936. What then, did Hitler get for his money?

The great hall was about 20m long and 17m wide, dominated at one end by the famous picture window. Either opposite the window, or on one of side walls, stood a large fire place. The walls were hung with Gobelin tapestries and several paintings by Italian masters, including nudes by Titian and Bordone, which hung either side of the entrance to the dining room. The dining room was also 20m

---

Table 14-1: Berghof Purchases, 1932-42

Date	Property	Owner	Price	B.	P.
32.09.17	Haus Wachenfeld	Winter	40,000	AH	51
33.11.25	Gasthof zum Türken	Schuster	165,000	MB	47
34.08.25	Bodenlehen (part of)	Brandner	13,160	AH	45
35.10.19	Landhaus Sonnenköpfl	Cornelius	79,000	MB	78
35.10.28	Clubheim	Arnhold'scher Pensionverein	125,000	MB	54
35.11.06	Villa Bechstein	Bechstein	170,000	MB	66
36.01.27	Bezirk Berchtesgaden	?	1,485	AH	96
36.07.20	Bodenlehen (part of)	Brandner	150,000	MB	45
36.10.10	Brandstattlehen (part of)	Irlinger	124,905	MB	84
36.10.15	Brandstattlehen (part of)	Irlinger	123,527	MB	84
36.10.15	Breilerlehen	Angerer	348,146	MB	82
36.10.15	Fichtenhäusl	Rasp	25,000	MB	80
36.10.15	Mooslehen	Rasp	180,000	MB	81
36.10.16	Scheberlehen	Walch	114,000	MB	79
36.10.19	Weißenlehen	Kastner	106,478	MB	68
37.01.05	Freidinglehen	Liegnitz	81,500	MB	56
37.01.06	Haus Hess	Hess	68,000	MB	43
37.03.01	Bodenlehen (part of)	Hudler	198,331	MB	46
37.03.02	Baumgartlehen	Linde	131,590	MB	64
37.03.02	Haus Unterwurf	Schmidtlein	100,000	MB	50
37.03.03	Antenberglehen	Marine-Offiziersverband e.V.	1,107,950	MB	72
37.03.03	Marienhäusl	von Rüxleben	55,200	MB	44
37.03.05	Pension Lindenhöhe	Dienemann	57,460	MB	57
37.03.05	Pension Moritz	Büchner	260,000	MB	53
37.03.06	Baumgartmühle etc.	Luchner	66,000	MB	63
37.03.06	Wesenheim	von Holstein	35,000	MB	62
37.03.08	Gasthof Hintereck	Kurz	61,000	MB	33

long, parallel to the great hall, and 13m wide. Off the dining room was an enclosed winter garden – one of the few places in the *Berghof* where smoking was allowed. Upstairs, bedrooms and offices were arranged either side of a long corridor. Hitler's private suite consisted of a sitting room, study, bedroom, and bathroom. The latter, which was made of Italian marble and had gold plated fittings, may have formed the link to Eva Braun's suite which was, according to Gun:

> *. . . heavily furnished with a sofa below a picture of a nude for which she is supposed to have posed. The walls were hung with silk and the whole thing was reminiscent of one of those chambres separées in Franz Lehár's operettas. There was a portrait of Hitler hanging opposite the nude which would have given nightmares to most women.*[21]

Table 14-1 (continued)

Date	Property	Owner	Price	B.	P.
37.03.08	Haus Eckerbrunn	Walch	60,000	MB	41
37.03.08	Haus Salzburgblick	Zotz	30,000	MB	58
37.03.08	Pension Buchenheim	Paulsen	85,000	MB	65
37.03.09	Gasthof Steiner	Kurz	140,000	MB	60
37.03.09	Haus Georgi	Walch	55,000	MB	42
37.03.09	Haus Mittertratten	Rappold	70,000	MB	59
37.03.09	Haus Mitterwurf	Schwarz	30,000	MB	49
37.03.09	Hinterecklehen	Hölzl	74,750	MB	32
37.03.09	Kindersanatorium Dr. Seitz	Seitz	240,000	MB	37
37.03.09	Obertallehen	Irlinger	105,060	MB	85
37.03.09	Oberwurflehen	Hölzl	70,930	MB	48
37.03.23	Feuerwehrhaus	Freiwillige Feuerwehr Salzberg	60	MB	35
37.05.12	Hitler-Jugendheim	NSDAP	2,000	MB	34
37.08.23	Unterklauslehen	Kurz	103,100	MB	87
37.09.02	Berghanghäusl	Fendt	36,500	MB	73
37.09.02	Berghäusl	Lochner	40,000	MB	77
37.09.10	Waltenbergerheim	Sandner	90,000	MB	74
37.09.21	Meisterlehen	Walch	87,335	MB	76
37.10.22	Oberklauslehen	Rasp	111,260	MB	86
40.04.03	Postgebäude	Deutsche Reichspost	16,835	MB	34
40.04.03	Spornhof	Guggenbichler	22,870	MB	94
40.07.03	Buchlehen	Brandner	70,000	MB	89
40.07.03	Wagnerlehen	Grois	45,000	MB	90
40.08.30	Fürstenbichllehen	Walch	70,000	MB	91
41.08.14	Landhaus Alpenruhe	Amort	16,000	MB	88
42.03.25	Halbes Kedermann- oder Gschwandgütl	Renoth	27,732	MB	92
		Total:	5,687,164		

Contemporary photographs show Hitler's study as a simple, rather cluttered room, with a desk that seems minute when compared to the theatrical monstrosity that he had in Berlin. On the desk – sometimes in his bedroom – stood a portrait of Hitler's mother.[22] One curious note: there is an ashtray on the desk of Hitler, the fanatical anti-smoker. Traudl Junge, in a post-war conversation with Gun, said:

> The only comfortable room was the library on the first floor, which in the old house had been Hitler's private sitting room. It was rustically furnished, with beer mugs placed here and there for decoration. The books at everybodys' disposal were of no great interest: world classics that no one seems to have read, travel atlases, a large dictionary, albums of drawings, and of course copies of Mein Kampf bound in gold and morocco leather.[23]

These were, presumably, the books later looted by the Americans. In the cellar, there was a small bowling alley. Elsewhere, a fully equipped cinema was installed and frequently showed two films nightly.[24] According to Gun, there was a dental surgery and:

> . . . carved cupboards stuffed with parchments proclaiming Hitler an honorary citizen of more than five thousand German and foreign towns, the attics with their accumulation of presents from the four corners of the globe, including fifty or so cushions with Ich liebe Sie embroidered on them, and many other gifts of which undoubtedly the most mystifying was the sword of the Landshut public executioner.[25]

Over time, Bormann bought up the surrounding land until Hitler owned almost 280 hectares around the *Berghof*. In some cases, owners were paid more than their land was worth to encourage them to move quickly.[26] In most cases, farmers were willing to sell; the soil was poor and the prices Bormann was prepared to pay offered the chance to purchase better land elsewhere. Some refused, having the peasant's sentimental attachment to land which had been in their families for generations. Schwarzwäller claims that there were forced evictions and this is probably true, but his lengthy, detailed story of the eviction of a farmer named Heinz Jager [sic] is somewhat suspect: no mention of Jager (or alternative spellings such as Jäger or Jaeger) can be found in Schörner's extensive study of land transactions around the *Berghof*, nor in Chaussy's history of the region (see also Table 14-1).[27]

Beginning in late 1936, a sprawling complex of buildings was added: SS barracks; kitchens; staff quarters; a communications centre; and a farm. The latter was of little interest to Hitler, but did once provide him with some amusement. When Bormann proudly showed him around the farm, remarking on the cleanliness of the pigs, it became obvious even to Hitler that the enterprise could not be profitable. After checking the account books he remarked to Bormann that it was not nearly as expensive as he first thought; a litre of milk from the farm 'only' cost twenty times the market price. The quasi-vegetarian Hitler was more pleased with the hothouses, which supplied fresh vegetables year-round.[28] The mushroom farm was a failure and had to be transferred to a brewery in Bad Reichenhall. The hundred-hive apiary had to be rebuilt to suit the harsh winter climate – during which sugar had to be brought in to feed the bees! Only the cider mill worked properly, but few apples grow in the Obersalzberg.

The *Berghof* complex was still under construction – and was to remain so for the next seven years – when the Austrian Chancellor Schuschnigg arrived for his fateful meeting on the night of 11 February 1938. The roads were in such a poor state, made worse by snow, that the visitors had to travel in half-track vehicles, threading their way through the construction site of the new SS barracks.[29] Another of the *Berghof*'s dramatic moments was the meeting between Hitler and the British Prime Minister Neville Chamberlain, which began on 15 September 1938. By this time, the roads had been improved, there was no snow, and Chamberlain's party reached the *Berghof* in ordinary cars. Chamberlain was impressed by the grandeur of the *Berghof* and admitted his disappointment that low cloud prevented seeing the famous view from the picture window. Chamberlain and his party did not stay at the *Berghof*, but in an hotel in Berchtesgaden.

Hitler spent most of August 1939 at the *Berghof*, far from Berlin where the invasion of Poland was being planned without any real knowledge of when – or even if – it should take place. Europe slipped towards war while Hitler ate cream cakes and played with his dogs. On 10 August, Albert Forster, *Gauleiter* of Danzig, was summoned to the *Berghof*, along with Carl Burckhardt, the League of Nations High Commissioner for Danzig. On arrival, Burckhardt was driven past the *Berghof*, up the winding road to the *Kehlsteinhaus*. This folly on top of the Kehlstein mountain was a gift organised by Bormann for Hitler's fiftieth birthday earlier that year.[30] The *Kehlsteinhaus* was only used on visitors who needed to be seriously impressed; and impressive it was. From the car park, the visitor entered through double bronze doors and walked along a 124 metre marble-lined tunnel to the lift which, in 41 seconds, would carry him (rarely her) to the summit of the 1,837 metre high mountain, about 800m above the *Berghof*. Some writers have confused the *Kehlsteinhaus* with a 'tea-house', which it was not, possibly because it was called the 'D-Haus' for *Diplomaten Haus*, an indication of its real purpose: to entertain and impress visiting diplomats, usually in tête-à-tête conversations with the *Führer*.[31] Begun in 1936, it was completed in the summer of 1938. During that time, about 3,500 men worked on its construction, at a total cost of about RM 30 million.[32] According to Hoffmann, the funds were provided by 'German Industry' (i.e. the *AH Spende*) and the *Arbeitsfront* (i.e. money confiscated from the trade unions when they were abolished in 1933). Hitler did not like the *Kehlsteinhaus* and complained that the air was too thin, and bad for his blood pressure, preferring the less dramatic tea-house just below the *Berghof* itself. He also worried about failure of the lift and about accidents on the rather precarious road up to the lift shaft. After 1939, it remained mostly empty, unused. The

Kehlsteinhaus was one of the few buildings to survive the air raid of April 1945 relatively intact, and it still can be visited today. The French ambassador François-Poncet has given a graphic description of the place, ending with the comment:

> *Was this the Castle of Monsalvat where the Knights of the Grail lived, . . . or simply a refuge where brigands rested and stored their treasure? Was this the work of a normal mind or that of a man tormented by megalomania, by obsessive fear of domination and solitude, or, simply, tortured by fear?*[33]

During construction of the *Kehlsteinhaus*, a curious incident is said to have occurred: a piece of rock shaped like a hand was found. There is nothing unusual in that; in rocks, as in clouds, any desired shape may be found if one looks hard enough. The curious structure was brought to the notice of Hitler, who is said to have named it 'The Hand of Wotan' and had it mounted in a glass case.[34]

The mountains, witnesses themselves to so many dramas, were also the source of drama, notably on 24 August 1939, after the signing of the Nazi-Soviet pact when, at about three in the morning, Hitler and his entourage were on the terrace of the *Berghof* – no longer the simple wooden veranda where Hitler allegedly cuddled his half-sister in 1936, but a broad expanse of stone and concrete capable of accommodating several hundred people. According to Speer:

> *Northern Lights of unusual intensity threw red light on the legend-haunted Unterberg across the valley, while the sky above shimmered in all the colours of the rainbow. The last act of* Götterdammerung, *could not have been more effectively staged. The same red light bathed our faces and our hands. The display produced a curiously pensive mood amongst us. Abruptly turning to one of his military adjutants, Hitler said: "Looks like a great deal of blood. This time we won't bring it off without violence."*[35]

Although the *Aurora Borealis* is rarely visible so far south, the event is corroborated by astronomical records.

As has already been noted, the *Berghof* was somewhat isolated and communications with the outside world, other than by land-line or radio, were far from easy. It was not well served by road or rail, though the line to Bad Reichenhall (about 20km from the *Berghof*) was improved and the station enlarged to accommodate Hitler's and Göring's private trains. Air travel was equally unsatisfactory. When, on 22 August 1939, Hitler called his top generals to a conference at which he would outline his plans for the conquest of Poland, most flew into Salzburg, rather than to the small airfield at Berchtesgaden itself. So as not to draw attention to themselves, they were ordered to come in civilian clothes; characteristically, Göring obeyed the letter of the order, if not its intent; he arrived in full hunting outfit.[36]

Once the Second World War began, Hitler spent more and more time at the *Berghof* and his relationship with Eva Braun became more open, at least to those with access to the Führer. Eva began to be addressed by the staff as *die Chefin* – wife of the boss – while Hitler was referred to, though rarely openly, as *der Chef*

– the boss. According to Hoffmann, who by now, like Hanfstaengl, was falling out of favour with Hitler on account of his drunken buffoonery, Hitler, convinced that the Soviet Union was planning to attack Germany, more-or-less abandoned the *Berghof* after 1940, though the evidence does not support this, adding:

> Notwithstanding our departure, work on the vast underground network of tunnels continued with undiminished speed at Obersalzberg. These tunnels . . . were also a safe asylum for a large and very valuable collection of works of art and important State documents.[37]

Another of the many dramatic moments at the *Berghof* occurred on the morning of Sunday, 11 May 1941, when Hitler received news of Heß's flight to Britain. This event marks a convenient turning point in the fortunes of the *Berghof* and, as the war dragged on, it seemed that the spirit of the place began to wane: no longer did decisions taken here lead to success; more and more they led to failure. Hitler was at the *Berghof* on 27 May 1941 when he received news of the loss of the battleship *Bismarck*. It was from the *Berghof* that Hitler denied von Paulus permission to withdraw from Stalingrad. It was there that Hitler took a sleeping pill one night, and gave orders that he should not be wakened on the following morning, 6 June 1944. It was there, on 29 June, that Hitler refused Rommel's suggestion to withdraw to a fighting line on the natural barrier of the river Seine.

By 1942, the extensive building work at the site was causing great concern to Speer, who was nominally in charge of all major construction projects within the *Reich*. Speer tried to get the work stopped and the workers transferred elsewhere and even managed to get a *Führerprotokoll* (*Führer* Order –5-6 March 1942, Point 17.3) to that effect.[38] Bormann simply ignored the order. Speer attempted to intervene on several later occasions, notably in September 1944, when he provoked a major row with Bormann.[39]

Traudl Humps (later Junge) has given a good account of the *Berghof* in early 1943, when she first arrived there as one of Hitler's secretaries, and worth repeating in its entirety:

> They started on the second floor where the Führer lived. The walls of the hallway were decorated with paintings by the old masters, beautiful pieces of sculpture, and exotic vases. Everything, thought Traudl, was wonderful but strange and impersonal. There was deadly silence since the Führer still slept. In front of one door were two black Scotch terriers — Eva's dogs, Stasi and Negus. Next came Hitler's bedroom. The two rooms, it seemed, were connected by a large bathroom and it was apparent that they lived discreetly as man and wife. Traudl was taken downstairs to the large living room which was separated from the famous picture-window room by a heavy velvet curtain. The furnishings were luxurious but despite the beautiful Gobelins and thick carpets she got the impression of coldness.[40]

Dinner was served in the dining room, with guests retiring to the great hall, where a large fire burned, for coffee and liqueurs. Food at the *Berghof* appears to have been wholesome, but uninspiring. Hitler's vegetarian meals were cooked in Berchtesgaden itself – some 15 km away by road – under the supervision of a Dr.

Werner Zabel, brought to the *Berghof*, and re-heated.[41] Secretaries were allowed to join Hitler for dinner at the *Berghof*, though not at the Reich Chancellery in Berlin, where a more formal atmosphere prevailed. Eva Braun was kept at either Hitler's or her Munich residence or at the *Berghof*, and it was only at the latter that she was permitted to behave as 'one of the family'. Even so, whenever important visitors were entertained, Eva was kept out of sight.

In March of 1943, following the disaster of Stalingrad, Hitler made one of his last public speeches on Heroes' Memorial Day. The speech was short, uninspiring, and widely criticised, even – especially – within the Party. Questions began to be asked: Where was the old Hitler, the inspiring speaker of yore? Answers began to be rumoured: the speaker was a substitute; Hitler had had a nervous breakdown and was now under house arrest at the *Berghof*. Alas, it was not true. For three months of 1943, Hitler was at the *Berghof*; most of the rest of the time he was at Rastenburg, his headquarters in East Prussia; only a few days were spent in Berlin, the nominal seat of government. In June, Hitler cut short a visit to East Prussia and returned to the *Berghof* because of concerns about his health; evidently he still had faith in the curative properties of the mountains.

In late February 1944, Hitler left Berlin and returned to the *Berghof*, bringing with him his whole headquarters staff; this was to be no relaxing interlude in the mountains. As Allied air-raids on Berlin increased in frequency and severity, it was decided to strengthen the Chancellery and the bunkers beneath it. Hitler did not return to Berlin until mid-July. Even the *Berghof* had now taken on the character of a military fortress; it was covered by camouflage netting, partly blacked-out, and its essential services were slowly re-housed underground, in a complex network of bunkers even more extensive than those below Berlin. There was even a bunker for Blondie, Hitler's Alsatian bitch.

On 14 July 1944, Hitler left the *Berghof* for the last time; however, the place continued to figure in the saga of Hitler's Fortune right up to the very end. On 9 February 1945, Hitler ordered Eva and Gretl to the *Berghof*, to take charge. Eva did not stay long, returning to Berlin on 23 February. It was the last the *Berghof* would see of its extraordinary first lady. As Russian troops approached Berlin in April 1945, many of his entourage urged Hitler to flee to the comparative safety of the *Berghof*, from where the war could be directed just as easily. Hitler, who had now developed a sentimental attachment to Berlin – the city he had derided so roundly to the landlady of the *Pension Moritz* in 1923 – exceeding his former attachment to the *Berghof*, refused. He would live or die in Berlin.

Many did flee south to the Obersalzberg, including Göring, who had sent his wife and children and a few of his most treasured possessions (i.e. several train-loads) south some two months earlier. He had also taken the precaution of moving half a million *marks* to his account in Berchtesgaden. Most of Hitler's staff fled to Berchtesgaden in twenty flights from Berlin's Gatow and Staaken airfields. The penultimate act in the saga of the *Berghof* was symbolic; it was named as part of a 'National Redoubt' from where fighting would continue after the fall of Berlin. Created by Goebbels' propaganda, the idea seems to have been readily taken up by Allied intelligence:

Here [Obersalzberg], *defended by nature and by the most efficient secret weapons yet invented, the powers that have hitherto guided Germany will survive to reorganize her resurrection; here armaments will be manufactured in bombproof factories, food and equipment will be stored in vast underground caverns and a specially selected corps of young men will be trained in guerrilla warfare, so that a whole underground army can be fitted and directed to liberate Germany from the occupying forces.* [42]

No doubt the anonymous writer had a successful post-war career as a Hollywood scriptwriter. On 25 April 1945, 318 Lancaster bombers of the RAF attacked the complex and the *Berghof* received a direct hit, destroying one wing. Hitler's last known reference to Obersalzberg, made to Goebbels the same day, is telling: *I'd regard it as a thousand times more cowardly to commit suicide on the Obersalzberg than to stand and fall here.* The mountain had shrunk to a mole hill.

According to some accounts, the SS flooded the *Berghof* with gasoline and set light to it on 4 May 1945, shortly before the arrival of American troops on 5 May. I can find no evidence for any such deliberate burning, and American eyewitness accounts make no mention of it. American troops discovered about 2,000 books from Hitler's personal library, hidden in one of the salt mines near Berchtesgaden. Hoffmann claimed that his *Führer* owned 60,000 books. [43] That, of course, is possible, but it should not be taken to mean that Hitler <u>bought</u> 60,000 books, let alone read them. Most were gifts, either from the authors or from admirers. To suggest, as Waite does, that keeping the books is an indication of approval of their contents is naïf, as any book reviewer will testify. [44]

After the War, the properties comprising the Berghof were deemed to be the property of Bormann, acting as proxy for the NSDAP, or, in certain cases – such as Göring – the property of individual Nazis. The Allies seized the properties and most were eventually transferred to the State of Bavaria. Surprisingly, the Bavarian Finance Ministry claims that no valuation was ever made. [45] Few, if any, of the properties were returned to their original owners since it could not be proved that they had been purchased under duress and in most cases it was decided that the sellers had received a fair market price.

Analysis

All these points leave a number of important questions outstanding with regard to Hitler's personal fortune: Did he own the *Berghof?* Did he own the land on which it stood? Did he own the surrounding land, forming the Berchtesgaden complex? To each of these questions must be added the supplementary question: If so, how much was it worth? The rest of this chapter tries to supply some answers.

Did Hitler own the Berghof?

At first sight, there seems to be little doubt that he did and several facts support this conclusion. Firstly, he definitely bought the original *Haus Wachenfeld* from its original owner, Frau Winter. Since the *Berghof* was built from *Haus Wachenfeld*, in the absence of any property transfer records to the contrary, the *Berghof* must have been one of his personal possessions. Indeed, Fest says that the whole of the *Berghof* complex was still entered in the land registry in Hitler's name in 1945.[46] The only doubt thrown on this is the question of whether or not Angela Raubal was part owner. While she appears to have been joint lessee before the property was bought, it is not clear whether she was party to the subsequent purchase.

The second fact which supports Hitler's ownership of the *Berghof* is his will of 2 May 1938. This will bequeathed all his personal possessions, the *Berghof*, his furniture and his pictures.[47] Presumably he would not have bequeathed something that was not his to give.

Another fact somewhat indirectly supports Hitler's ownership of the *Berghof*, or, at least that he regarded it as his personal home. Around 1940, Hitler had the *Kläsheim Palace*, near Salzburg, furnished as an hotel and reception centre for visiting heads of state, claiming that the *Berghof* was no longer an appropriate place for such meetings.[48]

What did it all cost?

According to one estimate, Hitler spent well over 100 million *marks* on the *Berghof* and 100 million for the artworks.[49] The only known, official estimate of the worth of the *Berghof*, which is said to have comprised 87 buildings, together with the house at Braunau where Hitler was born and his parents' home at Leonding, is given in Bormann's 1949 denazification trial in Linz, Austria, as '1.5 million *marks*'.[50] This estimate must be in *Deutschmarks*, which came into force on 20 June 1948, at a rate of 1 DM to 10 *Reichsmarks*.

There is no great mystery about what land and buildings were purchased, when, and by whom during the creation of the *Berghof*; everything was properly documented in the local land registry, where the documents remain to this day. An excellent summary, complete with photographs, has been compiled by two local historians, from which Table 14-1 is derived.[51] "P." refers to the page in Schöner and Irlinger where the data may be found. "B." indicates whether Adolf Hitler (AH) or Martin Bormann (MB) is the named buyer. The dates given are those for property registration, which is not necessarily the date of purchase. Thus, almost six million *marks* was spent on property comprising the *Berghof* complex. This is certainly consistent with the fifteen million *Reichsmarks* implied by Bormann's denazification trial.

Who paid?

Until Bormann was put in charge of the major expansion in 1936, it seems likely that Hitler paid for the work out of his own pocket: purchase of *Haus Wachenfeld*; the 1929 alterations; the 1933 alterations; and probably some land purchases. Once Bormann was put in charge of the work, he took it upon himself to raise the necessary funds, appropriating the *AH Spende*. Whether Hitler knew that the fund was being used to finance his own projects is not known, but it is highly probable that he did. If Hitler did know, it would go some way toward explaining his choice of Bormann, who administered the *AH Spende*, to oversee the expansion of the *Berghof*.

Other Property

The Berghof was not the only property owned by Hitler; at least four other properties were in his possession (though not necessarily in his name) in 1945: his Munich apartment; Eva Braun's Munich apartment; his birthplace in Braunau; his former family home in Leonding; and an estate in eastern Mecklenburg.[52] There is also a suggestion that Hitler and Eva Braun had bought land in Linz and Munich for their future retirement homes, but there is no concrete evidence for this.[53] Bormann, in his letters, also implies that Hitler owned property at Stolpe, outside Berlin.[54]

Hitler's Munich apartment

Hitler rented a nine-room (plus two kitchens and two bathrooms) apartment on the third floor Prinzregentenplatz 16, Munich, from September 1929 until he bought the building outright in 1938. The building was owned by Hugo Schühle and the lease, dated 10 September 1929, was to run until 1 April 1934.[55] Annual rental was 4,176 marks. Hugo Bruckmann arranged the deal, but it is unclear from the records whether he guaranteed the lease or paid it.

In December of 1938, Hitler purchased the entire building and the Munich real estate registry shows that it was held in his own name – not Bormann's as some suggest.[56] The purchase price was 175,000 marks; the money presumably came from the *AH Spende*.[57] The apartment took up the whole third floor of the four storey building (five storeys, if one counts the attic rooms, some of which appear to be substantial). The entire ground floor was taken up by security staff and other services. Surprisingly few people have left their impressions of this apartment, but one such is the Welsh Liberal MP Thomas Jones:

We might have been in Park Terrace, Glasgow, in a shipowner's drawing-room in 1880.[58]

Such comments suggest that the furniture was sombre, the decorations fussy and lacking in artistic merit. Lüdecke seems to have visited the apartment only once, but offers a few details:

> *This flat showed for pure legend the idea that Hitler was still living simply. The furniture had been designed by Ludwig Troost, the architect of the Braunes Haus, and Hitler would not have accepted such a service for nothing, since he always made a point of refusing important gifts. . . .*
>
> *. . . With visible pride, Hitler conducted me to his library, an attractive, cosy room, lined with several thousand books, many of them gifts, ranged in built-in bookshelves. . . . He waved me on into his study, a room which, despite its simple and practical furnishings, somehow reminded me of a college-boy's study fitted out by rich parents.*[59]

Gun gives a fairly comprehensive description, presumably based on his conversations with Annie Winter and his own inspection of the premises, adding that:

> *The apartment was furnished in the style that characterises the rich bourgeois homes of Munich, with an abundance of armchairs, sofas, lounge chairs, pedestal tables, chests of drawers, writing desks, clocks, frames, light brackets, and other bric-a-brac mass-produced in factories in careful imitation of period pieces. The effect was completed by pseudo-oriental carpets, heavy velvet curtains, damask hangings, and vitrines full of statuettes.*[60]

In late 1942, Munich was bombed and Hitler's apartment is said to have been damaged. According to Goebbels, the Führer was pleased; it would not have looked good otherwise.[61] Gun, however, contradicts this statement, claiming that the building was one of the few in Munich to remain undamaged.[62] Certainly, the building today shows no signs of any serious bomb damage. Post-war, the building was first used by the US Army, later passing to the Bavarian government.

Eva Braun's Munich residences

In March 1936, Hitler purchased a small two-storey suburban villa at Wasserburgerstraße 12 for the use of Eva Braun and her sisters.[63] In keeping with the secrecy which surrounded Eva, the house was held in the name of Heinrich Hoffmann, for whom Eva nominally worked as an assistant. Hoffmann is said to have paid RM 30,000 for the villa in payment for photographs which the sisters had taken, but there is little doubt that the money was Hitler's.[64] The girls moved in on 30 March 1936 and in 1937 the property was transferred to Fräulein Eva Braun, profession: secretary, and the documents duly notarised. Eva's salary, paid by Hoffmann, was RM 450 a month (it continued to be paid to the end of the war), insufficient, as Gun notes, to pay the taxes on the property. Somewhat nondescript, the house had only two interesting features (apart from its occupant and the art collection): a television set – one of the first in Germany – and an air-raid shelter. The television was probably a gift from the Telefunken company; the air raid shelter was built to military standards. The house was slightly damaged during an air raid on Munich in 1944, and an inmate of Dachau was sent there to help with repairs. Ca. 1948, the villa was confiscated and donated to a fund for compensating victims of Nazism. In 1952 it became the property of the State of Bavaria; its current status has not been revealed.

Hitler's birthplace in Braunau

Hitler was born in an inn on the River Inn, the *Gasthof zum Pommer*, a modest residence, named after the family which owned it. Following the *Anschluß*, Hitler purchased the rather modest building, using Bormann as proxy, closed down the bar on the ground floor, and turned it into a shrine. The Pommer brothers, both NSDAP members, drove a hard bargain: the purchase price was an outrageous RM 150,000.[65]

Hitler's former family home in Leonding

In November 1898, Alois Hitler bought a house in Leonding, Austria, five kilometres from Linz, for 7,700 *kronen*. His widow, Klara, sold the house in June of 1905 to a Herr Hölzl for 10,000 *kronen*, of which she received 7,480 *kronen* after the outstanding mortgage had been paid.[66] In 1938, following the *Anschluss* with Austria, Hitler purchased the Leonding estate and turned it into his 'official' ancestral home and a place of pilgrimage.[67] Although the purchase price is not recorded, it is unlikely to have been more than that paid for the *Gasthof zum Pommer*.

Mecklenburg

Known formally as 'Agricultural Estate North', the eastern Mecklenburg estate was held in Bormann's name and administered as part of the Obersalzberg complex. Occupying over 10,000 hectares, the estate included a castle, Schloß Stolpe, which Bormann remodelled for Hitler's personal use, and the Manor of Möllenbeck, which Bormann kept for his own use. Located about 100km northwest of Berlin, Bormann claimed the estate was necessary to ensure Hitler's vegetable supplies. It also served as a convenient place for Bormann to conduct his many extramarital affairs when in Berlin. Hitler never visited the place. In March of 1945, Hummel visited the estate and ordered the castle to be burned if it was threatened by the advancing Russians. It was.

What was it all worth?

As noted above, two estimates of the value of the *Berghof* put it at between 100 and 150 million *marks*. Neither estimate is well documented and it is not clear what each considers to be the *Berghof*. Pool's estimate seems to include only the house, while that at Bormann's denazification trial seems to be that property registered in his name – i.e. the property listed in Table 14-1. I have chosen the latter approach; if it was inside the security perimeter, then it was the *Berghof*. This all-inclusive approach brings its own problems in distinguishing between what was and was not Hitler's. In some cases, the question is clear: the house belonged to Hitler, as did the *Kehlsteinhaus*, the Tea House, and the properties listed in Table 14-1. Things such as the SS Barracks, the guard houses, and other military installations were clearly government property. But what of the underground air-raid shelters, whose construction costs must have been enormous? Were these paid for by Hitler's funds or state funds? There is no evidence either way, but I am inclined to think the latter.

The purchase prices of the various items of real estate comprising the *Berghof* are well documented (see Table 14-1.) The 1933 improvements were probably paid for out of Hitler's income from *Mein Kampf* since the *AH Spende* had only just got started, and was then being used for party purposes, and the *Eher Verlag* itself was only just beginning to make substantial profits. Hitler's income from *Mein Kampf* was RM 1.3 million for 1932-3; it has been assumed that he used half of it, all of it, or all of it plus a RM 1 million advance.

The cost of the *Kehlsteinhaus* has been given as RM 30 million on the basis of evidence apparently from Bormann's papers. This is one of the few figures available for the major works after 1936. This was a difficult and expensive engineering feat; consequently I have taken ±20% for the cost uncertainty.

The cost of the *Kehlsteinhaus* also allows a guess at the costs of the 1936 rebuilding of the *Berghof*. Most of the work on the *Kehlsteinhaus* was excavation, rather than construction, and the cost of the building itself (excluding the lift) would have been about ten million *marks*. On the advice of an architect colleague, who has actually designed a house similar in construction to the *Berghof*, one *Berghof* is equal to about eight *Kehlsteinhausen*. A figure of 80 million, −30%/+50%, has thus been assumed for the 1936 remodelling costs.

Finally, there are the other properties to consider at the *Berghof*, the 'grace and favour' residences: Bormann's house; the farm; Speer's studio; houses kept for visitors; and the *Platterhof*. (Göring's property was his own, though within the *Berghof* estate.) Somewhat surprisingly, Bormann's house was about the same size as the *Berghof* itself, and built out of an existing building, *Haus Hudler*, a small house formerly owned by a Dr. Seitz. It was more luxuriously furnished than Hitler's home, and probably cost about the same – 80 million *marks*. The farm was extensive and luxurious, fitted with the most modern equipment, and a cost of 100 million has been suggested. The remodelling of the *Platterhof*, botched by Bormann so that a major part had to be redone, probably cost about 30 million. Speer's studio was quite modest and probably cost around 15 million, with the tea house costing a similar amount because of its difficult construction site. The results of this analysis are shown in Table 14-2.

For Hitler's other property, the estimation is somewhat simpler because more is known. The Munich apartment building cost RM 175,000 in 1938; by 1944, the value should have increased 10-20 percent. A similar argument applies to Eva's villa (the air-raid shelter must have been added value). The RM 150,000 paid for Hitler's birthplace in Braunau was extortionate; I have therefore taken this as the high figure, reducing it by 25-50 percent. No purchase price is known for the Leonding property, but it is unlikely to have been anywhere near as expensive as that in Braunau and I have assumed 75% of the Braunau figures – but it makes little difference to the results.

Which leaves the 10,000 hectare Mecklenburg estate. The first question is whether or not this was his property. If it was not, then that establishes a minimum value of zero. Unfortunately, I have been unable to find any records of land prices for that area. Land prices around the *Berghof* were about RM 22,000 per hectare, including the property. The Mecklenburg estate, however, had few properties, so the price per hectare could have been much lower, though the land was better quality than that in the Obersalzberg. Similar estates in East Prussia – where the land was also poor – seem to have been valued at around 3-5,000 marks/ha. Consequently, I have used 15% and 30% of the *Berghof* figures. The results of these estimates are shown in Table 14-3.

From all of this rather shaky evidence it can be concluded that the value of Hitler's property holdings in 1944 lay somewhere between 240 and 500 million marks, with 340 million as the most probable value.

In addition, there is the question of what it cost to run. Although information exists on the staffing of the *Berghof*, the author has not been permitted to see it.

Table 14-2: Estimated value of the Berghof *estate*

Item	Value (million RM)		
	Min	Probable	Max
Berghof initial property	5.69	5.69	6.26
1933 Improvements	0.65	1.30	2.30
1936 Rebuilding	56.00	80.00	120.00
Kehlsteinhaus	24.00	30.00	36.00
Platterhof	21.00	30.00	45.00
Bormann house	56.00	80.00	120.00
Farm	70.00	100.00	150.00
Speer's studio	10.50	15.00	22.50
Small tea house	10.50	15.00	22.50
Totals	243.84	341.99	502.06

Table 14-3: Estimated value of other real estate

	Value (million RM)		
Item	Min	Probable	Max
Munich apartment	0.18	0.19	0.21
Eva Braun's villa	0.03	0.03	0.04
Birthplace in Braunau	0.08	0.11	0.15
Leonding family home	0.06	0.08	0.11
Mecklenburg	0.00	32.71	65.42
Totals	0.34	33.13	65.93

However, scattered information suggests the structure shown in Table 14-4.[68] Using these figures, which are derived from denazification records, the total salary bill for 1933-44 comes to about 1.5 million marks. Other running costs — food etc. — must have been comparable.

Table 14-4: Estimated staffing

	1933–36		1937–44	
Position	Number	Salary	Number	Salary
Butler	1	6,000	1	8,000
Sr. Valet	1	6,000	1	8,000
Jr. Valets	2	3,000	3	3,500
Sr. Cook	1	6,000	1	8,000
Jr. Cooks	1	5,000	2	6,000
Kitchen staff	2	2,000	9	2,500
Cleaning	2	1,800	5	2,200
Maintenance	1	2,500	3	3,000
Secretaries	2	3,000	4	3,500
Pro. waiters	2	3,000	4	3,500
Jr. waiters	2	2,000	8	2,200
Others			4	3,000
One-year salary total		55,100	One-year salary total	164,600
Four-year salary total		220,400	Four-year salary total	1,316,800

Notes

1   KERS98, p. 199, citing Hanfstaengl, *15 Jahre*, 108; Auerbach, *Hitler's politische Lehrjahre*, pp. 38-9; and TOLA76, pp. 142-3; SHIR60, p. 73; HITL53, p. 217. Night of 16–17 January 1942. Hitler says that Eckart was on the run from the police at the time and tells dramatic stories of police surveillance and aborted raids. There seems to be no evidence to substantiate this and Hanfstaengl, who was there, makes no mention of it. Heiden (HEID44, p. 222) says that Hitler wanted to be close to the Austrian border so that he could escape, should he be sought by the Bavarian police. In view of the fact that he was no less welcome in Austria, this does not seem very likely. Shirer calls the inn the *Platterhof*, but this name was not assumed until at least 1926.

2   TOLA76, pp. 142-3.

3   TOLA76, pp. 211-212. HITL53, p. 220, Night of 16-17 January, 1942.

4   KERS98, p. 283.

5   HITL53, p. 216, Night of 16-17 January, 1942. Hanfstaengl (HANF57, p. 132), Domarus, Heiden and Toland all put the date at 1925. Given that mention of Hitler's rental do not occur in his tax returns or in the land registry until 1929, I am inclined to accept 1928 as the correct date.

6   HEID44, p. 223. Heiden also seems to be mistaken about the date of the original rental, putting it at 1925. von Lang (LANG79, p. 93) and Domarus (DOM62a, p. 568) say that the house was registered in Angela Raubal's name; this may have been so, but the land registry clearly shows Hitler as the owner in 1932.

7   A copy of the deed of sale can be found in SCHO89, pp. 109-112. It is dated 17 September 1932.

8   HITL53, p. 216, Night of 16-17 January, 1942. Hitler seems unsure of the date, but puts it at 1917. Gun (GUN68, pp. 108-9) implies that the house was built during 1916-17.

9   HITL53, p. 222, Night of 16-17 January, 1942.

10 TOLA76, pp. 282-3. Date of the full moon according to the US Naval Observatory Astronomical Applications Department.

11 TOLA76, pp. 317-8.

12 MASE73, p. 120. Maser's information came from a fellow pupil of Heinz.

13 The author was once snow-bound for four days in a country cottage whose owner had no reading matter except the entire works of Zane Gray – in Finnish – and a beginner's guide to playing the accordion.

14 KERS98, p. 485, citing BHstA MA-106670, RPvOB, 19 August 1933; and Heiber, *Rückseite*, p. 9.

15 TOLA76, pp. 394-5. Toland attributes the recorded conversation to Ilsa Heß, citing Ziegler, Hans Severus. *Wer War Hitler?* Tübingen: Grabert, 1970. Ilsa's close friendship with both Angela and Paula lends some credence to the story.

16 TOLA76, p. 395, citing his 1970 interview with Hans Hitler.

17 DIET57, pp. 196-7.

18 DIET57, pp. 197-8.

19 SPEE70, p. 86.

20 GUN68, p. 114.

21 GUN68, p. 116.

22 KERS00, p. 12, citing Waite (WAIT77), p. 141. Waite cites an interview with Friedlinde Wagner, OSS Source book, p. 940; Karl Wilhelm Krause, *Zehn Jahre Kammerdiener bei Hitler* (Hamburg, early 1950s), p. 52; and conversations with Hanfstaengl, Munich, May 1967. Waite also says that Hitler carried a photograph of his mother with him at all times.

23 GUN68, p. 117.

24 TOLA76, p. 741.

25 GUN68, p. 117.

26 LANG79, pp. 94-95.

27 SCHW89, p. 173; SCHO89; CHAU01.

28 DIET57, p. 199. It is interesting that, in one of his letters to his wife (TREV57, p . 13), Bormann frets that were he to die, his wife and children would lose access to the hothouses and their produce. He also tells his wife, in the same letter, that she would have to leave their home at the Berghof. This suggests that neither the Berghof residence nor 'Bormann's farm' were his personal property. In another letter (TREV57, p. 28), Bormann writes to his wife: 'I have no money or property, but I have you, so I have far greater riches!'

29 TOLA76, p. 433; LANG79, pp. 97-98.

30 The building was never known as the *Adlerhorst*, or Eagle's Nest, a name which seems to have been coined by François-Poncet.

31 KERS00, note 109, p. 898.

32 LANG79, p. 104. KERS00, note 190, p. 898, citing Ernst Hanisch, *Der Obersalzberg: das Kehlsteinhaus und Adolf Hitler*, Berchtesgaden, 1995, pp. 18-21.

33 FRAN46, pp. 342-3. Author's translation. So far as is known, the design was not by Hitler.

34 WAIT77, p. 6, citing Frederick Oechsner, *This Is the Enemy*, New York, 1942, p. 77. The story appears in no other source, and may well be apocryphal. Such behaviour is not unusual: the author once found a piece of driftwood that resembled an eighteen-inch penis, albeit with a large crack down the middle, on the New Jersey shore. He took it home, mounted it on a wooden plinth, stuck it on top of a book-case, and called it Nixon, because it was a tricky dicky.

35 SPEE70, p. 162.

36 KERS00, p. 207.

37 HOFF55, pp. 126-7.

38 SPEE70, p. 216.

39 TREV57, pp. 103-4.

40 TOLA76, pp. 738-40.

41 TOLA76, p. 739.

42 SHIR60, p. 1313. Shirer cites a SHAEF intelligence summary of 11 March 1945, giving his source as Wilmot, p. 690.

43 WAIT77, p. 61, quoting Hoffmann, Hitler, p. xiv.

44 WAIT77, pp. 61-2.

45 STMF03, which is the source for most of this paragraph.

46 FEST70, p. 193. Fest cites "judicial proceedings in Linz" without saying what they were.

47 TOLA76, p. 460, citing evidence from Linge.

48 DIET57, p. 223.

49 POOL97, p. 146. Poole gives no supporting evidence for this figure.

50 Bormann was, of course, tried *in absentia*. Bormann's residence for tax purposes, in 1945, fell within the Linz jurisdiction, though his family was living – at least part of the time – on the Schluchsee, in the southern Black Forest.

51 SCHO89.

52 There is no truth in the wartime Finnish joke that Hitler purchased the famous Hotel Kämp, in Helsinki, and thereafter referred to it as 'Mein Kämp'. (The Finnish letter 'ä' is pronounced as a short 'a', not as a German a-umlaut.)

53 GUN68, p. 218.

54 TREV54, p. 183. Also known as *Ausweichquartier Nord* (roughly, North Sanctuary Area), Trevor-Roper, in his notes to Bormann's letters, says that this was a refuge Hitler had planned for himself before the war as a place to retire to when he needed a rest. Although there are several 'Stolpe' in Germany, the context of Bormann's letter suggests the one NW of Berlin.

55 All information is from the *Stadtarchiv*, Munich.

56 LANG79, p. 91.

57 Munich, Property Register 124, Haidhausen, p. 86, Folio 3235.

58 TOLA76, p. 390.

59 LÜDE38, pp. 454-5.

60 GUN68, p. 7.

61 KERS00, p. 535, quoting from an apparently as yet unpublished section of Goebbels' diary for 42/09/29 and 30. According to the US historian J. McKillop (personal communication to the author) the only raid on Munich in that month was on the night of 19/20 September. About 40 percent of the crews dropped bombs within 5km of the city centre, but most of the bombs fell in the western, southern and eastern suburbs.

62 GUN68, p. 5.

63 The street has since been re-named Delphstraße, in honour of a Jesuit priest executed by the Nazis.

64 GUN68, p. 141; TOLA76, p. 394.

65 LANG79, p. 112.

66 MASE73, p. 42.

67 SCHW89, p. 10.

68 Prepared with the assistance of the former butler to the British Ambassador, Berlin.

Chapter Fifteen

HITLER'S ART COLLECTION

With books and money plac'd for show
Like nest-eggs to make clients lay,
And for his false opinion pay.
Samuel Butler (1612-1680)
Hudibras. Part iii. Canto iii. Line 624.

Adolf Hitler often described himself as an artist and, as described in Chapter 2, he did make a modest living as a copyist and illustrator. There is evidence that Hitler resumed painting after his release from hospital in 1918 – suggesting that the damage to his eyesight was not too severe, though this is far from conclusive – but on a less prolific scale than before, and these paintings were sold for him by a former army colleague Hans Mend.[1] There is again evidence that Hitler still entertained thoughts of a career as an artist in late 1919 and sought the opinion of Max Zäper, a well-known Munich artist, about whether he should continue with his efforts. Zäper is reported to have been impressed and sought the opinion of Prof. Ferdinand Staeger, an artist of Czech extraction, whose mystical-romantic works are said to have first come to Hitler's attention at the *Vienna Secession* exhibition of 1898.[2] Staeger's verdict was also favourable. In later years, Hitler bought six of Staeger's paintings and it is said that he was himself painted by the artist in 1933. However, Otto Dietrich, in his post-war memoirs, claims that the only portrait Hitler ever sat for was painted by a Prof. Heinrich Knirr, who stayed at the *Berghof* expressly for the purpose; all other portraits, according to Dietrich, were painted from photographs.[3] Hitler's efforts as an artist are only of passing concern to this story, though it is interesting to note that even as early as 1930 there was a lucrative trade in forged 'Hitlers', a business which still goes on today. Following the establishment of the *Hauptarchiv der NSDAP* in 1934, attempts were made to collect and catalogue all of Hitler's paintings. The operation was a failure; fewer than fifty works were obtained. Many of the works collected turned out to be forgeries and were destroyed. For the few genuine works, the NSDAP was obliged to pay up to RM 8,000 – about €15,000 in 2003. Hitler called such prices insane, claiming that RM 200 was a more reasonable sum.

Adolf Hitler did not know much about art (certainly not as much as he claimed), but he knew what he liked – and what the German people should like.[4] To be fair, Hitler did support the arts and encouraged the public to buy paintings, discussing the matter on several occasions; unfortunately, much of what he recommended was mediocre.

Believing himself to be a talented artist (he was only moderately so) and an educated critic (he was not at all) he set out to dictate the artistic taste of the Third Reich and to collect and preserve what he considered the 'best' paintings for posterity. Around 1928 – the dating is uncertain, but a careful reading of Hoffmann suggests no earlier than this date – Hitler had sufficient disposable income to begin to collect paintings seriously.[5]

It seems fairly certain that when he began collecting he did so purely for his own pleasure, without any thought of creating a major collection; however, at some time he decided to create a collection that after his death would be given to the Austrian city of Linz, the place he regarded as his spiritual home. It seems that this decision must have been made after 1938, for his will of that year explicitly leaves his paintings to the Nazi party.[6] Hitler decided not only that his personal collection should go to Linz, but also that Linz should become the greatest art gallery in all Europe – a Greater German Europe, as conceived by himself. (Hitler's grandiose projects for Linz – apart from the art collection – do not concern this story; descriptions are given in Kershaw [KERS00] and Speer [SPEE70].) With this decision began one of the greatest exercises in mass plunder since the days of Napoleon. In some respects, it is not yet finished.

The Linz Collection and the Personal Collection (these names will be used from here on to avoid confusion) were two separate entities, even though Hitler intended the Personal Collection to go to Linz after his death, and explicitly says so in his 1945 will, stating:

> My pictures, in the collection which I have bought in the course of years, have never been collected for private purposes but only for the establishment of a gallery in my home-town of Linz on the Danube.

The two collections were officially financed separately: the Personal Collection from Hitler's funds; the Linz Collection by state funds and looting. Unfortunately, the two are intertwined, with the same agents and organisations not only collecting for both, but also making gifts to their *Führer* whose financing, provenance, and intended destination are not always clear. Thus it becomes necessary to consider both the Linz Collection and the Personal Collection together, while attempting to separate the two, for it is only the Personal Collection that can be considered to be part of Hitler's Fortune.

Hitler was remarkably generous, if fickle, towards the artists, sponsoring operas, sculpture, photography, cinema, architecture and, above all, painting.[7] According to Spotts, citing a variety of sources, in 1938 Hitler approved a list of 773 artists, from all fields, whose income taxes were to be cut by up to forty percent.[8] The sculptor Arno Breker, who was earning a million *marks* a year at the time, was permitted to pay taxes on no more than fifteen percent of his income. Speer received a studio and a tax-free honorarium of seven million *marks* for his work on planning the reconstruction of Berlin. Gerdy Troost, widow of the architect, received RM 300,000 over three years. Goebbels recorded in his diary for 30 May 1942: *The Führer gives me an explicit instruction to provide the most generous funding to retired [artists] so that their final years can be spent in comfort.*

The Personal Collection

One of Hitler's personal conceits was that he was an expert at re-discovering long forgotten artists such as Friedrich Stahl (of whom he bought twenty examples) and Karl Leipold (more than twelve examples).[9] Among others on whom he considered himself an expert were Carl Spitzweg (1808–85), Hans Thoma (1839–1924), Wilhelm Leibl (1844–1900) and Eduard Grützner (1846–1925). In his 'Secret Conversations', Hitler has much to say on this and other themes:

> *I have several original scores of Richard Wagner, which was something that not even Dönicke could overlook . . . Liebel is a personality. He doesn't yet know that I've found the Goblet by Jamnitzer for him. He supposes it's still in the Hermitage. The Jews had sold it, and I bought it back in Holland at the same time as the objects of the Mannerheimer collection.* [10]

Wentzel Jamnitzer (1508–1585) was a famous Nuremberg goldsmith. The goblet may well have been the famous piece in the form of a Moor's head which was part of the treasure of the House of Wettin (no relation to the author, alas). In October 1996, two treasure-hunters discovered the goblet, near Moritzburg (Saxony), along with about 50 pieces of gold and silver work, 150 pieces of nineteenth century silver and a coin collection – all belonging to the House of Wettin.[11]

A month later, Hitler is reported to have said:

> *The way in which Hoffmann can do me a service is by finding a Rottmann, for example, for my collection.* [12]

The 'Hoffmann' referred to is almost certainly Heinrich Hoffmann, the photographer, to whom Hitler often turned for advice on purchasing art. Hoffmann's memoirs seem to be the principal source of information on Hitler's art collection for most writers.[13] This is unfortunate, because Hoffmann's memoirs, like those of Dietrich and Speer, are more an *apologia pro vita sua* than serious history. As far as the author has been able to ascertain, no exact inventory of Hitler's possessions was ever made and it has been necessary to concatenate several accounts to arrive at an estimate of Hitler's personal collection. This estimate is undoubtedly pessimistic.

Speer implies that Hitler was buying two or three paintings a month at up to 5,000 *marks* each.[14] Ironically, in view of the later wholesale forgery of Hitler's own work, some of these paintings — those by Spitzweg in particular — may well have been forgeries.

Rosenberg has surprisingly little to say on Hitler's artistic tastes, confining himself largely to a critique of his master's architectural fantasies:

> . . . *he set about with an ever growing passion to acquire 19th-century paintings, which he intended to assemble some day in a gallery in the City of Linz, which was to be completely rebuilt. . . . An intensive hunt was started for works by Spitzweg and also for anything by the Grützners, who were placed on almost the same high level as Keller, Raabe and Busch. . . . That the Führer bought several large paintings by Zäper is still understandable; . . .* [15]

One vexed question which must be addressed is whether or not Hitler paid for the artworks he owned (other than those given as gifts) and to what extent the Personal Collection consisted of looted works. There is little hard evidence, but there is much anecdotal evidence to suggest that Hitler paid for most of what he owned. According to Hoffmann, Hitler refused priceless, looted work on at least one occasion:

> *Alfred Rosenberg . . . thought he would give Hitler great pleasure by presenting him with two most valuable pictures; one was the famous Vermeer van Delft,* Der Astronom, *from the Rothschild gallery, and the other the no less famous* Madame Pompadour *by Boucher, from the Louvre. . . . Hitler . . . was anything but pleased. "Tell Rosenberg", he said stiffly, "that I am not in the habit of accepting presents such as these. The proper place for these paintings is an art gallery, and a decision as to their fate will be made when the war ends!"* [16]

To assess the extent of Hitler's personal collection, it seems best to work chronologically. In 1934, Hitler purchased what became for him a holy icon: an oil painting of Frederick the Great by Anton Graff, for 34,000 *marks*. The importance of this painting, which travelled everywhere with Hitler, is well described by O'Donnell:

> *It was packed in a special, rather bulky, crate, and it was one of Chefpilot Hans Baur's chores to see to it that it was handled with tender care. It took precedence in the Fuehrer's plane over passengers, including general officers.* [17]

Shortly before his suicide, perhaps to atone for all the inconvenience which the painting had caused, Hitler gave it to Baur as a parting gift. Baur rolled up the painting and strapped it to the knapsack on his back prior to his attempted escape from Berlin on 1-2 May.[18] Even when he was shot and seriously wounded, Baur kept the portrait; what became of it is not known; presumably it was either destroyed or passed into Russian hands. The painting was the only picture to hang on the walls of Hitler's study in the Berlin bunker. A further observation is offered by O'Donnell from his interview with Rochus Misch, the operator of the telephone switchboard in the bunker:

Alone, the Fuehrer now spent long silent sessions gazing at his painting. He was looking, he said, for inspiration. . . . [Misch] once disturbed one of these reveries by accident. He hurriedly and discreetly withdrew. "It was very late, and I thought of course that the Fuehrer had already retired. I went into his study to find something. There was Der Chef, gazing at the picture by candlelight. He was sitting there, motionless, his chin buried in his hand, as if he were in a trance. Hitler was staring at the king. The king seemed to be staring right back. I had barged in, but Hitler took no notice of me. So I tiptoed out. It was like stumbling upon someone at prayer."[19]

In 1937, Hitler received Spitzweg's *The Serenade*, which was purchased in Prague.[20] According to Dietrich, Hitler found Makart's colossal painting *The Entrance of Charles V into Antwerp*, in a store-room at Hamburg Town Hall and had it transferred to a prominent place in an unnamed gallery.[21] Whether Hitler appropriated the picture is not clear from Dietrich's account. In the fall of 1940, Hitler acquired Franz von Stuck's *Siren with a Harp*.[22] Earlier, in the 1930s, he had bought von Stuck's *Die Sünde* (Sin), which he hung in his Munich apartment.[23] Mussolini presented him with *Plague in Florence*, by Hans Makart and it is said that Hitler ordered his secretaries to admire this rather gruesome scene with him.[24]

Hitler once boasted that he had acquired a Grützner for RM 5,000, though Speer thought it was only worth 2,000. He eventually acquired over thirty Grützners.[25] Amongst other paintings Hitler is known to have had in his Personal Collection are a Löwith, given to him by Hoffmann and the nude by Bordone that hung at the *Berghof*. Among the many works which Hitler acquired from the dealer Karl Haberstock were: Bordone's *Venus and Amor*; van Dyck's *Jupiter and Antiope*; *Santa Maria della Salute*, by Canaletto; Rubens' *St Peter in the Boat*; *La Danse*, by Watteau, which cost RM 900,000; and Boecklin's *Italian Villa*, for which he paid RM 675,000.

Over several years Hitler bought six paintings by Prof. Ferdinand Staeger, an artist of Czech extraction, whose mystical-romantic works had first come to Hitler's attention in Vienna, and Hitler was himself painted by the artist in 1933.

The Cartoons

An unusual facet of Hitler's art collecting is that he seems to have collected cartoons of himself – a not uncommon hobby of politicians and not necessarily confined to those with sadomasochistic tendencies. In 1933 Hanfstaengl had the idea of using the cartoons for propaganda purposes: reproduce the cartoons but add a commentary explaining the 'truth' behind the cartoonists 'lies'. Hitler liked the idea and gave his permission for the project. The result was a 174-page book entitled, rather cumbersomely *Hitler in der Karikatur der Welt: Tat gegen Tinte : ein Bildsammelwerk von Ernst Hanfstaengl.* (Hitler in the caricature of the world: Fact versus Ink: a picture compilation by Ernst Hanfstaengl) but usually known simply as *Tat gegen Tinte.* It appears that Hitler donated some of the cartoons to Hanfstaengl, or at least allowed him free use of them. The profits from the book, however, were his own and Hitler received no part of them. The book was not even published by the *Eher Verlag* but rather by *Verlag Braune Bucher, Carl Rentsch*, whose name suggests that it might have been associated with the SA. The work was so popular that a second edition was issued in 1934 and in 1938 *G. Wiese Verlag*, acting under license for *Verlag Braune Bucher*, brought out a mass-market edition.

One wonders what became of the original cartoons. It is unlikely – though not impossible – that they remained in Hanfstaengl's possession, though after his escape to England his property was confiscated and subjected to a fine of RM 42,000 as 'tax on flight from the Reich'. Perhaps they were sold to pay the fine. Equally likely, they may lie forgotten in someone's attic.

Other Valuables

Among the other valuables which Hitler possessed were an extensive library, estimated at up to 250,000 works, sculptures, antiques, musical scores, coins, and armour. Many of these were gifts; other than the library, their extent and value is impossible to assess. As noted in Chapter 14, much of Hitler's library was looted, but 3,000 items are still held by the US Library of Congress.

The Linz Collection

Following the exhibition of 'degenerate art', which opened on 19 July 1937, Hitler ordered, through Goebbels, the removal of all modernist works from German galleries. In the latter half of 1937, almost 5,000 paintings and 12,000 other works were removed from public galleries (private collections were left untouched at this time) and brought to a collection depot in the Köpenicker-straße, Berlin. Here, Hitler spent a few hours inspecting them in January 1938, commenting to Goebbels that the only thing to be done with these works was to exchange them abroad for some 'decent Old Masters'. A committee was set up under Goebbels to do just that. When Göring pointed out that it would be simpler to sell these paintings and buy Old Masters with the proceeds, Hitler promptly authorised both sales and exchanges. Over 1,000 paintings and sculptures and 3,825 other works are said to have been destroyed in March 1939.[26] In his report to Hitler, Goebbels stated that sales had brought £10,000, $45,000 and SFr 80,000, with trades amounting to the equivalent of RM 130,000. In his diary for 4 November 1939, Goebbels noted:

> *Degenerate art has brought us a lot of foreign exchange. It will go into the pot for war expenses, and after the war will be devoted to the purchase of art.*[26]

While these events may have awakened Hitler to the possibility of wholesale art collecting, the idea for the Linz Collection may have begun as early as 1937, when Hitler began seriously to contemplate *Anschluß* with Austria. Certainly one of Hitler's first acts on entering Austria on 8 April 1938 was to visit the Provincial Museum in Linz and hold a long discussion with its director, Theodor Kerschner. However, it seems to have been during or following his state visit to Italy in May of 1938 that Hitler's ideas for Linz took final form and the original conception of a gallery devoted to nineteenth century German painting expanded into a grandiose scheme for a collection of the greatest works of all pre-twentieth century European schools.

Possibly at the suggestion of the Berlin art dealer Karl Haberstock, one of whose best customers was Adolf Hitler, Hitler went to Dresden on 18 June 1938 and interviewed Hans Posse, former director of the city's gallery. Posse was re-appointed to his former position (he had been dismissed for 'supporting degenerate art') and in June of 1939 he was put in charge of acquisitions for Linz. In gratitude, Posse bought over one hundred paintings from Haberstock. Hitler set up *Sonderauftrag Linz* (Linz Special Commission), under Bormann, with Lammers in charge of finance and Kurt Hanssen responsible for administration, the latter being later replaced by Helmut von Hummel (see also Chapter 13). A staff of about twenty included persons responsible for cataloguing, restoration and storage, and special curators for books and autographs, armour, and coins.

In April, 1941, despite Hitler's being preoccupied with the preparations for Operation *Barbarossa*, the invasion of the Soviet Union, he took time to intervene in the selection of paintings for the Linz Collection. As Speer records:

> He sent his art dealers into the occupied areas to comb the picture market there, with the result that there was soon a bitter contest between his dealers and Göring's. The picture war had begun to take a nasty turn when Hitler finally reproved his Reich Marshal and thereby once and for all restored the order of rank even in regard to art dealers. [27]

This is optimistic on Speer's part; despite Hitler's dressing-down of Göring, the art war never ended. Speer also seems to be failing to differentiate between Hitler's private collection and the Linz Collection. He goes on:

> In 1941 large catalogues bound in brown leather arrived at Obersalzberg. They contained photographs of hundreds of paintings which Hitler personally distributed among his favourite galleries: Linz, Königsberg, Breslau, and other eastern cities. At the Nuremberg Trials, I saw these volumes again as evidence for the prosecution. The majority of the paintings had been seized from Jewish owners by Rosenberg's Paris office. . . . But Hitler did not utilize his authority for his private ends. He did not keep in his own possession a single one of the paintings acquired or confiscated in the occupied territories. [28]

This rather thin evidence does tend to support the idea that the two collections were separate – as indeed they were – but Speer seems scarcely aware of the fact. Speer goes on to muddy the waters:

268

Hitler's purchases of paintings stopped after he had appointed the head of the Dresden Gallery, Dr. Hans Posse, as his agent for building the Linz collection. Until then Hitler had chosen his purchases himself from the auction catalogues.[29]

But the paintings for the Linz Collection were only ever <u>chosen</u> by Hitler and were paid for not out of Hitler's pocket but out of state funds. Are we then to believe that Hitler stopped adding to his personal collection after 1941 or that he no longer involved himself in selecting the paintings for Linz? Indeed, there is solid evidence that Hitler was still buying paintings in late 1944. A subsequent passage by Speer fails to resolve the question:

Shortly after the appointment of Posse, Hitler showed him his previous acquisitions, including the Grützner collection. . . . Hitler went on about his favourite paintings in his usual way, but Posse refused to be overpowered either by Hitler's position or by his engaging amiability. Objective and incorruptible, he turned down many of these expensive acquisitions: "Scarcely useful" or "Not in keeping with the stature of the gallery, as I conceive it." . . . Posse rejected most of the pictures by painters of Hitler's beloved Munich School.[30]

There is no doubt that the Grützner collection was Hitler's own; as noted earlier in this chapter, Grützner was Hitler's great passion. We also know, from Hitler's will, that his collection was intended to pass to the city of Linz after his death. The situation is further complicated by Speer's muddled chronology. Posse was put in charge of acquisitions for the Linz Collection in June, 1939, yet Speer specifically refers to 1941 when describing the photograph albums. It is unlikely that Speer is mistaken as to the latter date, since no art had been acquired by June 1939, except from Austria and Czechoslovakia.

On 28 April 1942, at dinner in Berlin with Speer and *Gauleiter* Forster, Hitler expounded at length on his plans for Linz and his art collection:

After the French campaign and the occupation of Serbia and the Russian territories, Liebel, the Mayor of Nuremberg, approached me and requested the return to Nuremberg of all the works of art to which he could possibly stake a claim.

. . . I know my Viennese inside out! The moment we start to consider a Rembrandt or two taken from the Jews, they will at once start to try, in that gentle, naïve way of theirs, to persuade me to leave all the works of the Great Masters in Vienna, arguing that the works of lesser painters will be quite good enough to ensure the happiness of the museums of Linz or Innsbruck.

. . . But I am determined to make of Linz a German town on the Danube which surpasses [Budapest], and by so doing to prove that the artistic sense of the Germans is superior to that of the Magyars. . . . On the banks of the Danube there will be a great hotel reserved for the "Strength through Joy" organisation, municipal buildings designed by Professor Giesler, a Party House designed by the architect Fick, a building for Army Headquarters, an Olympic Stadium and many other things . . .

As regards the Party House and the Provincial Parliament, Reichsleiter Bormann made a handsome offer which delighted me. As soon as he heard that the plans had been completed, he volunteered to provide the money for the projects. As the Party Treasurer has already undertaken to defray these expenses, I did not feel justified in accepting Bormann's offer; but I am none the less grateful to him.

In 1942, Posse collected just 122 paintings for Linz and this relatively small number may have been the result of his ill-health. In December he died suddenly of cancer and was given a state funeral. Hermann Voss, who had been dismissed from his post at the Kaiser Friedrich museum for 'cosmopolitan and democratic tendencies and friendship with many Jewish colleagues', was appointed to both of Posse's former posts. Although the Linz project was still kept secret from the German public, Hitler signed a decree in October 1942 formally giving the gallery and its contents to the nation.

Relations between Hitler and Voss were not as easy as they had been with Posse, and Voss found it expedient to give a generous present to Hitler at the end of 1943, along with a reminder that he had procured 881 paintings for Linz, and noting that this was considerably more than his predecessor. One account suggests the number was somewhat greater, claiming that 3,000 paintings were collected for Linz in 1943-4 at a total cost of RM 150 million.[31] In April, on the occasion of Hitler's birthday, a small corner of the veil of secrecy surrounding the Linz project was lifted. In what was clearly a propaganda move, readers of the art magazine *Kunst dem Volk* were told that their *Führer* was 'giving thought' to an art gallery in Linz.

In 1944, the *Mannheimer Collection* was purchased for RM 6 million and the partial ledgers of *Sonderauftrag Linz* note that expenditure for 1944 was RM 548,766.[32]

The last entry in the ledgers is for 1 March 1945 and records that an additional RM 53,094 had been spent for the year up to that date.[33]

Nor was Linz the only city where Hitler interested himself in its museums:

> I must do something for Königsberg. With the money Funk has given me, I shall build a museum in which we shall assemble all we've found in Russia. I'll also build a magnificent opera house and a library.[34]

This is presumably a reference to Economics Minister Walther Funk. Tantalisingly, this leaves many questions unanswered: What money? How much? Is this money something given to Hitler personally or as Head of State? Could it be a reference to the treasury contributions to the Cultural Fund (see Chapter 13). Had the conversation taken place a few months later, it would be tempting to assume a reference to the notorious 'Max Heiliger' account, which was under Funk's control. Alas, we do not know.

Galleries

Linz was not the only intended home of the various collections. Indeed, the projects for Linz were never realised (Hitler always intended them to take place after the war – presumably to give himself something to do in his retirement) and the collection was never housed there. However, several galleries were built and these form part of this story.

The Haus des Deutsches Kunst

The House of German Art in Munich was designed by Troost under Hitler's direction and was formally opened on 18 July 1937.[35] A large, white, ugly, building in the obligatory neo-classical style, it still stands today and is known locally as the *Weisswurstpalast* – the White Sausage Palace, an allusion both to the shape and number of its columns and to a Munich delicacy. Above the entrance was a motto apparently written by Hitler himself: *Die Kunst ist eine erhabene und zum Fanatismus verpflichtende Mission* (Art is a noble mission committed to fanaticism.[36])

Hitler is reported to have financed the *Tag des Deutsches Kunst*, which was held in Munich every summer from 1937 through 1944, from the Cultural Fund. Since he personally chose the rather mediocre artworks, it is perhaps fitting that he should have paid for inflicting them upon the public. (In reality, it was the public who paid.) However, such patronage did serve a useful purpose since most of the works exhibited were for sale and usually at modest prices: oil paintings for as little as RM 250, drawings for as little as RM 130.[37] Hitler bought at least 1,100 paintings from the exhibition between 1937 and 1944, suggesting an expenditure of over 330,000 *marks* if the lowest price is taken. If other figures quoted are correct, Hitler spent almost four million *marks* over this period.[38]

The Führerbau

One of the few contemporary paintings that Hitler purchased was Adolf Ziegler's *The Four Elements*, a triptych of four rather sexless nude women.[39] The French ambassador François Poncet said it should have been re-named *The Four Senses*, since taste was lacking. After Ziegler fell from grace by suggesting peace negotiations in 1943, the painting was removed. Its present whereabouts are mercifully unknown. Menzel's *Frederick the Great Travelling* (a gift from Himmler) and Spitzweg's *The Serenade* also hung in his office.

The cellars of the *Führerbau*, which had been built as air-raid shelters, were later used as a repository for artworks – one of the few not identified by the Allies by early 1945. 3,423 works were evacuated from there to Kremsmünster and Alt Aussee in 1944-5; at least some of these formed part of the Personal Collection.[40] When American troops entered Munich, 723 works, including the 262 paintings of the Schloss Collection, were stored there. No attempt was made to safeguard these treasures and the building was looted by both locals and US troops; only 148 pictures were ever recovered, of which only 22 were from the Schloss Collection.

Hitler's Munich apartment seems to have been home to his favourite works, which included Lenbach's *Bismarck in Cuirassier Uniform*, Feuerbach's *Park Landscape*, Stuck's *The Sin*, and a Ziegler. There is a suggestion that several Spitzwegs were housed here:

> On both sides of the fireplace hung Hitler's prized possessions, the paintings of Spitzweg. He had [sic] ordered all art dealers to make a hunt for Spitzweg's pictures and the six that were hanging there were his prized possessions. Miss Wagner commented it seemed that the great Dictator who was always striving to make everything he did of monumental size should worship the painter who glorified "Des Spiessburgertums" [bourgeois-ness].[41]

Eva Braun's Munich Apartment

Like her lover, Eva Braun also possessed a substantial art collection and, according to Gun, these were detailed in her will and included:

> . . . landscapes by Fischbach, Rickelt, Baskon, Midgard; one by Wax, a large painting by Gradl, a canvas by Gallegos, another by Franke, portraits by Rosl, Popp, Hugo Kauffmann, and Gallegos. Eva's favourites were a watercolour by Hitler, "The Asam Church", a portrait of Hitler by Bohnenberger, a north Italian landscape by Bamberger and also a head of a young girl that Martin Bormann had given her for her birthday. There was a valuable painting attributed to the school of Titian, which was a gift from Mussolini to Hitler, another portrait of the Führer by Knirr, and a Reinhardt. Several other Bohnenbergers, including a portrait of Eva, a landscape of Rimini, some old watercolours of Venice and canvases by Tiedgen, Hoberg, Krauss, and Hengeler Hilbakt completed the collection. To this inventory . . . should be added several valuable rugs, including a Samarkand and a Gobelin (these may well have been imitations, however).[42]

Quite a remarkable collection. Its fate is unknown.

The Chancellery

Several artworks owned by Hitler were on view at the Reich Chancellery in Berlin. The grand dining room contained six landscapes which Hitler had commissioned from Hermann Gradl. These have been described as 'essentially wallpaper'.[43] Elsewhere hung Kaulbach's *Entry of the Sun Goddess*, Schwind's *Bacchus Festival*, a Füger, a Lenbach portrait of Bismarck (presumably different from the one in the Munich apartment), and a work by Angelica Kauffmann, one of the few female painters whom Hitler admired. A large proportion of the paintings on display – and intended to be viewed by visiting dignitaries – were not Hitler's, but were on loan from public galleries in Berlin and Vienna.

The *Führerbunker*, beneath the Chancellery, hardly qualifies as a gallery, but some art works were kept there – notably Graf's portrait of Frederick the Great – and the mysterious collection of Hitler's private papers that was later to cause so much trouble.

The Berghof

Much of the Personal Collection was kept at the *Berghof* and visitors and residents have left many accounts of the works on display there. The works assembled at the Berghof seem to have been chosen to impress, rather than the more personal selection found in Hitler's Munich apartment. Several persons have left their impressions of the works on display. Schuschnigg, the Austrian Chancellor, records seeing a Madonna by Dürer and that Hitler boasted of having 'the best collection of . . . Spitzweg in the world' and of paying RM 80,000 for a Defregger.[44]

Otto Dietrich gives a brief description of the salon at the *Berghof* and some of the art which it housed:

> The walls around the room glowed with the rich colours of classical paintings by German and Italian masters. Over the mantelpiece a madonna [sic] by an unknown Italian looked down upon the company. On the left was Feuerbach's Nana and a portrait of King Henry, the "founder of cities", holding compass and rule; on the right a female nude by Botticelli and the sea-nymphs from Boecklin's Play of the Waves. In the dark background of the room the bronze bust of Richard Wagner seemed to come to life.[45]

According to Speer, the paintings at the *Berghof* included a nude attributed to Bordone and another attributed to Titian, Feuerbach's *Nana*, an early landscape by Spitzweg, a landscape by Pannini, and an altar painting by Eduard von Steinle.[46]

Elsewhere

In addition to the above, Hitler made grandiose plans for galleries in territories conquered by the *Reich*; Königsberg (present-day Kaliningrad) was to receive all the loot from the Soviet Union, including 40,000 artworks from the imperial palaces around Leningrad (St Petersburg). In France, the cathedral of Strasbourg was to become a monument to German culture. Vienna, as punishment for having failed to recognise Hitler's artistic talents in 1907-8, was to be culturally diminished and eclipsed by Linz.[47] Perhaps the strangest 'cultural' project of all was destined for Norway:

> In the far north, in a project especially dear to his heart, he planned an entirely new city in Norway, near Trondheim. Originally to be called Nordstern (polar star) and then renamed Drondheim, it was to be wholly German with a population of 250,000 – three times larger than Trondheim at the time. It would have an opera, theatres, libraries, a large art gallery – for exclusively German masters – and other cultural requisites. Hitler himself chose the specific site and by 1945 planning was at an advanced stage.[48]

As the Allied bombing campaign over Germany mounted in 1943, it was realised that the various collections were vulnerable and so they were dispersed to various repositories (see Maps 1 and 2; the key to the repositories is given in Table 15-1.) Many of these were also soon considered unsafe and a permanent refuge was established in the old Steinberg salt mine at Alt Aussee, in Upper Austria (Number 93 on Map 2). Much, though not all, of the Linz Collection was hidden there and according to an official US report, this cache comprised 6,755 paintings and 257 cases of books.[49]

Table 15-1: Key to the repositories

Ref	Location	Contents
1	Loerrach	Karlsruhe institute
2	Hinterzarten	Library of the Univesity of Freiburg
3	Sankt Blasien	Paintings, Grüssau monastery.
4	Schwarzwald	Library of the Univesity of Freiburg
5	Rastatt	Karlsruhe institute
6	Emmendinghem	Karlsruhe institute
7	Beuren	
8	Konstanz	Library of Archbishop of Freiburg.
9	Lindau am Bodensee	Paintings, Grüssau monastery.
10	Tuttlingen	
11	Birnau, Kloster	
12	Heilingenberg	
13	Meersburg	
14	Salem, Kloster	
15	Salem, Schloß	
16	Ravensburg	Official storage.
17	Weingarten	
18	Isny	
19	Leutkirch-Wangen	
20	Pforzheim	Jewelry and library.
21	Ludwigsburg	Stuttgart museums.
22	Muehlheim	
23	Bebenhausen	
24	Hausen	
25	Bietigheim	Libraries, archives.
26	Sigmaringen, Schloß	
27	Hohen-Urach	
28	Saulgau	
29	Obermarschtal	
30	Biberach	Government property.
31	Erbach	
32	Ochsenhausen	
33	Wiblingen	

The shelters beneath the *Berghof* seem to have housed at least part of the Personal Collection, including part of Hitler's library.

How much?

The question which is important to this book is: How much did Hitler spend on his Personal Collection? To answer that one needs to know the number of paintings, sculptures, and books and their average price.

Table 15-1 (continued)

Ref	Location	Contents
34	Bad Mergentheim	Storage?
35	Bruchsal	Karlsruhe institute.
36	Menzigen	
37	Möckmühl	
38	Neunstein, Schloß	Stuttgart museums.
39	Neresheim	
40	Amstetten	ER.
41	Baden-Baden	Göring.
42	Seebach	
43	Aschhausen	Army museum, Wien.
44	Ehingen	Gewerbe Museum, Stuttgart.
45	Heilbronn	Material from Southern Germany.
46	Riedlingen	Gewerbe Museum, Stuttgart.
47	Bad Kissingen	Libraries.
48	Bad Kissingen	Frankfurt museum.
49	Egglkofn	Grand Duke of Hesse-Darmstadt
50	Weisee	Bavarian state library
51	Tegernsee	Bavarian state library, Army library.
52	Nordlingen	
53	Treuchlingen	
54	Berchtesgaden	Führer archive.
55	Berchtesgaden	Government archives, Pinakotheken, Munich.
56	Cham	Grand Duke of Hesse-Darmstadt; miniature .- collection; Holbein Madonna.
57	Nickelsburg (1)	
58	Kogl (2)	ER.
59	Augsburg	ER.
60	Buxheim	Deposit for artworks collected by E.R.
61	Arnsdorf, Schloss	Pictures, furniture.
62	Füssen	ER.
63	Gemund	Bavarian state library, Army library.
64	Schwanenwerder Schloß, Berlin	Goebbels' personal possessions.
65	Berlin, Wannsee	Files of General Staff
66	Potsdam	Files of General Staff. Files on ER.

Estimates of the number of works in the Personal Collection range from 3,000 to 30,000; in the author's opinion, 10,000 is a more reasonable upper limit. As noted earlier, Backes identifies 3,423 works moved from the cellars of the *Führerbau*, Munich, some of which were part of the Personal Collection. Thus, it seems reasonable to take 3,000 as the lower limit of the collection. There were also 144 paintings, bought by Hitler at the *Große Deutsche Kunstausstellung* (GDK), for RM 367,530 – an average of RM 2,552 – which seems low until it is remembered that the works exhibited at the GDK were by contemporary artists.

Table 15-1 (continued)

Ref	Location	Contents
67	Vierzehneiligen	Valuable books.
68	Laubach, Schloß	Hesse state mus.
69	Kuenzell	ER.
70	Phillipsthal	Five boxes of books.
71	Frankfurt am Main	French collections.
72	Hersfeld	Material from Kassel.
73	Kassel	Arch. for Kassel and Hessen-Nassau.
74	Allendorf an der Lahn	Wallenraf-Richarts Museum, Cologne.
75	Königshof	
76	Sigmaringen, Schloß	Artworks from Aachen, Cologne.
77	Bremen	Private libraries.
78	Bremen	Labour unions library.
79	Trier	Various collections.
80	Stotzheim	Alsatian works of art.
81	Eifel Mts.	Archives, German chemical industry.
82	Bonn	Part of Köln University library.
83	Remagen	Part of Köln University library.
84	Mari**laach	Part of Köln University library.
85	Marienstatt, Kloster	
86	Burg Reichenstein	Archived art: Koblenz
87	Bad Godesburg	Part archived in Trier.
88	Burg Untermaubach	Part Cologne museum.
89	Ehrenbreitstein	Archives Luxembourg, Osnabrück.
90	Dresden	Government archives.
91	Hamburg	Hamburger Kunsthalle.
92	Wandsbeck	Hamburg state archives.
93	Alt-Aussee, Bad Aussee	Linz museum, ER., Austrian collections.
94	Weimar	Works of art.
95	Schwarzach	Archives of SD for southern Thuringia.
96	Rudolstadt	Art archive., Weimar.
97	Feldkirch	*Reichsfinanzschule*
98	Dortmund	Art from western provinces?
99	Grafschaft	*Kunstmuseum*, Düsseldorf; art from Belgium, France, Holland.
100	Letmathe	*Westfalen* art archive.
101	Muenster	Films & photos from *Westfalen* Museum.

The author has been able to identify the amounts spent on 184 paintings and these are what is called in statistics log-normally distributed. Using this data, it is possible to estimate the value of a collection of three, five, and ten thousand works. In addition, there are the minor paintings Hitler purchased at the *Tag des Deutsches Kunst*, noted above, which one author claims totalled four million *marks*. To this author, 330,000 *marks* seems a valid minimum. The most probable value has been taken as the average of these two. To these must also be added a few sculptures, of which the most important were an Italian copy of *The Discus Thrower*,

Table 15-1 (continued)

Ref	Location	Contents
102	Arnsberg	Archive, Munster.
103	Warstein	Valuable material.
104	Siegen	Cathedral of Metz.
105	Schnan	Artworks from Paris.
106	Mehrerau	Art from monastery of Grüssau.
107	Vaduz	Art from Liechtenstein, Wien.
108	Maria-Waldrast, St.	Unknown.
109	Schwaz	Unknown.
110	Salzburg	Art from Paris.
111	Salzburg	Ministry of Transport archives.
112	Werfen	Libraries from Berlin.
113	Linz	Führer museum.
114	Linz	
115	Gaming, Schloß	
116	Rothschild Jagdschloß	
117	Graz	Steiermark province collections.
118	Sitzenberg-Reidling	Italian artworks.
119	Laxenburg, Schloß	*Museum für Volkerkunde*, Wien.
120	Kefermarkt	Linz archives.
121	Klosterneuburg, Stift	
122	Nikolsburg (Czech Mikulov)	
123	Eisgrub, Schloß	
124	Feldsberg, Schloß	
125	Eisenach	
126	Kogl (I)	ER.
127	Bregenz	Archives.
128	Hohenschwangau, Schloß	See also Füßen.
129	Neuschwanstein, Schloß	See also Füßen.
130	Dietr am Zell	
131	Kinzel	
132	Nikolausberg	
133	Undine	Archive.
134	Vienna, Schönbrunn palace.	Archive,. German Foreign Office.

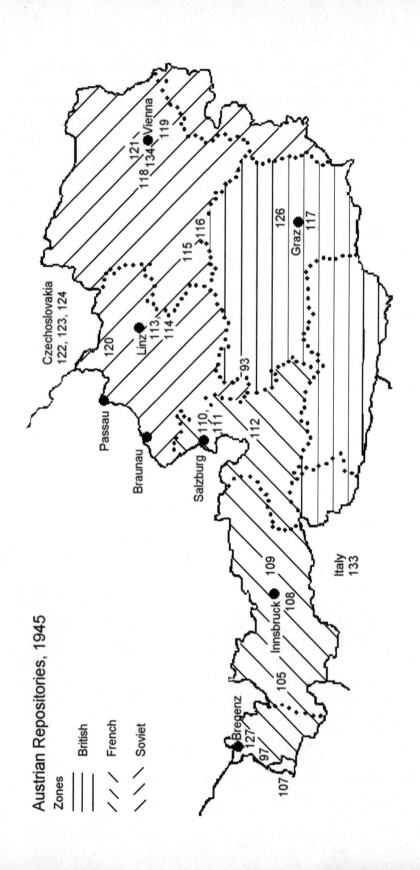

Austrian Repositories, 1945

Zones

British
French
Soviet

Czechoslovakia
122, 123, 124

120

Passau

Braunau

Salzburg

110,
111

Linz

113,
114

115

116

93

112

126

Graz

117

118
134
121
119

Vienna

105

Innsbruck

108

109

Bregenz
127

97

107

Italy
133

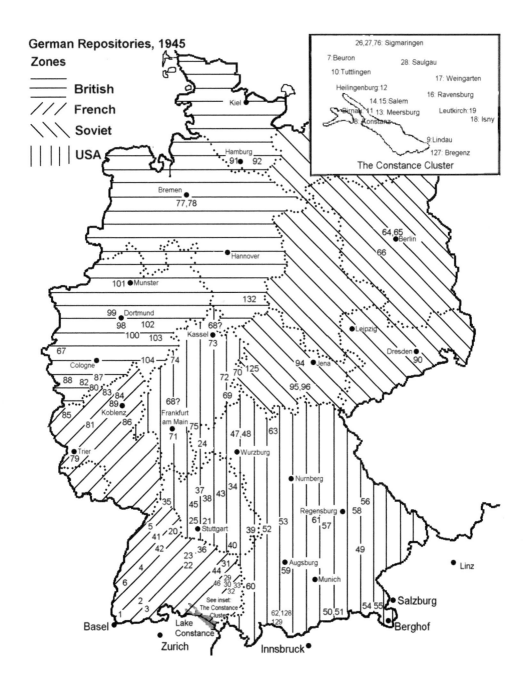

German Repositories, 1945

Zones

British
French
Soviet
USA

The Constance Cluster

26,27,76: Sigmaringen
7:Beuron   28: Saulgau
10:Tuttlingen
                              17: Weingarten
Heilingenburg:12
                      14.15:Salem   16: Ravensburg
Birnau 11 13: Meersburg   Leutkirch:19
8: Konstanz   18: Isny
                    9:Lindau
                      127: Bregenz

Kiel

Hamburg
91   92

Bremen
77,78

Hannover

Berlin
64,65
66

101 Munster

132

99 Dortmund
98   102
100 103

Leipzig

67
Cologne   104   74
88 82   87   70 125
80   72
83 84   69   95,96
89   68?
85   Koblenz   Jena 94
81   86   Dresden
Trier   90
79

1
Kassel
73

68?

Frankfurt
am Main
71

75

47,48   63
24
Wurzburg

37   34
45 38 43
35
          Nurnberg
5 20
41   53   Regensburg 56
42   39 52   61 57   58
25 21 Stuttgart
23 36   40   49
22 31
4   44   Augsburg
6   29   59   Munich
46 30 33 60
2 32
3   See inset:
1   The Constance
          Cluster   62,128   50,51   54 55
Basel   129   Berghof
          Lake
Zurich   Constance   Salzburg

Linz

Innsbruck

279

Table 15-2: Artworks and books

Value in million RM

	Minimum	Probable	Maximum
Major paintings	87.29	145.49	290.98
Minor paintings	0.33	2.17	4.00
Sculpture	1.44	2.16	3.24
Books	0.24	1.32	2.40
Total	89	151	301

bought for RM 707,400 and a torso, bought for RM 734,151.[50] These have been used to establish a minimum value for sculpture. The probable figure has been taken as fifty percent higher, and the maximum as fifty percent higher still.

Finally, there is the question of Hitler's library. Estimates of the size of this vary between 30 and 150 thousand books. Since they do not represent a significant sum compared to the artworks, a minimum average price of RM 8 has been taken with a maximum price of RM 16, and the average taken for the most probable.

The results of these speculations are shown in Table 15-2, which suggest that the value of Hitler's artistic possessions lay somewhere between 90 and 300 million *marks*.

Notes

1   MASE73, p. 53. The author has a friend, an architect, the retinas of whose eyes have been so badly damaged by illness that he can no longer drive or read a newspaper, yet he still paints well.
2   This is improbable, since Hitler would have been nine years old at the time of the exhibition. It is, of course, possible that Hitler became familiar with the works through illustrations.
3   DIET57, p. 192.
4   The whole question of Hitler's attitude to the arts has been thoroughly examined by Spotts, SPOT03.
5   HOFF55, Chapter 8 and passim. The date is consistent with his income from *Mein Kampf* and that declared in his tax returns.
6   TOLA76, p. 460.
7   A much more detailed study is given by Spotts, SPOT03.
8   SPOT03, p. 80.
9   MASE73, p. 62.
10 HITL53, pp. 162-4. 17 December 1941. Walter Dönicke was a *Kreisleiter* and mayor

of Leipzig. Liebel, Mayor of Nuremberg, fancied himself as an art collector and was always agitating for the transfer of works to the city collections. Hitler does not seem to have had a high opinion of Liebel.

11 Spoils of War International Newsletter. No. 3. December 1996. *Koordinierungsstelle der Länder für die Rückführung von Kulturgütern beim Senator für Bildung, Wissenschaft, Kunst und Sport.* D-28195 Bremen.

12 HITL53, p. 176. Night of 2-3 January 1942.

13 HOFF55.

14 SPEE70, pp. 81-82.

15 ROSE49, pp. 249-50.

16 HOFF55, p. 180.

17 ODON78, p. 39.

18 BAUR58, pp. 189-90.

19 Ibid., p. 39.

20 SPOT03, p. 194. It is uncertain whether Hitler bought this himself or whether it was bought by others and presented as a gift.

21 DIET57, p. 177.

22 WAIT76, p. 68. The best that can be said about Franz von Stuck (1863-1928) is that he was 'a bit odd'. He had a passion for painting naked women entwined with large snakes, and the words 'sin', 'evil', and 'depravity' feature regularly in their titles. The well-known 1960's poster of Nastassia Kinski, entwined with a snake, could easily have been inspired by a von Stuck painting – and possibly was.

23 WAIT76, p. 68; POOL97, p. 141. Now in the *Neue Pinakothek*, Munich.

24 POOL97, p. 143. WAIT76, p. 67, which quotes 'a secretary' but references Speer.

25 SPEE70, pp. 43-44; HOFF55, p. 168.

26 SPOT03, p. 168, citing Rave, Paul, *Kunstdiktatur in Dritten Reich* (1991), p. 68, and Roh, Franz, *'Entartete Kunst: Kunstbarbarei im Dritten Reich*, (1962), p. 53.

27 SPEE70, p. 178.

28 Ibid., p. 178.

29 Ibid., p. 179.

30 Ibid., p. 179.

31 WAIT76, p. 67.

32 WAIT76, p. 67, apparently quoting from FAIS45.

33 WAIT76, p. 67, apparently quoting from FAIS45.

34 HITL53, p. 215, night of 15-16 January 1942.

35 The building was ill-omened from the start. While laying the foundation stone in October 1933, Hitler tapped the stone with a ceremonial silver hammer. The hammer broke. Troost, the building's architect, died suddenly, three months later. Hitler believed the two events were connected.

36 Author's translation. Waite (WAIT76, p. 67) translates this as: 'Art is an ennobling mission demanding fanaticism', which is subtly different.

37 SPOT03, p. 175.

38 Ibid., pp. 173-4.

39 According to von Lang, Ziegler was referred to as 'the master of German pubic hair' – something which appears to be notably lacking in the work in question.

40 BACK88, p. 93. Backes is not always careful to distinguish between Hitler's prop-
    erty and the Linz Collection, but he tries.
41 Office of Strategic Services, *Hitler Source Book*, Interviews with Friedlinde [sic]
    Wagner, New York City.
42 GUN68, pp. 145-6.
43 SPOT03, p. 180.
44 Schuschnigg, Kurt von. *Austrian Requiem*. New York, 1946. p. 20. Franz Defregger,
    b. April 30, 1835, at Strontach, in the Austrian Tyrol; d. January 2, 1921, in Munich.
    Defregger was a competent, but uninspiring, academic painter who painted mainly
    simple, homely peasant scenes.
45 DIET57. p. 215.
46 SPEE70, p. 142. It would be interesting to get a rough valuation of these works.
47 According to Henriette von Schirach, in her book *Der Preis der Heerlichkeit*, (1956), p.
    17, Hitler's last message to Vienna was to order 'his' collection of antique armour
    to be moved to safety at the *Berghof*. However, there is some evidence that this collec-
    tion was evacuated to Aschhausen (43 on the map of German repositories.)
48 SPOT03, p. 33.
49 FAIS45, passim.
50 BACK82, p. 100.

Chapter Sixteen

THE LAST DAYS

Vicissitudes of fortune, which spares neither man nor the proudest of his works, which
buries empires and cities in a common grave.
Edward Gibbon (1737-1794)
Decline and Fall of the Roman Empire (1776). Chap. lxxi.

The end began on 22 April 1945, when Hitler had his famous tantrum, hurling coloured crayons at the maps and screaming 'The War is lost!'. A few hours later, Schaub was called to help sort through and destroy Hitler's personal documents from the safe. (It is a measure of Schaub's position in Hitler's entourage that he held the second key to Hitler's personal safe in the Berlin bunker.) Except for some unidentified papers which Hitler entrusted to Schaub, the material was carried up to the Chancellery garden and burned.[1] Hitler is reported to have witnessed the event and said:

> *What have I lost! My dearest memories! But that's the point — sooner or later you have to get rid of this stuff.*[2]

Earlier, apparently on 20 April, Hitler's fifty-sixth birthday, it had been decided to evacuate about eighty members of Hitler's staff, together with some government archives and some of Hitler's personal papers, to Berchtesgaden, in an operation code named *Seraglio*. A detailed description of this operation and its aftermath has been given elsewhere.[3] On the night of 22-23 April, two tri-motor Ju352 aircraft left Berlin with the first group of passengers and documents, the latter packed into steel boxes; only one aircraft eventually reached Salzburg, the other, piloted by Major Friedrich Gundlfinger, crashed en route near the Czech border.[4] Among those on board was *SS Scharführer* (Sergeant) Wilhelm Arndt, one of Hitler's valets, who was accompanying his master's private papers. When news that the aircraft was missing reached General Hans Baur, Hitler's chief pilot, he broke the news to Hitler:

> *Hitler was very upset at this, because one of his favourite personal servants was with this plane.*
> *'And I entrusted him with extremely valuable documents which would show posterity the truth about my actions!' he exclaimed in dismay.*[5]

283

Hitler's comments on hearing of the loss of the aircraft carrying his papers and on seeing his remaining papers burned has led to much speculation and no little trouble, particularly the *Hitler Diaries* fraud.[6] Even today, one can only speculate as to what was so important to Hitler that it was worth the risk of evacuating it to Berchtesgaden. In the case of financial records, the papers of principal importance to this book, three groups of such records can be identified: working records; papers of authority; and correspondence relating to funding.

Working records include account books, receipts etc. It seems most unlikely that these would have been regarded by anyone, even Hitler, as worthy of preservation and they were either destroyed or abandoned. There is little doubt that they are lost forever, unless they are lurking in some Russian archive.

Papers of authority include details of bank accounts, the authority for those needing access to them, property deeds, etc. Given Hitler's lack of interest in day-to-day financial matters, it is unlikely that he would have taken personal charge of such papers. Consequently it seems unlikely that they would have been evacuated on Hitler's orders (though they could have been evacuated on the orders of someone else) and equally unlikely that anyone would take the trouble to destroy them; if any group of records were to be preserved, this is it. Such papers would also be prime candidates for theft.

Any correspondence relating to funding – letters, promissory notes, etc. – would have been considered of great historical interest and, to say the least, political dynamite. Where such papers concerned Hitler personally, rather than the NSDAP, they would most probably be held in his personal archive, either in Berlin or at the *Berghof*. If any financial papers were marked for evacuation from Berlin or for complete destruction, it was these.

There is also the intriguing question of Eva Braun's papers. On 22 April, Eva wrote what she intended to be her final letter to her lifelong friend Herta Ostermeyr. The letter is printed in full in Gun; the following constitute merely the relevant passages:

> *My dear little Herta,*
>
> *These are the very last lines and therefore the last sign of life from me. I don't dare write to Gretl; you must explain all this to her with due consideration for her state. I'm sending you my jewelry, to be distributed according to my will, which is in the Wasserburgerstraße. I hope that with this jewelry you'll be able to keep your heads above water anyway for a time. . . . With fondest love and kisses,*
>
> *Yours,*
>
> *Eva*[7]

This letter effectively appointed Herta as executrix of Eva's will. The passage '. . . with due consideration for her state' refers to Gretl's pregnancy, which was nearing term. The following day, 23 April, Eva changed her mind and wrote to Gretl:

My dear little sister, . . .

The faithful Liesl refuses to abandon me. . . . I should like to give her my gold watch, but unfortunately I've bequeathed it to Miezi. Perhaps you could give Miezi something of equal value from my jewelry. I'm sure you'll find a satisfactory solution. I want to wear the gold bracelet with the green stone until the end. Then, it can be removed and you must wear it always as I have worn it. It's also destined to Miezi in the will, so make another substitution. My diamond watch is unfortunately being repaired. I'll write the exact address at the bottom of the letter. Maybe you'll be lucky and manage to retrieve it. I want it to go to you, because you've always admired it. The diamond bracelet and topaz pendant, Hitler's gift for my last birthday, are also for you. I hope my wishes will be respected by the others.

In addition, I must ask you to attend to the following things: Destroy all of my private correspondence and above all the business papers. On no account must Heise's [Eva's dressmaker] bills be found. Also destroy an envelope which is addressed to the Führer which is in the shelter, in the safe at the villa. Please don't read it. I want you to make a water-resistant packet of the letters from the Führer and the copies of my replies (blue leather notebook) and bury them if need be. Please don't destroy them. I owe the Heise firm the enclosed bill. There may be other requests, but not for more than 1,500 marks. I don't know what you propose to do with the films and albums. At all events, please only destroy them at the last moment, except for the private letters and the envelope addressed to the Führer. Those you can burn immediately.

. . . Has Arndt[9] arrived with the letter and the case? We heard here that the plane was late. I hope Morrel[10] [sic] delivered the jewelry to you. It would be terrible if something had happened. . . .

Eva

. . . The watchmaker's address: SS Unterscharf. Stegemann, SS Lager Oranienburg evacuated to Kyritz.[8]

The final grim touch: the diamond watch was being repaired at Oranienburg concentration camp.

Leaving aside Eva's fervent desire to suppress the evidence of her dressmaker's bills, this letter raises many questions about Eva Braun's financial affairs. Not least of which is the question: what 'business papers' and were they relevant to Hitler's personal finances? There are at least two strong possibilities. Firstly, Hitler is known to have given an allowance to Eva, and possibly to her sister, Gretl. Though such an arrangement does not qualify as 'business' in the sense of commerce, it would be useful to know just how much Hitler allowed Eva, where the money was paid from, and who administered it. The second possibility is Eva's business relationship with her employer, the photographer Heinrich Hoffmann who published a book of photographs by Eva and Gretl, the profits going to the two sisters. It is possible that there were other deals.

Who, then are the likely candidates for possession of such papers, bearing in mind Hitler's paranoia about his financial affairs and his policy of 'divide and rule'? The most likely candidates are, in alphabetical order, Bormann, Bouhler, Lammers, Meissner, and Schaub. These five – and, in some cases, their staffs – left the Berlin bunker in the following order: Lammers, 27 March; Meissner, 21 April; Schaub, 25/26 April; Bouhler, Unknown; Bormann, 1/2 May. Of this unholy quintet, Lammers seems an unlikely candidate since he left well before the evacuation of the bunker. However, as will be seen, Lammers did take important papers.

On 26 April, Schaub arrived at the *Berghof* where he had been sent to destroy the rest of his master's personal papers, together with those in Munich. (Hitler's naval adjutant, Admiral Karl-Jesko von Puttkamer, had been sent on a similar mission.) Drunk, and on the arm of his mistress, Schaub handed to Gretl Braun the letter which had been entrusted to him two days earlier.

On 1 May, Gretl set out to comply with her sister's wishes, at least with regard to the letters. Gretl enlisted the assistance of *SS Sturmbannführer* (Major) Johannes Göhler, who assigned one of his subordinates, *SS Haupsturmführer* (Captain) Erwin Haufler to the task. Haufler collected the trunk, plus a clothes basket, from Gretl and took them to his office for safe keeping. After a few days, Haufler's curiosity got the better of him and he opened the trunk and basket. According to Haufler, the trunk was about three quarters full of letters from Hitler to Eva Braun, which he estimated to total about 250, plus up to 40 postcards. Haufler claimed that he gave the trunk to another of his assistants, *SS Haupsturmführer* Franz Konrad, ordering him to burn the contents to prevent their falling into the hands of the advancing Americans. Konrad, who had acquired a reputation for looting in Warsaw, disobeyed orders and sent two suitcases or bags and the trunk, together with other loot, to his brother's house in Schladming, Austria. There they were discovered on 24 August 1945 by agents of the US CIC (Combat Intelligence Corps or Counter-Intelligence Corps) who were almost certainly acting on a tip-off. The soldiers seized Hitler's uniform that he had worn during the assassination attempt of 20 July 1944, Eva Braun's twenty-three private photograph albums, her silverware, some notes of hers, and an album containing examples of stamps with propaganda themes.[11] In October, CIC agents retrieved a second cache of effects from Konrad's mother's home, including twenty-eight reels of colour film, shot by Eva Braun. All this material was taken into US Army custody and shipped to the United States. However, the trunk of letters has never been found, though David Irving believes that they were found by one of the CIC officers, stolen by him, and eventually sold to a collector in the USA. There are also doubts as to whether or not Schaub did carry out his mission; in a post-war interrogation, Gretl claimed that Schaub took some of the more interesting papers and kept them; in the nineteen-seventies, David Irving claimed that Schaub sold the papers to 'a former magistrate now living on Lake Starnberg in Bavaria'.[12]

Meanwhile, on the evening of Saturday, 28 April, Adolf Hitler married Eva Braun. As Gun records:

> *The formalities were brief. The wedding rings were too big. They had been hard to find. Nobody in the bunker had wanted to give up a ring, for gold was precious in case of flight. Finally, they were obtained from the Gestapo treasury. Quite possibly they were rings confiscated from gassed victims.*

The next day Eva sent hers to her friend Herta. A photograph of this ring will be found in the documentary part of this book. Hitler kept his on his finger.[13]

By 'documentary part', Gun is referring to the illustrations between pages 176 and 177 of his book on Eva Braun. The third from the last photograph shows a plain wedding ring lying on a typewritten letter – from the text, that sent to Herta Ostermeyr, parts of which are quoted above. This letter lies on top of another letter, only parts of which are visible, but the last paragraph reads:

Yesterday I, probably, held the last conversation with Gretl. Since today no more connection is available. But I am firmly convinced, all this will again turn to the good and he is as hopeful as ever.[14]

This letter is clearly not to Gretl; presumably it was to Herta. The long-distance telephone lines to the Berlin bunker were cut on 26 April, repaired after a few hours, and finally cut on 27 April.[15] This suggests that the letter – Eva Braun's final 'final letter' was written on 28 April. The ring clearly went to Herta, as Gun records:

[On April 29] she called back Liesl, who was tidying the bathroom, and said to her, "Liesl, dear, I've a last service to ask you. When I'm no longer with you, I want you to go to see my friend Herta in Munich – not immediately but whenever it's possible and there's no longer any danger. Give her my wedding ring and this nightdress – they'll be easy to hide. I know I can trust you. Take this ring in memory of me. . . . " Liesl, moved to tears, kissed Eva's hand.[16]

Gun makes no precise mention of the maid Liesl in his acknowledgements, but he does refer to 'his maid' – presumably Hitler's – so he may have had the story direct. Equally, he may have had it second-hand from Herta, whose assistance he explicitly acknowledges. What is clear – if the wedding ring really was Eva Braun's – is that it reached Herta, along with what may be the final 'final letter' and was probably in Herta Ostermeyr's possession in 1967. Its present whereabouts are unknown, as are those of the night-dress – the latter doubtless eagerly sought by cloning enthusiasts.

In the early hours of 29 April, Hitler dictated his will and political testament. Both documents (there were three copies of each) were signed at about 04:00 and witnessed by Goebbels and Bormann for the Nazi party and by Burgdorf and Krebs for the Army; the will was additionally witnessed by Colonel von Below, Hitler's Luftwaffe adjutant. The relevant passage reads:

My possessions, in so far as they are worth anything, belong to the Party, or, if this no longer exists, to the State. If the State too is destroyed, there is no need for further instructions on my part.

The paintings in the collections bought by me in the course of the years were never assembled for private purposes, but solely for the establishment of a picture gallery in my home-town of Linz on the Danube.

It is my most heartfelt wish that this will should be duly executed.

As my executor I appoint my most faithful Party comrade, Martin Bormann. He is given full legal authority to make all decisions. He is permitted to hand over to my relatives[17] anything which is of worth as a personal memento, or is necessary for maintaining their present standard of living; especially for my wife's mother and my faithful fellow-workers of both sexes who are well known to him. The chief of these are my former secretaries, Frau Winter, etc., who helped me for many years by their work. [18]

On 30 April 1945, Adolf Hitler and his wife Eva committed suicide.

The 'Other' Testament

Before considering what happened to Hitler's will and political testament, it must be remembered that there was an earlier will, drafted in 1938, and a decree of 29 June 1941, which nominated Göring as Hitler's successor, presumably replacing or confirming a similar nomination of 31 August 1939. At least one of these documents was in the possession of Dr Hans Heinrich Lammers, head of the *Reichkanzlei* (Reich Chancellery), there being three other chancelleries: the *Präsidialkanzlei* (Presidential Chancellery) under Otto Meissner; the *Parteikanzlei* (Party Chancellery) under Martin Bormann; and Hitler's personal Chancellery under Philipp Bouhler. A secret British document of 1945 describes Lammers:

In the obsequious person of this rather revolting old man, many of the characteristics of the "good German" accessory to the revolution and its outcome can be seen at their worst. [19]

 By March of 1945, Lammers no longer had direct access to Hitler and his sole duty was to countersign decrees and laws signed by Hitler. Although he claimed to the British that he had not resigned his post because he feared either being shot out of hand or sent to a concentration camp, there is little to support these claims and Lammers stayed at his post until Berlin became too unhealthy for his liking. In any case, resigning from any high post in the Third Reich was impossible; Hitler's attitude can be summarised as 'If I can't resign, then you can't resign'. On 27 March 1945, Lammers' physician signed a statement to the effect that his patient was seriously ill with high blood pressure, recommending that he be allowed to go to Berchtesgaden to rest. The request was granted. Lammers claimed during his interrogation by US intelligence that he had tried to persuade Hitler to leave Berlin for Berchtesgaden and that for this he was held in disgrace. However, he made no such claim to the British, saying instead that he had decided not to return to Berlin on 17 April, when he learned that Hitler was leaving Berlin and coming to Berchtesgaden. This, of course, did not occur, but Göring and his entourage arrived on 23 April. According to the British account:

Goering arrived in Berchtesgaden on April 23rd and now for a short hour or so the Chef der Reichkanzlei came into his own. Goering had reported that the Fuehrer was a broken man determined to remain in Berlin, where perhaps he was already dead, and that would raise the question of succession.

The Fuehrer's testament, drafted with his help some years before, was still in Lammers' safe keeping as trustee, and he was not slow to realize his duty and his right in this crisis to stay at Goering's side and to advise him. [20]

The significant point here is that the report refers to Hitler's 'testament' in Lammers' possession as 'trustee'. Just what his functions were as trustee are uncertain, since Schwarz, the party treasurer, was named as executor, with Bormann as deputy executor; probably the designation is to be taken literally, in that Lammers was merely responsible for the document's safe keeping. There is sufficient ambiguity to raise the question as to whether this was a political or personal testament, or both. The statements in the American report are more explicit with regard to Lammers 'advising' Göring:

Dr. E. [sic] Lammers, describes himself as "one of the traitors of April 23rd" whose execution ordered by Hitler personally was only prevented by the sudden collapse of the Hitler Regime. . . . Lammers proposed Goering to succeed the Führer; or so he claims. (Dr. Walter Funk and Reichs Marshal [sic] Goering also claim to have been 'Traitors of April 23rd'.)

What is well known is that on 23 April, Göring, believing that Hitler might well be dead or captive, sent a telegram to Berlin asking for confirmation – either positive or by default of a reply – that he should take over as Head of State. The situation described by Trevor-Roper is slightly different:

Goering felt himself in a very delicate position. By decree, he was Hitler's successor; now, according to Koller's account, Hitler had resigned and devolved his powers upon him. The legal position was quite clear. Goering sent for a tin box, and from it extracted the text of Hitler's decree of June 1941. All agreed that the meaning was unmistakable. [21]

Here, Göring or his staff – Lammers was not a member of Göring's entourage and was present only by chance – have the copy of the 1941 decree; an entirely logical situation. What, then, did Lammers have – if, indeed, he had anything? Was it the 1938 will? Was it a later will and political testament? Alas, we do not know.

The Odyssey of the Testaments

To return to the 1945 will, Wagnerian documents deserve a suitably dramatic history and so it was to be for the three copies of Hitler's will and political testament. Three men were charged by Bormann with taking these documents to the outside world:[22]

- SS *Standartenführer* Wilhelm Zander, Bormann's military adviser, was to take them, together with Hitler's and Eva Braun's marriage certificate, to Admiral Karl Dönitz, Hitler's successor as head of state and at that time located at Flensburg, in northern Germany. Subsequent events, together with the fact that he also carried the marriage certificate, suggest that Zander had the original documents while Johannmeier and Lorenz had copies.

- *Major* Willi Johannmeier, Hitler's Army adjutant, was to carry them to *Feldmarschall* Ferdinand Schörner, the new Army C-in-C whose HQ was near the Czechoslovak border.
- Heinz Lorenz, a former journalist and now an official of the Propaganda Ministry. Lorenz was also given Goebbels' appendix to Hitler's Testament. His orders were also to attempt to take the documents to Dönitz; if that proved impossible, he was to escape to British or US territory and from there to deposit them in the party archives in Munich.[23]

Johannmeier, Zander, Lorenz and a Corporal Hummerich left Hitler's bunker at about noon on 29 April. They were ill-prepared for their journey, having no food, no money, and no documents. Johannmeier and Corporal Hummerich wore Army uniform; Zander wore SS uniform; and Lorenz was in civilian clothes. With Johannmeier and Hummerich leading, they left the Chancellery via the garages on Hermann Göring Straße and went west along Charlottenburger Chaussee, passing through Russian lines near the Victory Column. From there, they went south-west for a short distance, passing through more Russian lines near the Zoo U-bahn station. They then made their way westward to Pichelsdorf, at the north end of Lake Havel, where they passed through a third set of Russian lines, arriving in Pichelsdorf, where a detachment of Hitler Youth held the bridge, at around 17:00. Here, they slept in the commander's bunker until about 22:00.

In two boats, they then headed down the lake towards the Wannsee bridge-head, which was still held by the German 9th Army, arriving there in the early hours of 30 April. Johannmeier and Hummerich landed on the Wannsee bridge-head while Zander and Lorenz landed on the Schwanenwerder Peninsula; both parties stayed all day in bunkers, where Johannmeier radioed to Dönitz for an amphibious aircraft to fly them out. That night, they set forth by boat for Pfaueninsel, an island in Lake Havel.

At Pfaueninsel, Johannmeier and Zander changed into civilian clothes. There, they also met up with another escaping party: Maj. Baron Freytag von Loringhoven, adjutant to General Krebs; *Rittmeister* Gerhard Boldt, ADC to General Krebs; and Lt. Col. Weiss, adjutant to General Burgdorf. This trio, having no further duties in Berlin, had been allowed to escape to join the armies of Generals Wenck and Steiner. Shortly afterwards, they were joined by Col. Nikolaus von Below, Hitler's Luftwaffe adjutant and the last man to leave the bunker before Hitler's suicide. He was carrying a post-script to Hitler's Testament, addressed to the German Army and exhorting it to fight to the death.

On the night of I May, the Russians bombed or shelled the Pfaueninsel and Johannmeier; Zander, Lorenz and Hummerich took to a boat and paddled out into the lake for safety. There they boarded a yacht and waited. Presently, a seaplane landed and Zander paddled out to it in a canoe with Lorenz and Hummerich following in a second canoe; Johannmeier remained on the yacht, signalling to the aircraft with his pocket torch.[24] The pilot refused to shut off his engines and Zander could not make himself heard over the noise; in the confusion, he capsized and had to be rescued by his companions. The aircraft began to come under fire from the Russians and the pilot took off, returning to Dönitz's HQ where he reported that he had been unable to make contact with the party. So ended any attempts to bring Hitler's Will and Testament to Dönitz.

The quartet remained on the yacht for two more days, hoping that Dönitz would try again to reach them, but it was not to be. On 3 May, before dawn, the party took to their boats for the last time and paddled around to the Wannsee section of the lake, where they landed near the swimming pool and set off west towards Potsdam. They successfully reached Potsdam, then Brandenburg, and crossed the River Elbe at Parey, between Magdeburg and Genthin. Somehow disguised as foreign workers, they entered the British and US zones. By now, Dönitz had surrendered and the War was over; the quartet abandoned their mission.

Zander somehow travelled all the way to his home area of Bavaria. There he hid his copies of the Will and Testament in a metal trunk in the village of Tegernsee, began an elaborate deception plan to persuade everyone that he was dead, and began a new life as 'Friedrich-Wilhelm Paustin'. Johannmeier also returned to his family home at Iserlohn, Westphalia, where he buried his set of documents in a bottle in his garden. Lorenz temporarily disappeared from view.

In the summer of 1945, the British Military Government in Hanover was approached by Georges Thiers, a Luxembourg journalist, who was looking for employment, in exchange for which he claimed to be in possession of information about Hitler's last days in the bunker. Since Thiers could not substantiate his claims, he was ignored.

In mid-September, 1945, Hugh Trevor-Roper, then an officer in British Intelligence, later a distinguished historian, arrived in Berlin charged to determine the fate of Hitler: Was he dead or alive? Trevor-Roper, in his official report and in a subsequent book, concluded that the evidence for Hitler's death was overwhelming. The whereabouts of the body, however, could not be determined, though it has since been reliably established that it was taken by the Russians.

In mid-November, Thiers, the 'Luxembourg journalist', was arrested on suspicion of having false papers. Under interrogation, he revealed his true identity as Heinz Lorenz, formerly of the Propaganda Ministry in Berlin. A search of Lorenz and his effects revealed a set of documents sewn into his clothing: Hitler's Will, political Testament, and Goebbels' appendix to the latter.

Trevor-Roper, then on leave in Oxford, was hastily summoned back to Berlin by British Intelligence to examine the papers and determine their authenticity. Under interrogation, Lorenz readily revealed that there were two other copies of the documents, in the care of Johannmeier and Zander. Trevor-Roper took up the chase. What happened next superficially smacks more of James Bond than of Oxford academics though it must be remembered that few can be more blood-thirsty or determined than an Oxford don.

Johannmeier was soon located, living in his parents' home in Iserlohn, near Dortmund. By all accounts, Johannmeier was a straightforward, honest soldier with a strong sense of loyalty. All he would admit to was that he had been the military escort for Zander and Lorenz, denying all knowledge of their mission or of any documents. Realising that he would get no further with Johannmeier without further evidence, Trevor-Roper switched his attention to Zander.

Enquiries in the Munich area suggested that Zander had not been seen and was thought to be dead. His wife, who was found living with her parents in Hanover, claimed not to have seen her husband since before the end of the war. Through the usual inconsistencies in statements, Trevor-Roper became convinced that *Frau* Zander was shielding her husband who was really alive. Further inquiries began to throw suspicion on a 'Friedrich-Wilhelm Paustin' who had worked for a time as a market-gardener in the small Bavarian town of Tegernsee. A series of raids led to the capture of Paustin/Zander in the early hours of 28 December at Aidenbach, a small village near Passau on the Austrian border, where he was staying with Bormann's secretary. Under interrogation, Zander freely confessed to being a disillusioned ex-Nazi and spoke freely. His story confirmed that of Lorenz and the second set of documents was retrieved from the metal trunk in Tegernsee. Trevor-Roper now had all that he needed to confront Johannmeier.

However, Johannmeier, a loyal soldier in Trevor-Roper's opinion, steadfastly denied that he had any documents, despite the sworn statements of Lorenz and Zander. Eventually, however, Johannmeier gave in. As Trevor-Roper explains:

> In this pause, Johannmeier reasoned with himself and convinced himself. He decided (as he explained afterwards during the long drive to Iserlohn) that if his companions, old and highly-promoted party men, could so easily betray a trust which, to them, was connected with their alleged political ideals, then it was quixotic in him, who had no such party connections (for he was simply a regular soldier), to suffer longer in their cause or defend the pass which they had already sold. So after the pause, when the seemingly endless business began again, he observed at last "Ich habe die Papiere".

Captive and captors finally arrived in Iserlohn; it was dark. Johannmeier led them into the garden and hacked at the earth with an axe, eventually revealing a bottle. With a stroke of the axe, he chopped the neck off the bottle, revealing the last of the missing copies. The Odyssey of the Testaments was over; a new chapter was beginning.

Or was it? Much of the previous description is based on Trevor-Roper's 1947 work. Trevor-Roper, however, lacked a key witness: *SS Brigadeführer* Wilhelm Mohnke who attempted to escape from Berlin on 1/2 May and who was captured by the Russians and not released until October 10, 1955. Talking to O'Donnell in the early nineteen-seventies, Mohnke said:

> *Admiral Doenitz was now the new Reich president and I was supposed to deliver into his hands several documents of state that had been drawn up in the bunker during the last two days. These were a protocol drawn up by Reich Chancellor Goebbels on May first <u>and a copy of both the Hitler testaments of April thirtieth</u>.* [Emphasis added.]²⁵

Thus, if Mohnke is correct, there was a fourth copy of the personal and political testaments. According to Mohnke, Hitler's last order to him as military commander of the bunker was to deliver these copies to Dönitz. Mohnke continues:

> *Late in the afternoon of Tuesday, May first, I went into the Reich Chancellery casualty station to look for some kind of waterproof container for these documents and also for a leather sack for some diamonds I was carrying. . . . I knew we might have to swim the Spree and other rivers beyond. Finally I located some wax paper. I fashioned a kind of long packet, which I was able to sling about my neck so that it rested on my breast, under my uniform.*²⁶

Later on 2 May, while holed-up in the Schultheiß-Patzenhofer brewery, Mohnke passed the packet on to one of the women who were being led to safety by a Luftwaffe sergeant, with a request to deliver the packet to his wife. According to some accounts, Mohnke first entrusted the packet to Else Krüger, Bormann's secretary, but then changed his mind and gave it to a woman whom O'Donnell calls 'Elizabeth D.' for the simple reason that she was from the Lübeck area, where Mohnke's wife was living:

> *With adhesive tape, Mohnke strapped this fairly heavy packet between Elizabeth D.'s shoulder blades, under her bra strap.*²⁷

The women did escape, though they were savagely raped by Russian troops on the road to freedom but, according to O'Donnell, Elizabeth D. later told a woman friend that the rapists were in such a hurry that she managed to keep her bra on. Traudl Junge resisted and was beaten so badly that her skull was fractured. As for the diamonds and the testament copies, they were never seen again and, when interviewed by O'Donnell, Elizabeth D. denied all knowledge of them. As O'Donnell writes in a footnote:

> *I leave it at this: diamonds, as always, are a girl's best friend. Their worth, at best, was only a few thousand dollars.*²⁸

The Executor

No account of the testaments is complete without considering the fate of their executor, Martin Bormann, the man charged with ensuring that Hitler's wishes were carried out. Bormann left the bunker on the night of 1 May in the third group, which included Artur Axmann, leader of the *Hitlerjugend*, Hans Baur, Hitler's personal pilot, and Ludwig Stumpfegger, a giant of a man over two metres tall. Stumpfegger was one of Hitler's gaggle of personal physicians, having replaced Brandt and von Hasselbach after they were dismissed for objecting to Morell's treatment of Hitler. On the night in question, both Stumpfegger and Bormann – possibly Baur, too – were drunk. According to Baur, whose testimony was not available to Trevor-Roper since he had been captured by the Russians and would not be released until 1955, Hitler told him on 29 April:

> I have given Bormann several messages for Doenitz. See to it that you get Bormann out of Berlin and to Doenitz by means of your planes at Rechlin.[29]

Baur was also carrying Graf's oil painting of Frederick the Great, which Hitler had given him as a parting gift. In the event, none of the group made it to safety. Baur, still carrying the portrait, was severely wounded and lost a leg in Russian captivity. Bormann and Stumpfegger died near the Lehrter railway station – possibly by suicide. Whatever papers they were carrying disappeared.

Suppression

On Tuesday, 22 January 1946, Mr Maurice Edelman, Labour MP for Coventry West tabled the following question in the House of Commons:

> *213 Mr. Edelman, – To ask the Chancellor of the Duchy of Lancaster, whether he has obtained corroborative evidence from independent experts concerning the authenticity of documents purporting to be Hitler's will and marriage certificate discovered by intelligence officers at Tegernsee, Germany, on 26th December 1945.*[30]

Note that there is a slight inconsistency between Trevor-Roper's dating –28 December – and that of Edelman's question, which refers to 26 December. The question was passed to the Foreign Office for an official reply, and they drafted a memo (<u>not</u> the reply) which reads:

> We have no corroborative evidence about the documents discovered at Tegernsee which are in the hands of the American military authorities.

This is clearly not the whole truth. Trevor-Roper, while still a serving intelligence officer, had personally seen all three copies. The memo continues:

> We have however such evidence in the case of the replicas which were found in the British zone.

Both Hanover, where Lorenz was captured, and Iserlohn, Westphalia, where Johannmeier was found, were in the British zone of occupation; Tegernsee, where Zander was found, was in the American zone. It is probable that Zander had the original of the will – he also had the marriage certificate – while Lorenz and Johannmeier had copies. It is only in this sense that the papers can be considered 'replicas' and it is known that they were individually signed by Hitler. The memo continues:

> Of those copies Major-General Lethbridge informed the J.I.C.[31] "the authenticity of the signatures was vouched for by a British handwriting expert and that Otto Dietrich, Hitler's press chief had recognised them but not being a handwriting expert was not able to swear they were genuine". The story of the German Lorenz[32], who was found in possession of this copy of the will, has also been checked against all available evidence and appears to be entirely reliable.

The final paragraph of the memo is revealing:

> In general, we wish to limit as far as possible public interest aroused by the discovery of the wills, and to cease comment. It 'is therefore for consideration whether the question should not be withdrawn. I attach however a possible draft reply.

Clearly, in early 1946 the British government was opposed to any revelations about the will and its contents. The memo ends with a hand-written note from the 'German Dept.' – presumably of the Foreign Office. In so far as it can be deciphered, it reads:

> The Control Office have suggested that we might take this question and I think we should agree. I should doubt the need to get the question withdrawn.

The draft reply offered by the Foreign Office reads:

> No, Sir: these particular copies are in the hands of the American authorities. The will is, however, identical with a replica found in the British zone, the signature of which has been examined by a handwriting expert and pronounced to be authentic.

Interestingly, the reply implies that there was only one copy found in the British zone, whereas in fact there were two. The US State Department was also concerned to limit any publicity surrounding the documents and sent the following message to the Foreign Office, apparently via the British Embassy:

> Following is substance of memorandum (gp. undec.[33]) from State Department in reply.
>
> Department agrees with British Foreign Office "that the less public notice the documents receive in Germany or outside the better". Department has no present intention of mentioning these documents in broadcasts to or in Press releases for Germany.
>
> The Department has been informed by its political representatives in Germany that original signed text of Hitler's political and personal testaments which were in United States hands have been transmitted to the War Department. Mr. Murphy reported that United States Military Authorities (gp. undec. ? promised) to furnish copies of these documents to British, Russian and French military officials and also to give photostatic copies to representatives of the American Press.
>
> The Department recognises that it would be undesirable to have facsimiles of these documents distributed throughout Germany. It should be possible to prevent such distribution during period of Allied control over publications, publishing establishments and printing presses in Germany. In view of release of photostatic copies that has already taken place the Department does not see what steps could be taken at this time to prevent facsimiles from falling into German hands at some future date. [34]

In this respect, the British and American governments seem to have achieved a measure of success: facsimile copies of Hitler's will are rare.

Notes

1   ODON78, p. 114.
2   HARR86, p. 33; no source given.
3   HARR86, pp. 29-40.
4   There seems to be some disagreement as to the date of the fatal flight. Baur (BAUR58, p. 181) has 25 April. Harris (HARR86, p. 31) has 21 April. O'Donnell (ODON78, p. 116) implies that it was 22 April. The crucial event in establishing correct dating is Morell. Eva Braun's letter to Gretl, in which she asks whether Morell has arrived safely, is dated 23 April. Gerhardt von Boldt, who was also present, writes (BOLD48, p. 48) that he was told on the morning of 23 April that Morell had already left. Since Morell was in the aircraft which safely reached Salzburg, Baur's date must be wrong. It seems clear that *Seraglio* took place on the night of 22-23 April, and that is the date I have used.
5   BAUR58, p. 181.
6   For a full account, see HARR86.
7   GUN68, p. 252.
8   The full letter is in GUN68, p. 253. Passages irrelevant to this book have been omitted. Gun gives no reference to the source, but implies that it is Ilse Braun.
9   The escort for the ten trunks of papers which were lost when the aircraft was shot down, as described at the beginning of this chapter.
10 Hitler's personal physician. Evacuated south in Operation *Seraglio*, it is known that he arrived safely. So, then, must the jewellery – unless he entrusted it to Arndt. Did it reach Gretl (or Herta Ostermeyr)? We do not know.
11 There is some occasional confusion over these photograph albums. Those seized by US forces were the 23 albums of original photographs. Secondly, Eva and Gretl would often use copies of this material to make presentation albums for their friends; these occasionally surface on the market for Nazi memorabilia as "Eva Braun's photo album". Finally, there were the books, printed by Hoffmann, on which Eva and Gretl received royalties; these are not albums in the sense meant here.
12 HARR86, p. 33.
13 GUN68, p. 268.
14 The original German reads: *Gestern habe ich, vermutlich, das letzte Gespräch mit Gretl geführt. Seit heute ist kein Anschluss mehr zu bekommen. Aber ich bin fest überzeugt, das sich alles wieder zum Guten wenden wird und er ist hoffnungsvoll wie selten.* The translation is by the author.
15 BOLD48, p. 50 says that the lines were cut on 26 April, but on p. 54 it says that this was only the first interruption and subsequent statements imply that the connection was finally lost on 27 April.
16 GUN68, pp. 270-71.
17 The official US Government translation renders this as 'brothers and sisters'. *Nazi Conspiracy and Aggression*, Government Printing Office, Washington, 1946-8, Vol. VI, pp. 259-60.

18 Translation from document JIC/1910/45, dated 28 December 1945. Copy supplied by Mr J. Gray of the Cabinet Office, London. According to Shirer, although Hitler did not specifically name these 'relatives' mentioned in the last paragraph, he made it clear to his secretaries that he was thinking of his sister, Paula, and his mother-in-law.

19 Document dated 7 July 1945, entitled *Lammers, Hans Heinrich – Head of the Reich Chancellery*. The document is unsigned, but the phrasing smacks of Trevor-Roper. In file WO208/4482, Public Record Office, Kew, UK.

20 Ibid.

21 TREV47, pp. 134-5.

22 TREV47, pp. 189+.

23 It does not seem to have occurred to Bormann to question whether or not there still <u>was</u> a party archive in Munich, nor that the British or US authorities might not be too keen on the idea.

24 According to Trevor-Roper (TREV47, p. 221) it was a Ju52, probably a Ju52/3m, the only variant made as a float-plane. Even so, this seems unlikely as there were better aircraft suited to the task.

25 ODON78, pp. 271-2.

26 Ibid. p. 272.

27 Ibid. p. 292.

28 Ibid. p. 292.

29 Ibid. p. 296.

30 Extract from Hansard attached to the reply dated 18 January 1946. In file FO371/55477, Public Record Office, Kew, England. Note that questions are submitted several days in advance of when they are formally asked in front of the assembled House; there is no inconsistency in the reply to the question having been answered four days before it was formally asked.

31 Joint Intelligence Committee. A British government committee which coordinated the efforts of Army, Navy, and Air intelligence, the Secret Intelligence Service (SIS or MI6), the Security Service (MI5) and other intelligence bodies. The Foreign Office, which drafted this reply, is responsible for the SIS.

32 In the original document, this has been spelled as 'Laurenz' and then corrected by hand. A note in the margin says 'See Flags'. This refers to additional information which would be given to the Minister replying to the question in the House; unfortunately, it is not in the file.

33 Presumably 'group undecipherable'.

34 Decrypted message to the Earl of Halifax, received 3 February 1946. In file FO371/55477, Public Record Office, Kew, England.

Chapter Seventeen

THE INHERITORS

To heirs unknown descends the unguarded store,
Or wanders heaven-directed to the poor.
Alexander Pope (1688-1744)
Moral Essays. Epistle ii.

The previous chapters have shown the origins and extent of Adolf Hitler's considerable fortune. The question which now remains is: What happened to it? As this, and subsequent chapters, show, the answers are complex and, in some cases, rather surprising. For example:

- The US Treasury once profited from the royalties of *Mein Kampf*.
- Hitler's family is still fighting for what it claims is its rightful share of his estate.
- The German state of Bavaria lays claim to most of the estate and actively tries to prevent anyone else from profiting.
- Significant parts of the estate are still missing.

The first thing to establish is who stood to gain, and who <u>did</u> gain, from Hitler's estate? These apparently simple questions remain uncertain almost sixty years after Adolf Hitler's death. To give even partial answers to these questions, eight major groups need to be examined: the Nazi party; Hitler's relatives; his friends and employees; the Allies; post-war institutions; publishers; foreign banks; and others. One must also consider the question of looting.

The Nazi Party

As far as has been established, Hitler made only two personal wills: one in 1938, and one shortly before his suicide in 1945.[1] The 1938 will left all Hitler's personal possessions to the Nazi party.[2] It could thus be argued that Hitler's use of money from the *AH Spende* – which had originally been established to finance the political campaigns of the NSDAP – to finance the *Berghof* and its contents –

was not entirely fraudulent if the items purchased were to revert to their morally rightful owner at the end of Hitler's life. His 1945 will implies the same intention, but is less specific:

> *My possessions, in so far as they are worth anything, belong to the Party, or, if this no longer exists, to the State. If the State too is destroyed, there is no need for further instructions on my part.*

In this will, Hitler's <u>personal</u> art collection was disposed of separately, to the city of Linz, Austria, which he regarded as his spiritual home (see *Post-war Institutions: Linz*, below). The Nazi party effectively ceased to exist with Hitler's suicide, and the German surrender on 4 May, 1945. When the NSDAP <u>legally</u> ceased to exist is rather vague.

The War in Europe formally ended on 8 May 1945, but Admiral Dönitz's administration remained legally in effect until around the end of May. (The *Wehrmacht* – the German armed forces – actually remained a legal body until 20 August 1946). Bracher claims that the NSDAP was dissolved by the Allied *Control Council* on 4 June 1945.[3] However, this is not consistent with the Allies' *Potsdam Declaration* of 17 July 1945, which established the *Control Council* which was to govern Germany. Among its stated objectives is Article 3 (III) which states:

> *To destroy the National Socialist Party and its affiliated and supervised organizations, to dissolve all Nazi institutions, to insure that they are not revived in any form, and to prevent all Nazi and militarist activity or propaganda.*

While this states an intention, it does nothing to define the legal status of the NSDAP. The records of the International Military Tribunal (capitalisation as in the original text) merely confuses the issue:

> *The following are named as groups or organizations <u>(since dissolved)</u>* [emphasis added] *which should be declared criminal . . . DAS KORPS DER POLITISCHEN LEITER DER NATIONALSOZIALISTISCHEN DEUTSCHEN ARBEITERPARTEI (LEADERSHIP CORPS OF THE NAZI PARTY) . . .*[4]

On this basis, it can be concluded that the NSDAP ceased to exist some time between 4 June 1945 and 18 October 1946. However, a further factor comes into the equation, which makes questions of the legal ending of the Nazi party somewhat academic: for a will to come into effect the testator must be legally dead. There is also the difficult question of which legal system should be applied to the will: that of Nazi Germany (which was in force at the time the will was made); that of the Control Council (which probably did not foresee such a question when the law was drafted); or the law in effect at the time the will was probated. Since the circumstances of the time meant that many wills made under one legal system were being probated under another, the question would have been a common one.

By 1947, Hitler's death was beyond reasonable doubt – to everyone except the legal authorities in Germany. In 1947, denazification proceedings were launched against Hitler, with the object of seizing his property in Bavaria on the grounds that he was a 'major offender'. The denazification court declared Hitler's 1945 will invalid but, in the spring of 1948, postponed a final decision on the disposition of his estate until his death could be established to the satisfaction of the court. After considering testimony from the Nuremberg trials and from other witnesses, the court decided that Hitler would have been classified as a 'major offender' for denazification purposes, had he been present at the trial. Consequently, the court ordered the confiscation of the property of Hitler and his wife. (In a bizarre incident typical of legal systems, two empty chairs were placed in front of the bench while the judgement was read.) Apparently the Munich police were not convinced and told the court that they still considered Hitler a legal resident of Munich – which he had been for tax purposes. In 1950, they are said to have seized several items of his from the house of 'a Munich merchant'. Just what these items were – if, indeed, they existed – their fate, and the identity of the merchant are not yet known.[5]

Hitler's sister, Paula, who had been trying to claim her share of the inheritance since 1948, began a legal process in 1952 to have her brother legally declared dead. Around the same time, Frau Anni Winter, formerly housekeeper at Hitler's Munich apartment, filed a lawsuit against the State of Bavaria to recover various gifts which she had received from her master and which, she claimed, had been illegally seized by the state. (See the following chapter.) The seizure by the Austrian authorities of a Vermeer which had once belonged to Hitler prompted both Paula Hitler and several Austrian Jews to challenge the decision and in 1952 the Austrian government asked the German government for a copy of Hitler's death certificate to substantiate their claim. It may have been these events which prompted the German authorities, on 24 February 1953, to make a formal request to the Allied High Commission for confirmation of Hitler's death, noting, with Teutonic formality, that:

> Investigations, made so far, show that the death of Adolf Hitler has not been registered with either the Registrar's Office I of Greater Berlin, Berlin N 54, Rückerstraße 9, or the Registrar's Office I in Berlin-Halensee, Albrecht-Achillesstraße 65/66 . . . [Therefore] the Amtsgericht in Berchtesgaden has asked that the result of the investigations, made by the Occupation Powers concerning the death of Adolf Hitler, be made available to it.[6]

Did the German government seriously expect that someone – Bormann, perhaps – would have forced their way through the encircling Russian forces to ensure that Hitler's death certificate was properly filed? Given that many soldiers were 'missing, presumed killed', some procedure must have existed for probating their wills without the necessity of a death certificate. One wonders why such a procedure was not applied in the case of Adolf Hitler. The Germans' request seems to have caused something of a stir in the High Commission, noting on 27 March 1953 that:

[The Political Affairs Committee has] *reached the conclusion that it would be inadvisable to meet the Federal authorities' request unless it were established that it stems from a real necessity under German legislation and procedures.* [7]

Various searches were made in the archives of the British Foreign Office and Cabinet Office, each claiming to have nothing. (In fact, this was not true: a file did and does exist of papers relating to the death of Adolf Hitler; it was held by the Cabinet Office and was only released to the public in 2001.) A formal reply was sent on 28 July 1953, noting that:

. . . the circumstances of Hitler's death are the subject of many publications and might be considered facts of common notoriety (offenkundige Tatsachen). There should also be available to the Court the statements of contemporary historians (Sachverstaendige fuer Zeit geschichte) as well as those of a number of witnesses who were present at the Chancellery at the relevant time and whose names can be obtained from books published on the subject. [8]

In July of 1955, the Berchtesgaden Lower Court was charged with the task of deciding whether or not Adolf Hitler and his wife really were legally dead. The timing was fortuitous; it came just as the Russians began releasing German Prisoners of War, including such key witnesses as Baur, Günsche, Linge, Mengerhausen (an officer in Hitler's personal police protection squad), Mohnke, and Rattenhuber (head of Hitler's personal police protection squad). Their testimony eventually satisfied the German authorities and Adolf Hitler was legally declared dead by the Berchtesgaden Lower Court on 25 October 1956. On 11 January 1957, the following entry was made in the Braunau parish register, Volume xix:

Declared dead, in fid. publ., in accordance with the ruling made by the Berchtesgaden District Court on 25 October 1956, II 48/52. Parish Presbytery, Braunau, 11 January 1957. [9]

One may therefore conclude, on purely practical grounds, that the Nazi party, as it existed in 1945, received nothing. That is not to say that none of Hitler's fortune passed to successor organisations. Perhaps it did, but no verifiable evidence has yet emerged to indicate so. Stories of leather-clad, whip-wielding, SS officers leaving the *Führerbunker* with truckloads of gold bullion and sailing off down the River Spree in a U-boat to found the Fourth Reich in the jungles of Argentina are the stuff of third-rate fiction.

Hitler's relatives

The question of who were or are not Hitler's relatives is examined in Appendix I. What is of interest here is those relatives who legally stood – or stand – to inherit Adolf Hitler's estate.

The Braun Family

Since Eva Braun was Hitler's legal wife in 1945 – though she almost certainly pre-deceased him, if only by minutes – it is possible that her family might have had a legal claim to her husband's estate. Both parents were still alive in 1945. Eva made a rather informal will in October, 1944, which seems not to have been witnessed and which she left in her Munich house on Wasserburgerstraße. The letter carried to the *Berghof* by Schaub (see Chapter 16), effectively left some items to her sister Gretl and there is no doubt that she did receive some of them. Did Eva have anything else to leave? She certainly received presents from Hitler – mostly cheap jewellery, but also cars, and her Munich villa – but whatever she had pales into insignificance beside the estate of her husband.

Under the terms of the 1945 will, Bormann was to give Eva's mother:

> . . . *anything which is of worth as a personal memento, or is necessary for maintaining their present standard of living . . .*

There is no evidence that she received anything. In Hitler's 1938 will, Eva's sisters, Gretl and Ilse, were granted RM 12,000 a year for life. No specific provision was made for either in the 1945 will.[10]

Hitler, Alois Jr.

Rather surprisingly, in view of the trouble caused by his son, Alois Jr. was awarded a lump sum of RM 60,000 under the terms of Hitler's 1938 will, but is not mentioned in the 1945 will.[11] However, under the terms of the February 1960 grant of inheritance (see below under Hitler, Paula) he was granted a one sixth share of the estate – four years after his death. His son Heinz was already dead and does not appear to have been mentioned in the October 1960 determination of Paula Hitler's heirs; neither was Patrick.

Hitler, Hans

The mysterious Hans Hitler is one of the present claimants to the estate and Toland implies that Hans acted as spokesman for the family during the 1970s, when Toland was in contact with them.[12] Clearly, Hans was close to the surviving family members, as evidenced by the photographs which he provided to Toland. The range of these photographs suggests that Hans Hitler owned, or had access to, the Hitler family albums.

Hitler, Paula (alias Wolf)

Hitler certainly made provisions to support his sister long before 1945. According to Toland:

> He gave her 250 marks a month, raising that figure to 500 in 1938. In addition he gave her a present of 3,000 marks every Christmas and helped her buy a villa.[13]

Whether the monthly payment of RM 500 continued after April 1945, and where it was paid from, are not known; answering these two questions would be a significant step towards untangling Hitler's finances. Under the terms of Hitler's 1945 will, Bormann was empowered to give her, as with Eva Braun's mother: *anything which has a sentimental value or is necessary for the maintenance of a modest standard of living* ... But Bormann was dead and could not execute his master's wishes; Paula had to wait fifteen years for the first acknowledgement of her status as an heir to Hitler's estate.

Paula made her first attempt to claim her inheritance in 1948, at which time a Munich court declared Hitler's 1945 will to be invalid on the grounds of 'formal legal deficiencies'.[14] In 1954, a court case arose over the publication of Hitler's 'Table Talk' or 'Secret Conversations' (see Chapter 7) and a Düsseldorf court ruled that Hitler's will had to be respected 'to the letter'. (Due to Germany's federal constitution and legal system it is possible for a court in one state to make a ruling contrary to that in another state.) On 10 January 1960, she wrote:

> My dearest wish is that I may at long last get the probate certificate which would enable me to move into a nice, sunny flat so that for the remainder of my days I could perhaps enjoy the warmth and comfort I have so long craved in vain.[15]

On 17 February 1960, the Munich Lower Court finally granted an inheritance certificate to Paula Hitler (note that the name is Hitler, not Wolf, suggesting that the pseudonym was never formally adopted):

> ... concerning the hereditary succession of Adolf Hitler, after Reich Chancellor Adolf Hitler, who died in Berlin on April 30, 1945, on the basis of a testament, following the elimination of the fiduciary heir, the NSDAP.[16]

To the author, the phrase *'following the elimination of the fiduciary heir, the NSDAP'* suggests that the will was considered valid – at least for the purposes of this judgement – despite its having been declared invalid in 1948 by a court in the same jurisdiction. This certificate granted her two thirds of the property, with one sixth each going to Alois Jr. and Angela Hammitsch, who had re-married after the death of her first husband, Leo Raubal. Paula died on 1 June 1960, apparently without receiving anything.[17] Later that year, on 25 October, the Berchtesgaden Lower Court ruled (File VI, 108/60) that:

> Heirs of Paula Hitler who died in Schoenau on June 1, 1960, are the sibling children Elfriede Hochegger (née Raubal) and Leo Raubal, at one half each.[18]

It is not clear from this whether 'one half each' refers to the whole estate or just Paula's two thirds. Presumably Elfriede and Leo received half each of their mother's one sixth, but that ought to have been a separate matter. According to Trevor-Roper, Paula sold her rights to Hitler's copyright – if, indeed, she

303

possessed them at the time of sale – to the Swiss lawyer, François Genoud (see below).[19] To whom the 'rights' passed on Genoud's death in 1996 is not known.

Hitler, William Patrick

There is no evidence that Patrick or his sons ever tried to claim the one sixth share granted to Alois Jr.

Loret, Jean-Marie

Although Maser's claim that Jean-Marie Loret is the illegitimate son of Adolf Hitler has long been disproved, surviving members of the Hitler clan seem to recognise him as one of their own.[20] Some time after the death of Leo Raubal (q.v.) in 1979, Loret laid claim to the fifty percent inheritance that the courts had granted to Leo. It is doubtful that any court would support a claim against Hitler's estate, though the Hitler family might.

The Raubal family

In his 1938 will, Hitler wrote:

> To my sister Angela I entrust the appointments of the room in my Munich flat formerly occupied by my niece Geli Raubal.[21]

Since the room in question had been maintained by Hitler as a shrine to his dead love, it seems that Hitler was conferring responsibility on Angela, rather than giving her anything of value.[22] Angela received nothing under the terms of the 1945 will. However, under the terms of the February 1960 grant of inheritance she received a one sixth share of the estate – eleven years after her death. The October 1960 determination of Paula Hitler's heirs names Angela's surviving children, Elfriede and Leo, as heirs, each receiving one half of Paula's inheritance plus, presumably, one half of their own mother's.

According to Ryback, Elfriede (Friedl) once stated she had no intention of making any claims, but it is not clear when this was said, nor whether this refers just to the *Mein Kampf* royalties or to the estate as a whole.[23]

Leo received half of Paula's estate under the terms of the October 1960 determination. Subsequently, in the mid-sixties, he emerged as the spokesman for the family. Maser and Leo corresponded extensively and met several times, mostly discussing the subject of *Mein Kampf* and its royalties, and Maser tried to bring together the different elements of the family, but, according to Ryback, without success:

> At first, Raubal thought that he could win back the confiscated Mein Kampf royalties. As a precondition, Maser says, he insisted that the family claim only those royalties that were generated between 1925, when the book first appeared, and 1936. After that, Mein Kampf replaced the Bible as the official wedding gift presented to German couples. "Since these were forced sales, and the money came from public sources, I insisted that all these royalties be donated to orphanages or Holocaust survivors,"

Maser says. Whether it would have been possible to divide the money with such precision is doubtful, but in any case the question was moot because the relatives could not agree on who would get what. Leo Raubal added a complication by insisting that the entire amount be paid to him, and that he would disperse the money based on lineage. "Raubal wanted fifty percent for himself," Maser told me. "But I protested, saying that he could not justify that to the rest of the family." The Schmidts themselves did not complain. Maser recalls one of them saying, "Als Hitler lebte, bekamen wir nichts; nun dass er tot ist, bekommen wir erst recht nichts" – "While Hitler lived, we got nothing; now that he's dead, we'll certainly get nothing."

The Schmidt Family[24]

Anton Schmidt wrote to Werner Maser in the mid-sixties, enquiring about the status of the copyright of *Mein Kampf*. Shortly after, he contacted several other relatives, including Leo Raubal. After Leo Raubal's death he seems to have become the principal spokesman for the surviving heirs.

Others

According to Toland, Hitler's 1938 will made bequests (unspecified) to 'relatives in Spital'. These could have been the Schmidt family or, equally probably, other relatives on Hitler's mother's side. Maser also mentions 'Hitler's relatives, the Sillip family' who were related to the Schicklgrubers. When Maria Ann Schicklgruber died on 7 January 1847, it was at the house of one of the Sillip family in Klein-Motten. It seems doubtful whether any of these could have a claim on the estate.

Hitler's friends and employees

Several individuals received bequests under Hitler's wills of 1938 and 1945; these are listed below in alphabetical order. Technically, Hitler's 1945 will empowers Martin Bormann, as his executor, to provide for:

. . . my faithful fellow-workers of both sexes who are well known to him. The chief of these are my former secretaries, Frau Winter, etc., who helped me for many years by their work..

The following names have been selected on this basis.

Brückner, Lt. Wilhelm

Hitler's chief personal adjutant until he was dismissed in 1942, probably for some amorous adventure, having served him faithfully since at least 1923. The 1938 will asked the party to take good care of him for life; he was certainly not included in the 1945 will.[25]

Christian, Gerda (née Daranowski)

One of Hitler's general-purpose secretaries who occasionally deputised for Wolf or Schröder, she may have been meant for inclusion in the 1945 will.

Lively, popular, fashionable, she was also noted for her stamina and servility towards Hitler. She married General Christian, one of Hitler's Luftwaffe adjutants. She is said by Brandt to have been something of a manipulator, persuading Hitler to send the secretaries Wolf and Schröder for lengthy health cures so that she could increase her influence in Hitler's circle.[26] She divorced her husband shortly after the war. In a post-war interview with O'Donnell, she said of her husband, who had left the bunker to join Göring in Bavaria while she remained in Berlin:

> Well, he went his way and I went mine. But that ended our marriage. I couldn't forgive that kind of desertion. I'm glad I survived, just to be able to divorce the lout.[27]

Junge, Gertrud (Traudl)
The youngest of Hitler's secretaries, she rose from assistant to full secretary after marrying Junge, a former servant of Hitler's.[28] There is little doubt that she was meant to benefit under the 1945 will. According to Brandt, she combined *naïveté* with slyness, but was treated in a fatherly fashion by Hitler, who often remarked that she would come to resemble Eva Braun as she grew older.[29] Of all the secretaries, she was closest to Eva Braun and this may be reflected in the fact that she received a silver fox coat from Eva Braun, a few hours before the latter's suicide, who gave it with the words:

> I always like to have well-dressed people around me. Take it, and I hope it will give you much pleasure.[30]

O'Donnell, however, tells a slightly different story, though both his and Toland's accounts are based on interviews with *Frau* Junge:

> She made her a present of her one fairly valuable fur, a silver fox wrap, saying, "Trudl, sweetheart, here's a present for next winter and your life after the war. I wish you all the luck in the world. And when you put it on, always remember me and give my very best to our native Bavaria — das schoene Bayern."[31]

Gertrud left the wrap behind when she fled the bunker and it most probably ended its days on the back of a Russian.

Linge, Heinz
Hitler's valet to the end in 1945 and one of the few people to see him daily. Like Schaub, Linge was one of the *Chauffeureska* and a valued employee who was certainly intended to benefit under the 1945 will. Captured by the Russians, he spent several years in prison, being released in 1955.

Manzialy (or Manziarli, or Martialy[32]), Konstanze (or Constanze)
Born of a Greek father and Tyrolean mother, *Fraulein* Manzialy started out as an employee of Prof. Zabel, who ran a vegetarian sanatorium in Berchtesgaden. She

came to run the kitchens at the *Berghof* after the departure of the previous cook who was alleged to be 'half Jewish'. Hitler often shared his meals with her, especially when in Berlin, and this appears to have been a source of friction between her and Eva Braun. It is not clear whether Hitler intended her to receive a bequest, since she is not specifically mentioned, but she seems to have been held in similar esteem to the secretaries and was probably an intended beneficiary under the 1945 will. She disappeared during the attempt to escape from Berlin, 1-2 May 1945, and is presumed to have been killed. Gerda Christian believed that she simply melted away into the civilian population of Berlin.[33] She was, after all, 'only a cook'.

Schaub, Julius

SS-Gruppenführer Julius Schaub was Hitler's bodyguard and valet for over 20 years. In Hitler's 1938 will, he received an unspecified bequest. Schaub, like Linge, was almost certainly one of the 'faithful fellow-workers' intended to benefit from the 1945 will. Like Linge, he failed to press any claim.

Schröder, Christa

The second of Hitler's personal secretaries and junior to *Fraulein* Wolf. Christa Schröder was noted not only for her intelligence and interpersonal skills, but also for her occasional open criticism of Hitler. According to Brandt, she was never close to Hitler and had 'a somewhat peasant servility'.[34] It seems possible that she was intended to benefit from the 1945 will.

Winter, Annie

The only person mentioned by name in Hitler's 1945 will. Annie Winter was cook/housekeeper at Hitler's Munich apartment from 1929 until, presumably, 1945. Post-war, she had an antique shop in Munich.[35] She seems to have occupied an important place in Hitler's immediate circle, passing on to him items of Munich gossip and passing back useful snippets to the secretaries, to whom she appears to have been close.[36] Annie's husband, Georg, acted as caretaker-handyman at the Munich apartment, but seems to have had no close relationship with Hitler and he is not specifically mentioned in either will. Nor are the other three members of the Munich staff.[37] In the 1938 will, Annie Winter received an unspecified bequest. In the 1945 will, she was granted:

> . . . *anything which is of worth as a personal memento, or is necessary for maintaining their present standard of living* . . .

Amongst the items which she received were: Hitler's gun licence; his Nazi party membership card; some of his water-colour paintings; a copy of *Mein Kampf*; and the original 1933 letter from German President Hindenburg, inviting Hitler to become Chancellor. Most of these items were confiscated by the State of Bavaria in 1951 when she tried to sell them to an American collector who had offered her $250,000.

Wolf, Johanna

The oldest of the secretaries and Hitler's personal secretary. Formerly secretary to Dietrich Eckart, she was recruited into Hitler's service by Rudolf Heß in 1924. According to Brandt, she lived a modest life, mostly occupying herself with her 80-year old mother.[38] She suffered from chronic heart and gall bladder complaints and Hitler paid for her treatment, apparently having a closer bond with her than with the other secretaries. She is reputed to have been offered $500,000 for her memoirs, but turned it down, saying: *I was taught long ago that the first and last duty of a confidential secretary is to remain confidential.*[39] There is little doubt that she was intended to benefit under the 1945 will.

The Allies

In 1946, the Allied Control Commission, the body which administered occupied Germany, issued Allied Control Directive No. 38, which dealt with the confiscation of assets of high-ranking Nazi party officials.[40] There is no evidence that any of Hitler's assets were formally seized, though some artwork was confiscated by the Americans, but not because it was Hitler's. A part of his library was seized and is now in the US Library of Congress.

Post-war institutions

Some sort of confiscation order was made in 1948, on the basis of Allied Control Directive No. 38, of 1946, transferring assets, including copyright of *Mein Kampf*, to various states, including Bavaria.[41]

Bavaria[42]

The majority of Hitler's assets were transferred to the German state of Bavaria between 1948 and 1951. No detailed account of this transfer has ever been published but the assets are known to have included: the *Berghof* and other property purchased by Hitler; the residue of his art collection; some money, possibly from the *Eher Verlag* accounts; and copyrights.

The State claims copyright to Hitler's published works (see Chapter 4) but this claim is disputed by Hitler's heirs and by Werner Maser (see below).[43] Today, the whole *Berghof* complex is under the trusteeship of the State of Bavaria, with the farm apparently being leased-out.[44] In 2001, Kurt Falthauser, Finance Minister of the State of Bavaria, announced that an hotel and golf course is to be built on a 106-hectare site, part of which will include Göring's former residence (of which only the foundations and the underground bunkers remain).[45] The $60 million development will include a 140-bed luxury hotel and will be developed by the US-based *Interconti* group, in collaboration with the *Bayerische Landesbank*, a bank owned by the Bavarian state. On the basis of this deal, the details of which are not yet clear, it appears that the state will benefit from both the sale and the financing.

Linz

As a post-war institution, the city of Linz, Austria, certainly existed, though in a somewhat battered state. Hitler was quite specific in his 1945 will that his art collection should go to 'my home-town of Linz'. The town never received its inheritance.

Publishers

The question of the copyright of *Mein Kampf*, and other publications, is dealt with in Chapter 7. Pirate editions of *Mein Kampf* abound, notably in middle-eastern countries and in states, such as Bosnia, which did not exist in 1945. It is self-evident that these directly benefit their publishers, without any benefit accruing to Hitler's heirs. The same may be said of various web-based editions, though most of these are available free.

Foreign banks

That Hitler had at least one foreign account, as account holder for the *Eher Verlag*, is certain; that he had other accounts is highly probable, though at least one seems to have been held by Amann, as Hitler's proxy. Either directly, or through the *Eher Verlag*, he was receiving royalties for *Mein Kampf* from a variety of foreign sources. After 1939, many of these sources, even though in countries not formally at war with Germany, would have had difficulty in transferring funds directly to the Reich. This problem would have become much more acute by, say, 1943 and the logical solution would have been an account in a neutral, though friendly, country such as Switzerland. That Hitler purchased paintings in Switzerland with his own money is well established and strengthens the case for his having an account there, though such an account would be unlikely to be in his own name. A search of dormant Swiss bank accounts at the Swiss-American Chamber of Commerce has not produced any startling revelations, but why should it? Any account would undoubtedly be under an alias and anyway, need not necessarily be in Switzerland; Sweden or Portugal would have served just as well, maybe even better as they are less well known as havens for hidden accounts. As noted in the introduction to this work, there have even been allegations of an account in London and Hitler certainly transferred money to a London account for purchasing artworks.

All this still leaves open the possibility that somewhere there may still be accounts owned by Hitler, steadily accumulating interest under an alias. Equally possible is that the accounts have been identified and seized by the host country; after all, their original owner is unlikely to come back to claim them.

Others

There is also a rather heterogeneous group of individuals – rather than institutions – who have, legally or illegally, claimed or obtained a part of Adolf Hitler's fortune.

Genoud, François
A shadowy Swiss lawyer, alleged to have been a pro-Nazi with links to the Palestine Liberation Organisation (PLO). According to Trevor-Roper, quoted in Rosenbaum, Genoud bought the rights to Adolf Hitler's copyright from Paula.[46] Copyright to Hitler's existing work was seized by the German authorities, but Paula was an Austrian citizen. Genoud secured the copyright on 'Hitler's Second Book' for himself by bringing out a translation in French – which he, as translator, could copyright separately – and then having the translation translated into whatever languages he chose. To whom these various rights passed on Genoud's death in 1996 is not known.

Heidemann, Gerd
One of the principal characters in the 'Hitler Diaries' fraud of the early nineteen-eighties. On 18 June 1981, he secured a contract with Maser which apparently read:

> Prof. Dr. Werner Maser receives, as the administrator of Hitler's will on behalf of Hitler's descendants, a fee of 20,000 marks, paid in cash. For this sum he allows Gerd Heidemann the rights to all the discovered or purchased documents or notes in the hand of Adolf Hitler, including transcribed telephone conversations and other conversations which have so far not been published and which could be used for publication. Prof. Dr. Werner Maser gives to Gerd Heidemann all the rights necessary for this, including personal rights and copyrights. Dr Maser affirms that he is empowered to do this on behalf of the family. This document is completed in the legal department in Hamburg and is valid in German law.[47]

Whether the rights were Maser's to give is uncertain, especially in light of Maser's comments about his negotiations with the Schmidt family.

Maser, Prof. Dr. Werner
If Heidemann is to be believed (see above), Maser is administrator of Hitler's will on behalf of his descendants. At first sight, there seems to be a legal problem here: Martin Bormann was explicitly named as executor of Hitler's 1945 will. However, Bormann's remains were found in Berlin in December of 1972 and he was legally

declared dead by the German Federal Government in 1973. Therefore, depending on the timing of the transfer, Maser <u>could</u> have the right to administer the estate. However, during the affair of *Hitler's Diaries*, the legal department of Gruner and Jahr, parent company of the magazine *Stern*, gave its opinion that Maser's claim had no basis in law. Furthermore, they could not state with certainty who did own the copyrights.

Looting

Any complete account of the disposition of Hitler's Fortune must consider the question of looting.

The map in Figure 14-1 shows the places identified by the Allies as housing artworks, books, money, archives, etc. evacuated to safety by the Nazi Government and their place in the zones of occupation in mid-1945. In addition one must also consider the *Berghof*, the *Führerbau* in Munich, the *Führerbunker* in Berlin, the Munich apartment, and the Leonding and Linz properties. As can be seen, the majority of Hitler's assets were in the US zone of occupation, though many of the public treasures were in the French zone – close to Switzerland. As far as their fate is concerned, six groups need to be considered: British, Americans, Russians, French, Germans, and Treasure Seekers.

The British forces in Germany in 1945 had little opportunity to loot any of Hitler's personal assets for the simple reason that they were in the wrong places: most of the assets were either in Berlin – taken by the Russians – or in Bavaria – taken by the Americans.[48]

American forces, and civilian visitors to the US zone of occupation, had plenty of opportunity to loot Hitler's personal assets. Fifty-five years after the end of the war, spectacular instances of US looting are beginning to be revealed as the looters die off and their families discover unexpected treasures in pop's old attic.[49] While there is nothing to suggest that US forces looted anything so valuable from Hitler's assets, there is plenty of evidence that they took the opportunity for petty looting on a grand scale.

The Russians, of course, took Berlin, and with it the *Führerbunker* beneath the Reich Chancellery. It is doubtful whether the bunker contained much of value by then (most things had been removed to safety long before) but it did contain much of interest. Unfortunately, the first troops to enter the bunker were more interested in Eva Braun's underwear than in artworks. What the Russians did get, of course, were most of the archives and these may have thrown some light on the location of Hitler's personal funds. Could Hitler's bank book be lying in some forgotten Russian archive? Only time will tell – unless, of course, it has already been found . . .

The French, like the British, were in the wrong places to have access to any of Hitler's Fortune and, in general, were most concerned with recovering their own property. However, as the Figure 14-1 map shows, rather a lot of artworks and archives were concentrated in the French sector, including the Constance Cluster of material which seems to have been cached for a quick getaway to Switzerland. The story of the French handling of the treasures under their control has never been told.

Where looting was concerned, the Germans had two advantages: they knew where everything was and they were there first. However, most of the repositories remained guarded by military or police until the last moment and when the guards fled in the face of the advancing Allies, the civilian staff – often museum officials – remained in place, guarding their treasures. In this, they were successful, at least until the Allies came. Also, there were more precious commodities for Germans to loot in May of 1945: cigarettes and food. Nor was there much – if any – looting by Germans of the Berlin bunker, though lesser bunkers and stores certainly suffered. The *Berghof*, however, is a different story.

Contemporary descriptions speak of the *Berghof* being stripped by the local civilian population within hours of the SS guards fleeing the site and many more hours before US forces took over to begin their own pillaging.[50] Quite how the locals dealt with the extensive minefields left behind is not known, but light fittings, furniture, and even flagstones from the patio where Hitler was so often photographed rapidly found their way into Berchtesgaden homes. No doubt so did more substantial loot. It is tempting to assume that this wholesale looting was an act of revenge, rather than opportunism. Perhaps it was; but was it revenge for having been dragged into the war or revenge for having lost it? Such judgements are left to the reader.

Finally, there remain the Treasure Seekers: combing the woods around lakes such as Toplitzsee and diving into its murky depths in search of fabulous hoards; picking over the site of the *Berghof* for scraps of plaster which may contain a molecule of *der Führer's* holy sweat; even – one is forced to admit it – snuffling through dusty archives in the hope of finding clues to the truth. Except in the latter case, as I hope this book shows, their efforts have proved fruitless. No dragon sleeps atop a golden hoard in some sealed-in *bunker des Niebelungen* beneath the *Obersalzberg*: true to his *Waldviertel* peasant origins, Hitler put his trust in real estate – which proved rather fragile beneath the bombs of the RAF – and second-rate art.

Notes

1   On each occasion he also wrote a political testament. He also wrote a political testament shortly before his arrest in 1923 but, so far as has been established, no personal will was made at that time.
2   TOLA76, p. 460.
3   BRAC70, p. 465.
4   Volume I, Page 28, dated 18 October 1946.

5   MCKA81, p. 105. In correspondence with the author, both the Bavarian Finance Ministry and the Munich Police deny all knowledge of this incident.

6   Correspondence with the Allied High Commission. PRO, Kew, England. File FO371/103736.

7   Note dated 27 March 1953, reference POL/Sec(53)5 PRO, Kew, England. File FO371/103736.

8   Letter from W. Neate, Secretary General of the Allied High Commission, to Herrn Ministerialdirektor Blankenhorn, Office of the Chancellor of the Federal Republic of Germany, dated July 1953. PRO, Kew, UK. File FO371/103736.

9   MASE73, p. 1.

10 TOLA76, footnote to p. 460.

11 DIET57, p. 221. Dietrich claims that Alois' name could not be mentioned in Hitler's presence.

12 TOLA76, footnote to p. 255.

13 TOLA76, footnote to p. 395. Toland's source reference cites his interview with Hans Hitler, but the words reported appear to be attributed directly to Paula.

14 RYBA00.

15 MASE73, p. 7. Maser is rather vague as to whether the letter is to herself or to the court.

16 SCHW89, p. 194. Maser has no reference to this certificate, which seems to be the probate certificate sought by Paula.

17 RYBA00.

18 MASE73, p. 350, note 17; SCHW89, p. 194.

19 ROSE98, p. 74.

20 RYBA00, quoting conversations with Werner Maser. The *Waldviertel* (lit. *Forest Quarter*) is the area of the German-Austrian border from which the Hitler family springs.

21 MASE73, p. 202.

22 BRAN45, p. 7, gives her name as 'Angelika'; this may be formally correct but the more common 'Angela' has been retained.

23 RYBA00.

24 All information from RYBA00.

25 Dietrich claims (DIET57, p. 249) that Brückner was dismissed for some trivial blunder while serving at table, but no other writer supports this view.

26 BRAN45, p. 4.

27 ODON78, p. 121.

28 Her husband was apparently killed in September 1944 in an air attack behind the lines on the Eastern Front. TREV57, p. 85.

29 BRAN45, pp. 4-5.

30 TOLA76, p. 885.

31 ODON78, p. 222.

32 Brandt (BRAN45, p. 5) describes Hitler's vegetarian cook in some detail, but gives her family name as 'Martiali', without giving her forename. Since he describes her as having a Greek father and 'Konstanze' could be taken as a Greek spelling, it has been assumed that 'Manzialy' and 'Martiali' are the same person. According to a Greek

colleague, 'Manzialy' is more likely as a Greek name than 'Martiali' but both are certainly transliterations from whatever the original was. Gun (GUN68, p. 251) has the name as 'Manziarli', but he is woefully inaccurate with names.

33 ODON78, p. 287.
34 BRAN45, pp. 4-5.
35 GUN68, p. 7.
36 BRAN45, pp. 5-6.
37 ROSE98, p. 101.
38 BRAN45, pp. 3-4.
39 HARR86, p. 70.
40 RYBA00.
41 RYBA00.
42 Unless otherwise noted, all information in this section is from STMF03.
43 SCHW89, pp. 193-194.
44 SCHW89, p. 193.
45 *Hitler's Alpine Lair to Become Hotel, Golf Course.* Reuters, Monday, July 02, 7:43 AM EDT.
46 ROSE98, p. 74.
47 HARR86, p. 159
48 The father of the author was a POW at Hohenfels, Bavaria and, on being liberated, looted a set of cutlery (cheap, aluminium alloy) and a book on lettering techniques for Gothic script from the officers' mess. It may be stretching a point to claim that, since he was head of state and head of the Wehrmacht, these were Hitler's property, but if any of the claimants to Hitler's assets want them back, I will be happy to oblige. In exchange for an exclusive interview.
49 The most spectacular example is, of course, the Quedlinburg Treasure, documented in *Treasure Hunt*, by William H. Honan. Dell Publishing, 1997. ISBN 0-385-33282-3.
50 e.g. Gun (GUN68, p. 260) writes that " . . . the local inhabitants rushed into Hitler's house and started pillaging frenziedly".

Chapter Eighteen

EINE ABRECHNUNG

O, *Weary reckoning!*
William Shakespeare (1564-1616)
Othello.

The title of this chapter is taken from the subtitle of the first volume of *Mein Kampf*; it seems a fitting title since one of the phrase's meanings is a settling of accounts – literally and figuratively.

What was there?

This book has gone to great lengths to estimate the extent of Hitler's assets at the end of 1944. The results are summarised in Table 18-1. Taking an 'exchange rate' of €4 per *Reichsmark* (RM), this puts Hitler's assets at somewhere between €1.35 and €43.5 billion. Against these somewhat staggering figures must be set the question: did his income justify this?

Table 18-1: Hitler's assets, January 1945

Asset	Minimum	Probable	Maximum	Ch.
	——— Value, million RM ———			
The *Berghof*	243.84	341.99	502.06	14
Other real estate	0.34	33.13	65.93	14
Artworks	89.30	151.14	300.62	15
Money in the bank	0.0	0.1	1.00	18
Subtotal	333	526	870	
Outstanding royalties	4.50	5.00	5.50	18
Equity in the *Eber Verlag*	–	600.00	10,000.00	4
Grand total	338	1,131	10,875	

315

Hitler's initial combined salary and expenses as Chancellor of the German Reich was RM 47,200 per year, which he drew for 11¼ years (he donated his first year's salary to charity). However, there are suggestions that his salary may have increased to RM 60,000 per year after 1938, but this is uncertain. Royalties from *Mein Kampf* are accurately known and are analysed in Chapter 7.

The question of profits from the *Eher Verlag* is more contentious and is discussed in Chapter 12. The author is convinced that Hitler did receive such profits, but what proportion is unknown. Amann, however, definitely received five percent, so the minimum figure in Table 18-2 assumes the same. The most optimistic assumption is that Hitler received the remaining 95% and this has been used to determine the maximum amount. The probable amount has been taken as the simple arithmetic mean of these two figures.

Add to this the estimated income from the *AH Spende* (Chapter 13) and the result is as shown in Table 18-2. Comparing income with expenditure gives Table 18-3. The minimum and probable values are in surprising agreement – suggesting that the analysis is not too far out, though coincidences do happen! For the probable case, the excess of income over expenditure could be accounted for by the many things which were not taken into account, such as motor vehicles, travel and food. There is no doubt that, at the beginning of 1945, Adolf Hitler was a wealthy man.

The Fate of Specific Items

As noted in the previous chapter, a denazification court ruled in 1948 that 'Hitler was an active Nazi' and his will was declared invalid, enabling the State of Bavaria to seize his personal property. Among the major items seized were Hitler's private apartment at Prinzregentenplatz 16, Munich; money (estimated at 5 million

---

Table 18-2: Hitler's income, 1933-45

Source	Minimum	Probable	Maximum	Ch.
	——— Income, million RM ———			
Salary as Chancellor	0.52	0.52	0.61	11
Royalties from *Mein Kampf*	7.72	7.72	7.72	7
Profits from the *Eher Verlag*	24.39	220.76	417.13	12
AH Spende	299.00	416.00	1,001.00	13
Totals without Culture Fund	332	645	1,426	
Culture Fund	268.59	273.74	322.63	13
Totals with Culture Fund	600	919	1,749	

Table 18-3: Income vs. Expenditure, 1933-45

| | Income − Expenditure | | |
	Minimum	Probable	Maximum
Income	332	645	1,426
Expenditure	333	526	869
Difference	-2	119	558

marks[1]) owed to him as royalties by the *Eher Verlag*; other royalties and several 'valuable paintings'. There is no mention of any seizure of the *AH Spende* or the Cultural Fund.

To try to make some sense of what became of Hitler's estate, the following sections follow the fate of several of his possessions, including: the Berchtesgaden complex; other real estate; the *Eher Verlag*; his art collection; literary rights; minor personal possessions; his personal bank accounts within Germany; and his personal bank accounts outside Germany.

The Berghof

This property was acquired by the US Government in 1945. In 1952, they returned the whole mountain to the Germans, but retained the *Platterhof*, re-naming it the General Walker Hotel and using it as a recreation centre for the armed forces. They also retained Bormann's farm, which they renamed the Skytop Lodge, and Speer's studio, which became the Evergreen Lodge – a VIP guesthouse for generals. The property was returned to the Bavarian State in 1996. In September 1998, the Bavarian authorities advertised the property for sale.[2] A luxury hotel is currently under construction on the site of Göring's former residence.

Other real estate

As noted in Chapter 14, Hitler's Munich apartment, having briefly been used by US forces, was transferred to the State of Bavaria. It is now a police station. The properties at Braunau and Leonding, being in Austria, were of no concern to the Bavarian government and seem to have reverted to private ownership. Requests to the Austrian authorities have not been answered. The former *Gasthof zum Pommer* in Braunau, Hitler's birthplace, is physically little changed. Hitler's birth is commemorated by a plaque which describes his crimes against humanity. The house in Leonding stood empty for many years and was recently on the point of being condemned as unsafe and razed. While some in the town want it to be

317

turned into a memorial to victims of the Holocaust, it seems that the local council has decided to turn it into a warehouse for coffins, since it is close to the cemetery.[3]

The Eher Verlag

The records of the *Eher Verlag* were — perhaps conveniently — destroyed during the latter stages of the War. Like the *Berghof* properties, the *Eher Verlag* was considered to belong to the NSDAP and its assets, whatever they were, were confiscated separately from those of Hitler. The Bavarian Finance Ministry would have us believe that no records were kept.

Hitler's art collection

Unfortunately, the contents of the Personal Collection and the Linz Collection were disposed of as if they were one, leading to much international squabbling, as detailed by Spotts.[4] Some of it went to the State of Bavaria, notably such pieces as were in Hitler's Munich apartment. Some was seized by the Americans, some was looted, some was returned to its original owners, and the rest was distributed in galleries around Germany. According to the Bavarian Ministry of Finance, no records exist of what was seized. A large part of Hitler's library was seized by US forces and is now in the Library of Congress.

Rights to Hitler's literary works

1973 saw the fortieth anniversary of the Nazis' rise to power. The so-called *Hitler Welle* (Hitler wave) of books about the dictator and his party led the German satirical magazine *Pardon* to hire an actor to impersonate Hitler and tour the stands of the Frankfurt International Book Fair, demanding his share of the royalties. He was arrested.

As noted in Chapters 7 and 17, the Bavarian state owns the rights to all works published prior to 1945, which in practice means *Mein Kampf*. The only book which falls outside this remit is the so-called 'Second Book', a new edition of which was announced as this manuscript was being finalised.

Hitler's minor personal possessions

Frau Anni Winter, Hitler's former housekeeper in Munich, died in 1972. As one of the legatees under his will she had received various items, apparently intended to ensure her comfort in her old age. Just who gave her these items is not known — certainly not Bormann — and it is possible that she merely appropriated them, which she was well placed to do; it is equally possible that they had been given to her prior to 1945. The majority of these were confiscated by the State of Bavaria in 1951. Following her death, such items as remained in her possession were auctioned in Munich. The exact sum realised and the recipient have never been revealed and most of the bids were by telephone and on behalf of anonymous clients. The lots included: family photographs; an eleven-word note made by Hitler for a forthcoming speech; a War Loans savings card; and several signed photographs of Hitler. For one of the latter, a successful bid of £450 was recorded.

Hitler's personal bank accounts within Germany

These were seized by the Bavarian state. According to the Bavarian Finance Ministry, they amounted to about RM 900,000. This has been rounded up to a million and taken as the maximum figure in Table 18-1; it makes little difference to the results.

Hitler's personal bank accounts outside Germany

In 1996, the London-based *Jewish Chronicle* revealed what many had long suspected: Adolf Hitler had a Swiss bank account.[5] The account, at the Bern Branch of the Union Bank of Switzerland, was held for Hitler by Max Amman and used for foreign royalties from Hitler's published works. The current state of the account is unknown; is it one of the accounts classed as 'dormant'? If it is not, then who has been using it since 1945? The fate of the Amsterdam bank account is unknown, and efforts to trace it have been unsuccessful. The London bank account for the purchase of artworks was not in Hitler's name, though it was supplied with Hitler's money, and was probably closed before the outbreak of war; certainly it was not seized by the Custodian of Enemy Property.

Eva Braun

What, then, of Eva Braun's legacy? The Braun family were, not surprisingly, interrogated by the Americans. They were, by some accounts[6], persecuted by the post-war German administration, though the evidence suggests little more than normal denazification procedures. Efforts to trace records of Fritz Braun's de-nazification trial have not succeeded, but it seems that he was probably judged to be a Category 2 offender, since he was deprived of his pension rights and fined, and his possessions, including houses and bank accounts, were confiscated. Any legacy that they received would no doubt also have been confiscated. Eventually Herr und Frau Braun were rehabilitated and lived out a peaceful old age together.

Herta Ostermeyr, it will be recalled from Chapter 16, had effectively been named as executor of Eva's will and almost certainly received the jewellery carried to the Berghof by Morell. It is said that she and Gretl hid the jewellery, along with the photograph albums and films, at Schloß Fischorn, Gretl's late husband's castle at Zell-am-Zee, Austria. From there, they passed into the hands of a German working for the US CIC – a story little different from that recounted in Chapter 16.

Ilse, widowed (her husband was killed in the Russian assault on Breslau) and penniless, went to court to suppress the fake diary of her sister, which mysteriously surfaced in 1947 in the hands of a Tyrolean actor by the name of Louis Trenker.[7] This ludicrous work, which has Eva wearing black leather underwear and sleeping between swastika-embroidered sheets, was exposed as a fake in a 1948 lawsuit brought by the Braun family. Subsequent investigations showed that large portions of the text had been copied, with appropriate name changes, from a book by Countess Larisch-Wallersee about the love affair between Archduke Rudolf of Hapsburg and Marie Vetsera. It is unlikely that Ilse received much in the way of legacy, and after the lawsuit she disappeared into obscurity.

The fate of the house on Wasserburgerstraße is curious. According to one account, it was occupied by Polish refugees, former inmates of Dachau, who more-or-less turned it into a souvenir shop selling (mostly fake) relics of its former mistress.[8] The villa was later seized by the Bavarian authorities and given to a charity for Jewish refugees. It is still there. Its current status is unknown.

Some unanswered questions

A work of this nature inevitably leaves many questions unanswered. The major questions are summarised below.

Hitler's financial records

That some sort of record of Hitler's personal financial records were kept is almost certain – even Al Capone kept financial records – but what became of them? Were they among the personal papers destroyed by Schaub in the Chancellery garden immediately before Hitler's suicide? Were they in the papers taken by Meissner and which may have found their way into the possession of his family? Or do they still exist in some unresearched, possibly Russian, archive? It should be remembered that a legacy can only be given if the legatee has clear title to the legacy. Therefore, Hitler's will would have been difficult – though not impossible – to enforce without documentary proof of ownership for the major items. Such documents must have been somewhere.

Legal anomalies

The previous chapter described the denazification trial of Adolf and Eva Hitler and the German government's attempts to prove – to their satisfaction – the death of the former. To this author, who is not an expert on German law, there seems to be an anomaly. Hitler and Eva were tried, *in absentia*, as husband and wife, which suggests that the court considered their marriage legal – despite the fact that the marriage was not registered with the Berlin city authorities. However, the German government did not consider Hitler legally dead <u>because</u> the appropriate papers had not been lodged with the authorities. This seems like a case of having your cake and eating it. Similarly, because it had not been filed with the appropriate office, Hitler's will was declared invalid because of 'legal deficiencies'. All of which suggests that the German authorities may have been a little flexible in their legal interpretations.

The NSDAP financial records

The NSDAP financial records are thought to have been destroyed on the orders of Schwarz, the NSDAP treasurer, shortly before US troops captured Munich. However, the NSDAP membership records – which were under Schwarz's control – were found intact, though orders had been given for their destruction.

Missing artworks

What was the true extent of the Personal Collection and what was its fate? Since no proper records have ever been found, the truth will probably never be known. Why proper records of ownership were not kept by the Allies is a mystery.

The AH Spende

The fate of the AH Spende remains the biggest mystery of all. Where were the records? Where were the bank accounts and in whose name? Was the account with Delbruck, Schickler & Co., as was the *National Treuhand*, discussed in Chapter 13, or was it with the *Bayerische Hypotheken-und Wechselbank*, Munich, where most NSDAP accounts seem to have been held? Lack of documentary evidence leaves open the possibility that the account still exists, gaining interest. A substantial prize for anyone who can track it down.

Notes

1   Hitler must go down as one of the few writers in history who failed to collect his royalties. Is this a record?

2   Louise Potterton. *Hitler's old holiday home is for sale . . . but don't tell anyone.* The Sunday Telegraph, 27 September, 1998.

3   George Jahn. *House Where Nazi Dictator Grew Up Haunts Residents of Austrian Town.* AP, 6 July, 2002.

4   SPOT03, p. 220.

5   6 September, 1996. The material was based on recently de-classified US documents.

6   e.g. GUN68, pp. 288-290.

7   GUN68, pp. 80-81 HARR86, p. 49.

8   GUN68, p. 289.

Appendix One

THE HITLER FAMILY

The question of Hitler's ancestry has been studied by many authors, but most works seem to be based almost entirely on Heiden and Shirer, neither of which is complete and both of which contain errors; the exceptions are Maser and Jetzinger, who have done considerable research into the subject. However, few authors have considered the question of his collateral descendants, and on this question there is less information and even more uncertainty.[1] Since questions of inheritance (examined in Chapter 17) are important to this study, the network of Hitler's relatives needs to be plotted in some detail (see Figure A1, Sheets 1-4). Anyone seeking information on ancestors, rather than descendants, should consult the authors named above. Note that in the following text I have used the name by which a person was generally known – e.g. Angela Raubal – rather than following strict genealogical practice. Dates of birth, marriage and death are given in the family tree in the form {year.month.day} and, for brevity, are not repeated in the text.

Some of the minor characters in the family tree can be disposed of briefly. Johann Georg Hiedler was nominally Alois Hitler senior's real father. He seems to have had no other legitimate issue. Klara Hitler (née Pölzl) was Hitler's mother.[2] Franziska (Fanni) Matzelsberger was first the mistress, and then the wife of Alois Sr., whom she married in 1883, having already given him a son, Alois Jr. Adolf Hitler had several siblings who died in childhood: Gustav died of diphtheria; Ida also died of diphtheria; Otto was born and died in the autumn of 1887, of unknown causes; Edmund apparently died of measles. The family tree of Figure A1 is based on the following information, which is listed in alphabetical order by family name.

Braun family
Eva's parents were Fritz and Franziska. They had three daughters: Ilse, Eva, and Margarethe (better known as Gretl). Ilse was the oldest sister and in 1942 she married a Dr. Fucke-Michels from Breslau and thereafter played little part in Eva's life. Eva was Hitler's mistress, becoming his legal wife in 1945. Margarethe Franziska Bertha was Eva's younger sister. According to Gun, she was 'not over particular in the matter of men'. Nonetheless, Hitler made several attempts to

323

marry her off, finally succeeding in 1944, when she married *SS Obergruppenführer* Fegelein, Himmler's liaison officer to Hitler, taking the style *Frau* Braun Fegelein. She gave birth to a child on 5 May 1945, but Gretl was so promiscuous that there is some doubt as to whether or not the child was Fegelein's.[3] The child, a girl named Eva, committed suicide in 1975.[4] Gretl subsequently remarried, becoming plain *Frau* Berlinghoff.[5]

Hiedler, Lorenz

This person, only referenced by one author, seems to have been an elder brother to Hiedler, Johann Georg and Hütler, Johann Nepomuk.[6] It is possible, though not proven, that some of the unidentifiable members of the Hitler clan – e.g. Hans – descend from him.

Hitler, Adolf [7]

Adolf was born in Braunau-am-Inn, Austria, and died in Berlin, shortly after marrying Eva Braun. This union had no issue and, despite rumours to the contrary, there is no evidence that Hitler had any illegitimate issue.[8]

Hitler, Alois Jr.

The illegitimate son of Alois Sr. and Franziska Matzelsberger, he bore her name until being legitimised in 1883. Alois Jr. left home in 1896, aged fourteen, and embarked upon a career as a waiter and petty criminal, being twice imprisoned for theft and once for bigamy. There is some evidence that he may have married, or at least lived with, two other women before 1910, but little, if anything, is known about them. In 1909 or 1910, he moved to Britain, where, in 1911, he married an Irish woman, Brigid Elizabeth Dowling (q.v.), whom he had met while working in Dublin.[9] In 1913, he abandoned Brigid and their son, William Patrick Hitler (q.v.), and returned to Germany.[10] Shirer met the man, and offers a personal reminiscence:

> The coming to power of the National Socialists brought better times to Alois Hitler. He opened a Bierstube – a small beerhouse – in a suburb of Berlin, moving it shortly before the war to the Wittenbergplatz in the capital's fashionable West End. It was much frequented by Nazi officials and during the early part of the war when food was scarce it inevitably had a plentiful supply. I used to drop in occasionally at that time. Alois was then nearing sixty, a portly, simple, good-natured man with little physical resemblance to his famous half brother and in fact indistinguishable from dozens of other little pub keepers one had seen in Germany and Austria. . . . Alois himself, I remember, refused to be drawn into any talk whatsoever about his half-brother – a wise precaution but frustrating to those of us who were trying to learn all we could about the background of the man who by that time had already set out to conquer Europe. [11]

Shirer makes no mention of a wife. In 1924, Alois Jr. was sentenced to six months jail for bigamy, suggesting that he had married again by that date, and Adolf was not best pleased, calling on his lawyer Hans Frank to hush up the incident.[12] One wife is said to have been called Hedwig, the other Maimée; however, it is possible that these were the same person.[13]

One of these gave birth to Heinz, also, like Leo Raubal, said to have been Adolf's favourite nephew. After completing his training at the National-Political Education Centre in 1938, he wanted to become a professional soldier, but this was forbidden by Adolf. In the end, he was conscripted and served as an NCO with the 23rd Potsdam Artillery Regiment and was either killed in 1943, or captured at Stalingrad and died in captivity.[14]

When Adolf Hitler's name came into the international news, Brigid attempted to regain contact with Alois Jr., whom she had thought to be dead. On 30 November 1930, an article appeared in the *American*, a publication of the Hearst empire, entitled 'Adolf Hitler' and purportedly written by 'Alois Hitler'. This article appears to be a collaboration between Patrick and Alois Jr., the latter possibly acting in collaboration with Adolf himself.[15] The most significant statement, for an analysis of the Hitler family, is Alois' assertion that he is 'the son of a cousin of Adolf's father'. This is clearly a lie.

Hitler, Alois Sr.

The illegitimate son of Maria Anna Schicklgruber and an unknown man, possibly Johann Georg Hiedler, but probably Johann Nepomuk Hütler, who later adopted him. Legitimised from Schicklgruber to Hitler in 1876 and, curiously, not on his alleged father's marriage to his mother in 1842.[16] Married: (1) Anna Glasl-Hörer, the adopted daughter of a customs official; no issue.[17] Married: (2) Franziska Matzelsberger; one son, one daughter. Married: (3) Klara Pölzl; three sons, two daughters. He also had one illegitimate child by a woman named 'Thelka' (family name unknown) in the 1860s.[18]

Hitler, Brigid Elizabeth (née Dowling)[19]

The first, or possibly even third, wife of Alois Jr. and mother of William Patrick. According to some accounts, she attempted to extort money from Adolf in the 1920s and 1930s, though it is more likely that the extortion, which seems to have been quite mild, was practised by Patrick (who seems to have preferred his second forename), though possibly at his mother's suggestion. In 1939, she went with her son to America, where, supported by Patrick's earnings on the lecture circuit, she did voluntary work for the British War Relief Society – to the consternation of some American citizens.[20] She left an unpublished 'memoir' much of which is palpably fake and the rest of which is of doubtful accuracy.

Hitler, Hans

So far as has been established, only Toland and Ryback mention this mysterious character. Nine photographs in Toland are credited to Hans, yet his name does not appear in the Acknowledgements, though the Sources refer to a taped interview in 1971, and the only references to him in the text are footnotes. In the first and second footnotes, Hans is referred to as a 'second cousin' and as 'speaking for the family'.[21] The third footnote is most interesting and deserves to be quoted in full:

> *Hitler had two other relatives on* [the Russian] *front: Hans Hitler, whose father was the Führer's first cousin; and Heinz Hitler, son of his half-brother, Alois Jr. Hans escaped to Germany; both Leo* [Raubal] *and Heinz were captured. According to Stalin's daughter, the Germans proposed exchanging one of their prisoners (it could have been either Leo or Heinz) for her brother, Yasha. But Stalin told her, "I won't do it. War is war." Reportedly young Stalin was shot by the Germans. Heinz Hitler died in captivity but Geli's brother returned home in 1955, reconciled to the fact that his uncle had done nothing to save him and more than ever convinced that Hitler was "absolutely innocent" of his sister's death.* [22]

From this account, if Toland is to be believed, Hans Hitler was not the son of Alois Jr. For Hans' father and Adolf to have been first cousins, either their fathers must have been brothers (or step-brothers) or Hans' father was the illegitimate son of a woman bearing the name 'Hitler'. For brothers or step-brothers, this leaves three possibilities, since the identity of Adolf's grandfather is in doubt: male offspring of Johann Georg Hiedler; Johann Nepomuk Hütler; or the mysterious Lorenz Hiedler. These are identified as 'D1' in the family tree. The other possibility, that Hans' father was born illegitimately to the female offspring of Johann Georg or Johann Nepomuk, is identified as 'D2' in the family tree. Whatever the case, the standard Hitler family trees, as recorded in Shirer, Kershaw, et. al., are incomplete.

Jetzinger indirectly suggests another possibility: in his book, a portrait of Hitler's father, dated 1893, is said to belong to 'an illegitimate grandson of Alois Hitler'.[23] Unfortunately, Jetzinger does not say which Alois, but it is probable that he means Hitler's father, rather than his half brother.

Hitler, Paula (alias Wolf)
Paula, Hitler's sister, lived mostly in Vienna, where she had business interests, though at times she served as Hitler's housekeeper. She never married.

Hitler, William Patrick
Patrick (the name by which he preferred to be called) was the son of Alois Jr. and Brigid Dowling. He was therefore Adolf's half-nephew, and consequently one of his closer surviving relatives in 1945.

Prior to the Second World War, Patrick made many attempts to capitalise on his famous namesake – with no great success – and attempted to extort money from his Uncle Adolf, also with little success. After 1939, he went to the USA where he tried to capitalise on his supposed knowledge of Nazi Germany, again with little success. He was eventually taken into the US Navy – possibly as a less controversial alternative to preventive detention – where he spent all his time ashore at training camp. He was discharged in 1946 and disappeared into obscurity.

Patrick had four sons. The first born was named Alexander.[24] Three sons were still alive in 2000 (one died in the nineteen-eighties) and living in the New York metropolitan area. They guard the secret of their ancestry well, and refuse to give interviews. William Patrick Hitler is buried in a Long Island cemetery; his gravestone bears no last name.

Hüttler, Johann Nepomuk[25]

Brother of Johann Georg Hiedler who adopted Alois Schicklgruber and legitimized his family name to Hitler in 1876. He married Eva Maria Decker, by whom he had a daughter, Johanna, who married Johann Pölzl, and their daughter, Klara, married Alois Sr.[26] There is no evidence of any other children in the available biographies, but these tend to concentrate solely on the lineage of Klara Pölzl and Alois Sr. There is no evidence that Johann had any other children; equally, there is no evidence that he did not; the question remains open. Any male issue of his would have been legal brothers to Alois Sr. and would have borne the name of Hitler, or one of its variants. Such descendants could be the ancestors of the mysterious 'Hans Hitler'. His granddaughter was Klara Pölzl, who married Alois Sr., they being second cousins by blood but, if the adoption of Alois Sr. was legal, first cousins from the point of view of inheritance.

Another factor in the case of Johann is the estate that he left. By astute management he amassed a respectable estate, including the only inn in the village of Spital, and on his death his relatives had 'great expectations'. They were disappointed. The executor's statement notes: 'Liquid assets: none.'[27] Rather curiously, in 1888 Alois Sr. bought a substantial property for 4,500 *gülden*, money which he could only have saved from his salary with difficulty. The supposition is that Johann Nepomuk's estate had passed to Alois Jr. some time before the former's death, thereby strengthening the possibility that Alois was in fact his son.[28]

Loret, Jean-Marie[29]

Born in Wavrin, a small village in northern France, Jean-Marie Loret claimed to be the son of Adolf Hitler, from a liaison during the First World War with a French peasant girl named Charlotte. His claim to paternity is dubious and genetic tests were inconclusive.[30] The author, along with most historians, doubts the claim, and Loret would not have been mentioned here were it not that surviving members of the Hitler clan seem to have recognised him as one of their own.[31] Loret is not included in the family tree.

Pölzl, Johanna

Known to Hitler as 'Hanitante', Johanna is said to have been irascible, hunch-backed, and schizophrenic, though the latter seems unlikely, given the substantial sum which she is said to have amassed.[32] Unmarried, she lived in the household of Theresia Schmidt, serving as her house-maid. She provided Adolf with funds prior to 1911 and left a substantial sum, most of which he received.

Pölzl, Theres(i)a

Sister of Klara, Theresa[33] is of interest through her marriage to a Herr Schmidt, from whom the various members of the Schmidt family are descended and who currently form the major group of claimants on Hitler's estate. Of the present-day relatives of Hitler, Maser writes:

> *[Johann Nepomuk] Hüttler died in 1888 and today not even his direct descendants know what he looked like. The most that can be said is that there is a distinct family resemblance between Hitler's relations in Spital, Mistelbach, and Langfeld, the Schmidts and Koppensteiners, who can be shown beyond doubt to be descended from Johann Nepomuk. The fact that some of them look surprisingly like Adolf Hitler is readily explicable, for his mother, Klara Pölzl, was a granddaughter of Johann Nepomuk Hüttler and the sister of Theresia Schmidt, a Pölzl from Spital and forbear of the present Waldviertel Hitlers.[34]*

The immediate question is whether Maser is implying that there are people in the *Waldviertel* today who bear the name Hitler. If so, then either they changed their name to Hitler or somehow intermarried with a male bearing the Hitler name. Either could explain the mysterious Hans Hitler and others that have been hinted at. Maser's account later contains a statement which seems clearly in error or, at least, enigmatic:

> *. . . Alois always kept a mistress, and it seems probable that he handed over this sum to Therese Schmidt, his illegitimate daughter, on the occasion of the birth at Schwertberg of her son, Fritz Rammer who, incidentally, bore a striking resemblance to Alois junior.[35]*

The sum in question, according to Maser, was 600 *gülden*, which Alois borrowed before disappearing to Vienna for about a month in 1892.

Raubal, Angela[36] (née Hitler)

Married: (1) Leo Raubal, a revenue official; (2) Professor Martin Hammitzsch, director of the State School of Building Construction in Dresden, 29 February, 1936.[37] He was subsequently killed on the Eastern Front. Angela acted as Hitler's housekeeper at the *Berghof* from 1928 until 1935.

Raubal, Angelika ('Geli')

Hitler's niece and lover, she died in mysterious circumstances, inside the traditional locked room, at his Munich flat, with a pistol. On the authority of

Gürtner, the Bavarian Minister of Justice and a Nazi sympathiser, an inquest was dispensed with and her body was embalmed and shipped to Austria with surprising haste. Her body, sealed in a metal coffin, was interred in a prominent position in Vienna's Central Cemetery. Himmler and Röhm represented Hitler at the interment, accompanied by Alfred Frauenfeld, the self-appointed Nazi Gauleiter of Vienna.[38] Surprisingly – since Catholic doctrine is opposed to suicide – a Catholic priest, said to have been a friend of the Raubal family, blessed the remains.[39] Hitler was not present at the ceremony, which was no doubt well publicised, and some authors have seen this as evidence of indifference, even callousness, on Hitler's part. However, Hitler had a good reason for not attending the ceremony: he was banned from entering Austria. Post-war research by Toland has revealed that Hitler did visit Geli's grave, a day or so after the burial, after the fuss had died down, slipping over the border with Schreck, his chauffeur and double, and Hoffmann, and meeting Frauenfeld, who drove them to the cemetery in a less obtrusive car than Hitler's Mercedes.[40] There, shortly after dawn, Hitler placed flowers on the grave which bore the inscription:

Here Sleeps Our Beloved Child
Geli
She was Our Ray of Sunshine
Born 4 June 1908 – died 18 September 1931
The Raubal Family

The latter part of the story is not entirely credible since headstones are rarely erected at the moment of burial; they take time to make and the ground around the grave must stabilise before the stone can be erected. The inscription either belonged to a temporary marker or was added later and Frauenfeld's memory is false. Toland's interview with Frauenfeld took place in 1971, four years after Gun's book on Eva Braun had been published, and Gun's work contains exactly the same details from the headstone, which he claims to have found in the course of his researches.[41] What the inscription does suggest is that the headstone was paid for by the Raubal family; this is plausible, but it must not be forgotten that Geli's mother was working for Hitler at the time, as his housekeeper at the *Berghof*. After the war, the coffin was moved – on the grounds that 'the Hitler family' was no longer in a position to make the necessary annual payments – to an unmarked pauper's grave.[42]

Raubal, Elfriede (Friedl)
Younger sister of Geli, she married a lawyer named Hochegger and had at least one daughter.

Raubal, Leo Rudolf

One of the better educated of the Hitler clan and, according to Maser, Hitler's favourite nephew, he took a degree in chemistry and worked post-war at the Linz steelworks.[43] It seems that Hitler regularly sent Leo money at Christmas, and probably other gifts. Hanfstaengl seems to have met Leo towards the end of 1922 or, more probably, at the beginning of 1923:

> One morning when I came in [to Hitler's room on Thierschstraße] rather unexpectedly, a big lump of a boy stood in the open kitchen door. He turned out to be Hitler's nephew, the son of his half-sister who had married a man named Raubal and still lived in Vienna. He was an ill-favoured lad and Hitler was somewhat displeased that I had seen him. [44]

In January of 1943, as a second lieutenant in the engineers, he was captured at Stalingrad. The Germans offered to exchange Leo or Heinz Hitler for Stalin's son Yasha (Jacob), but the offer was refused.[45] He survived and returned to Germany in 1955, settling in Linz. Subsequently, in the mid-sixties, he emerged as the spokesman for the family. According to Maser:

> Most of the Hitler heirs were poor, uneducated farmers. Leo was the intellectual among them. . . . He was a very pleasant man, but I could tell right away that he wanted to keep a certain distance. [46]

Rommeder, Walburga (née Hüttler)[47]

Walburga married in 1853 and lived the rest of her life in Spital, where she died, wealthy and childless, probably after 1906, leaving her entire estate to her sister Johanna. In the event of Johanna predeceasing Walburga (which she did) the estate was to pass to Johanna's three daughters, Klara (mother to Adolf and Paula), Johanna and Theresa.

Schmidt, Anton[48]

Anton wrote to Werner Maser in the mid-sixties, enquiring about the status of the copyright of *Mein Kampf*. Shortly after, he contacted several other relatives, including Leo Raubal. After Leo's death he seems to have become the principal spokesman for the surviving heirs.

Schmidt, Eduard[49]

He is said to have been a hunchback with a speech defect. Arrested by the Russians in 1945, he died in captivity.

Schmidt, Johann Sr.[50]

Arrested by Soviet troops in May of 1945 and taken to Vienna for questioning. Died in captivity.

Schmidt, Johann Jr.[51]

Son of the above, he was arrested by Soviet troops in June of 1945 and taken to Moscow, where he was charged with 'co-operating with the Führer', and sentenced to 25 years imprisonment, together with 'several other' relatives. He was released under a general amnesty in 1955. According to Paula, in a letter written to the publisher Hans Sündermann in December of 1955, as quoted in Ryback:

> *"My nephew has returned home from Russia and with him a young Waldviertel relative, and seven people have legally returned." Five other Hitler relatives, Paula noted, had perished. "The same fate as hundreds of thousands of others," she wrote. "My brother would have found it fitting that we were also not spared."*[52]

Here, it must be noted that Johann Sr. was undoubtedly first cousin to Adolf and Hans' father is also described as being a first cousin. The name 'Hans' is occasionally used as a diminutive for 'Johann' or 'Johannes', which raises the remote possibility that Johann Schmidt Jr. adopted the surname 'Hitler' – legally or as an alias – and is, in fact, 'Hans Hitler'. The fact that Anton, who may be his brother, is currently the family spokesman slightly strengthens this supposition.

Schmidt, Theresia

Born Pölzl, she is said by Maser to be 'forbear of the present *Waldviertel* Hitlers'.[53] If this is literally true – i.e. that she is the ancestor of those who today bear the name 'Hitler' – then either she re-married someone named Hitler, one of her descendants married a Hitler, or one of her descendants changed his name to Hitler.

Notes

1 As far as this author has been able to determine, only Maser (MASE73), Toland (TOLA76), Harris (HARR86), and Ryback (RYBA00) have given much attention to the question.
2 Some writers seem to be confused over the year of death. Klara's tombstone clearly states 1907, but Heiden (HEID44, p. 37) has the year as 1908, as does Dr. Eduard Bloch, Hitler's mother's physician, in his statements to the OSS on March 5, 1943. Bloch, who is most unreliable on dates and times, states that Hitler was 18 at the time of his mother's death, which would put the year at 1907.
3 SHIR60, p. 1332; TOLA76, p. 881; GUN68, pp. 226-8; p. 291.
4 ODON78, p. 186.
5 GUN68, p. 282.
6 The only reference to this person is in the family tree published at http://history1900s.about.com/homework/history1900s/library/holocaust/nhi tanc.htm

7   Heiden (HEID44, p. 42) has the baptismal name as 'Adolfus' but no other author does so.

8   Brandt (BRAN45, p. 2) refers to rumours that Eva Braun had two children before her marriage, but states that the children so identified were actually those of a Frau Schneider, who lived at the *Berghof*, though what purpose she served there, Brandt does not say.

9   TOLA76, p. 245; ROSE98, p. 19; HEID44, p. 41. The essential facts are confirmed in FBI-Hit.

10 Rosenbaum (ROSE98, p. 19) says 'shortly before World War I'. Hitler (FBI-Hit, 1942 interrogation) claimed 1913.

11 SHIR60, p. 23. As with all who have tried to investigate the tangled web of the Hitler family, Shirer's frustration is evident.

12 ROSE98, p. 19; p. 33.

13 RYBA00.

14 MASE73, p. 350, note 15.

15 Quoted and analysed in Rosenbaum (ROSE98, p. 183).

16 For a detailed analysis of the legitimisation, see MASE73, p. 15ff.

17 Some writers, such as Kershaw (KERS98) and Waite (WAIT77) give the name as 'Glasl' or 'Glassl'; the author has chosen to accept the evidence of Maser (MASE73, p. 1).

18 KERS98, p. 10; WAITE77, p. 132.

19 The dates of birth and death are unclear. There appear to have been at least two – possibly 3 – Brigid Dowlings born in the relevant time period in Dublin. One listed as December 29, 1865, parents Thomas Dowling and Anne Clear. A second listed for December 29, 1866, parents Thomas Dowling and Anne Clease. A third listed for July 3, 1891, who died in November 1969 in the USA. I have chosen to use the latter since she is known to have been issued a US social security number in New York.

20 FBI-Hit. The FBI received an anonymous letter, dated 30 June, 1941, from 'An American Citizen' in Spring Lake, New Jersey. Attached to a newspaper clipping from the *New York Tribune* of Wednesday, 25 June, 1941, reporting Brigid's voluntary work, it states: *If the enclosed clipping hasn't come to your notice it merits investigation. This Hitler woman can glean much from the British Society and relay it to Germany. Is her presence in the U.S. legal? The Eagle screams – the Stars and Stripes protect her presence in the Land of the Free!*

21 TOLA76, pp. 255 and 395.

22 TOLA76, p. 730. The third relative was Leo Raubal, brother of Geli. Recent research suggests that Stalin's son committed suicide. See: Craig, Olga. *How Stalin's brutal massacre at Katyn shamed his PoW son into suicide.* The Sunday Telegraph, 30 July 2000.

23 JETZ58, illustrations between pp. 104-5.

24 Toland (TOLA76, footnote to p. 365) claims that the first son was named Adolf, basing this on a photograph of William holding the baby and captioned 'baby Adolf', but this seems to have been no more than a family joke.

25 Heiden (HEID44, pp. 36-39) has the name as von Nepomuk, after the national

saint of the Czech people; later authors do not perpetuate the "von" and I have chosen to do likewise for the sake of consistency.

26　HEID44, p. 37.

27　MASE73, p. 20.

28　MASE73, pp. 20-1.

29　Most of the following information is from RYBA00, except where otherwise referenced.

30　It is not yet known what these tests were but, since Loret died in 1985, they were unlikely to have been DNA-based and were probably simple blood type tests.

31　RYBA00, quoting conversations with Werner Maser.

32　WAIT77, p. 171. Hamann (HAMA99, p. 7) refers to her as 'apparently feeble-minded', citing Jetzinger as evidence. JETZ58, p. 86, refers to her being 'slightly hump backed'.

33　The spelling varies among authors; I have adopted the more common spelling.

34　MASE73, p. 18.

35　MASE73, p. 24.

36　BRAN45, p. 7, gives her name as 'Angelika'; this may be formally correct, but the more common 'Angela' has been retained. Hoffmann (HOFF55, p. 187) gives her year of death as 1948, but most other authors have 1949. Goebbels (GOEB48, p. 179) has the unusual spelling 'Angelea'.

37　Shirer (SHIR60, p. 23) is the only one to give the husband's occupation. BRAN45, p. 7, and MASE73, p. 350, give the second husband's name as 'Hammitsch', which seems more likely, but enquiries have failed to shed any light on this matter and other authors use the spellings "Hamitzsch" or "Hamitsch". GOEB48, p. 179, implies the date of her second marriage, though it could have been a day before or after.

38　TOLA76, p. 255.

39　HEID44, p. 307.

40　TOLA76, pp. 255-256, citing correspondence and an interview with Frauenfeld. Heiden (HEID44, p. 306) however, states that the Austrian government gave Hitler special permission to visit the grave and he paid his visit a week later, in the evening. Heiden's story is repeated almost verbatim by Shirer (SHIR60, p. 168).

41　GUN68, pp. 15-16.

42　ROSE98, p. 202. Rosenbaum says that the coffin was zinc; Hanfstaengl (HANF57, p. 166) says that it was lead; the latter seems more probable.

43　RYBA00. Formerly the Herman Göring steelworks.

44　HANF57, p. 48. The story seems a little odd; Leo Raubal was not especially big and Hitler's room on the Thierschstraße did not have a kitchen. Is it possible that Hanfstaengl is recalling a later encounter with William Patrick at Hitler's Munich apartment on Prinzregentenplatz and has confused the timing and parentage? Certainly, Patrick could be well described as 'a big lump of a boy'.

45　TOLA76, footnote to p. 730; RYBA00.

46　Conversations with Ryback, quoted extensively in RYBA00.

47　All information from MASE73, pp. 42-3.

48　All information from RYBA00.

49   All information from WAIT77, p. 171.
50   All information from RYBA00.
51   All information from RYBA00.
52   RYBA00.
53   MASE73, p. 18.

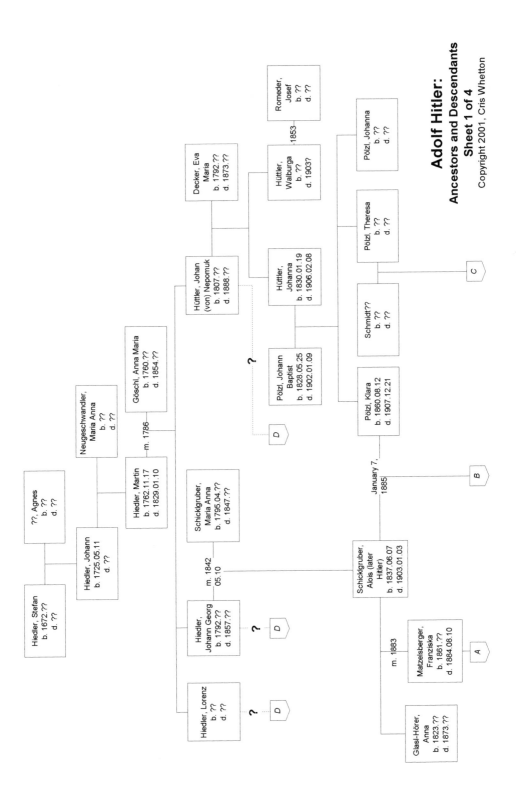

Adolf Hitler:
Ancestors and Descendants
Sheet 1 of 4
Copyright 2001, Cris Whetton

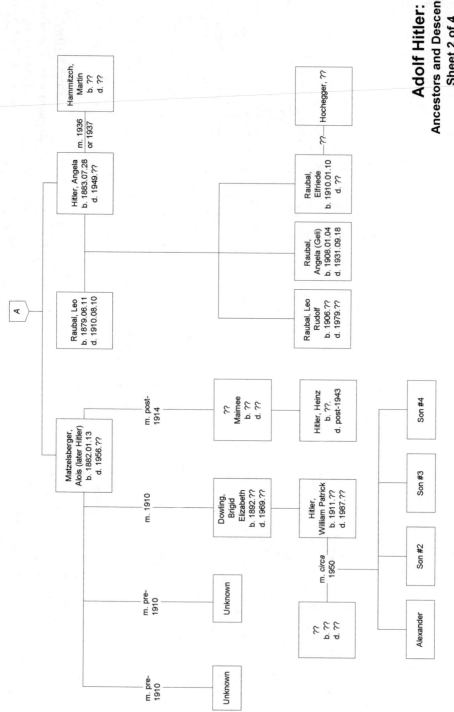

Adolf Hitler:
Ancestors and Descendants
Sheet 2 of 4
Copyright 2001, Cris Whetton

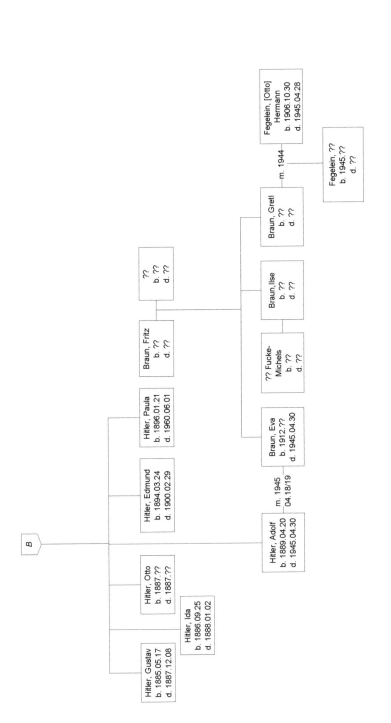

Adolf Hitler:
Ancestors and Descendants
Sheet 3 of 4
Copyright 2001, Cris Whetton

B

Hitler, Gustav
b. 1885.05.17
d. 1887.12.08

Hitler, Ida
b. 1886.09.25
d. 1888.01.02

Hitler, Otto
b. 1887.??
d. 1887.??

Hitler, Edmund
b. 1894.03.24
d. 1900.02.29

Hitler, Paula
b. 1896.01.21
d. 1960.06.01

Hitler, Adolf
b. 1889.04.20
d. 1945.04.30

m. 1945
04.18/19

Braun, Eva
b. 1912.??
d. 1945.04.30

?? Fucke-
Michels
b. ??
d. ??

Braun, Ilse
b. ??
d. ??

Braun, Fritz
b. ??
d. ??

??
b. ??
d. ??

Braun, Gretl
b. ??
d. ??

m. 1944

Fegelein, [Otto]
Hermann
b. 1906.10.30
d. 1945.04.28

Fegelein, ??
b. 1945.??
d. ??

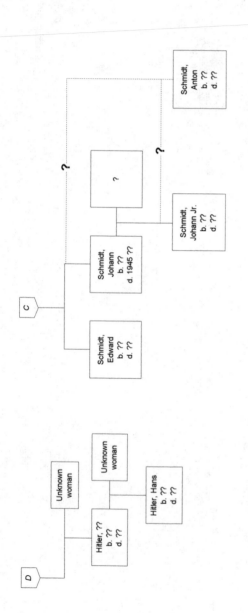

THE *THULE GESELLSCHAFT*

The *Thule Gesellschaft* was founded in 1917-18 as a right-wing, anti-Semitic, Pan-German nationalist club, successor to the earlier *Germanen Orden*, founded in 1912.[1] As the society's name implies, it was connected to Thule, a legendary island somewhere in Arctic waters, long since disappeared. A Nordic counterpart to Atlantis and, like Atlantis, the seat of an ancient and highly advanced civilisation; in the case of Thule, German civilisation. It was from the supposed knowledge of this civilisation – how they acquired it remains a mystery[2] – that the society developed its peculiar brand of Pan-Germanism. Many authors[3] have proposed theories for the origins of organisations such as the *Thule Gesellschaft*, but few have remarked on the common factor: something in male psychology finds secret societies attractive. The majority of secret societies – Freemasons, Rosicrucians, the Order of Skull and Bones, the Elucidated Brethren of the Ebon Night – are exclusively male; little boys, of any age, seem drawn to ritual, secret handshakes, mysterious symbols, and coded greetings that they hope their mothers cannot understand.[4] Some of course, are drawn to comradeship; either echoes of the comradeship of war, or the latently homosexual comradeship of exclusively male societies. Some just want to get away from their wives and families and have a few beers without being reminded that the lawn needs cutting or the tap on the kitchen sink needs a new washer. In short, men join societies such as the *Thule Gesellschaft* for a variety of reasons, few of them connected with world domination or the creation of a new social order. Such facts should be borne in mind when resisting the temptation to read over-sinister motives into the activities of the *Thule Gesellschaft*.

The *Thule Gesellschaft* was never a paramilitary organisation though it had close connections to many of them, especially the *Kampfbund*, which some regard as the society's paramilitary wing. Based in Munich, the few hundred members of the *Thule Gesellschaft* were mostly rich and included Julius F. Lehmann, Gottfried Feder, Dietrich Eckart, Karl Harrer, Hans Franck, Rudolf Heß, and Alfred Rosenberg.[5] Some writers claim that Amann was also a member. Of these, Feder, Eckart, Franck, Heß and Rosenberg would all become prominent members of the Nazi party. Interestingly, Lehmann, Feder, Eckart, and Rosenberg were all connected with publishing, Lehmann owning his own imprint. It was the *Thule Gesellschaft* which, despite its quasi-mystical mumbo-jumbo, decided that its ideas should be brought to the masses. For this, the German Workers' Party was created on 5 January 1919. Some highly coloured accounts have been written about the *Thule Gesellschaft* and its relationship with Hitler and the Nazi party.[6] However, it is fair to say that the society was not without influence and several of its members were certainly Hitler's backers – morally or materially.

President of the *Thule Gesellschaft* was the self-styled Rudolf Freiherr von Sebottendorf, a wealthy adventurer who had made a fortune through financial deals in Turkey and marriage to a wealthy heiress. Born Alfred Rudolph Glauer in 1875, he emigrated to Turkey where he was adopted by the real Freiherr von Sebottendorf. Such practices were not at all uncommon among German aristocrats who had no issue, but who wished to preserve their family name. During the Balkan Wars of 1912-13 he had an important position in the Turkish Red Crescent, the Moslem equivalent of the Red Cross. While in Turkey, he was initiated into the secret society of the *Rosicrucians* by a Jewish merchant named Termudi. In 1917, he returned to Germany a wealthy man, but was compelled to leave in 1919 on suspicion of espionage. In 1933, he returned to Germany and in 1934 published a book *Bevor Hitler Kam* – Before Hitler Came – which was immediately banned on Hitler's orders and Sebottendorf left Germany for the last time. He spent the Second World War in Turkey, where he operated as an ineffective agent of low credibility for the *Abwehr*, though there are claims that he was also in the pay of the British. On the day that Germany surrendered, 7 May 1945, he drowned himself in the Bosporus. It was Sebottendorf who, in July 1918 at a cost of RM 1,000, bought and presented the *Münchener Beobachter* to the *Thule Gesellschaft* as its propaganda organ.[7] From the beginnings, Nazism and publishing were closely linked.

The *Thule Gesellschaft* had more than adequate funds and was prepared to put money into almost anything, provided it satisfied the society's *Völkisch*, anti-Semitic aims. Sebottendorf, never a reliable witness, speaks of the society having an annual income of thirty to seventy thousand *marks*.[8] It is said to have financed the *Freikorps Oberland* with the assistance of a wealthy Munich paper manufacturer called Theodor Heuß (not to be confused with the first President of the German Federal Republic, 1949-59) who was also one of the earliest members of the DAP. It is said to have funded genealogical research (and it has been suggested to the author that it still does), research into ancient German law, and the *Bürgerwehr*, a private sabotage and intelligence organisation.

Just what financial support the *Thule Gesellschaft* gave to the DAP and later to Hitler is not known, but the evidence suggests that it was very little. The fact is that from its inception the DAP was starved of funds and if the *Thule Gesellschaft* was not prepared to give money to its creation, it was even less likely to do so to the unknown who had come to take control of it.

What is certain is that some *Thule Gesellschaft* members were members of the DAP. Most prominent of these was Dietrich Eckart, who would play an important part in shaping Hitler's career. Eckart, who often lived the life of a bohemian tramp, came from a wealthy family and was a successful journalist and translator. His translation of *Peer Gynt* brought him substantial royalties and he was the owner and publisher of a mildly satirical, but rabidly anti-Semitic, Pan-German magazine called *Auf gut Deutsch* (In plain German).

Another *Thule Gesellschaft* member who became prominent in the Nazi party was Alfred Rosenberg. Rosenberg had come to Germany in 1918 as a refugee from Tallinn (Reval), Estonia. The penniless Rosenberg was not at first sight a natural candidate for membership of the *Thule Gesellschaft*, but his anti-Semitic and anti-Communist writings brought him to Eckart's attention and, through Eckart, into the society, where his views, mixed with plenty of Nordic mysticism, found ready acceptance.

Max Amann is also said to have been a member of the *Thule Gesellschaft*, though it is hard to square the image of the no-nonsense Amann with the society's ideas. Pool's assertion that Amann was appointed to the board of the *Eher Verlag* at the insistence of the *Thule Gesellschaft* is pure conjecture, especially as Sebottendorf remained on the board.[9]

Another member of the society was Dr. Ernst Pöhner, head of the Munich police department. This is thought to account for the lenient attitude which the police showed towards Hitler and has led to claims, never wholly substantiated, that many of the Munich police were members of the NSDAP.

The final character connected with the Thule Gesellschaft was Scheubner-Richter. Born in Riga, Latvia, 1884 as Maximilian Erwin Richter, he fought for the Imperial Russian army as an officer in a Cossack cavalry regiment during the 1905 revolution. He afterwards married Mathilde von Scheubner. Since her father had no sons, he joined his wife's family name to his own, in accordance with the practice of the time. He came to Munich in 1910 to study engineering, joined a light cavalry regiment, and became a German citizen. He served during the First World War on the Western Front and in the Middle East, becoming German consul in Erzerum, Turkey towards the end of hostilities.[10] After the war, Scheubner-Richter was active in circles where business and anti-Bolshevik politics overlapped, eventually becoming the link between a group of German businessmen and White Russian forces under General Wrangel, which still controlled much of southern Russia. According to a German report, White Russian industrialists and oil traders such as Gukason, Lenison, and Baron Köppen, and industrialists such as Nobel, all passed funds through Scheubner-Richter to the NSDAP.[11] He also had extensive connections among the Russian émigré community and, through Princess Alexandra, wife of Prince Kyrill, heir to the Russian throne, he acquired funds on behalf of Ludendorff, part of which may have been diverted to Hitler.

Notes

1   A comprehensive description of the *Thule Gesellschaft* is provided by Bracher, BRAC70, pp. 80-83.

2   The gullible may wish to search the novels of Dennis Wheatley for clues.

3   e.g. HEID44, pp. 9-24 and *passim;* MASE73, pp. 109-11.

4   According to Bracher (BRAC70, p. 81) applicants for membership of the *Thule Gesellschaft* had to complete a questionnaire which required, *inter alia,* data on the hairiness of the applicant's body parts as proof of 'Aryan' descent.

5   KERS98, p. 138.

6   e.g. Schwarzwäller's *The Unknown Hitler* [SCHW89].

7   There is evidence that he remained on the board of the *Eher Verlag* until at least 1924. Maser (MASE73, p. 111) is the only source for the RM 1,000 figure.

8   SEBO34, *passim.*

9   POOL78, pp. 34-35.

10 KERS98, p. 189.

11 *Bericht über die Russische monarchistische Organisation in der Emigration.* Dated 18 October 1935. In the US National Archives. EAP 161-b-12/139 Folder 148.

REFERENCES

The following lists the major source material used in this work, together with the reference (in boldface type) used as an abbreviation in the footnotes. Documents cited less than three times are referenced in full in the end notes to each chapter. Some comments on the accuracy of the sources are also given.

Primary Sources

AMAN24 Statement dated 2 June 1924. Currently in *Staatsarchiv München*, SpkA *Karton* 20, Max Amann I-3

AMAN46 *Vernehmung* (cross-examination) *des Reichsleiters* Max AMANN *durch* Mr FEHL *am 6. Dezember 1946 – von 10.30 – 12.30* for Mr. DICKINSON, Ministry Section. Currently in *Staatsarchiv München*, SpkA *Karton* 20, Max Amann I-3.

AMAN49 Judgement (*Spruch*) dated 11 July 1949. *Berufungskammer* Registration No. 166/49. File I/3617/48. Currently in *Staatsarchiv München*, SpkA *Karton* 20, Max Amann I-3.

AMAN50 Decision (*Beschluß*) dated 19 October 1950. *Berufungskammer* Registration No. 166/49. Currently in *Staatsarchiv München*, SpkA *Karton* 20, Max Amann I-3.

BAUR58 Baur, Lt. Gen. Hans. *Hitler's Pilot*. London, 1958, Frederick Muller Ltd.

BICK17 Bickhardt, H. *Georg v. Seidlitz*. Memorial article printed in a special edition of *Entomologischen Blättern*, 1917 – possibly July or August.

BOLD48 Boldt, Gerhard von. *In the Shelter with Hitler*. London, 1948, The Citadel Press. (Originally published as *Die Letzten Tage*, 1947, Ernst Rowohlt.)

BRAN45 Brandt, Dr. Karl. *Women Around Hitler*. An eight page note written by Brandt, who was Reich Commissioner for Hygiene and Public Health, while interned at Kransberg (code name 'Dustbin') and dated 21 August 1945. Public Record Office, Kew, UK. File FO1031/102.

> Brandt's rather chatty little note gives some interesting insights into the women at the Berghof. Brandt himself entered Hitler's circle through his

friendship with Anni Rehborn, an Olympic swimmer. At that time a resident in Berlin's famous Charité Hospital, Hitler appointed Brandt as his personal physician and later civilian head of the Wehrmacht medical services.

DEUE62 Deuerlein, Ernst. *Der Hitler-Putsch: Bayerische Dokumente zum 8./9. November 1923.* Stuttgart, 1962, *Deutsche Verlags-Anstalt.*

DIET34 Dietrich, Otto. *Mit Hitler in die Macht. Persönliche Erlebnisse mit meinem Führer.* Munich, 1934, Eher Verlag.

DIET57 Dietrich, Otto. *The Hitler I Knew.* London, 1957, Methuen. [Originally published as *Zwölf Jahre mit Hitler.* Munich, 1955, Isar Verlag.]

FAIS45 Faison, S. Lane Jr. *Linz: Hitler's Museum and Library.* Consolidated Interrogation Report No. 4, 15 December, 1945. Office of Strategic Services, U.S. War Department.

FBI-Hit Refers to the whole file compiled by the US Federal Bureau of Investigation on Brigid Elizabeth and William Patrick Hitler during their time in the USA between 1942 and 1946.

FBI-Lüd Refers to the whole file compiled by the US Federal Bureau of Investigation on Kurt Lüdecke, 1936-59.

FRAN46 François-Poncet, André. *Souvenirs d'une ambassade à Berlin: Septembre 1931 – Octobre 1938.* Paris, 1946, Flammarion.

FROM43 Fromm, Bella. *Blood and Banquets: A Berlin Social Diary.* London, 1943, Geoffrey Bles.

GOEB48 Goebbels, Josef. (Ed. Louis P. Lochner.) *The Goebbels Diaries.* London, 1948, Hamish Hamilton.
Rather surprisingly, since he was a journalist who had worked in Berlin, Lochner's notes and commentary to Goebbels' text contains many errors.

HANF33 Hanfstaengl, Ernst. *Hitler in der Karikatur der Welt: Tat gegen Tinte: ein Bildsammelwerk von Ernst Hanfstaengl.* Berlin, 1933, Verlag Braune Bucher, Carl Rentsch, pp. 174.

HANF57 Hanfstaengl, Ernst. *Hitler: The Missing Years.* London, 1957, Eyre and Spottiswoode.

HAP *Hauptarchiv der Partei.* The archive documents of the NSDAP, now held in the US National Archives, Washington. References are to the microfilm copy of the files.

HITL53 Hitler, Adolf. (Attributed to) *Hitler's Secret Conversations: 1941-44.* New York, 1961, Signet Books. All page references are to this paperback edition. However, to accommodate the various editions of this book, each reference includes the date of the conversation.

HOFF55 Hoffmann, Heinrich. *Hitler Was My Friend.* Tr. Lt. Col. R.H. Stevens. London, 1955, Burke Publishing Co. Ltd.

KAAV82 Kaavere, Vello. *Georg Seidlitz: Zoologe und Darwinist.* Article published March 1982 in the Estonian journal *Loodus* (Nature) in a special edition celebrating the 350th anniversary of the University of Dorpat (Tartu).

LÜDE38 Lüdecke, Kurt G. W. *I Knew Hitler: The Story of a Nazi Who Escaped The Blood Purge.* London, 1938, Jarrolds Publishers (London) Ltd.

MEIS50 Meissner, Otto. *Staatssekretär unter Ebert – Hindenburg – Hitler.* Hamburg, 1950.

ROSE49 Rosenberg, Alfred. *Memoirs of Alfred Rosenberg. With commentaries by Serge Lang and Ernst von Schenck.* Chicago, 1949, Ziff-Davis Publishing Company.

Some authors, notably Cecil [CECI72] have cast doubts on the authenticity of parts of this text; fortunately, these are in areas which do not concern this narrative. However, it must be noted that this book is a translation – possibly only partial – of Rosenberg's memoirs, interspersed with commentary. Although the publishers have used a different size of font to distinguish commentary from the original, the difference is only one point size and the reader needs a sharp eye to determine where the text ends and the commentary begins. Some authors do not seem to have had 20/20 eyesight, attributing to Rosenberg statements which rightly belong to Lang and von Schenck.

SEBO34 Sebottendorf, Rudolf von. *Bevor Hitler Kam: Urkundliches aus der Frühzeit der Nationalsozialistischen Bewegung von Rudolf von Sebottendorf.* Munich, 1934.

SPEE70 Speer, Albert. *Inside the Third Reich.* London, 1970, Macmillan. (Page references are to the 1981 Macmillan-Collier paperback edition. ISBN 0-02-037500-X).

Speer's record is invaluable in that it is one of the few which covers the years 1933-45 in any detail. However, his account suffers from two major problems: firstly, some parts have been shown to be untrue and this must cast doubts on the rest of the work; secondly, and most important to this study, Speer rarely sticks to a strict chronology of events. This problem has been particularly acute in trying to unravel the events recounted in Chapters 10 and 15.

TREV54 Trevor-Roper, H.R. (Editor) *The Bormann Letters: The private correspondence between Martin Bormann and his wife from January 1943 to April 1945.* London, 1954, Weidenfeld and Nicolson.

TURN85a Turner, Henry Ashby Jr. (Editor) *Hitler – Memoirs of a Confidant.* Yale University Press, 1985, ISBN 0-300-03294-3.

This interesting book is actually the memoirs of Otto Wagener, compiled while in a British POW camp in 1946 and originally published as Turner, Henry Ashby Jr. *Hitler aus nächster Nähe. Aufzeichnungen eines Vertrauten 1929-1932.* Berlin, 1978.

Turner gives a comprehensive analysis of the accuracy of this work in his introduction (pp. xv-xix). Most of the material on Hitler's finances from this source relates to Hermann Göring and his industrial connections. It must be stressed that Wagener clearly hated Göring and his statements about Göring and money transferred to Hitler must therefore be subject to careful scrutiny.

Secondary Sources

BACK88 Backes, Klaus. *Hitler und die bildende Künste: Kulturverständnis und Kunstpolitik im Dritten Reich.* Köln, 1988, DuMont, ISBN 3-7701-1912-6.

BRAC70 Bracher, Karl Dietrich. *The German Dictatorship: The origins, structure and effects of national socialism.* New York, 1970, Praeger Publishers Inc.
  It is somewhat difficult to know what to make of this work, which is often Marxist in phrasing without being always Marxist in content. I have tried to restrict usage to verifiable references.

BULL62 Bullock, Alan. *Hitler, A Study in Tyranny.* London, 1962, Pelican Books. Page references are to the 1990 Penguin edition: ISBN 0-14-013564-2.

BURL00 Burleigh, Michael. *The Third Reich.* Macmillan, London, 2000, ISBN 0-330-48757-4. All page references are to the 2001 paperback edition by Pan Books.

CASS70 Cassels, Alan. *Mussolini's Early Diplomacy.* Princeton, 1970, Princeton University Press.

CECI72 Cecil, Robert. *The Myth of the Master Race: Alfred Rosenberg and Nazi Ideology.* London, 1972, B.T. Batsford Ltd., ISBN 0-7134-1121-X.

CHAU01 Chaussy, Ulrich. *Nachbar Hitler: Führerkult und Heimatzerstörung am Obersalzberg.* Berlin, 2001, Christoph Links Verlag, ISBN 3-86153-240-9.

COMP68 Compton, James V. *The Swastika and the Eagle: Hitler, the United States, and the origins of the Second World War.* London, 1968, The Bodley Head Ltd.

CROS61 Cross, Colin. *The Fascists in Britain.* London, 1961, Barrie and Rockliff. (Page references are to the 1963 US edition, published by St Martin's Press, NY.)

DAVI77 Davidson, Eugene. *The Making of Adolf Hitler.* New York, 1977, Macmillan, ISBN 0-02-529700-7.

DIAM74 Diamond, Sander A. *The Nazi Movement in the United States, 1924-41.* Ithaca, 1974, Cornell University Press.

FEST70 Fest, Joachim. *The Face of the Third Reich.* New York, 1970, Ace Books. (Originally published as *Das Gesicht des Dritten Reich,* Munich, 1963.)

FRAN62 Franz-Willing, Georg. *Die Hitlerbewegung: Der Ursprung, 1919-1922.* Hamburg, 1962, R. v. Decker's Verlag G. Schenck.

GORD72 Gordon, Harold J. *Hitler and the Beer Hall Putsch.* Princeton, 1972, Princeton University Press, ISBN 0-691-05189-5.

GUN68 Gun, Nerin E. *Eva Braun: Hitler's Mistress.* New York, 1968, Meredith Press.
  Although considered by some to be the definitive work on Eva Braun, this book contains so many errors of fact in matters peripheral to the

story of Hitler and his mistress that it is difficult to have confidence in the facts presented about Eva Braun and her family.

HALE55 Hale, O.J. *Adolph Hitler, Taxpayer*. American Historical Review, July 1955, pp. 830-42.

HALE64 Hale, Oron J. *The Captive Press in the Third Reich*. Princeton, 1964, Princeton University Press, LCC No. 64-12182,

HAMA99 Hamann, Brigitte. *Hitler's Vienna: A dictator's apprenticeship*. Oxford, 1999, OUP, ISBN 0-19-512537-1 (Page references are to the 2000 paperback edition.)

HARR86 Harris, Robert. *Selling Hitler*. London, 1986, Faber & Faber. Page references are to the Arrow paperback edition: ISBN 0-09-979151-X.

HEID36 Heiden, Konrad. *Hitler, a Biography*. London, 1936, Constable & Co. Page numbers refer to the 1975 reprint by AMS Press Inc., New York.

HEID44 Heiden, Konrad. *The Fuehrer*. London, 1999, Robinson Publishing Ltd. (Paperback edition, said to be a 1944 translation.) ISBN 1-84119-082-9. The first major, scholarly biography of Hitler, much drawn upon by other writers and well worth consulting. However, post-war documents have proved many details to be inaccurate and the book should be used with great care.

HERR95 Herring, Phillip F. *Djuna: The Life and Work of Djuna Barnes*. New York, 1995, Viking Penguin, ISBN 0-670-84969-3.

HIGH83 Higham, Charles. *Trading With the Enemy: An exposé of the Nazi-American money plot 1933-49*. New York, 1983, Delacorte Press, ISBN 0-440-09064-4.
In the best tradition of conspiracy books, this work, by a well-known writer on Hollywood and its stars, is over-dramatic and inaccurate. All the 'good guys' are clean cut, athletic, while all the 'bad guys' have some physical deformity.

JETZ58 Jetzinger, Franz. *Hitler's Youth*. London, 1958, Hutchinson & Co.

KERS98 Kershaw, Ian. *Hitler 1889-1936: Hubris*. London, 1998, Penguin Books, ISBN 0-713-99047-3.
I have drawn extensively on this text and the subsequent volume. Kershaw is a professional scholar and his work is thoroughly referenced. As a guide to Hitler's pre-1936 career, the work is invaluable.

KERS00 Kershaw, Ian. *Hitler 1936-45: Nemesis*. London, 2000, Penguin Books, ISBN 0-713-99229-8.
While up to the standards of scholarship of the previous volume, this book is of less use as a source of information on Hitler's fortune since it concentrates more on the man in a political context than on his personal life.

LANG79 von Lang, Jochen. *Bormann: The Man Who Manipulated Hitler*. London, 1979, Weidenfeld and Nicolson. Originally published as *Der Sekretär*. 1977, *Deutsche Verlags-Anstalt*. All page references are to the British edition.

MASE73 Maser, Werner. *Hitler*. London, 1973, Allen Lane, ISBN 0-7139-0473-9.

MCKA81 McKale, Donald M. *Hitler: The Survival Myth*. New York, 1981, Stein and Day. Page references are to the 1983 paperback edition.

MOSL74 Mosley, Leonard. *The Reich Marshal: A biography of Hermann Goering*. London, 1974, Weidenfeld and Nicolson, ISBN 0-297-76810-7.

NOLL56 Noller, Sonja. *Die Geschichte des "Völkischen Beobachters" von 1920-23*. Doctoral dissertation, München, 1956.

ODON78 O'Donnel, James. P. *The Bunker*. New York, 1978, da Capo Press, ISBN 0-306-80958-3. Page references are to the 2001 Edition.

ORLO69 Orlow, Dietrich. *The History of the Nazi Party: 1919-1933*. Pittsburgh, 1969, University of Pittsburgh Press.

ORLO73 Orlow, Dietrich. *The History of the Nazi Party: 1933-45*. Pittsburgh, 1973, University of Pittsburgh Press, ISBN 0-8229-3253-9.

PLAU46a Plaut, James S. *Loot for the Master Race*. The Atlantic Monthly, September 1946.

PLAU46b Plaut, James S. *Hitler's Capital*. The Atlantic Monthly, October 1946.

POOL78 Pool, James and Suzanne. *Who Financed Hitler?* New York, 1978, Dial Press, ISBN 0-8037-9039-2.

> This is an annoying and flawed book, though useful in establishing lines of inquiry. The scholarship of the book has been called into question by Turner (TURN85, p. 362, note 3) and this author sees no reason to disagree. The authors frequently draw conclusions from documented sources that are different from what is actually written in those sources.

POOL97 Pool, James. *Hitler and his Secret Partners: contributions, loot and rewards, 1933-1945*. New York, 1997, Pocket Books, ISBN 0-671-76081-5.

PRYC76 Pryce-Jones, David. *Unity Mitford: A Quest*. London, 1976, Weidenfeld and Nicolson. (Page numbers refer to the US edition, ISBN 0-8037-8865-7.)

ROSE98 Rosenbaum, Ron. *Explaining Hitler*. New York, 1998, Random House. Page references are to the 1999 'Papermac' edition, ISBN 0-333-75078-0.

RYBA00 Ryback, Timothy W. *Hitler's Lost Family*. The New Yorker, July 17, 2000, pp. 46-57.

SCHO89 Schöner, Helmut and Irlinger, Rosl. *Der alte Obersalzberg bis 1937*. Berchtesgaden, 1989, *Verlag Berchtesgadner Anzeiger*, ISBN 3-980-2241-0-4.

SCHW89 Schwarzwäller, Wulf. *The Unknown Hitler*. New York, 1989, Berkley, ISBN 0-425-12133-X. (Originally published as *Hitlers Geld*. Paperback edition: Vienna, 1998, *Verlag Carl Ueberreuter,*. ISBN 3-8000-3700-9.)

> While Schwarzwäller contains a wealth of interesting information, little of which is referenced, it is written in a chatty, rather sensational style, and many of the conclusions the author draws are dubious. Because of

the lack of references to sources, I have tried to avoid using the text except where no other source exists.

SHIR60 Shirer, William L. *The Rise and Fall of the Third Reich*. London, 1960, Secker and Warburg. Page references are to the 1964 Pan paperback edition: ISBN 0-330-70001-4.

> Shirer is an invaluable reference, especially as the author was resident in Germany during much of Hitler's rise to power. There are some minor errors and omissions, mostly the result of material not being available at the time. Where these are relevant to this story, I have tried to indicate them in the footnotes.

SNYD76 Snyder, Louis L. *Encyclopaedia of the Third Reich*. New York, 1976, McGraw-Hill Inc., ISBN 1-85648-219-7.

SPOT03 Spotts, Frederic. *Hitler and the Power of Aesthetics*. Woodstock, 2003, The Overlook Press, Peter Mayer Publishers, Inc., ISBN 1-58567-345-5.

STEE37 'Steel, Johannes'. *Escape to the Present*. New York, 1937, Farrar and Rinehart Inc.

> I have classed this book as a secondary source because I have some doubts as to its authenticity, though the author claims to have worked for the 'Industrial Intelligence Service' of the Weimar Republic. Some parts of this pseudonymous work appear to be pure fantasy; some, where the facts can be verified, are clearly wrong. .

STMF03 Correspondence between the author and the *Bayerische Staatsministerium der Finanzen*.

THYS41 Thyssen, Fritz. *I Paid Hitler*. London, 1941, Hodder and Stoughton. I have relegated Thyssen's much-quoted memoir to a secondary source since there is some doubt as to how much of it he actually wrote.

TOLA76 Toland, John. *Adolf Hitler*. Ware, 1976, Wordsworth Editions, ISBN 1-85326-676-0.

> A significant portion of Toland's work is based on tape-recorded interviews made ca. 1970. This alone makes it an invaluable source, as many of those involved are now dead.

TREV47 Trevor-Roper, Hugh R. *The Last Days of Hitler*. London, 1947, Macmillan.

TURN85b Turner, Henry Ashby Jr. *German Big Business & the Rise of Hitler*. Oxford, 1985. ISBN 0-19-504235-2 All references are to the 1987 paperback edition.

> The author restricts himself to 'big business' and is careful to define what that includes. Within this rather narrow scope the book is invaluable. It is therefore unfortunate that the author has made so many minor mistakes over peripheral characters, outside his scope of study but not outside that of this book.

WAIT77 Waite, Robert G. L. *The Psychopathic God.* New York, 1977, Basic Books, ISBN 0-465-06743-3.

    This book well documents some aspects of Hitler's early life and family and I have drawn on it for some parts of Chapter 2: Father to the Man and Chapter 16: The Inheritors. However, some of the conclusions drawn by the author, while perfectly sensible to a psychiatrist, are laughable to a lay-person and the reader is urged to exercise judgement and common sense.

WILL72 Williams, Robert C. *Culture In Exile: Russian Émigrés in Germany, 1881-1941.* Ithaca, 1972, Cornell University Press.

INDEX

1st Bavarian Infantry Regiment, 16

2nd Demobilisation Company, 20

Abegg, Baroness, 241
Abel, Werner, 132, 188
Adolf Hitler Cultural Fund, 194, 197, 201, 208n, 230–31, 236, 271, 317
Adolf Hitler Spende der Deutsche Wirtschaft (Adolf Hitler Fund of German Business), 5, 69, 82, 135, 194, 196–97, 203, 225–37, 243, 247, 253, 256, 298, 316–17, 321
AH Spende, see *Adolf Hitler Spende der Deutsche Wirtschaft*
Ahrenburg, Prince, 32
Alexandra, Princess, 341
Allied Control Commission, 308
Altenberg, Jacob, 14
Aman (Bavarian politician), 170
Amann, Max, 16, 25, 29, 34, 45, 47, 49, 51, 52, 55, 56, 58, 63, 93, 111, 113, 125–26, 132–33, 135, 141, 188, 199, 209–12, 213–14, 216–19, 223n, 339, 341; control of Hitler's finances, 5, 6, 58, 93, 207, 209, 210, 212, 215, 232, 309, 316, 319; personal profits, 31, 38, 45, 209, 217–19, 316; rivalry with Bormann, 6, 207, 232–34
American Aid Committee, 172
Anschluß, 202, 255, 268
Appleby, Sir Humphrey, 8n

Arco-Valley, Graf Anton von, 19
Arndt, Wilhelm, 283
Association of Bavarian Industrialists, 173
Asthaber, von (Bavarian industrialist), 189
Atlantic, Hotel, 69
Auer, Erhard, 180
August Wilhelm 'Auwi', Crown Prince, 96, 172, 173
Aussenpolitische Amt (Foreign Policy Bureau), 136
Austria (*and* Austrian), 6, 14, 15, 38, 56, 63, 66, 67, 73, 81, 90, 116, 126, 187–88, 202, 231, 234, 239, 241, 247, 252, 255, 263, 268, 269, 273, 274, 282n, 286, 292, 299, 300, 309, 310, 313n, 317, 320, 322n, 324, 329, 333n
Auwi *see* August William, Crown Prince
Aust, Hermann, 62, 173
automobile (*see also* car; Mercedes; Selve), 51, 66, 67, 69
Axmann, Artur, 108n, 294

Baltic (*and* Balt), 107 (n.45, n.47), 184; Baltic German, 22, 98, 172, 185; Baltic Nationalist movement, 100
Bang, *Finanzrat* Dr., 131, 150, 177
bank accounts, 2, 4, 5, 56, 93, 210, 232, 309–10, 317, 319
Barbarossa Bund, 129
Baur, Gen Hans, 37n, 82, 90, 170, 265, 283, 294, 296n, 301

Bavaria(n), 19, 25, 28, 31, 33, 42, 51, 65, 100, 104, 113, 126, 140, 169, 170, 173, 176, 177, 212, 220, 239, 242, 259n, 291, 306, 311, 314n, 329; authorities, 5, 182; Finance Ministry, 57, 120, 123n, 313n, 318; Finance Office, 71, 84n; government, 111, 117, 119, 120, 121, 254; paramilitary units (*e.g. Freikorps*), 20, 24, 30; separatism; 27, 168, 186–88; State of, 57, 115, 119, 210, 251, 298, 300, 308, 309, 316, 317, 319
Bavarian People's Party, 145, 170, 221
Bayerische Reichswehr Gruppenkommando No. 4, 21
Bayreuth Festival, 103, 183
Bechstein, Carl Edwin, 93, 174
Bechstein, Hélène, 91–92, 93, 106n, 174, 176
Bechsteins, the, 23, 26–27, 32, 74, 88, 94, 97, 182, 239–40,
Breker, Arno, 264
Below, Col Nikolaus von, 287, 290
Berchtesgaden, 49, 91, 96, 239–40, 248, 250, 283–84, 288
Bergbauverein, 143, 148, 157, 161
Berghof, 4–5, 7, 206, 234, 239–58, 260n, 275, 282n, 284, 286, 302, 307, 308, 311–12, 317, 329, 332n; appearance and decoration, 243–46, 248, 249, 273; costs and value, 244–45, 252, 256, 257, 258, 315;

Berghof, (continued)
  financing, 4–5, 122n, 209,
  234, 243, 247, 253, 298
Berlin, 7, 19, 21, 23, 26, 28,
  32, 66, 77, 78, 79, 82, 89,
  91, 96, 102, 126, 128,
  134, 136, 139, 140, 145,
  146–7, 152, 156, 159,
  160, 170, 173, 174, 176,
  177, 185, 186, 188, 196,
  199, 201, 203, 208n, 225,
  234, 239, 246, 247, 250,
  253, 255, 261nn, 264,
  265, 268, 272, 288–89,
  291, 300, 303, 306, 307,
  310, 312, 321, 324; *Eher
  Verlag* and *Völkischer
  Beobachter*, 52, 54–56, 58,
  131–32, 213–34;
  Führerbunker, 228, 283,
  285–86, 287, 311; Hitler
  fundraising in, 23, 26,
  31–32, 78, 176; newspaper
  format, 47
Berliner Illustrierte, 56
Bertelsmann Group, 117
Beyschlag, Rudolf, 21
Bialystock, Max, 106n
Bierbaumer, Käthe, 40, 42–44,
  176–77
Bingel, Rudolf,146
Biskupsky, Gen Vasili, 169–72
Bismarck, Count Gottfried von,
  146
Bissing, Dr. Baron von, 189
black leather *see* leather
blackmail, 74–5
Bloch, Dr. Eduard, 10
Blood Purge of 1934, 20, 25,
  74, 156
Boldt, *Rittmeister* Gerhard, 290
Bormann, Martin, 47, 67,
  108n, 112, 206–207, 228,
  232–35, 243, 255–56,
  260n, 261n, 268, 285,
  287–89, 293–94, 300,
  303, 305, 310, 317;
  control of Hitler's finances,
  5, 6, 102, 197, 206, 226,
  228, 233–34, 235, 243,
  246, 251–53; rivalry with
  Amann, 6, 207, 232–34
Borsig, Ernst von, 23, 28, 141,
  174–75
Bosch, Dr. Karl, 195
Bosdari, Alessandro de, 188
Bouhler, Philipp, 233–34, 285,
  288
Brandi, Ernst, 148, 161

Brandt, Dr. Karl, 108n, 294,
  306, 307, 308, 313n, 332n
Brasol, Boris, 180
Braun, Eva, 90, 100, 203, 220,
  242, 248, 284–87, 289,
  306–307, 311, 323–24,
  332n; legacies, 203, 284–5,
  302, 319–20; possessions,
  102–3, 201, 253, 254–55,
  272, 286–87
Braun, Franziska, 323
Braun, Fritz, 319, 323
Braun, Gretl, 102, 201, 220,
  286, 302, 324
Braun, Ilse, 203, 302, 323
Braun, Karl Alfred, 40, 43
Braun, Margarethe, *see* Braun,
  Gretl
Braun, Otto, 188
Braunau (am Inn), 13, 241,
  252, 253, 255, 257, 301,
  317
Braunes Haus, 53, 86n, 132,
  155, 161, 233, 235, 254
Brauschitsch, Gen Walther von,
  202
British Holocaust Education
  Trust, 118
British Red Cross Society, 117
British Union of Fascists, 184
Bruckmann, Hugo and Elsa, 23,
  27, 29, 63, 74, 88, 93–94,
  97, 101, 107n, 150, 172,
  175, 253
Brückner, Lt Wilhelm, 202,
  207n, 233, 305, 313n
Brüning, Heinrich, 80
Buch, Maj Walther, 199
Büchner, Elizabeth, 92, 107n
Bund Wiking, 169
Burckhardt, Carl, 247
Burgdorf, Gen Wilhelm, 287,
  290
Burhenne, Karl, 174, 177

Canaris, LCdr Wilhelm, 169
car (*see also* automobile;
  Mercedes), 30, 65, 68, 203,
  329
Cantacuza-Grant, Princess, 172
Cantacuzène of Romania,
  Princess, *see also* Bruckmann,
  Elsa, 93
Cautio GmbH, 214
Chamberlain, Prime Minister
  Neville, 197, 247
Cherep-Spiridovic, Count, 180
Christian, Maj Gen Eckard,
  306

Christian, Gerda, 305–306
cigars (*and* cigarettes), 21,
  54–5, 141, 155, 312
Claß, *Justizrat* Heinrich, 131,
  149–50, 177
Coburg, Duchess of , 97
Coburg, Duke of, 173
coffee, 141, 173, 203–6; gifts
  to Hitler, 203–6;
  manufacturers, 33, 47, 141,
  173, 176
Cohen, Richard, 117
Contraband Control, 203
Control Council, 299
Cossman, 28
Cramer-Klett, Theodor Freiherr
  von, 170
Cultural Fund, *see* Adolf Hitler
  Cultural Fund
Cura Treuhand un Prüfung GmbH,
  214
Curtis Brown Literary Agency,
  116

Dachau, 255
Daily Mail, 109, 185
Daily Telegraph, 117, 123n, 189
Darré, Walther, 199
Dawes Plan, 149
Dawson, Geoffrey, 185
*Deutsche Bank und Disconto-
  Gesellschaft*, 154
Degano, Alois, 242
Der Angriff, 51
Der Freundeskreis Himmler (The
  Circle of Himmler's
  Friends), 147
Der Stürmer, 66
Deterding, Sir Henri, 170,
  189–90, 193n
Deutsche Arbeiterpartei (DAP –
  German Workers' Party),
  21–22, 99, 167, 340 ;
  changes name, 23
Deutsche Arbeitsfront (DAF—
  German Work Front), 197
Deutsche Volkspartei (DVP –
  German People's Party),
  142, 144, 151, 153
Deutsche Werhgeist (German
  Military Spirit), 52
Deutsche Werkgemeinschaft (DWG
  – German Work
  Community), 28
Deutsche Zeitung, 26
Deutscher Nationale Volkspartei
  (DNVP—German
  Nationalist Party), 143,
  148, 150, 153

Deutscher Volksville, 28
Dickel, Dr. Otto, 28
Diehn, August, 161
Dietrich, Dr Otto, 3, 33, 58, 66, 79–80, 108n, 110, 142–44, 150, 163n, 173, 195, 206, 209–10, 213, 220, 228, 230, 243, 262, 264, 273, 295
Dietrich, *SS-Obergruppenführer* Josef "Sepp," 20
Dirksen, Frau Viktoria "Tory" von, 96, 101
Dodd, US Ambassador William E., 178
dog whip *see* whips
Dönitz, Adm Karl, 289–90, 293, 299
Drexler, Anton, 23, 26, 42–43
Dulles, Allen, 153
Duschnitz, von, 189
Dvorak, Pavel 121

Eckart, Dietrich, 22–23, 24, 25, 26, 41–44, 89, 91, 125, 177, 182, 222, 239–40, 259n, 339, 341; financial support for Hitler, 22–23, 29, 175–76
Eckart, Simon, 41, 59n, 176–77, 182, 191n
Eden, Hotel, 33
Eder, 43
Eher Verlag, 3, 4–5, 22, 24, 35n, 38–41, 43–45, 48, 50, 52–54, 56–57, 63, 75, 85n, 97, 116, 130, 131, 135, 154, 166, 169, 210–15, 217–21, 225, 226, 267, 308, 309, 316–18; Hitler's income from, 4, 5, 38, 53, 72, 82, 109, 111, 158, 194, 201, 207, 212–13, 217–19, 232, 256; ownership, 44–45, 57–58, 99, 211; purchase of, 25, 39–45, 176–77
Eher, Franz, 39
Ehrhardt, Capt Hermann, 169
Eisner, Kurt, 19
Elefanten, Hotel zum, 142
Enabling Act, the, 196
Epp, Gen Ritter von, 20, 24, 32, 41–43, 75
Erzberger, Mathias, 131, 169
Esser, Hermann, 20, 70, 127, 212
European Web, 177, 184–190

Faber, Maj Wilhelm, 24
Faure, Paul, 187
Feder, Gottfried, 20, 40, 43, 52–53, 94, 153, 156, 339
Fegelein, *SS Obergruppenführer* Otto Hermann, 324
Feilitzsch, Freiherr Franz von, 40, 43
Feldzeugmeisterei, 24
Fick, Roderich, 244
Fickler, Erich, 152
Fighting League for German Culture, 228
Finck, August von, 161
Finland (*see also* Finnish), 48, 98, 99
Finnish (*see also* Finland), 5, 31, 48, 97, 98, 99, 107n, 119, 259n, 261n
Flick, Friedrich, 145
Ford, Henry, 3, 76, 129, 131, 166, 172, 178, 180, 182, 191n, 192n, 202
Forster, Albert, 247
France (*and* French), 15, 114, 119, 126, 184, 185, 186, 273, 327
François-Poncet, Ambassador André, 248, 260n, 271
Frank, Hans, 72, 231, 339
Frank, Richard, 33, 37n, 47, 92–93, 174, 176, 190
Frankenberg, Conrad von, 81
Frauenfeld, Alfred, 329
Freemasonry, 33, 35n
Friedrich-Wilhelm, Crown Prince, 30
Freikorps Eberhardt Brigade, 30
Freikorps Oberland, 340
Freikorps, 20, 30, 32, 140, 169
Frick, Wilhelm, 85n, 142
Funk, Walther, 29, 139, 144, 147, 153, 156, 160–62, 214, 235, 270, 289

Gansser, Dr. Emil, 26–28, 31–32, 47, 50, 174, 176–77, 241; fundraising from Switzerland, 27, 32, 176–77, 190
Gattineau, Heinrich, 147, 152
Gelsenkirchen Bergwerks, 150
Gengler, 51
Genoud, François, 112, 304, 310
German Welfare Council 117–18
German National Defense and Offensive League, 27

Gestapo, 30, 136
gifts, given by Hitler, 6, 133, 202; received by Hitler, 32, 63, 67, 184, 203
Gissibl, Fritz, 67
Glaser, Alexander, 140
Goebbels, Josef, 53, 81–83, 100, 131–32, 134–135, 162, 195, 199, 229, 251, 254, 264, 267, 287, 290; publishing ventures, 44, 52, 213–15
Göhler, *SS Sturmbannführer* Johannes, 286
Gömbös, Gyula, 126, 127, 131
Göring, Hermann, 27, 63, 79, 82, 126, 134, 142, 143, 154, 187, 199, 213, 233, 248, 250, 251, 256, 267–68, 288–89; financial affairs, 30, 63, 67, 155, 156–60, 189, 195–96, 212, 225
Göring, Karin, 67, 158
Grandel, Dr. Gottfried, 25, 28, 41–44, 59n, 177, 191n
Grauert, Ludwig, 157, 160, 162
Großmann, Stephan, 186
Günsche, Maj Otto, 301
Gutberlet, Dr. Wilhelm, 40, 42–43, 57
Gutmann, Lt Hugo, 16

Haberstock, Karl, 268
Hailer, Fritz, 202
Hajek, Jiri, 120
Hamburg-Amerika Line, 177
Hammitsch, Angela, 303; *see also* Raubal, Angela
Hammitsch, Prof. Martin, 242, 333n
Hanfstaengl, Egon, 241
Hanfstaengl, Erna, 95
Hanfstaengl, Ernst "Putzi", 3, 7, 27, 28–32, 36nn, 46, 63, 65, 75, 80, 81, 84n, 89, 96, 101, 107n, 113, 114, 122n, 124, 127, 134, 163n, 189, 190, 198, 203, 211, 220, 236, 240, 249, 266–67, 330; and Hitler's finances, 7, 29, 31, 50, 92–93, 110, 139, 176, 185; and purchase of rotary press, 47–49, 97–98
Hanfstaengl, Hélène, 94–95, 104, 241
Haniel, Karl, 152

Hanisch, Reinhold, 12–13, 17nn
Hanssen, Kurt, 268
Hanussen, Erik Jan, 70, 85n, 241
Harrer, Karl, 21, 23, 339
Hasselbach, Dr Hans-Karl von, 294
Hauffe, Hotel, 7
Haufler, *SS Hauptsturmbannführer* Erwin, 286
Haus des Deutsches Kunst, 271
Haus Wachenfeld, 73, 240–43, 252, 253
Haushofer, Prof Karl, 214
Hearst, William Randolph, 29, 77, 110, 114, 180, 192n, 325
Hecker, Ewald, 146
Heidemann, Gerd, 310
Heiliger, Max, *see* "Max Heiliger"
Heinrichsbauer, August, 160–61
Held, Heinrich, 65
Helfferich, Karl, 146
Helldorf, Count Wolf von, 85n, 152
Hermine, Princess 96
Herting, 200
Heß, Rudolph, 25, 63, 67, 70–71, 75–76, 78, 104, 112, 134, 157, 199, 206, 214, 225–26, 228, 233–35, 240, 249, 308, 339
Hesse , Grand Duke of, 173
Heuß, Theodor, 40, 43, 48, 99, 340
Hiedler, Johann Georg, 323, 327
Hilfskasse (Relief Fund), 86n, 198, 233
Hilpert, 28
Himmler, Heinrich, 103, 147, 160, 199, 206, 215, 242, 324, 329
Hindenburg, Paul von, 80, 131, 144, 145, 307
Hitler Jugend Zeitung, 52
Hitler, Adolf. To give individual page entries would be a waste of space; however, the reader may consult the following entries in this index for details of Hitler's fortune and his personal life: Adolf Hitler Cultural Fund; *Adolf*

Hitler Spende der Deutsche Wirtschaft; Amann, Max; automobile; bank accounts; *Berghof*; car; coffee; *Eher Verlag*; gifts; leather; libel; looting; *Mein Kampf*; Müller, Adolf; postage stamps; Schaub, *SS Gruppenführer* Julius; Seidlitz, Frau Gertrud von; taxes; underwear; *Völkischer Beobachter*; whips; wills
Hitler, Alois (Aloys), Sr., 16n, 255, 323
Hitler, Alois, Jr., 75, 202, 302–304, 313n, 324–25
Hitler, Angela, *see* Raubal, Angela
Hitler, Brigid Elizabeth (*née* Dowling), 325, 332n
Hitler, Hans, 108n, 302, 313n, 325–26
Hitler, Heinz, 241, 259n, 302, 325, 326, 330
Hitler, Klara, 10, 255
Hitler, Paula, 10, 13, 100, 104–105, 112, 202, 300, 302–304, 313n
Hitler, William Patrick, 75, 302, 304, 324, 326–27, 333n
Hitlerjugend, 294
Hitler-Mutti, 90–91
Hochegger, Elfriede (*née* Raubal), 303
Hofbräuhaus, 23, 35n
Hoffman, Heinrich, 25, 30, 35n, 47, 64, 70, 84n, 108n, 203, 213, 219–21, 233, 238n, 240, 249, 251, 254, 329; art collecting, 230, 263, 264, 265, 266; Hitler's finances, 5, 23, 102, 143, 197, 209, 247; photographer and publisher, 33, 50–51, 102, 197, 209, 224n, 230, 254, 285
Hoffmann, Carola, 91, 105
Hoffmann, Gen Max, 170
Hohenzollern monarchy, 172–3; *see also* August-Wilhelm, Friedrich-Wilhelm, Kaiser Wilhelm II, Rupprecht
Houghton Mifflin publishers, 118
House of German Art, *see Haus des Deutsches Kunst*

Hugenburg, Alfred, 77, 79–80, 140, 148–150, 152, 153
Hummel, Helmut von, 23–4, 268
Humps, Traudl, *see* Junge, Gertrud
Hungarian, 2, 14, 102, 126–7, 187
Hungary, 121, 126, 127, 130, 137 (n.12)
Hutchinson, William, 116
Hüttler, Johann Nepomuk, 327

IG Farben, 39, 81, 136, 141, 147, 151–52, 158, 161, 177, 195
Ilgner, Max, 147, 152
Imam of Yemen, 204–6
Illustrierte Beobachter, 51–52, 56, 70
Interessantenpresse, 39
International Military Tribunal, 299
Italy, 70, 102, 126, 128, 187, 268; funds from, 126, 187

Jamnitzer, Wentzel, 264
jewellery (*and* jewelry *in quoted US text*), 33, 89, 90, 92, 101, 102, 103, 106n, 172, 174, 284, 285, 296n, 302, 320
Johannmeier, Maj Willi, 290–92
Jouvenel, Bertrand de, 114
Junge (*née* Humps), Gertrud (Traudl), 246, 249, 306

Kahr, Gustav Ritter von, 25, 28
Kaiser Wilhelm II, 173
Kaiserhof, Hotel, 77, 79, 82, 86n, 135, 139, 142, 145, 147, 159, 161, 164n, 196
Kalle Kreis (Kalle Circle), 151–52
Kalle, Wilhelm, 152
Kampfbund (Fighting League), 20, 30, 187, 339
Kampfund für Deutsche Kultur (Activist Association for German Culture), 175
Kampfverlag, 52
Kampfzeit (Time of Struggle), 79
Kannenberg, Arthur (Willi), 201
Kapp Putsch of March 1920, 23, 148, 170, 177
Kapp, Karl, 202

Kapp, Wolfgang, 24, 170
Kauert, Herbert, 161
Kauffmann, Angelica, 272
Kempka, Erich, 82, 237
Keppler Circle, 145–47
Keppler, Wilhelm, 144, 146, 160, 235
Kerschner, Theodor, 268
King Edward VIII, 186
King Ludwig III of Bavaria, 15
Kirdorf, Emil, 72, 74–77, 85n, 86n, 93, 141, 148, 149, 150–51, 175
Klagges, 81
Klintzsch, Lt Hans Ulrich, 30, 36n, 169
Klöckner, Peter, 81, 152
Klotzbach, Arthur, 152
Knepper, Gustav, 160
Knirr, Prof. Heinrich, 262
Komission zur Sammlung, Verwaltung und Verwendung des Industriellen Wahlfunds (Commissiion for the Collection, Management and Use of Industrial Election Funds), 140
Konrad, SS Hauptsturmführer Franz, 286
Körber, Adolf Viktor von, 34n, 111
Körner, Oskar, 42, 59n
Kränzchen, 147
Krause, Gertrud (See also Gertrud von Seidlitz), 98
Krebs, Gen Hans, 287, 290
Kristallnacht pogrom, 104, 161
Krogmann, Karl Vincent, 146
Krosigk, Schwerin von, 195, 199
Krüger, Else, 293
Krupp (company), 148, 152, 177
Krupp von Bohlen und Halbach, Gustav, 81, 135, 152, 162, 177, 195–96, 226
Krupp, Alfried, 226
Kubizek, August ('Gustl'), 17n, 202
Kuhlo, Dr., 33, 62, 173
Kunze, Dora, 40, 42, 43, 44, 176–77
Kuratorium für dem Wiederaufbau des Deutschen Wirtschaftslebens (Trust for the Rebuilding of German Economic Life), 140
Kyrill, Prince, 341

Laffert, Sigrid von, 101
Lammers, Dr. Hans Heinrich, 199, 202, 214, 234, 268, 285–86, 288–89, 297n
Landsberg am Lech (Prison), 63, 65, 91 112–13, 216, 221, 236
Lauböck, Frau Theodor, 91, 105
Lauböck, Fritz, 31
Law for the Safeguarding of the Unity of Party and State, 44–45
League of Bavarian Industrialists, 173
leather, 92, 94, 100, 119, 246, 268, 285, 293, 301; underwear, 320
Lechfeld, 21
Lehmann, J.F., 25, 26, 167–68, 339–40
Leibl, William, 264
Leipold, Karl, 264
Leonding, 10, 11, 202, 253, 255, 257, 311, 317
Ley, Robert, 83, 141, 197, 199, 229
libel, 27, 40, 42, 62, 76, 86, 131, 135, 141, 186, 188
Linge, Heinz, 261n, 301, 306
Linton-Orman, Miss Rotha, 184
Linz, Austria, 6, 10, 11, 13, 14, 15, 17nn, 18n, 66, 126, 202, 208n, 252, 253, 255, 261n, 265, 274, 282n, 287, 299, 309, 311, 330; Linz Collection, 7, 197, 231, 263, 267–70, 318; Linz Gallery, 230; Linz Provincial Museum, 268
Lizius, Dr., 200–201
London, 1, 4, 56, 117, 130, 184, 189, 309, 319
Loomis, Mrs. Henry, 134
looting (and loot), 263, 273, 286, 298; for or by Hitler, 3, 203, 265; of Hitler, 246, 267, 271, 311–12, 314n, 318
Lord Mayor's Fund, 117
Lorenz, Heinz, 290–91, 294–95
Loret, Jean-Marie, 304, 327
Loringhoven, Maj Baron Freytag von, 290
Lossow, Gen Otto Hermann von, 32
Low, David, 198

Löwenstein, Hans von, 148, 157
Lüdecke, Kurt, 3, 23, 24, 27, 28, 31, 32–33, 40, 50, 63, 88–89, 93, 94, 114–15, 124–37, 158, 172, 182–85, 190, 211–13, 220, 221, 254; Eher Verlag, 53, 58, 132, 211; finances, 125, 127, 132, 177, 212; Henry Ford, 76, 129, 182–83
Ludendorff, Gen Erich von, 23, 28, 30, 33–34, 65, 81, 155, 170, 341

Mannheim, Ralph, 116
Manzialy, Kostanze, 306, 313n
Maser, Prof. Dr. Werner, 10, 310–11
Maurenenbrecher, Max, 26
Maurice, Emil, 31, 63, 70, 71, 73, 101, 112, 240
"Max Heiliger" , 160, 270
May, Karl, 241
Mayr, Capt Karl, 21, 24–25, 35n, 167
Mayrhofer, Josef, 11, 14
Mecsér, András, 127
Mein Kampf, 52, 63, 67–68, 93, 100, 111, 112–122, 133, 209–10, 215, 217, 225, 232, 240, 246, 256, 304, 307, 308, 315, 316, 318; Hitler's income from, 4, 35n, 65, 70–71, 72, 73, 76, 78, 80, 83, 115–16, 122n, 194, 198, 209, 232, 256, 280n, 316
Meissner, Otto, 170, 285, 288, 320
Mend, Hans, 262
Mengerhausen, Erich, 301
Mercedes (see also automobile; car), 62, 65, 66, 67, 72, 76, 90, 102, 142, 201, 203, 329
Merchant's Guild, 173
Meyer, Emil, 146
Milch, Field Marshal Erhard, 234
Mirre, Dr. Ludwig, 200–201
Mitford, Jessica, 103
Mitford, Nancy, 103
Mitford, Unity Valkyrie, 6, 103–104, 184
Möhl, Generalmajor von, 21
Mohnke, SS Brigadeführer Wilhelm, 292–93, 301

Möllendorf, Wichard von, 147
Morell, Dr, Theodor, 108n, 294, 296n
Morgenstern, Samuel, 14
Müller u. Sohn printers, 217, 219, 221
Müller, Adolf, 45, 47, 53, 55, 56, 60nn, 64, 125, 209, 210, 221–22
Müller, Prof Karl Alexander von, 93
Münchener Beobachter, 22, 39
Münchener Neuste Nachrichten, 28
Münchener Post, 26–27, 49, 89, 163n, 177, 186, 191n, 192n
Munder, *Gauleiter*, 70, 73
Munich, 4, 7, 9, 14–15, 19–25, 27–9, 33, 34, 39, 40, 48, 49, 52, 53, 55–9, 59n, 62, 63–6, 67, 72–74, 76, 89–92, 94, 97, 99, 103–5, 106n, 108n, 110, 114, 116, 127, 130, 132, 133, 150, 155, 157, 159, 167, 170, 172, 173, 182, 183, 186–88, 211, 218, 220–22, 230, 236, 244, 250, 260n, 261nn, 262, 266, 269, 271, 276, 282n, 286, 287, 290, 292, 297n, 303, 311, 339, 340; bank accounts in, 19, 92, 93, 174, 321; beer halls, 21, 22, 23, 28, 34, 35n, 106n, 125; corporation court, 40, 43, 44, 57; police, 51, 193n, 300, 313n, 341; property in, 62, 72, 73, 75, 101, 102, 220, 253–5, 257, 272, 302, 304, 307, 316, 317, 318, 328, 333n; tax affairs in, 14–15, 18n, 67–9, 70–71, 72–3, 76, 78–9, 80, 83–4, 84n, 198–201
Munich Hansa Bank, 41
Musin-Pushkin, Count, 172
Mussolini, Benito, 28, 70, 125–26, 184, 187–88, 202
Mutschmann, Martin, 83, 87n

National Socialist Party, 27, 74, 154
National Socialist Press Service, 133
National Treuhand (National Trust), 196, 225, 321
Nationalklub von 1919, 69

Nationalsozialistdstische Briefe, 52
Nationalsozialistische Bewegung (National Socialist Movement), 113
Nationalsozialistische Duetsche Arbeiterpartei (*See* NSDAP)
National-Zeitung, 156–57, 159, 162
Negrelli, Leo, 187
Nikolai, Grand Duke, 170
Norman, Montagu, 185
Northumberland, Duke of, 130
NSDAP *Nationalsozialistische Deutsche Arbeiterpartei* (NSDAP) (Nazi – *see also* National Socialist Party), 9, 20, 25–34, 44–46, 52, 66, 67, 72–78, 88–89, 91, 99, 105, 126, 129, 131–33, 142, 146–48, 166–69, 171–74, 176–78, 180, 184–90, 195–96, 201–202, 211–13, 216, 221, 232–36, 251, 255, 284, 298–99, 321; *Eher Verlag* and *Völkischer Beobachter*, 44, 46, 52, 54–55, 82, 201, 318; finances, 23, 25, 26, 27, 31, 32, 46, 62–64, 69–70, 73, 75, 80, 83, 88, 93, 97–98, 125, 135, 139–40, 143–45, 148–62, 166–69, 176–78, 183, 195, 226, 233; Hitler's 'expenses', 25, 77–78, 110
NSDAv *Nationalsozialistische Deutsche Arbeitverein*, eV (National Socialist German Workers' Society), 42, 44, 58, 59n
Nuremberg, 28, 33, 65, 75, 98, 145, 150, 197, 217, 264, 269, 280n; Nuremberg Laws, 217; Nuremberg Rally, 75; Nuremberg Trials (*and* testimony), 5, 76, 98, 145, 160–61, 163n, 164nn, 209, 210, 217, 223n, 226, 234, 237n, 268, 300

Obsersalzberg, 239, 250–51
Ohnesorge, Wilhelm, 31, 95, 197, 230, 236
Order of St. John of Jerusalem, 117
Organization Consul, 169

Ostermeyr, Herta, 284, 287, 319

Pan-German League, 35n, 138n, 149
Panholzer, Rudolf, 11
Papen, Franz von, 82
Paris, 103, 125, 130, 186, 268
Patrons Web, 172–77
Patton, Gen George S., 217
Paulus, FM Friedrich von, 249
"Paustin, Friedrich-Wilhelm", 291–92
Pension Moritz (*later* Platterhof), 67, 92, 197, 239–40, 250
Pfeffer von Salomon, Franz, 233
Philipp of Heße, Prince, 30
Phoney War, 203
Pietsch, Albert, 65
Platterhof (*formerly* Pension Moritz), 67, 240, 256, 259n, 317
Poensgen, Ernst, 152
Pöhner, Dr. Ernst, 51, 341
Political Testament, 34, 202, 287–93, 295, 312n
Pölzl, Johanna, 10, 13–14, 17n, 328
Pölzl, Theresa, 328
Popp, Josef, 15
Popular Block, 64
Posse, Hans, 268–70
postage stamps, 4, 5, 32, 197, 201, 227, 230, 237n, 286
Potsdam Declaration, 299
presents: *see* gifts
press, rotary: *see* rotary press
Prussia, 71, 75
Putsch of November 1923, 34, 98, 113, 127, 173, 187–88, 190, 212, 236
Puttkamer, Adm Karl-Jesko Otto von, 286

Quandt, Dr. Günther, 131, 161

Rastenburg, 250
Rathenau, Walther, 27, 169
Ratibor-Corvey, Prince, 173
Rattenhuber, *Gruppenführer* Johann, 301
Raubal, Angela, 13–14, 73, 104–5, 202, 241, 242–43, 252, 259n, 304, 328
Raubal, Angelika "Geli", 72, 73, 74–75, 95, 100–101, 213, 221, 304, 328–29

Raubal, Elfriede, 304, 329; *see also* Hochegger, Elfriede
Raubal, Leo, 303, 304–305, 328–30
Redesdale, Lord, 103
Reemtsma, Philipp, 54–55
Rehse, J.F.M., 74–75
Reich Labour Front, 141
Reichert, Maria, 75
Reichsbank, 79, 142, 160, 170, 225
Reichskulturkammer (Reich Chamber of Culture), 229
Reichslandbund, 149
Reichstag, 73, 82
Reichsverband, 148
Reichswehr, 35n, 166
Reichswehr Web, 166–69
Reinhardt, Fritz, 198, 199–200, 214
Reinhart, Friedrich, 146
Reiter, Maria (Mimi), 100
Reusch, Paul, 140, 145–46, 152, 170
Reventlow, Ernst Graf zu, 131
Rhenisch-Westfälisches Kohlensyndikat, 150, 151
Ribbentrop, Joachim von, 226
Richter, Maximilian Erwin, 341
Riehl, Walter, 126
Robbins, Warren, 28
Roder, Lorenz, 127
Röhm, Capt Ernst, 24–25, 35n, 40, 132, 160, 167, 199, 223n, 329
Roller, Prof Alfred, 12
Rommeder, Walburga (*née* Hütler), 10, 330
Rommel, *Feldmarschall* Erwin, 249
Ropp, Baron Wilhelm de,185
Roselius, Ludwig, 141
Rosenberg, Alfred, 22, 29, 38, 49, 51–53, 59n, 63, 75, 78, 85n, 97, 98, 107n, 100, 132–33, 135–36, 140, 162n, 170, 172, 175, 184, 185, 188, 189, 199, 212, 216, 228, 339, 341
Rosterg, August, 146, 161
rotary press, 31, 47–48, 60n, 97–99
Räterepublik, 20–21
Rothermere, Lord, 109–110, 185
Royal Dutch Shell, 3, 54, 55, 166, 170, 189–90

Ruhr, 34, 140–42, 148, 152, 156, 157–60
Ruhrlade (Ruhr Chest or Treasury), 140, 148, 152–53, 161
Rupprecht, Crown Prince, 28

SA (*Sturmabteilung*), 30, 32, 67, 77, 96, 125, 141, 145, 152, 161, 167, 177, 198, 212, 233, 267; Relief Fund, 226
Sachsen-Anhalt, Duchess Eduard von, 96, 172
Sauckel, Fritz, 223n, 234
Saxony, 71, 74, 87n
Schacht, Hjalmar, 57n, 79, 142, 146, 160, 178, 191n, 195–196, 225–26
Schaub, *SS Gruppenführer* Julius, 5, 70, 79, 108n, 110, 195, 198, 200, 207n, 210, 233, 236, 237, 283, 285–86, 302, 307, 320
Schaumberg-Lippe, Prince Friedrich Christian Fürst zu, 172–73, 191n
Schenck, von, 49, 170, 187
Scheubner-Richter, Mathilde, 172
Scheubner-Richter, Maximilian Erwin von, 23, 34, 169–70, 184, 190n, 341
Schickedanz, Arno, 172
Schicklgruber, Alois, 327
Schirach, Baldur von, 199
Schleicher, Gen Kurt von, 80, 152
Schmidt family, 330–31; Anton, 305
Schmidt, Ernst, 16, 20
Schmitt, Dr. Kurt, 136, 161
Schnitzler, Arthur, 195–96
Schönaich-Carolath, Prince 96
Schörner, *Feldmarschall* Ferdinand, 290
Schreck, Julius, 20, 82, 233, 236–37, 238n, 329
Schreiber, Berndt, 120
Schröder, Adm August Ludwig von, 26, 176
Schröder, Baron Kurt von, 146, 153
Schröder, Christa, 307
Schuschnigg, Kurt von, 247, 273
Schüßler, Rudolf, 212
Schutzstaffel (SS), 145, 198, 251
Schwartz, Franz Xaver, 3, 6,

53, 57, 64, 74–75, 77, 82, 132, 158, 199, 201, 212–13, 223n, 233, 235, 289, 321
Sebottendorf, Rudolph Freiherr von, 36n, 39–40, 50, 60n, 168, 216, 340
Second Marine Brigade, 169
Seidlitz, Frau Gertrud von (*See also* Gertrud Krause), 7, 27, 29, 31, 48, 62, 88, 97–99, 107n, 184, 190n
Seidlitz, Georg Karl Maria von, 98, 100
Seidlitz, Gerhard Karl Lamarck Darwin von, 98–100
Seldte, Franz, 149, 199
Selve (car), 30, 31, 66
sex, 74–75, 90, 91; intercourse, 89
Shell *see* Royal Dutch Shell
Silverberg, Paul, 152
Simon, Sir John, 189
Sinclair, Upton, 178
Skoda, 187, 189
Social Democrats (*see also* SPD), 82, 214
Sonderaktion Linz, 6
South Tyrol, 187–88
Spain, 121, 126
Spanish, 92, 119, 130; Civil War, 187–88
SPD (*Sozialdemokratische Partei*), 20
Speer, Albert, 3, 108n, 151, 201, 203, 232, 234, 243, 248, 249, 264–65, 268–70
Spital, Austria, 13, 17n, 202, 305, 327, 328, 330
Spitzweg, Carl, 264–66
Springorum, Fritz, 152, 160–61
Stadelheim prison, Munich, 27
Staeger, Ferdinand, 262, 266
Stahl, Friedrich, 264
Stahlhelm, 23, 149
Stauss, Emil Georg von, 142, 153–54
Steinbrinck, Otto, 145
Steiner, Gen Felix, 290
Stempfle, Fr. Bernhard, 74–75, 113–14, 122n
Stinnes, Hugo, 141, 149
Stolzing-Czerny, Josef, 51, 113
Stoßtrupp Adolf Hitler, 20, 223n
Strasser brothers: *see below*, Gregor and Otto
Strasser, Gregor, 52, 113, 160
Strasser, Otto, 26, 74, 112–13

Streicher, Julius, 28, 66, 70, 188, 212
Stuchlik, Josef, 121
Stuck, Franz von, 266, 272, 281n
Stumpfegger, Ludwig, 294
Sturmabteilung: see SA
Sudeten Germans, 189
Swiss, 27, 33, 47, 92, 112, 153, 176, 232, 304, 312; bank accounts, 5, 188, 310, 319; fundraising, 32, 97, 190
Switzerland, 121, 130, 137n; bank accounts, 232, 310, 319; fundraising, 27, 32, 98, 176, 190
Sydenham of Combe, Lord, 130

Tat gegen Tinte (Facts versus Ink), 198, 266
taxes, 53, 142, 190, 219, 254, 261n, 263–4, 267; Hitler's, 4–5, 6, 15, 17n, 30, 35n, 62, 65, 66, 67–9, 70–1, 72–3, 73–4, 76, 78–9, 80, 83–4, 84n, 85n, 93, 97, 196, 198–201, 209, 235, 236, 259n, 280n, 300
Tegernsee, Bavaria, 217, 221–22, 242, 291–92, 294
Tengelmann, Ernst, 161
Terboven, Josef, 75, 148
Teutonia Society, 67, 177
"Thiers, Georges", 291
Thoma, Hans, 264
Thost, Dr. H., 184
Thule Gesellschaft, 20–22, 25, 26, 35n, 39, 48, 99, 100, 167–69, 176, 339–41
Thyssen, Fritz, 8n, 34, 37n, 58, 74, 76, 79–81, 85n, 141, 143–44, 149–50, 152, 154–55, 162, 164n, 170, 195
Thyssen Gold, 2
Trevor-Roper, Hugh, 291–92, 294, 303, 310
Troost, Gerdy, 264
Troost, Ludwig, 93, 271, 281n
Truman-Smith, Captain, 28, 36nn
"Twenty-five Points", Hitler's, 38

UFA film company, 149
Ullstein publishing company, 213–15
Ullstein, Hugo, 188
underwear, 100, 103, 311; leather, 320
United States Web, 172, 177–80
Uschla (NSDAP court), 55, 61n, 136

VB see *Völkischer Beobachter*
Versailles Treaty, 24, 32, 166
"Vicky", 198
Vienna, 9–15, 16nn, 17n, 58, 63, 103, 105, 114, 127, 262, 269, 272–73, 282n, 326, 328, 329, 330; Academy of Fine Arts, 11; Handicrafts School, 12
Vierjahreszeit, Hotel des, 167
Vigny, Alfred de, 33
Villa Silberblick, 95
Vladimirovich, Grand Duchess Victoria, 97, 171
Vladimirovich, Grand Duke Kyrill, 97, 130, 170–72, 180
Vogl, Adolf, 73
Vogl (Tax Inspector), 199–200
Vögler, Albert, 152, 160–61, 195
Völkischer Beobachter (VB), 22, 24, 25, 29, 30–31, 33, 34, 38–39, 40–41, 44–57, 65–66, 74–75, 77, 82, 109, 111, 113, 115, 132, 156, 169, 170, 174, 176, 184, 198, 213, 216, 222; Hitler writing for, 26, 44, 51, 53, 66, 95, 109, 199
Voss, Hermann, 270

Wachenfeld: *see* Haus Wachenfeld
Wagemann Circle, 147
Wagemann, Ernst, 147
Wagener, Otto, 3, 53, 75, 76, 146–47, 154, 156–60, 161, 209, 236
Wagner, Richard, 94, 239, 264
Wagner, Siegfried, 63, 95, 129, 182–83

Wagner, Wieland, 95
Wagner, Winifred, 63, 75, 95, 129, 182–83
Wales, Prince of, 186
Wartenburg, Count Yorck von, 26
Weber, Christian, 49, 127
Wehrsport Programme, 152
Weimar Government, 27
Weiß, Lt Col Rudolf, 290
Weiß, Wilhelm, 50, 51, 55
Wenck, Gen, 290
whips, 90, 93, 95–96, 239, 301
White Russian Web, 169–72, 189
Wiedemann, Fritz, 16, 90, 202, 233
Wilhelm, Crown Prince August, 172–73
wills, 10, 13, 17n, 34; Eva Braun's, 103, 203, 272, 284–85, 302, 304, 319–20; Hitler's (*see also* Political Testament), 7, 75, 202, 252, 263, 269, 287, 289, 291, 294, 296, 298–308, 316, 318, 320
Windsor, Duke of, 186
Winkhauss, Fritz, 152
Winkler, Dr. h.c. Max, 214–15
Winter Relief, 210
Winter, Anni, 75, 202, 254, 300, 318, 307
Winter, Georg, 75
Winterbotham, Maj F.W., 185
Wirtschaftspolitischer Pressedienst, 156
Witthoeft, Franz Heinrich, 146
Wolf, Johanna, 308
Wolff, Otto, 195
Wolfsschanz, 206
Württemberg, 20, 153

Yemen, Imam of: see Imam of Yemen
Young Plan, 149–50, 153, 155

Zabel, Werner, 250
Zander, *SS Standartenführer* Wilhelm, 289–92, 294
Zäper, Max, 262
Zeman, Milos, 120
Ziegler, Adolf, 202, 281n
Zitko, Michal, 119–21